PARTNER IN EMPIRE

DWARKANATH   TAGORE

PARTNER IN EMPIRE

*Dwarkanath Tagore and the Age of
Enterprise in Eastern India*

by BLAIR B. KLING

UNIVERSITY OF CALIFORNIA PRESS
BERKELEY · LOS ANGELES · LONDON

University of California Press
Berkeley and Los Angeles, California

University of California Press, Ltd.
London, England

Copyright © 1976, by
The Regents of the University of California

ISBN 0-520-02927-5
Library of Congress Catalog Card Number: 74-27293
Printed in the United States of America

To Julia

CONTENTS

vii

PREFACE

The story of Dwarkanath Tagore first came to my attention in a seminar conducted by Richard Park at Berkeley twenty years ago. I was intrigued by the discovery that the grandfather of the poet Rabindranath and the father of the saintly Debendranath was an astute business tycoon who owned fleets of ships, coal mines, insurance companies, banks, and indigo plantations. At once I sensed the likelihood of a dramatic conflict between the worldly father and his other-worldly son and imagined Dwarkanath's profound disappointment when Debendranath refused to carry on the hard-won business empire. In this case research confirmed my guess. On another point, however, I was proven wrong. I had anticipated that the adulatory historians of the Tagore family had exaggerated Dwarkanath's achievements, and I was surprised to discover that he was all they had said and more. In a British-dominated business world, a Bengali Brahmin indeed stood at the pinnacle of power.

My research was supported by generous grants from the American Institute of Indian Studies, the American Philosophical Society, and, at the University of Illinois, by the Center for International Comparative Studies, the Graduate College Research Board, the Department of History, and the Center for Asian Studies.

In India, I could not have proceeded without the help of my cherished friend, Professor Gautam Chattopadhyay. Other friends and colleagues who were generous in their aid were Samaren Roy, Professor Panchanan Saha, M.K. Chaudhuri, Tarun Mittra, K.L. Mukhopadhyay, Amritamaya Mookerji, Tridib Ghose, and Professor N. Majumdar. Those who helped me in an official capacity included Hiranmay Banerjee, Vice Chancellor of Rabindra Bharati University; S.N. Bhomik, Rabindra Bharati Museum; J.C. Goswami, Keeper of the Records, and T.K. Mukherjee, Assistant Director of Archives, West Bengal State Archives; Y.M. Mulay, Librarian, and

Chittaranjan Banerji, Deputy Librarian, National Library of India; S.R. Das, Vice Chancellor, and H.C. Bhattacharyya, Registrar, Visva-Bharati University; Sovan Lal Ganguly, Curator, Rabindra Sadhana; S.V. Desika Char and Sourin Roy of the National Archives of India; A.D. Ogilvie, B. Mitter and W.J. Jameson of Andrew Yule and Company; S.K. Banerjee, Registrar, Calcutta High Court, and the staff of the High Court Archives; W.D. Bryden, Secretary of the Bengal Chamber of Commerce; and G.B. Ghosh, Geological Survey of India.

In England, S.C. Sutton and his efficient staff at the India Office Library were especially helpful. I also wish to thank the staffs of the numerous other libraries and archives at which I worked in Britain for their courteous assistance.

I am especially grateful to Professors K.N. Chaudhuri of S.O.A.S., John B. McLane of Northwestern University, and John H. Broomfield of the University of Michigan, as well as to my colleagues at the University of Illinois—Charles Hall and Professors Lloyd Eastman and Koji Taira—for reading all or part of the manuscript and suggesting improvements. I am also indebted to those who as students helped me in the research—David Schob, Robert Neiss, Sultana Krippendorf and Nancy Peshkin.

For their patience during the long gestation period I want to thank my children, Joanna and William; and, for her relentless prodding, my mother. Finally, I am eternally grateful to my wife, Julia, for her help and inspiration.

ABBREVIATIONS

BM British Museum
IO India Office Library
KNT Kshitindranath Tagore Collection, Rabindra
      Bharati University
NAI National Archives of India, New Delhi
PRO Public Record Office
WBSA West Bengal State Archives, Calcutta

In America, until recently, many potential poets and philosophers became businessmen . . . and the paradox is that these misplaced individuals who do not really belong are often the ones who shape the character and style of the sphere in which they operate. It was not conventional businessmen but misplaced poets and philosophers who set in motion the vast combinations and the train of ceaseless innovation which gave American business its Promethean sweep and drive. To a philosopher who finds himself immersed in a milieu of sheer action, all action will seem of one kind and he will shift easily from one field of activity to another. He will combine factories, mines, railroads, oil wells, etc. the way a philosopher collates and generalizes ideas.

Eric Hoffer,
The Temper of Our Time
(New York, 1964)

Why, one asks, are the Tatas unique—or nearly so? Where were the *entrepreneurs* of the same calibre, whether Indians or Englishmen, who should have been doing what they did, and much more of the same kind, fifty or sixty years earlier?

H.N. Brailsford,
Subject India
(New York, 1943)

INTRODUCTION

During the first half of the nineteenth century, the armies of the East India Company extended British rule into every corner of the Indian subcontinent. Confronted with the totally unfamiliar task of administering a vast oriental empire, the British responded by converting India into a giant social laboratory. They experimented with transplanting their institutions onto Indian soil and applying current western economic and social philosophies to Indian conditions. Through trial and error they tested schemes for the administration of local government and land-revenue systems, fashioned codes of law and grappled with the question of interfering with religious customs they considered unacceptable. In contrast to the later nineteenth century with its bureaucratized, imperial leviathan, the first half of the century was a period of flexibility when alternative systems of relationships between ruler and ruled seemed possible. One of these alternatives was presented by a prominent Bengali merchant, Dwarkanath Tagore.

Dwarkanath Tagore (1794–1846), a western-educated Bengali Brahmin, was the acknowledged civic leader of Calcutta during the 1830s and 1840s. Though a brilliant entrepreneur, he subordinated his business activities to political and social ends. Tagore envisioned a future India that was westernized and industrialized and whose inhabitants enjoyed without discrimination the rights and liberties of Englishmen. He would lay the foundations for this new India in his own day by promoting an all-encompassing interracial partnership of Britishers and Indians. One component would be the community of British settlers who, like the colonists in America, Australia, New Zealand, and South Africa, would strike roots in the country and develop local allegiances. The other component would be progressive-minded Indians who would associate with the British as equals in business, social, cultural, and political activities. Together they would form a single community with local loyalties. Upon this provincial partnership would be built an imperial partnership in which India would join with other dominions of the British empire in a common, worldwide empire of equals. Tagore's vision was not as fanciful as it may appear. He and his contemporaries were products of eighteenth-century rationalism and nineteenth-century liberalism, ideologies that supported such concepts as progress, liberty, and internationalism. Even more to the point, Tagore was a businessman, and business was the traditional area for interracial collaboration in India.

Indo-British business collaboration began in the seventeenth century, when the East India Company first established its major trading posts at Madras, Bombay, and Calcutta. These coastal enclaves attracted Indian merchants from all corners of the subcontinent, who came to take advantage of the opportunities created by the British. Some worked as agents and brokers, others joined the Europeans as partners in commercial ventures and still others developed their own merchant houses. One of the attractions of the British ports must have been the security of living in a town ruled by a company of merchants who understood and respected property rights and the sanctity of contract. In these British enclaves, a number of Indian business communities rose to wealth and prominence. Bombay on the west coast attracted Gujarati trading castes as well as Parsis, Jains, and Muslim Bohras. To Madras came the Chettiyars of Tamilnad and the Komatis from Andhra.

In Calcutta, Bengali trading castes, such as the Subarnabaniks, were joined by Brahmins and Kayasthas who worked as agents, brokers, and contractors for the British. Among the Brahmin families who came to seek their fortune in Calcutta were the ancestors of Dwarkanath Tagore. From farther afield came other traders—Armenians and Bagdadhi Jews who settled in all three cities. Also participating in the British network were inland trading communities such as the Marwaris of Rajasthan and the Khatris of the Punjab, who linked the port of Calcutta with northwestern India. By the late eighteenth century the East India Company's coastal enclaves had become wealthy and prosperous centers of power from which the British were able to launch their conquest of the subcontinent.

The British conquest of India coincided with the industrial revolution and both events radically changed the entire context of Indo-British economic relations. The conquest united into one dominion two nations at opposite ends of the industrial-technological spectrum. Whereas Great Britain led the world in industrialization and in the application of modern technology, India's peasants and artisans worked with tools that had been passed down virtually unchanged for thousands of years. Because of the technological disparity of the two countries, the British conquest exposed India to uncontrollable economic pressures. British factory-made textiles replaced indigenous products in the local bazaars, and to pay for these new imports, landlords converted cropland and jungle to commercial agriculture. Exporters developed overseas markets for such Indian products as opium, indigo, sugar, tea, coffee, and cotton. India became an integral part of the world economy, and the Indian peasant found himself dependent for his well-being on the demands of a distant consumer.

Among the great unknowns in the flux and uncertainty that characterized early-nineteenth-century India was whether British rule would bring prosperity or poverty. By sharing with India their skills, entrepreneurs, capital, and technology, the British could develop the country's abundant natural resources and encourage manufacturing as well as commercial agriculture. Their alternative was to exploit India as a dumping ground for manufactured goods and as a source of cheap raw materials for home industries. By the end of the century it was evident that the economic impact of British rule had not been the same in all parts of India or in all periods of British rule. When and where industrial development did, in fact, occur depended to a large extent on the vitality and commitment of the local business entrepreneurs, European and Indian.

In eastern India, Dwarkanath Tagore and a handful of like-minded contemporaries of both races provided the entrepreneurship. One of Tagore's goals was to carry over the commercial partnerships and other organizational forms of the mercantile age into the industrial age. A second goal was to import the industrial revolution into India and to adapt the steam engine to commercial use. Tagore organized the first coal-mining company and the first steam-tug and river-steamboat companies, and was among his country's pioneer railway promoters. To facilitate these enterprises he launched a commercial bank, insurance companies, and commercial newspapers. He engaged in ocean shipping, under both steam and sail, and tried his hand at applying modern technology and organization to tea planting, salt manufacturing and sugar refining. In all of these undertakings he associated with British partners.

By 1840 it appeared that Calcutta and its hinterland were on the threshold of a small-scale industrial revolution. Then a series of commercial crises shook the Calcutta business community and by 1850 the momentum failed, the interracial coalition fell apart, and, though Calcutta continued to grow as a commercial and financial center, the city lost its industrial leadership to Bombay. Calcutta became an enclave port with stronger economic ties to Europe than to its own regional hinterland. The development of new industries such as iron and steel, heavy machinery and tool manufacturing, glass, paper, rails, and rolling stock had to wait until the twentieth century. By that time, eastern India had lost the competitive advantage that comes with early industrialization. The tragic irony is that, in terms of resources, eastern India—the present-day economically depressed states of West Bengal, Bihar, and Assam and the nation of Bangladesh—is the richest area in south Asia. The region contains vast deposits of coal, iron ore and other minerals, a fertile soil, a large number of educated people and a potentially large skilled labor force. If the dynamism of the "age of enterprise" had been sustained, if the industrial revolution of the 1840s had not been aborted, eastern India might have developed indigenous industries commensurate with its natural and human resources.

Why did the dream of Dwarkanath Tagore fail to materialize? Why did the industrial development of eastern India lag so far behind its potential? One reason is that the enterprises undertaken during the period from 1830 to 1850 were poorly managed and failed to make the proper use of modern technology. On the macroeconomic level the failure can be attributed to the adverse effects of Bengal's heavy commodity-trade imbalance on prices and investments and to the fact that the types of products exported from the area were particularly susceptible to severe market fluctuations. The government, too, was responsible for the industrial lag by its failure to enact a law of limited liability or to underwrite public-service enterprises designed to develop an industrial infrastructure. But more deep-seated were social and cultural factors. The indigenous Bengali elite turned its back on business and left modern industry and international commerce in Calcutta to Europeans, who controlled it until well into the twentieth century and after independence transferred it to non-Bengali business communities.

It is possible that the literature on entrepreneurship has overlooked an important factor determining investment decisions. This factor can be called "local commitment," and the lack of it is the essence of economic imperialism. The alien entrepreneur, one suspects, has little interest in reinvesting his profits in local enterprises or social overhead. He is like a farmer who refuses to replenish the soil with nutrients, taking but never giving, exploiting but never contributing. Furthermore, he lacks knowledge of and interest in the region's economic potential. He would rather import his managers and materials from regions in which he feels "at home." Third, colonial industries seem to attract marketing rather than production specialists. Alien businessmen are more familiar with importing and exporting than with the production process, which requires a deeper understanding of local conditions. For the full and balanced economic development of a region, a locally based and locally committed group of businessmen is essential.

After the death of Dwarkanath Tagore, such a group was wanting in Bengal, and in the late nineteenth century the indigenous elite played only a minor role in the modern sector of Bengal's economy. In part, the blame for this can be ascribed to British racism and, perhaps, to official policy, but to a large extent it lies with the antibusiness attitudes inherent in the dominant culture of Bengal. This dominant culture reflected the values of the Bengali *bhadralok,* literally, the "respectable people," who composed the western-educated middle class. It included a preference for occupations requiring education, the ownership of land, and an idealization of the casual, simple, and graceful life of a country gentleman. Bhadralok culture is peculiar to Bengal and grew out of historical circumstances. [1]

Bengal is the home of one of the distinctive subcultures of south Asia. The region was originally the eastern frontier of the Indic heartland in the Ganges Valley, and, in isolation from the heartland, Bengal became a haven for non-Aryan religions such as Buddhism and Jainism. Her first great indigenous dynasty, the Palas, who ruled the country from A.D. 750 to 1150, were ardent Buddhists. Under their rule the merchant communities of Bengal enjoyed a high status and grew wealthy in trade with Ceylon and Southeast Asia. In contrast, the succeeding dynasty, the Senas (1150–1250), supported Brahminism and suppressed Buddhism and, by re-establishing Brahmanic orthodoxy, degraded the merchant castes. In the thirteenth

[1] For a definition and description of the bhadralok, see John H. Broomfield, *Elite Conflict in a Plural Society: Twentieth-Century Bengal* (Berkeley: 1968), pp. 5–20.

century the Muslim invasion dealt a final blow to Buddhism in
Bengal. The lower classes were converted to Islam and the upper
classes reacted with even more vigorous support for orthodox
Brahminism. Brahmins continued to dominate the caste system to
the detriment of the merchant castes. As a result, the caste hierarchy
of Bengal was bifurcated. At the top were the learned castes—Brahmins, Baidyas, and Kayasthas. Because the orthodoxy recognized no
middle-range castes, the merchant castes—Subarnabanik, Gandha-
banik, and Tantubanik—were classified as Sudras. Thereafter Bengali culture was dominated by Brahmin and Kayastha values. The
Brahmins were teachers, priests, and administrators; the Kayasthas
primarily administrators, and the Baidyas, physicians. These castes
were employed as administrators by Muslim officialdom and the
great landholders of both religions. Commercial occupations were
considered beneath their dignity.[2]

It was the European traders who removed at least part of the
stigma from commerce. The East India Company had both trading
and governmental functions, and at first there was no clear
distinction between mercantile and administrative service. In the
seventeenth and eighteenth centuries the East India Company and
individuals in its service employed—along with Bengali merchant
and artisan castes—Brahmins, Kayasthas, and Baidyas as agents and
contractors. On the one hand, many Brahmins and Kayasthas
became traders, commission agents, and brokers as well as administrators; on the other, Bengalis from merchant castes became administrators as well as traders. Men of both groups alternated between
commercial activity and employment in such agencies as the salt and
opium departments and the mint. The entire group of Indians who
worked as British agents were called *banians,* the Indian equivalent of
compradors, and took on certain common characteristics. Although
upper and lower castes were still separated with regard to Hindu
rituals and marriage alliances, all enjoyed the reflected prestige of the
new rulers, were more or less wealthy, and were interested in
European culture.

With the banian, the bhadralok style began to evolve in the
eighteenth century. It included associating with the Europeans and
taking an interest in acquiring the linguistic, legal, and administra-

2Satindra Narayan Roy, "Bengal Traditions of Trade and Commerce," *Journal of
the Anthropological Society of Bombay,* vol. XIV, no. 4 (1929), pp. 431–58; and Nripendra
Kumar Dutt, *Origin and Growth of Caste in India,* vol. II (Calcutta: 1965), pp. 82 ff.

tive skills necessary to advance in British employment. Although commercial activity in association with the Europeans was considered respectable, upper-caste Bengalis were still partial to administrative, professional, and intellectual occupations. As the expansion of British rule increased the demand for people trained in these areas, young Bengalis flocked to the colleges to prepare themselves for careers in administration, law, medicine, journalism, and education. In Dwarkanath Tagore's day, business was still a possible component of the bhadralok life style, but after the middle of the nineteenth century, training for a profession was usually substituted for entering business. Not only were there more opportunities in the professions, but these careers were more in accord with the bhadralok value system.

The final component of the bhadralok life style, landholding, was also introduced by British rule. In 1793, the government, in conformity with Whig doctrines of private property, assigned and guaranteed property rights in the land to a class of landlords designated *zamindars*. To encourage the zamindars to improve their estates the government pledged that the annual tax on each estate would remain fixed in perpetuity. Initially, however, the tax assessments were too heavy, and, when many of the old large estates failed to meet their assessments, they were put up for auction and purchased by wealthy banians. Gradually, as inflation effectively brought the assessments down to reasonable levels, the estates increased in value. The zamindar became a small raja, the effective ruler of all the villagers encompassed by his estate, and ownership of a zamindari became another measure of social status. Though he might still reside in Calcutta and perform his mercantile or administrative business, the zamindar acquired a country home where he could house his dependents and celebrate his holidays. Zamindari rents became the source of a regular income independent of the vicissitudes of trade. The zamindar's sons were not raised in the bustle of city mercantile life, but were brought up as young gentry. Imbued with the traditional respect for education, they were expected as a matter of course to enter either a local college, or Calcutta University, or, later in the century, a college in Britain.[3] As a result, the bhadralok, including the descendants of Dwarkanath Tagore, lost their "instinct for business." No Bengali was more

3 Pradip Sinha, *Nineteenth Century Bengal: Aspects of Social History* (Calcutta: 1965).

passionate in his denunciation of the bhadralok value system than Prafulla Chandra Ray, a professor of chemistry and founder of the Bengal Chemical and Pharmaceutical Works. In 1932 he wrote:

The Bengali has learnt to look upon a University degree as the *summum bonum* of his ambition. . . . He has been traditionally averse to commercial or industrial pursuits as he looks upon them as something derogatory. No wonder that the market is flooded with starving degree-holders. . . . The misfortune of Bengal is that she has allowed herself to be all but ousted from her trade and commerce, internal and external. Her intelligentsia, barring a handful of successful lawyers and placemen, are now reduced to a race of ill-paid and ill-fed schoolmasters and quill-drivers; while taking advantage of her ineptitude and weakness, the powerful and enterprising foreign and non-Bengali traders and merchants have captured all her avenues to wealth.[4]

Whereas the Bengalis lost control of the modern sector of the economy of their city, that of Bombay remained firmly in Indian hands. Asok Mitra, as superintendent of census operations for West Bengal, compared present-day Bombay and Calcutta and attributed Calcutta's troubles to the Bengalis' economic weakness.[5]

[Calcutta's] big industrialists and businessmen came from elsewhere with no thought of a stake in the city to start with. . . . The bulk of them have been content to get the most of what the city has had to offer but have hardly ever thought of placing themselves as a group at its service. Thus developed an unfortunate dichotomy. The city's councillors have been mostly drawn from the liberal professions, the academics, bureaucrats, owners of real estate, rentiers, who sprang from the middle classes, to whom their primary charge was themselves and their kin, and not the producer or entrepreneur.

In contrast, "Bombay's affairs were quickly taken over by a band of dedicated industrialists, businessmen and entrepreneurs who were large in vision, big in money and unsparing of effort. Bombay was their passion, their destiny, and apart from straining all their surplus energy for the good and prosperity of the city, they gave away their own money in trusts and charities to make Bombay strong, cultured, beautiful."

The businessmen of Bombay were drawn from traditional western Indian trading castes—Hindu, Jain, and Muslim Gujaratis—or were Parsis whose traditional occupations had been agriculture and

4 Prafulla Chandra Ray, *Life and Experiences of a Bengali Chemist,* 2 vols. (Calcutta. 1932, 1935), I, pp. 499–500.
5 Asok Mitra, *Calcutta India's City* (Calcutta: 1963), pp. 38–40.

carpentry. In contrast to those of Bengal, the traditional merchants of western India always enjoyed a high social status. They had no interest in administration, and under the British these posts in the Bombay Presidency were filled by Maharastrian Brahmin and Kayastha castes that had served in the bureaucracy of the old Maratha empire. Nor had the merchants of Bombay any opportunity for investment in rural estates, for the area around the city had been settled directly with peasant yeomen. Thus the merchants of Bombay had no other home but the city itself. In Bengal one could attain status and power through a zamindari or a profession, but in Bombay, success in business was the chief road to status. The indigenous city leaders of Bombay were the *shetias,* the wealthy businessmen, and if a man were to lose his money he would forfeit his standing in the social and political life of the city. Under these circumstances the businessman of Bombay grasped at new opportunities when old investments began to lose money. Thus in the 1850s the Parsis, who were losing ground to new commercial groups and suffering displacement from technological innovations, took the lead in establishing the cotton-mill industry in Bombay. 6

Ironically, those who compared the two cities in the period 1825 to 1850 usually believed that Calcutta and not Bombay could look forward to the more glorious future. In 1839 the *Bombay Gazette* complained that "instead of maintaining the lonely icicled state of magnificence in which we exist, [in Calcutta] the thaw of social harmony has produced a permeative process of coalescence, which is spreading in every direction, and resolving into one community both Europeans and Natives."7 The zamindari system had given an aristocratic flavor to Calcutta's civic life by providing for the continuity of elite families who patronized cultural institutions. In addition to becoming a cultural center, Calcutta in 1850 appeared to be on the threshold of becoming a progressive center of trade and industry under the control of local merchants of both races. The career of Dwarkanath Tagore illuminates both the dream and its failure.

6Christine Dobbin, *Urban Leadership in Western India* (Oxford: 1972) is a detailed study of Bombay city in the nineteenth century.

7Quoted in *Bengal Hurkaru,* 22 Oct. 1839.

Chapter I

THE HOME AND THE WORLD

Two major influences shaped the character of Dwarkanath Tagore: one was his family and the other his friend and "guru," Rammohun Roy. The Tagore family emerged from obscurity at the beginning of the eighteenth century, when it migrated from Jessore to the newly founded British settlement at Calcutta. As priests the Tagores earned their livelihood ministering to the lowly fishermen of Govindapore, one of the fever-haunted villages scattered in the swamp near the British fort. The poor fishermen, who could induce only degraded Brahmins to serve their ritual needs, were so pleased to have priests that they honored them with the title *thakur,* meaning "lord." During the eighteenth century, Calcutta grew rapidly into the leading port of south Asia, and the first settlers prospered with the city. The men of the Tagore family gave up their priestly role to serve as commercial agents for the East India Company and amassed a fortune providing supplies to the commissariat at Fort William and to captains of merchantmen anchored in the river. They invested their money in land, first within the rapidly growing city, then, toward the end of the century, in rural estates acquired from a declining aristocracy. During the nineteenth century these descendants of humble priests would themselves become aristocrats—the "Medici" of Calcutta, the most gifted and versatile of families; civic leaders, philanthropists; merchant princes, patrons of the arts, prophets and theologians, musicians, artists, and poets. [1]

1 The history of the Tagore family that follows is based upon Amritamaya Mukherjee, "Thakur Barir Itikatha," in *Samakalin,* Posh 1365, (December-January 1958–59); Jogendra Nath Bhattacharya, *Hindu Castes and Sects* (Calcutta: 1896), pp. 119 ff.; Lokenath Ghosh, *The Modern History of the Indian .Chiefs, Rajas, Zamindars* 2 vols. *(Calcutta: 1879–81),* II, 160–85; James W. Furrell, *The Tagore Family,* 2nd ed. (Calcutta: 1892); *A Brief Account of the Tagore Family* (IO Tract 137, Calcutta: 1868); *The Tagores of Calcutta* (Calcutta: 1869 [?]); *The House of the Tagores* (Calcutta: 1963); Kissory Chand Mittra, *Memoir of Dwarkanath Tagore* (Calcutta: 1870); and Kshitindranath Thakur, *Dwarkanath Thakurer Jabini* (Calcutta: 1969).

The Tagores were similar to a score of Bengali families that rose to wealth and prominence in eighteenth-century Calcutta. In two respects, however, they differed. The first was the intensity of their drive for achievement and status within Bengali society; and the second, their fondness for things novel and fashionable, especially when these were European. Dwarkanath once attributed their extraordinary energy and ambition to a "sense of injury" resulting from the "separation . . . between my family and the more bigoted classes of my countrymen."[2] The Tagores belonged to a degraded Brahmin subcaste called "Pirali Brahmin," and, although in the secular world of the frontier metropolis they could rise to the highest level of power and influence, in the Brahmanic world of social stratification based on pollution and pedigree they were irredeemable pariahs. They met the challenge in two ways: at times they rejected Hindu tradition and adopted European manners and values; at other times they tried to prove their caste legitimacy by hyperorthodox behavior.

Orthodox Hindu social leaders rigorously enforced the ostracism of the Piralis. In the late eighteenth century, a Brahmin who had done nothing more than take a meal with a Pirali had to donate fifty thousand rupees to his priests to be readmitted into his own caste. Another Brahmin who unwittingly had married his daughter to a Pirali was abandoned by his friends and died of grief; and a Kayastha, in status slightly lower than a Brahmin, spent thousands of rupees to be restored to his caste after marrying a Pirali girl. Many Piralis, including some of the Tagores, tried unsuccessfully to buy their way into society with huge sums of money.[3] As late as the mid-nineteenth century, the Tagores, in spite of their immense wealth and prestige, could not break the caste barrier; and when, in 1852, the nephew of a leading Kulin Brahmin married the grand-daughter of Dwarkanath, the boy was expelled from his family. A contemporary noted that "any child married into any of the Tagore families loses from the moment of his union the privileges of the society of which his relatives are members. He holds as much an isolated position as a Hindoo convert, and entails on the head of his new connexions the necessity of maintaining him and his progeny."[4]

2Dwarkanath Tagore to Lord William Bentinck, 20 Aug. 1834, in Bentinck Papers, Portland Collection, Nottingham University Library, Ref. no. PW JF 2091. Cf. Everett E. Hagen, *On the Theory of Social Change* (Homewood, Illinois: 1962).

3Shib Chunder Bose, *The Hindoos as They Are* (Calcutta: 1881), p. 173.

4*Bengal Hurkaru*, 6 May 1852.

The story of the way in which the ancestors of the Tagores fell from a state of purity exists in a number of versions, all of which involve association with the Muslim rulers of Bengal. According to their family traditions, they had been high-ranking orthodox Kulin Brahmins until the fifteenth century, when one Purushottama brought lasting disgrace upon his family. Some say he lost caste status because, in the course of attending a feast given by a Muslim official, Pir Ali Khan, he was tricked into inhaling the forbidden aroma of cooking beef. In another version, Purushottama lost caste when he rashly entered into a love match with a beautiful daughter from a family of Brahmins who had been converted to Islam.[5]

A more plausible account is given in the *Chaitanyamangala* of Jayananda, composed in the sixteenth century. Husain Shah, ruler of Gaur at the turn of the sixteenth century, was told that the Brahmins of Navadvipa were arming to overthrow his rule. He looted their property, desecrated their shrines, and forced those in the nearby village of Pirulya to take water from the hands of Muslims. Thereafter the Pirulya (or Pirali) Brahmins were considered polluted and unfit for marriage into other Brahmin families.[6] Still another explanation is that the ancestors of the Tagores were among those Brahmins employed by the Muslims as tax collectors and became unpopular with their fellow Brahmins either for implementing harsh revenue assessments or associating too freely with Muslims.[7] Whatever the origin of their degradation, the descendants of Purushottama were ostracized from Brahmin society, subjected to insults, and hounded from place to place. They had great difficulty marrying off their daughters and could serve as priests only to low castes that other Brahmins would not serve.

But the Tagores refused to accept an inferior status, and when an opportunity appeared to improve their position, they seized it. The first Tagore to emerge from legend into history was Panchanan, the great-great-grandfather of Dwarkanath. Toward the end of the seventeenth century he left the ancestral home at Narendrapur in Jessore and migrated to Govindapore. Panchanan was alert to economic opportunities, and at the turn of the eighteenth century he and his family began serving the Europeans as banians or compra-

5*Brief Account of the Tagore Family.*

6Dinesh Chandra Sen, *History of Bengali Language and Literature* (Calcutta: 1954), pp. 409–11.

7Bhattacharya, *Hindu Castes,* pp. 121–22.

dores. Thanks to commissions earned supplying provisions and arranging commercial transactions, Panchanan became a wealthy man and built a fine home and a temple to Siva.

The British appointed Panchanan's son, Joyram, Amin of the 24–Pargannas and Head *Sarkar* of the Paymaster's Department. Joyram added to the Govindapore property and built a second house for himself in Dhurumtullah, but his advance was momentarily interrupted by the capture of Calcutta by Sirajah-daulah in 1757. After the reconquest of the city, the government requisitioned both his Govindapore and Dhurumtullah properties for the site of the new Fort William and in compensation appointed Joyram contractor to construct the new fort. Soon he had recouped his fortune and built a fine house at Pathuriaghatta.

Joyram died in 1762, leaving four sons (see the accompanying genealogical chart). The eldest, Anunderam, who was the first Tagore to receive an education in English, was excluded from his father's will because of an impious act. [8] Gobinderam, the youngest son, who took over his father's lucrative position in the building of Fort William, had no descendants. The two middle sons, Darpa Narayan and Nilmony, were left to carry on the family name. Darpa Narayan amassed a fortune as banian for the French East India Company at Chandernagore and augmented his wealth by purchasing zamindaris or rural estates auctioned for arrears of revenue, including the Nattor Raj, an estate of 249 square miles situated in Rajshahi District.

His brother, Nilmony, sought his fortune upcountry, where he served as *sheristadar* of the district court in Chittagong. He remitted his salary to Darpa Narayan for investment, but upon his return from Chittagong the two brothers quarreled over the amount due Nilmony, and they divided their joint household. Nilmony left the ancestral dwelling at Pathuriaghatta and built a new home at Jorasanko. Although eventually the two brothers ended their quarrel, the division of the family into a senior branch at Pathuriaghatta and a junior one at Jorasanko was final. [9]

Nilmony died in 1791 and left three sons, Ramlochan, Rammoni, and Ramballhab. The middle son, Rammoni, married Menoka

8Supreme Court Report for 19 July 1836 in *Calcutta Monthly Journal,* 1836, pp. 332–33.

9Nilmony's name is included in a list of forty Indian names as tax farmers for the East India Company's pargannas in 1767. WBSA, Proceedings of the Select Committee, Fort William, 4 Nov. (347–50) 1766.

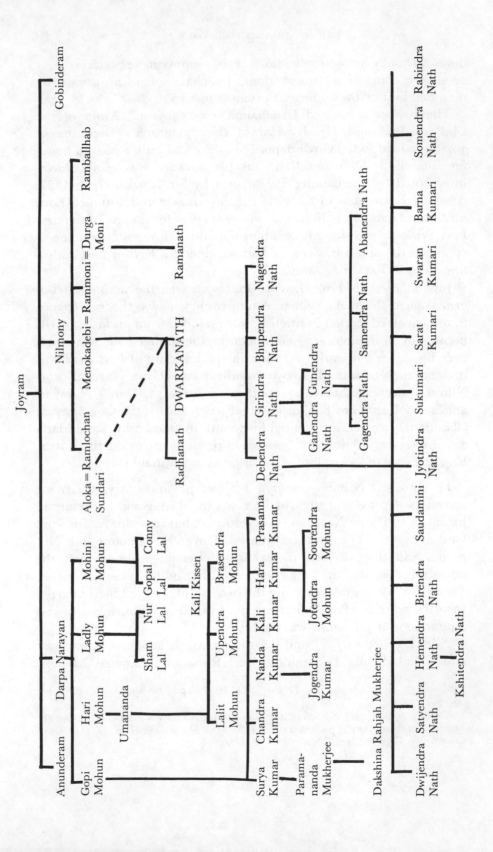

Debi, who bore him two sons: the first was Radhanath; the second, born in 1794, was Dwarkanath. Soon after Dwarkanath's birth, Menoka Debi died and Rammoni took a second wife, Durga Moni, who gave him a third son, Ramanath. Meanwhile, Dwarkanath's uncle, Ramlochan, now head of the Jorasanko branch of the family, had married Aloka Sundari, a sister of Dwarkanath's mother. Because they were childless, Ramlochan and Aloka Sundari were allowed to adopt Dwarkanath as their own in 1799. Thus Dwarkanath was raised by his father's elder brother and his mother's sister with the economic advantages of an only son.

Ramlochan provided his adopted son with the schooling customary for an upper-class, western-oriented Hindu. Dwarkanath learned his Bengali letters at a *pathsala* and received an elementary English education at Mr. Sherbourne's, one of a score of small English-medium schools run by Eurasians that catered to upper-class Hindu boys.[10] In 1807, when Dwarkanath was only thirteen years of age, Ramlochan died and left Aloka Sundari, Dwarkanath, and his natural father, Rammoni, to carry on the household at Jorasanko. [11] To Dwarkanath he bequeathed a substantial inheritance—estates in Orissa, which Ramlochan and his two brothers owned jointly, urban property in Calcutta, and, most important, a large zamindari called Berhampore situated in Jessore and Pabna districts, all held in trust by his stepmother. [12] At eighteen, Dwarkanath came into his property and, following the family custom, married a girl from the Pirali community of Jessore. The girl was Digambari, the daughter of Prawn Nauth Roy Chowdry of Narendrapur. [13] Dwarkanath's marriage—that of a worldly esthete with an orthodox, pious woman——would parallel the marriage of Ramlochan and Aloka Sundri.

Although of opposite temperaments, Ramlochan and Aloka Sundari each left an imprint on the character of Dwarkanath. Ramlochan was the most financially successful of the brothers, a dashing man of fashion who patronized poets, musicians, and singers and set

10Kissory Chand Mittra, *memoir*, p. 5.

11Satyendranath Tagore and Indira Devi, trans., *The Autobiography of Maharshi Devendranath Tagore* (Calcutta: 1909) p. 14; and notes in Bengali edition: Satischandra Chakravarty, ed., *Shrimanmaharshi Devendranath Thakurer Atmajibani* (Calcutta: 1927), pp. 297–98.

12The will of Ramlochan was collected by Amritamaya Mukherjee and published in *Samakalin,* Posh 1365 (December-January 1958–59), pp. 549–50.

13*Annual Register,* 1846 (London: 1847), "Chronicle," pp. 272–74; and Kshitindranath Thakur, pp. 71–76.

the standards of contemporary taste among the more urbane Calcuttans.[14] Aloka Sundari, who survived her husband by thirty years, was a devout Vaisnavite who staged festivals at Jorasanko and went on pilgrimages to the Vaisnavite shrines at Puri and Brindaban. According to her grandson, however, "there was a certain freedom of mind in her, together with her blind faith in religion."[15] Dwarkanath appears to have acquired from her some of his liberal religious and social attitudes—his preference for simple garb during worship, his democratic personal relationships, and his advocacy of the emancipation of women. During her last illness, when she was taken to the Ganges to die, Dwarkanath, her favorite, was on a trip upcountry. "If Dwarkanath had been at home," she complained, "you would never have been able to carry me away."[16] At her *sraddha* or funeral ceremony, Dwarkanath, as was the custom, distributed alms to fifty or sixty thousand people.[17]

Beyond Jorasanko, Dwarkanath's life was shaped by his kinship in the larger Tagore *paribar* or extended family. The Tagores were the most open-minded, free-spirited, and venturesome of the great Calcutta families; and many of the new paths Dwarkanath was to follow had been broken earlier by his elders and ancestors. While Dwarkanath was still a child his kinsmen had formed business partnerships with Britishers, supported liberal causes, adopted elements of western culture, entertained Europeans in their homes, and associated with social reformers. The Tagores had been divided into two households since the 1760s, but in matters affecting family honor, social status, and to some extent, economic well-being, the *paribar*

14Amritamaya Mukherjee, "Thakur Barir Itikatha."

15*Autobiography of Maharshi Devendranath Tagore,* p. 2.

16Ibid., p. 3. There may have been some relationship between the Tagores and three of the six Gosvamins who became the leading Vaisnava theologians in the sixteenth century. The three were *pirali* Brahmins who at one time had been converted to Islam or had somehow lost caste through association with the Muslims. See Edward C. Dimock, Jr., "Doctrine and Practice among the Vaisnavas of Bengal," in Milton Singer, ed., *Krishna: Myths, Rites, and Attitudes* (Honolulu: 1966), pp. 44, 219–20, no. 17. The Tagores of Jorasanko practiced Vaisnavism; those at Pathuriaghatta were Saivites.

17*Asiatic Journal* (London). Vol. 26, August 1838, p. 216. Both the *Calcutta Courier* of 21 Mar. 1838 and the *Bengal Hurkaru* of 13 Mar. 1838 mention the death of Dwarkanath's mother in 1838. Debendranath, however, wrote that his "Didima" died in 1757 *Shak* (1242 B.S.), which corresponds to the year 1835, and, according to Satischandra Chakravarty's notes in the Bengali edition, "Didima" refers to Aloka Sundari. See *Autobiography of Maharshi Devendranath Tagore,* p. 2; also Satischandra Chakravarty edition, p. 297.

acted together under the leadership of the eldest of the senior branch. In Dwarkanath's youth, the family head was Gopi Mohun, the eldest son of Darpa Narayan. Gopi Mohun was not only the head of the Tagore family but also the *dalapati* or leader of the Tagore "party" or *dal,* which included families from other castes who looked to the Tagores for patronage and leadership. At Pathuriaghatta the *dalapati* held court to settle questions within the family regarding ritual observances, marriage, property, and social behavior.[18]

Gopi Mohun was a highly educated man, conversant in English, French, Persian, and Sanskrit, and prominent among the founders of Hindu College. [19] He had been banian to Edward Wheler, a member of Warren Hasting's council, and, like his father Darpa Narayan, served as banian to the French at Chandernagore and added extensive estates to his inheritance. An orthodox Hindu, generous with *pandits,* and a builder of temples to Siva and Kali, he was also a personal friend of Joseph Barretto and other European merchants and was one of the small number of Hindus who invited foreigners into their homes.[20] He was tolerant of new ideas and may have counted himself as one of the friends of the notorious iconoclast, Rammohun Roy.[21] Possibly he attended the meetings of the Atmiya Sabha (Friendly Society) formed by Rammohun Roy in 1815 and may have taken along his youngest son, Prasanna Kumar, then fourteen years of age. Because the way had been cleared by the dalapati, Dwarkanath too would have been free to attend the meetings.

When Gopi Mohun died in 1818 his brother, Hari Mohun Tagore, became family head. Hari Mohun was *dewan* of the Export Warehouse, one of the higher government posts an Indian could hold.

18On the *dal* as a social unit in nineteenth-century Calcutta, see S.N. Mukherjee, "Class, Caste and Politics in Calcutta, 1815–1838," in E. Leach and S.N. Mukherjee, eds., *Elites in South Asia* (Cambridge: 1970), pp. 33–78; and Shib Chunder Bose, *The Hindoos As They Are* (Calcutta: 1881), pp. 169n., 170, and 176.

19In 1833, when his house burnt down, it was reported that among the articles lost was his library of over 3,000 volumes. *Indian Gazette,* 15 May 1833.

20Furrell, *Tagore Family,* pp. 69–76; Lokenath Ghosh, *Modern History,* II, 163–66; *Bengal Past and Present,* vol. 30, ser. no. 59–60 (July–December 1925), p. 199.

21Gopi Mohun is mentioned as an early supporter of Rammohun Roy, but the evidence is not conclusive. He is listed among the "Friends and Followers of Rammohun" by Manmatha Nath Ghosh, in app. D of Satischandra Chakravarty, ed., *Father of Modern India Commemoration Volume, 1933,* (Calcutta: 1935), pt. II, p. 131. Ghosh notes that Gopi Mohun was a patron of Kali Mirza, a musician who also gave lessons to Rammohun Roy and whose songs "strengthened him in his fight against idolatry."

Bishop Heber, who once visited him in his country villa, remarked on the "decidedly European" character of his house, furnishings, and carriages. "He is a fine old man, who speaks English well, is well informed on most topics of general discussion and talks with the appearance of much familiarity on Franklin, chemistry, natural philosophy, etc." [22] Unlike Gopi Mohun, however, he had no patience for Rammohun Roy's attacks on Hindu orthodoxy, and in 1822 he joined with Radha Kanta Deb in proposing a vote of thanks to Lord Hastings for his protection of *sati*. [23]

When Dwarkanath and his cousin Prasanna Kumar defied the dalapati and opted for the camp of Rammohun Roy, they created a new breach in the paribar which cut accross the old one between Jorasanko and Pathuriaghatta. The young renegades were not yet important enough to polarize the entire family, but in time their combined wealth and power would equal that of the orthodox party within the family and they would form their own dal in opposition to that of Hara Kumar, successor to Hari Mohun as Tagore dalapati. The lines were drawn by 1823 when Hari Mohun's son, Umananda (also known as Nandalal) directed the preparation of two tracts, the first attacking Rammohun Roy and the second aimed in all likelihood at Dwarkanath and Prasanna Kumar. The latter referred to "certain well known persons, fallen into bad company because of youth, wealth, power and thoughtlessness, [who] throw off fear of religion and of public opinion, cut their tuft of hair, drink wine and consort with Muhammadan women." [24]

Some of the other Tagores were won over to reformism in whole or in part. Chandra Kumar, the second son of Gopi Mohun, took up a position somewhere between those of Rammohun and Hara Kumar. He avoided the issue of sati but joined Rammohun, Dwarkanath and Prasanna Kumar in a petition against the press regulations, was later involved in the agitation against the Stamp Act, signed the petition favoring European settlement in India, and supported the movement for jury trial. Another cousin, Shamlal, participated in the anti-sati movement and, in 1831, together with Prasanna Kumar and

22Quoted in Furrell, *Tagore Family,* p. 153.
23R. Heber, *Narrative of a Journey through the Upper Provinces of India.* 3 vols. (4th ed., London: 1828), I, 92.
24Sushil Kumar De, *History of Bengali Literature in the Nineteenth Century,* 2d ed. (Calcutta: 1961), p. 526.

Ramanath, launched a weekly newspaper, *Reformer,* to advocate the views of Rammohun and his followers. [25]

Old and new divisions within the family did not prevent Dwarkanath from joining his Pathuriaghatta relatives in a number of business arrangements. As middlemen operating between the Indian and British business worlds the Tagores collaborated with European merchants in trade, banking, insurance, and plantations. [26] A family association that would be of particular consequence to Dwarkanath was the connection of Surya Kumar and Chundra Kumar Tagore, the two older sons of Gopi Mohun, with the agency house of Mackintosh and Company. [27] Among his Pathuriaghatta relatives, Dwarkanath was most closely involved in business arrangements with Ladly Mohun Tagore, youngest brother of Gopi Mohun. Ladly Mohun furnished the personal security for Dwarkanath when the latter was appointed Dewan of the Salt Department in 1828[28] and joined Dwarkanath in speculations involving John Palmer and Company and the Palmers of Hyderabad. [29] Ladly Mohun's fortunes declined, and when he died in 1833, Dwarkanath helped his sons Shamlal and Hurlal to pay their father's debts and establish themselves in business. [30]

Dwarkanath received little direct financial help from his family. In the 1820s, when he was launching his investments and speculations, the Tagores of Pathuriaghatta were in difficulties. The large estate left by Gopi Mohun had shrunk within a decade of his death in 1818, and his sons, led by Chandra Kumar, lost heavily in opium

25 Nirmal Sinha, ed., *Freedom Movement in Bengal* (Calcutta: 1968), pp. 28–30, 49; J.K. Majumdar, ed., *Raja Rammohun Roy and Progressive Movements in India* (Calcutta: 1941), pp. 44, 203, 212.

26 Hari Mohun Tagore joined with Gopi Mohun Deb and Ramdulal Day as the original Indian partners in the Saugor Island Society of 1818. G.A. Prinsep, "Sketch of the Proceedings and Present Position of the Saugor Island Society and Its Lessees" (IO Tract 146, Calcutta: 1831).

27 Atulchandra Gupta, ed., *Studies in the Bengal Renaissance* (Jadavpur: 1958), p. 546.

28 WBSA, Customs, Salt and Opium; Salt Proceedings, 17 July (22–23) 1832.

29 Palmer Papers, Engl. Lett. c 124, 11 Aug. 1833, and c 121, 25 July 1832.

30 Hurlal Tagore vs. Ashutosh Day, Supreme Court, 18 Apr. 1836, in *Asiatic Journal* (London), vol. 21, October 1836, p. 91. Although Shamlal had joined the Rammohun party a few years earlier, his younger brother, Hurlal, had turned his back on Dwarkanath and gone for financial help to the Day family, among the city's wealthiest orthodox Hindu families. Dwarkanath, undoubtedly angry with his kinsman for seeking help from a rival *dalapati,* later testified in court to Hurlal's weak character and improvident habits.

speculations and in law suits against Alexander and Company and Barretto and Sons. In 1829 the surviving brothers divided up the family property and liabilities and by the time Prasanna Kumar and Hara Kumar had recouped their losses and become wealthy men, Dwarkanath had made his own fortune.[31] It was not capital but intangible assets that Dwarkanath acquired from his Pathuriaghatta relatives: the family name and reputation, the business traditions, and the Tagore life style. The family molded his fundamental attitudes and values—his refined tastes, cosmopolitan outlook, and receptivity to new ideas. Nevertheless, in both business and public life, Dwarkanath transcended his family. His idealism, breadth of vision, and contribution to his country must be attributed largely to the influence of one outside the family—Rammohun Roy.

When he settled in Calcutta in 1815, Rammohun Roy at 43 was a full generation older than Dwarkanath. Although he had spent most of his life in the *mufassal,* accumulating a modest fortune in moneylending and land speculation, he was already well-known in Calcutta where his religious views had antagonized both Hindus and Muslims, whose sacred beliefs he attacked as irrational and superstitious. A few years later he would antagonize Christians too by ridiculing the concept of the Trinity. Even the sympathetic orientalist H.H. Wilson would describe his views as unreasonable and immoderate.[32]

Concrete evidence of the early association of Rammohun and Dwarkanath is sketchy. Dwarkanath may have attended the meetings of Rammohun Roy's Atmiya Sabha, for a newspaper report notes that a Sabha meeting in 1819 was attended by some members of "families, most eminent for wealth or learning amongst the Hindoo inhabitants, but we regret that we are not enabled to mention their names."[33] If the worldly young Dwarkanath did attend the meetings,

31*The Great Tagore Will Case* (Calcutta: 1872), p. 1. Eventually the Tagores of Pathuriaghatta became the wealthy branch and the Tagores of Jorasanko relatively modest in means. The chief reason for this was that Hara Kumar's property was divided between only two sons whereas the wealth amassed by Dwarkanath was eventually divided among the fourteen children of Debendranath.

32Sophia Dobson Collet, *The Life and Letters of Raja Rammohun Roy* (D.K.Biswas and P.C. Ganguli, eds.), 3d ed. (Calcutta: 1962), pp. 22, 27. Peary Chand Mittra, *Life of Dewan Ramcomul Sen* (Calcutta: 1880), p. 13.

33 J.K. Majumdar, ed., *Raja Rammohun Roy*, p. 18.

he probably had less interest in the readings from the Upanishads than in the strange maverick who conducted the meetings. 34

Dwarkanath was not faced with the need to commit himself fully to the camp of Rammohun Roy until 1818. In that year Rammohun launched his campaign against the "evils and disgrace" of sati by publishing two pamphlets, one in Bengali and one in English. 35 These "produced a commotion in Calcutta Hindu society" and brought forth a reply from the conservative intelligentsia and counter-replies from Rammohun. 36 The polarization of Hindu society intensified in the 1820s and reached its climax in 1830 with the formation of the Dharma Sabha, organized by the conservatives to defend sati. Sati, above all issues, became the cause that divided the friends from the opponents of Rammohun Roy, and if Dwarkanath and his kinsman Prasanna Kumar Tagore had been vacillating, they were now forced to choose their camp and to separate themselves from the elders of the Tagore family. 37

For a short period in the 1820s the two young Tagores even experimented with Christianity. In 1821, Rammohun Roy and the Reverend William Adam, formerly a Baptist missionary, gathered together a small group of friends and formed the Calcutta Unitarian Committee. There is no list of the original members, but in 1827 the

34One writer claims that Dwarkanath was at first an implacable foe of Rammohun Roy. *Fisher's Colonial Magazine* (London), August-December 1842, I, 393-99.

35Kalidas Nag and Debajyoti Burman, eds., *The English Works of Raja Rammohun Roy,* 6 pts., (Calcutta: 1945-51), pt. III, pp. 87 ff.

36A.F. Salahuddin Ahmed, *Social Ideas and Social Change in Bengal 1818-1835* (Leiden: 1965), p. 113.

37Perhaps the earliest concrete surviving evidence of an association between Rammohun and Dwarkanath is a letter from John Digby, Rammohun's old employer, to the Board of Revenue, dated 16 Nov. 1822. Digby had nominated a nephew of Rammohun to the post of Abkaree Teshildar (Excise-tax collector) of the Burdwan collectorship and wrote that "Dwarkanauth Takoor who is possessed of considerable landed property has offered himself as security" for the young man. See R. Chandra and Jatindra Kumar Majumdar, *Selections from Official Letters and Documents relating to the Life of Raja Rammohun Roy,* vol. I, 1791-1830 (Calcutta: 1938), p. 319. Politically, the first association between Rammohun and Dwarkanath may have been a petition to the Supreme Court dated 18 Mar. 1823, protesting the Press Regulation. Twelve years later, Dwarkanath reminisced: "When this regulation was first promulgated, I with three of my own relations and my lamented friend the late Rammohun Roy were the only persons who petitioned the Supreme Court against it." Quoted in Kissory Chand Mittra, *Memoir,* p. 45. In fact, the signers also included Gauri Charan Banerjee, a brother of orthodox-party leader Radhamadub Bannerjee, and Hurchunder Ghose. See Collet, *Raja Rammohun Roy,* p. 429.

members included Theodore Dickens, a Barrister of the Supreme Court; George James Gordon, a merchant of the firm of Mackintosh and Company; William Tate, an attorney; B.W. Macleod, a surgeon in the company's service; Norman Kerr, an uncovenanted servant of the company; Rammohun Roy; Dwarkanath Tagore; Prasanna Kumar Tagore; Radhaprasad Roy (eldest son of Rammohun); and William Adam. [38] Among the Britishers, George James Gordon and Theodore Dickens would remain lifelong friends of Dwarkanath.

Rammohun disbanded the Unitarian Committee in 1828 and replaced it with the Brahmo Samaj, composed exclusively of Indians. Dwarkanath emerged as the second in command, and after Rammohun departed for Europe in 1830 he assumed leadership of the Brahmo Samaj and the reforming party. Although proud to associate his name with that of Rammohun in social and political movements, Dwarkanath was less than enthusiastic about carrying on his iconoclastic religious ideas.

Dwarkanath's deepest religious convictions were Vaisnavite, with which he became imbued during his childhood at Jorasanko. His son Debendranath asserted that he had been "a staunch believer in the popular religion of the country," and that although Rammohun Roy undermined his faith in Hindu practices, "he never became thoroughly posted in the truths of theism as preached by Raja Rammohun Roy." [39] Throughout his life, Dwarkanath continued to perform *puja* to the family idols, but during Rammohun's lifetime, deference to his teacher took precedence over conventional worship. Debendranath recalled that whenever Rammohun approached Jorasanko, Dwarkanath would interrupt his daily puja to receive his friend and teacher. He attended Brahmo services and perhaps for a time even accepted Rammohun's theism, but he insisted on worshipping God in his own fashion. He alone would come to Brahmo prayer meetings informally attired, and once, when taken to task for his alleged disrespect for God, replied, "Having to spend the whole day in my office-dress, I cannot again put myself to the trouble and inconvenience of using it in the evenings, especially when I have come to worship God, to whom we should always appear in the simplest and humblest garb." [40] The anecdote reveals a view of the separation of secular and sacred quite different from that held by

38Collet, *Raja Rammohun Roy,* p. 131n.
39Chakravarty, ed., *Father of Modern India,* pt. II, p. 173; *Memoir,* p. 124.
40Chakravarty, ed., *Father of Modern India,* pt. II, pp. 175–76.

Rammohun. Rammohun believed that God was man's king and master and in going to His court, one must dress himself properly and must appear before Him as one fit to be present at the court of the Prince of Princes.[41] Dwarkanath associated wealth, luxury, and elegance with the secular world and with objects that could be assigned a price and that men could manipulate. The sacred he associated with humility, poverty, and simplicity.

Because he lacked Rammohun's zeal for religious reform, Dwarkanath was able to serve as a bridge between the Brahmos and the orthodox community. He and Prasanna Kumar joined the conservative leaders in the Gaudiya Samaj (Bengali Society) formed in 1823 to promote the Bengali language, defend Bengali culture against the attacks of the missionaries, and save the youth from the corrupt moral influence of both Christian and rationalist education.[42] In 1833, when the European business community appealed to the government to reduce the number of Hindu holidays observed in public offices, Dwarkanath joined his Hindu brethren to protest religious discrimination.[43] In the following year the chief magistrate of Calcutta issued orders prohibiting religious singing processions in the city streets. Dwarkanath and Radha Kanta Deb, leader of conservative society, united in opposition, and the order was rescinded.[44]

In his religious behavior, Dwarkanath was governed largely by a sense of propriety. He would follow the customs and traditions of his ancestors so long as they were not disgraceful or degrading to his self-respect. Much of what he did was done with an eye toward the reaction of the European community, for he craved their approval just as his orthodox kinsmen looked for approval to the Hindu caste leaders. Thus, while indifferent to theological reform, he was passionate in his support for the outlawing of sati. Most of his European associates saw it as a cruel, barbaric rite and questioned whether any nation that practiced it could be truly civilized. To a Bengali in daily contact with Europeans, the continued practice of sati was personally embarrassing.

After a long struggle, Rammohun and Dwarkanath won their victory against conservative opposition. In December 1829 Lord

41 Ibid.
42 Amitabah Mukherjee, *Reform and Regeneration in Bengal 1774–1823* (Calcutta: 1968), pp. 118–19.
43 *Bengal Harkaru,* 2 July 1834.

Bentinck and his council passed the regulation making sati illegal and its administration punishable in the criminal courts. The conservative leaders formed the Dharma Sabha and employed a group of lawyers to appeal the law before the Privy Council. Many years later one of the lawyers, McDougall, still had not been paid, and his Calcutta agent appealed to Dwarkanath and Prasanna Kumar, among others, to honor the debt. Ordinarily Dwarkanath would have been the first to respond to such a request; now he reminded the agent, John Storm, of the role he and Prasanna Kumar had played in the anti-sati movement. "You cannot, I am sure, for one moment suppose that I, or the Reformer [Prasanna Kumar] or any true son of humanity will contribute the smallest iota towards the payment of the sum. . on account of expenses attending the appeal against the abolition of that diabolical system of Suttee! I am proud to say, I stood among the first of those who. . .helped to suppress that species of murder. . .by proper representations to the Noble Lord our Ruler who has thereby, if no other act, immortalized his name here and wherever it was known that such barbarous atrocity was practiced in India." He suggested to Storm that Rajnarian Ray and Ashutosh Day, principal supporters of the Dharma Sabha, would "wipe off their responsibilities."[45]

Second only to sati as an issue that embittered the Bengali community against Rammohun Roy and his followers was their stand on European settlement. Rammohun and his followers joined the European mercantile community in advocating the abolition of restrictions on the holding of land by Europeans in the mufassal. At a public meeting in December 1829, Dwarkanath moved to support the petition of the Europeans, and both he and Rammohun spoke in favor of European settlement in India. The opposition, led by officials of the East India Company, included the majority of the Bengali community. Some of the Indians had unhappy experiences with disruptive European adventurers in the mufassal, others were xenophobic or harbored vague fears of religious pollution. They petitioned Parliament, and their newspaper, the *Samachar Chandrika*, editorialized that if colonization occurred, "the natives will lose

44*Calcutta Monthly Journal,* October 1835, p. 302.

45 Letter from Dwarkanath Tagore to John Storm, 19 Aug. 1841. Copy of full text exists in ms. copy of Kshitindranath Thakur, "Dwarkanath Thakurer Jabini," archives of Rabindra Bharati University, Calcutta. Hereafter referred to as KNT ms.

caste . . . their means of subsistence will be destroyed, and . . .
continual disputes will arise with the English relative to lands."[46]

The most articulate advocate of European colonization was
Rammohun Roy, who, with Dwarkanath in agreement, viewed the
question in the broad context of India's history and future place in
international society. They saw India as a vast subcontinent occupied
by many different communities, castes, tribes, sects, and nations.
Each of the subcontinent's foreign invaders had eventually made
India his home, entered into the Indian social fabric, and dropped
distinctions between conqueror and conquered. Rammohun expected
the most recent among the conquerors, the British, to follow the
pattern and foresaw, in time, an India that was Christian (if not in a
formal sense, at least in an ethical sense), modernized, prosperous,
and, in some measure, associated with England. The Indian empire
of the future was to be a realm of British-Indian partnership in all
spheres—political, economic, and cultural. In the future, wrote
Rammohun Roy, "the existence of a large body of respectable
settlers . . . would bring that vast Empire in the east to a level with
other large Christian countries in Europe, and by means of its
immense riches and extensive population . . . may succeed sooner
or later in enlightening and civilizing the surrounding nations of
Asia."[47]

In formulating his ideal of empire, Rammohun must have drawn
upon the Roman model as portrayed by Gibbon: "The grandsons of
the Gauls . . . commanded legions, governed provinces, and were
admitted into the Senate of Rome. Their ambition, instead of
disturbing the tranquility of the state, was intimately connected with
its safety and greatness."[48] Rammohun's view of the Mughal Empire
is strikingly similar, and he once wrote the King in Council
comparing the Mughal to the British policy: "Under their former
Muhammadan Rulers, the natives of this country enjoyed every
political privilege in common with Mussulmans, being eligible to the
highest offices in the state, entrusted with the command of armies
and the government of provinces and often chosen as advisers to their

46J.K. Majumdar, pp. 432–46. Restrictions on European settlement were
abolished, but few Britishers settled in India. Still, the opposition's contention that
Europeans would disrupt mufassal life in Bengal proved correct.

47Nag and Burman, *English Works,* pt. III, pp. 79 ff.

48Edward Gibbon, *The History of the Decline and Fall of the Roman Empire,* 7 vols., 2d
ed. (London: 1926), I, 40–41.

Prince, without disqualification or degrading distinction on account of their religion or the place of their birth . . . . Under British rule, the natives of India have entirely lost this political consequence." [49]

Thus far, the East India Company had not fulfilled the mission of creating a British empire in India. It was still at heart a trading company and its efforts had been primarily directed to extending the commercial structure of Britain. Because of its limited objectives, the company tried to effect as little social change as possible, and therefore insisted upon restricting free British settlers from coming to India and upsetting conservative Indian society. Rammohun believed that the presence of British settlers would force the government to broaden political participation and to introduce British political institutions into India, creating in the process a true British-Indian empire. [50]

Rammohun himself recognized the dangers and disadvantages of European settlement. He conceded that some of the indigo planters had "proved obnoxious to those who expected milder treatment from them" but that "no general good can be effected without some partial evil." At least the planters treated the peasantry better than did their own zamindars. They gave the peasants an alternative protector in the mufassal and "if any class of native 'would gladly see them all turned out of the country' it would be the zamindars in general, since in many instances the planters have successfully protected the *ryots* against the tyranny and oppression of their land-lord." Rammohun suggested that immigration be limited to Europeans of the "high and better educated classes," that all subjects be placed on the same judicial footing, and that cases be tried by juries composed impartially of both races. [51]

Furthermore, he had no illusions about the capacity of the British for racial arrogance and himself had encountered rude and overbearing behavior. He hinted at his deeper feelings in a letter to Prasanna Kumar from England: "Though it is impossible for a thinking man not to feel the evils of political subjection and dependence on a

49Nag and Burman, *English Works,* pt. IV, pp. 26–27. Dwarkanath did not share Rammohun's favorable view of Hindu-Muslim relations in the Mughal Empire, but he did envision an Indo-British empire in terms similar to those of Rammohun.

50Ibid., pt. III, p. 83.

51Collet, *Raja Rammohun Roy,* p. 270; Nag and Burman, *English Works,* pt. III, p. 83. David Kopf, perhaps unfairly, attributes Rammohun's support of colonization to "blind faith in the nobility of English intentions." David Kopf, *British Orientalism and the Bengal Renaissance* (Berkeley: 1969), p. 270.

foreign people, yet when we reflect on the advantages which we have derived and may hope to derive from our connection with Great Britain, we may be reconciled to the present state of things which promises permanent benefits to our posterity." [52] It was not westernization *in toto* that he advocated for India. He attacked Christianity for its own absurdities and irrationalities, favorably compared the "domestic conduct" of Indians to Europeans, and asserted that "in point of vices the Hindus are not worse than the generality of Christians in Europe and America." [53] His object was the regeneration of India and to accomplish this he would play upon the humanitarian, utilitarian, and evangelical instincts of the rulers. It was immaterial that high ethical behavior was no more pervasive in Europe than in India. To the extent their British rulers in India held high-minded sentiments they could be enlisted in the cause of Indian reform and regeneration.

Dwarkanath contributed to the debate by introducing an economic dimension. He told how indigo manufacture had improved the condition of both ryots and zamindars, how land had increased in value, and how he and his relatives had made a great deal of money from planting indigo. Unrestricted immigration would open the way for the manufacture of other articles that India was capable of producing "of an excellence and quality, as any other [country] in the world, and which of course cannot be expected to be produced without the free recourse of Europeans." [54] Along the same lines, the *Reformer* referred specifically to the entrepreneurial skills that Europeans would bring and anticipated that India would develop into a manufacturing country competing with Britain itself. [55]

Yet neither Rammohun nor Dwarkanath viewed India as the passive beneficiary of western civilization. If Britishers were to participate in the rejuvenation of Indian society, Indians must join in and help reform British society. It was to India's interest that its rulers were men who held enlightened principles. Just as he attacked orthodox Hinduism, Rammohun spoke out in criticism of the irrational in Christianity and formed his Unitarian society as his contribution to religious reform in the West. In politics he called for reform in the international passport and visa system that prevailed in

52Nag and Burman, *English Works,* pt. IV, p. 40.
53Collet, *Raja Rammohun Roy,* p. 249.
54J.K. Majumdar, ed., *Raja Rammohun Roy,* pp. 38–39.
55Ibid., pp. 453–55.

Europe and lobbied in favor of the Reform Bill of 1832. He did all this as an "insider," since he considered himself a British subject as well as an Indian. After the passage of the Reform Bill he wrote a British friend: "As I publically avowed that in the event of the Reform Bill being defeated I would renounce my connection with this country, I refrained from writing to you or any other friend in Liverpool until I knew the result. Thank Heaven, I can now feel proud of being one of your fellow subjects."[56]

From Rammohun, Dwarkanath learned that the affairs of the British were his own affairs. He would in time give his own expression to the concept of imperial partnership. British causes would become his own, he would donate liberally to their charities, patronize their arts and play a leading role in the civic life of the British community of Calcutta. Just as Rammohun had had the temerity to lend his hand in the reform of Christianity, Dwarkanath would take a leading role in the modernization of British-Indian business institutions. They both subordinated their particular ethnic loyalties to their identities as imperial citizens.

As a "British subject" Rammohun Roy was eager to observe the Reform Bill debates at first hand and to testify before the select committee of the House of Commons to consider renewal of the charter of the East India Company. In addition, he had undertaken to act as agent for the cause of the King of Delhi. When he left for England on 19 November 1830, Dwarkanath must have watched him sail off with a heavy heart. The leadership of the new sect, the Brahmo Samaj, and of the large number of dependents who constituted the party of Rammohun Roy now fell on his shoulders. Rammohun died in England on 27 September, 1832. "When the news of Rammohun Roy's death came," wrote Debendranath, "I was by my father, and he began to weep like a boy."[57]

56 Rammohun Roy to William Rathbone, 31 July 1832, quoted in Collet, p. 334.
57 Chakravarty, ed., *Father of Modern India*, pt. II, p. 176.

Chapter II

ZAMINDAR, DEWAN, AND BANIAN

By 1830 Dwarkanath was a man of wealth and influence, ready to shoulder the responsibility of leading the Brahmo faction. His position was built on three components—his increasing stature as a landowner, his official connections with the government, and his financial and commercial enterprises. Each of these must be dealt with separately, but Dwarkanath pursued his three careers simultaneously and his success in any one of them helped him to succeed in the others. As early as 1812, when he assumed personal supervision of the estates inherited from Ramlochan, he began to develop competence in land-tenure law and zamindari accounting. Perhaps because he saw an opportunity to serve other zamindars as advisor, he expanded his legal knowledge under the guidance of Robert Cutlar Fergusson, one of the small but important group of British advocates who practised before the Supreme Court in Calcutta. [1]

Under Fergusson, Dwarkanath mastered regulation law and the procedures of the Supreme, *sadr,* and *zilla* courts. He then set himself up as a legal agent and attracted as clients some of the leading zamindars of Bengal, among them Rajah Baradakant Roy of the

---

1. Robert Cutlar Fergusson was known to Dwarkanath as the attorney employed by Rammohun Roy's nephew, Govindpersaud Roy, in his lawsuit against Rammohun in 1817. A few years later, Fergusson acted in a cause friendly to Rammohun when he defended James Silk Buckingham, editor of the *Calcutta Journal,* against charges of libel and presented to the Supreme Court the appeal for freedom of the press. After his retirement to England, Fergusson served as a representative for the orthodox community and on their behalf presented a petition to the House of Commons against European settlement. R. Chandra and J.K. Majumdar, eds., *Selections from Official Letters and Documents relating to the Life of Raja Rammohun Roy,* I, pp. 63–70; J.K. Majumdar, ed., *Raja Rammohun Roy and Progressive Movements in India,* pp. 399, 433–44; Charles Moore, *The Sheriffs of Fort William from 1775–1926* (Calcutta: 1926), pp. 32–33; Ralph E. Turner, *The Relations of James Silk Buckingham with the East India Company, 1818–1836* (Pittsburgh: 1930), pp. 33, 42; C.H. Philips, *The East India Company, 1784–1834* (Manchester: 1940), pp. 278, 282, 285 and n., 293, ·336.

Jessore Raj, Durga Charan Mookerjie of Bagbazar, Harinath Roy of Cossimbazar, and Rani Kateyanee of the Paikpara Raj family.[2] In addition to his fees, Dwarkanath realized other financial advantages. For example, he borrowed Rs. 75,000 from Harinath Roy in 1827 at 4 percent when the market rate was 8 to 12 percent.[3]

Dwarkanath started his career as a zamindari agent in 1815, a watershed year in the land-revenue history of Bengal. After a generation of floundering, the zamindars were at last learning how to preserve their estates from the auction block and had begun to reverse the tide of sales that had begun with the Permanent Settlement of 1793. Although the regulation strengthened the zamindars by allowing them to seize the property of defaulting tenants, the original revenue demand set by Cornwallis in 1793 had been ruinous. Payment was enforced by a law of sale and implemented mercilessly. The government allowed no suspension of tax payments in case of natural calamity, and the British judicial concepts upon which the laws were founded were incomprehensible to most of the zamindars. By 1812, more than half the estates in Bengal had been wrested from the hands of their original owners and many were sold at auction to families with newly acquired wealth. Some districts were harder hit than others. In Jessore, for example, all of the 122 estates in existence in 1793 fell into arrears over the next decade and were subdivided and sold in parcels to the highest bidders. By 1800 there were 5,044 small zamindars in place of the 122 old aristocrats. Among the new zamindars were Darpa Narayan and Gopi Mohun Tagore, who participated in the dismemberment of the vast Nattor Raj.[4]

By 1815 the crest had been reached. The zamindars had become accustomed to the laws, and, to preserve their estates, both the old survivors and the new zamindars had learned to resort to every available legal stratagem and circumvention. The laws elaborating upon and modifying the original act of 1793 were in the form of highly technical regulations stating conditions under which estates in

2Kissory Chand Mittra, *Memoir of Dwarkanath Tagore,* pp. 7–9; Bengal District Gazetteers, *Murshidabad* (Calcutta: 1914), p. 195; J. Westland, *A Report on the District of Jessore* (Calcutta: 1874), pp. 100, 149; letter from Dwarkanath to Debendranath, 22 May 1846, Tagore Family Archives, Rabindra Sadana, Santiniketan.

3WBSA, Court of Wards, nos. 8–11, March 1837.

4N.K. Sinha, ed., *The History of Bengal (1757–1905)* (Calcutta: 1967), p. 423; Westland, *Jessore,* p. 145; M.N. Gupta, *Analytical Survey of Bengal Regulations* (Calcutta: 1943), p. 284; F.D. Ascoli, *Early Revenue History of Bengal and the Fifth Report,* 1812 (Oxford: 1917), p. 77.

whole or in part could be sold, village accounts could be obtained, and suits could be conducted against unfair collectors. They also defined the legal status of undertenures, the powers of zamindars over peasants, and conditions under which tax-exempt land could be reassessed by the government.[5]

These were the regulations that Dwarkanath mastered; and just as his ancestors had risen to wealth by interpreting the Indian market to western merchants, he earned his reputation interpreting the laws of the British government to anxious zamindars. As a zamindar himself, and scion of a prominent family with widespread estates, Dwarkanath was trusted as an insider and social peer. At the same time, he had entrée into the world of western law and commerce. He understood the implications of foreign legal concepts such as contract, a market in land, and the adversary system of justice. He knew there were legal limitations on the powers of the collector and magistrate, and he presented a legal brief in terms the British would respect. The young Tagore, at home in the new culture, was thus the teacher and counsellor of his elders.

Dwarkanath's own zamindari holdings, augmented and developed in a businesslike fashion, provided the basis for his strong financial position in the commercial world. The dual nature of his economic activities gave him his financial resiliency: among merchants he was a zamindar and among zamindars a merchant. He inherited from Ramlochan the largest and most important of his zamindaris, Berhampore, which straddled the districts of Jessore and Pabna and included within it the hinterland of the town of Commercolly, an important center for trade and for indigo and silk manufacturing. In addition, he inherited a group of estates in the Cuttack area of Orissa in the Pandua and Balia Taluks. In 1830 Dwarkanath purchased Kaligram in Rajshahi District and in 1834 Shahazadpur in Pabna District.[6]

The four zamindaris—Berhampore, Pandua, Kaligram, and Shahazadpur—were held without partners and placed in trust for his sons and their descendants in 1840 when Dwarkanath was in the prime of life (see accompanying chart).[7] Through purchase or default

5 M.N. Gupta, *Bengal Regulations,* pp. 275–301.
6 KNT ms., p. 58.
7 Will of Dwarkanath Tagore and other papers in "Case for Opinion, re: division of property of Debendranath Tagore requested by Hitendra Nath Tagore, et al.," Kshitindra Nath Tagore Collection, Archives of Rabindra Bharati University, Calcutta. Hereafter refferred to as KNT Collection.

CHART 2. PATRIMONIAL ZAMINDARIS

Estate, location, & date acquired	Gross income, 1834 (rupees)	Jumma* 1898	Gross income, 1900	Jumma, cesses & collection charges, 1900	Average, net income, 1900
Berhampore, Commercolly & Sadaka in Pabna, Nadia & Jessore D. 1807	50,000	16,887	1,73,891 (with Kaligram)	63,272 (with Kaligram)	1,10,650 (with Kaligram)
Pandua, Balia, Paharajpur in Cuttack 1807	20,000	16,043	Pandua: 36,911 B & P 19,350	Pandua: 24,814 B & P 13,485	Pandua 12,100 B & P 5,860
Kaligram in Rajshahi D. 1830	40,000	11,673	(included with Berhampore.........)		
Shahazadpur in Pabna & Rajshahi D. 1834	20,000	10,980	1,38,357	32,658	1,05,700
Total	1,30,000	55,583	3,68,509	1,34,229	2,34,310

Sources:
1834 figures from KNT ms., p. 58. Other figures from Case for Opinion, re: division of property of Debendranath Tagore requested by Hitendranath Tagore, et al., in Kshitindranath Tagore Collection, Archives of Rabindra Bharati University, Calcutta.
*Jumma: Total land revenue paid by zamindar to government. Under the Permanent Settlement, would have been little changed between 1834 and 1898.

on mortgages, Tagore acquired a number of other zamindaris, some of which he held in partnership with others. Finally, he acted at times as the general manager for the whole of the Tagore family estates scattered in every district of lower Bengal, estates that, in his own words, accounted for one-fifteenth of the total land revenue of the lower provinces.[8]

As a zamindar Dwarkanath was mercilessly efficient and business-like, but not generous. The editor of the *Bengal Hurkaru* once wrote: "We do not remember to have heard that . . . he differs much from the rest of his class. Have the ryots upon his estates been happier than those on the estates of his neighbours—has he done much to mitigate the sufferings of the laboring people—to lessen the amount of oppression and extortion, exercised almost universally on the estates

[8] WBSA, Criminal Department Proceedings, 15 December (1–3) 1840.

of native land-holders—has he done much to create the fairest of all sights on the face of nature—a happy tenantry?"[9]

At times his tenants complained to the government. In 1824, 116 ryots on his Berhampore estate submitted a petition asserting that during the rainy season they were trapped in their houses because their zamindar, Dwarkanath Tagore, would not build an embankment. Though Tagore contended that a new embankment would flood part of his fields and destroy 60 to 70 houses, the government and the head of the Embankment Committee supported the ryots.[10] Another incident occurred in 1833 when the ryots of Pargana Khashpore in the 24–Pargannas petitioned Bentinck against their "stoney-hearted zamindar," Dwarkanath Tagore, who tried illegally to raise their customary rents and, after losing a court decision, had turned to coercion. "He imprisons some and corrects others," but "on account of the said zamindar being affluent" the collector, commissioner, and magistrate "paid no attention to their piteable condition." The government referred the ryots to the courts for redress, but questioned the legality of Tagore's actions.[11]

Dwarkanath had no intention of acting the part of a benevolent and paternalistic landlord. He viewed the people on his estates as rent-payers or laborers, not dependents. To him zamindari was a business like any other, and he insisted on the businesslike and efficient management of his estates. Still, if only to keep his cultivators from absconding, he kept a close watch on the worst kinds of abuses by his *amla* or supervisory personnel. In 1836, for example, when the ryots of his Berhampore estate petitioned the judge of Jessore against oppressive treatment by his servants, Tagore instructed his manager, S.F. Rice, to obtain a copy of the petition and, "ascertaining the true nature of the case make me acquainted with the same. Are they actually ill-treated by the indigo *gomastas* or zemindary *amlahs*? Is the land, too, become so much impoverished that they cannot go on with the cultivation? I cannot, however, understand why the lands of Berhampore villages should turn out so unproductive when we do not hear of similar complaints from any

9*Bengal Hurkaru*, 6 Jan. 1843.
10WBSA, Territorial Revenue Department Proceedings, 9 Apr. (24) and 28 May (10–12) 1824.
11WBSA, Territorial Revenue Department Proceedings, 8 July (10) 1833 and 15 January (17) 1834.

other quarter, nor even from its adjacent villages. I suspect there must be some other cause for so many Istafas being at once tendered. From the way things are going on there, there will, I fear, in a few months hence, hardly remain any ryots at all. Pray make a full enquiry into the matter and write to me on the subject at your earliest convenience." [12]

Hard as he was with his peasants, he was even more so in his dealings with other zamindars and European indigo planters. He purchased Shahazadpur in Pabna from the heirs of Sibchunder Bhattacharya, who had fallen on bad times and were forced to sell their estate at auction. The heirs, including the mother of the zamindar, had tried to protect themselves by acquiring undertenures with permanently fixed rents. But Dwarkanath abrogated these and ousted them from the land.[13] As one of his estate managers, Alexander Forbes, recalled, Dwarkanath "made very hard bargains" with European planters and leased villages to indigo factories for more than they could realize in rental income. For example, he let a village to the Hizlabut Concern for Rs. 10,000 although the concern could collect rents from it amounting to only Rs. 7,000; but it willingly paid for the lease, expecting to make up for the loss in indigo production. In another case, according to Forbes, Tagore forced the same concern to lease a village from him by threatening to cut off the services of boatmen and carters from their other factories.[14] When planters were squeezed by zamindars they passed on the burden to the indigo cultivators, forcing them to give up their plant for little in return. Dwarkanath must be included among those zamindars who contributed to the oppressive nature of the indigo system.

Lower Bengal was a turbulent and unsettled province in Tagore's day, and many of the zamindars and indigo planters retained armed bands to decide disputes over the possession of territory. But Dwarkanath relied instead on his ability to command the resources of

[12]Dwarkanath Tagore to T.F. Rice, Sylhidah, Commercolly, dated Calcutta, 18 Apr. 1836, in KNT ms., p. 56. This may have been the incident referred to by Kissory Chand Mittra who relates that the ryots of Berhampore petitioned against Tagore and won the support of their magistrate, but that Dwarkanath obtained some information against him and by threatening him with blackmail into ignoring their petitions, forced the ryots to succumb. Kissory Chand Mittra, *Memoir*, pp. 16–17.

[13]*Bengal Hurkaru*, 30 Jan. 1837.

[14]*Report of the Indigo Commission* (Calcutta: 1860), pt. 3, pp. 60 ff.

two systems of power: he met the Europeans with the weapon of jurisprudence and over his own countrymen exercised a personal authority derived in part from his familiarity with the ways of the rulers. In one case, for example, Tagore had leased part of his Shahazadpur zamindari to an indigo planter, J. Marquez. Tagore's servants complained that Marquez had been bickering with them, had not paid his rent and had combined with the neighboring zamindars, the Bhattacharjee, to detach a parcel of land from his estates. In plain and forceful language Dwarkanath confronted the planter and insisted that he measure the lands in dispute, decide what he would consider fair rent and negotiate directly with him "instead of disputing with the amlahs there."[15] When Ramrutton Roy, head of the great Narail Raj of Jessore, tried to extort an extra fee from Dwarkanath's manager on renewal of the lease of a village, the manager refused and referred the matter to Tagore, who, he reported, "having so much influence over Baboo Ramrutton Roy, at once brought the matter to a satisfactory conclusion."[16]

In contrast to many zamindars who preferred to sublease their estates, Dwarkanath exercised direct control through a hired European manager. There is no indication, however, that he examined his zamindari accounts or had an intimate knowledge of his villagers. For example, he provided the new manager of Sajualpur zamindari, J.C. Miller, with rather conventional and general instructions. Miller was to survey the fields carefully and adjust the rents with "equity and justice," making sure that his own interests were not overlooked and "bearing at the same time in mind that the ryots be not oppressed." Waste lands were to be brought under cultivation and ryots induced to settle on them by the sacrifice of some rent that "might afterwards be raised as circumstances would admit to." The manager was not to displace local ryots with those from outside the estate. He was to enquire "as to the boundary lines . . . where they border on other zamindar's estates, so that encroachment may be prevented and where such have already taken place, restitution . . . obtained." To repossess lands illegally held, "you must endeavor to collect information as to the nature of the tenures . . . and of all circumstances bearing on the cases which might in any way prove useful to establish my right to repossession." The

15 Dwarkanath Tagore to J. Marquez, Mohungunge, Pabna, dated Calcutta, 16 Nov. 1835, in KNT ms.

16 *Report of the Indigo Commission,* pt. 3, pp. 60 ff.

manager was to sign all vouchers and accounts and transmit them to Dwarkanath.[17]

The government became aware of Dwarkanath's legal and managerial talents quite early in his career. In 1822, at the age of 28, Dwarkanath was appointed sheristadar or head Indian officer of the salt agency of the 24-Pargannas. In recommending him for the post, Trevor Plowden, the salt agent, described him as "a native of very high character and respectability; he has not been before employed in the service of government, but is a person of good education and fully qualified for the situation to which he is nominated."[18] His immediate predecessor in the position was Ramtanu Roy, a first cousin and close friend of Rammohun Roy.[19] It being customary in such appointments to permit an office holder to nominate a successor, the salt agency may well have been a stronghold of the Rammohun Roy faction.

Dwarkanath was to spend the next twelve years in the Salt Department under the Board of Customs, Salt, and Opium, which supervised the manufacture and wholesale distribution of salt. As a government monopoly the sale of salt provided a source of revenue second only to that of the land tax. There were six salt agencies in Bengal, situated in districts where the earth had a high saline content; one of these was in the 24–Pargannas, to which Dwarkanath was appointed sheristadar. The producers of salt, called *molunghees,* were often illiterate peasants who received advances from the agency headquarters and in turn hired coolies to help collect saline earth, boil it, and produce the salt. In April of each year, at the end of the salt-manufacturing season, the molunghees would bring their bags of salt to the agency headquarters and receive a payment from which the advance was deducted. Thereafter, until the next November, all manufacture of salt was illegal. The salt was delivered to the government salt warehouse in Howrah and there auctioned to merchants and retailers who came from all parts of Bengal.[20]

17 Dwarkanath Tagore to J.C. Miller, dated Calcutta, 14 Jan. 1836, in KNT ms., p. 56.

18 WBSA, Board of Customs, Salt and Opium, Salt Preceedings, no. 21, 14 March (1) 1823.

19 Ibid.; Collet, *Raja Rammohun Roy,* p. 60n.

20 H.R. Ghosal, *Economic Transition in the Bengal Presidency 1793–1833* (Patna: 1950), pp. 102 ff.

During the six years that Dwarkanath served as sheristadar, the average produce of his agency increased by 30 percent. According to Plowden, he was particularly zealous in recovering outstanding balances due the agency from molunghees who had received advances and had not covered them with sufficient salt. His remuneration was very low—perhaps Rs. 150 per month salary and a commission of eight rupees per 1,000 maunds annual increase in production—a commission that probably averaged Rs. 320 annually. [21] Dwarkanath could not have looked upon the rewards of his office in terms of money. Instead he sought prestige, a foothold in official circles, and an inside knowledge of governmental operations.

Plowden thought very highly of his sheristadar. In a letter dated September 24, 1828, transmitting an account of the commission due the native officers of the salt agency, he wrote of Tagore's "indefatigable exertions and the intelligence he has shown in the discharge of his duties . . . The zeal he has . . . manifested for the public service in the discharge of his official duties call for my unqualified praise and I hope will also be deserving the favorable consideration of the Board." [22]

A few months later, on December 1, Dwarkanath was promoted to the exalted post of dewan of the Board of Customs, Salt, and Opium, one of the three or four most important positions an Indian could hold in the government service. The man responsible for his appointment was Henry Meredith Parker, the junior member of the board. Dwarkanath, he wrote, "joined this office at my urgent request. I had just discovered the extensive and fraudulent combination which threatened such serious injury to the Salt Revenue—surrounded on all sides by intrigues and machinations, with scarcely an individual in the Office not implicated in the conspiracy, I received that assistance from the great talents, the industry, and I do not hesitate to say, the integrity of Dwarkanath Tagore, without which I should in all probability have struggled in vain against the difficulties into which the Department was plunged." [23]

Soon, however, Dwarkanath himself was accused of peculation and forced to defend his honor in one of the most trying episodes of his life. In 1833, certain molunghees of the Ballunda Aurang in the 24-Pargannas presented petitions complaining of extortion and

21 WBSA, Board of Customs, Salt and Opium, Proceedings, 7 Nov. (8–10) 1828.
22 Ibid.
23 Minute of H.M. Parker, 1 Mar. 1834, in ibid.

oppression by Gopi Mohun Mullick, the *darogha* or head of the customs station. The petitions alleged that the darogha had deducted credit from the molunghee's accounts for varying quantities of salt to enable him to "make good his agreement for 6,000 rupees with Dwarkanath Thakoor, the Dewan of the Salt Board." This deduction, wrote the petitioners, became popularly known among the molunghees as "Dwarkanath's *bundobust*" (settlement).

The acting magistrate of Baraset, Richard Herbert Mytton, was ordered to make a thorough investigation. The darogha having died, Dwarkanath was exposed without witnesses. Mytton reported that the darogha had indeed extorted from the molunghees, and, although "the legal proof of his [Tagore's] misconduct is somewhat imperfect, I have not considered it necessary to call upon him for explanations, still there are just grounds of suspicion that his name was not made use of without a cause." Mytton's conclusion was rejected by the Board, for neither C. Doyly, the senior member, nor Parker, the junior member, was willing to concede that any suspicion fell on Dwarkanath. Parker, in an overstated and lengthy minute, defended the integrity of Dwarkanath and attributed the allegations to attempts by the orthodox party to destroy his reputation.

Parker pointed out that once before, when Dwarkanath had been sheristadar of the 24–Pargannas, he had been accused of stealing government salt. At that time, Parker said, his accusers had been orthodox Hindus, encouraged by their Brahmins to harass him because of his association with Rammohun Roy, his intimacy with "impure" Europeans, his supposedly hedonistic way of life, and his refusal to propitiate the Brahmins with gifts, build temples, or endow shrines. They had presented a petition to the board stating that a deficiency of 9,000 *maunds* of salt had been discovered in the Nullooah Golahs, "of which Dwarkanath Tagore was cognizant and by which he had profited," but an investigation disclosed no shortage of salt and Dwarkanath was cleared [24]

Now, in the face of another accusation, Parker defended Tagore on grounds that the accusation was too vague, that the sum involved was small compared with the *lakhs* of rupees Dwarkanath could have taken illegally if he had so chosen, and that because of his high character the whole idea was absurd and distressing. As he was a

24 WBSA, Board of Customs, Salt and Opium, Salt Proceedings, 15 Apr. (41–44) 1834.

wealthy and well-known figure, Parker pointed out, his name could have been used by a lower officer in the service for the purpose of exaction. Above all, as the leader of the Brahmo party and the progressive Hindus, he must be supported by the British. He and his kind provided the justification for British rule in India—"for the sake of that civilization which the British Government profess it to be their first object to promote," the good name of Dwarkanath Tagore must be saved. He and his followers must be defended from attack by the bigots of orthodoxy. [25]

The governor-general-in-council reviewed the case and expressed less certainty of the complete innocence of Dwarkanath. Finally, the India Office in their turn studied the entire proceedings and argued *a priori* that not only Tagore but the darogha was completely innocent and that the charges were false. Their view was that it appeared from reference to the accounts that the "full produce of the *aurung* had been returned by the darogha and under his *kabooleat* he was bound to deliver this amount." He would, in fact, have lost money himself if he did not. Consequently, they held, apart from the minute of Mr. Parker, the Dewan was innocent and so was the darogha. [26]

It cannot be known for certain whether or not Dwarkanath used his position as dewan for personal gain. On the one hand, he had every opportunity for extortion, and he emerged from his job a wealthy man. On the other, petty thievery would have been out of character and grand larceny would have presented too great a risk of discovery. The accusers may indeed, as Parker contended, have been opponents of Dwarkanath for religious or party reasons. But perhaps Parker attributed too much to religion and party. It may well have been that Dwarkanath was, by local standards, over-zealous in stamping out petty illegalities among the molunghees and lower-echelon employees in his department. The molunghees were poor men, and the coolies who worked under them even poorer. Illicit salt manufacture was their only means of survival. To avoid prosecution they bribed the lower officials in the salt agency, and thus everybody in the system benefited from illicit manufacture. Into this situation stepped Dwarkanath Tagore, who combined British punctiliousness with a Bengali's inside knowledge of illegal operations—a dangerous combination. In the eyes of the molunghees and minor officials,

25 Ibid.
26 IO Records, Despatches to India and Bengal, vol. 8, pp. 701–16; Separate Revenue Department, Customs, Salt and Opium, 13 Apr. (4) 1836.

Dwarkanath was too much a man of the Raj, a collaborator interested more in pleasing his masters than in good-humoredly participating in a bit of harmless illicit manufacture and sale of salt. One need not look for religious motives to explain why the molunghees tried to rid themselves of their uncompromising dewan.

On August 1, 1834, Dwarkanath resigned his office as dewan, to be succeeded by Prasanna Kumar Tagore. [27] He had launched his own agency house in partnership with William Carr and gave as his reason for resigning "the pressure of private business." [28] From that time on he was finished with government service, and zamindari was to be only his secondary occupation. He was entering a new stage of his career as first and foremost a man of business—merchant, financier, entrepreneur.

Dwarkanath had been carrying on some business activity since the early 1820s, beginning in the most prosaic manner as a moneylender. [29] He started modestly enough, lending small sums of Rs. 2,000

[27] WBSA, Board of Revenue, Salt Department, Qriginal Consultations, 8 Aug. (15) 1834.
[28] K.C. Mittra, *Memoir,* p. 10.
[29] List of persons who received loans from Dwarkanath Tagore:

Name	Date of loan maturity	Amount (Rs.)
Muthoormohun Shaw	1820	2000
Chittoogossain	1820	2000
Bancharam Sikdar and other zamindars (DT and Benj. Preston)	1826	21,000
Richardson, Bengal C.S.	1826	21,032
John Brereton Birch, indigo planter	1829	20,000
Thomas Barfoot	1833	4000
Seetul Chunder Ghose	1833	14,000
R.C. Jenkins, merchant	1834	3000
Ronald McDonald, indigo planter	1835	10,000
John Armstrong Currie, shipbuilder	1835	1,00,000
John Baird	1837	1,00,000
John Freeman	1837	1,20,000
Archibald Bryce, indigo planter	1838	25,000
Bycauntnath Roy and Mootoonath Roy, et al.	1841	1,00,000
Hay Tweedale Stewart	1841	1,50,000
James Smith, indigo planter	1842	52,557
Rani Indranee and Annund Chundra Ghose	1843	2,80,000
Maurice Chardon, indigo planter	1846	1,20,000
Maharaj Cower Basdeo Sing	1846	50,000
William Storm	1849	2,00,000

Sources: Calcutta High Court, Plea Side; Tagore Family Archives, Rabindra Sadhana; Calcutta Supreme Court Civil Side; Calcutta Supreme Court, Plea Side.

or less. By the thirties his customary loan was closer to Rs. 20,000 and by the forties Rs. 200,000. The borrowers—Indian zamindars and British planters, merchants, and government officials—were charged the customary rate of interest, varying between eight and twelve percent.

In addition to moneylending he speculated in cargoes of indigo and silk bound for Europe, and in 1821 launched a more ambitious adventure, one that prefigured future bold undertakings. In partnership with a local merchant, John Lundrin Sanders, he outfitted a large ship, the 260–ton *Resolution,* and sent it to Buenos Aires with a shipment of rum, aniseed, and nutmeg. The cargo was left with an agent in Buenos Aires, Brown Rushausen Company, and the *Resolution* sailed on to Valparaiso, where, in February 1822, it loaded a cargo of copper for the return voyage. Brown Rushausen Company had a great deal of trouble selling the Indian goods, and it is doubtful whether the voyage was a commercial success. [30]

During his service in the Salt Department, Dwarkanath had been associated with one of the major agency houses of Calcutta, Mackintosh and Company. The Tagores had been involved in business with Mackintosh since the time of Gopi Mohun, and for Dwarkanath this connection was reinforced by Rammohun Roy, who also did business through the house. The founder, Aeneas Mackintosh, had been his personal friend, and the partners included George James Gordon, a member of Rammohun's Unitarian Committee, and James Calder, who served as an intermediary between Rammohun and Lord Bentinck during the backstage maneuvering over the bill to outlaw sati [32] Dwarkanath was neither a partner nor an employee of Mackintosh and Company, though he may have been considered a banian. His speciality was not trade but finance; that is, arranging for capital and credit to meet the firm's obligations. [33]

Dwarkanath's formal link with Mackintosh and Company was

---

[30]Brown Rushausen Company, Buenos Aires, to J.L. Sanders and Dwarkanath Tagore, dated 2 Aug. 1822, 26 Jan. and 16 Sept. 1823, in Tagore Family Archives, Rabindra Sadana. The *Resolution* is listed in *Bengal Annual Directory for 1822* (Calcutta: 1822), app., p. 5.

[31]Collet, *Raja Rammohun Roy,* pp. 406–20.

[32]A.F.S. Ahmed, *Social Ideas and Social Change in Bengal 1818–1835* (Leiden: 1965), p. 123.

[33]Henry Keller vs. Dwarkanath Tagore, et al., Supreme Court, 16 Feb. 1835, reported in *Bengal Hurkaru,* 18 Feb. 1835. Dwarkanath applied to Keller for a loan of Rs. 50,000 on behalf of Mackintosh and Company.

through the Commercial Bank, one of the three private western-style banks associated with Calcutta agency houses. The bank which opened in 1819, had been founded by a group that included Gopi Mohun Tagore, Joseph Barretto, whose house handled Portuguese business, and Mackintosh partners Gordon and Calder. Although originally conceived as a joint-stock bank to serve the needs of all the agency houses, the bank gradually became synonymous with the cash department of Mackintosh and Company, and by 1828 its only remaining proprietors were members of the firm and Dwarkanath Tagore.

In that year the partners of the Commercial Bank decided to revert to their original purpose and to start a new joint-stock bank that would be of equal benefit to all the traders of Calcutta engaged in international commerce. There was a critical need for such a bank. The other three banks in the city were the Bank of Hindoostan, founded in 1770, owned by Alexander and Company; the Calcutta Bank, founded by John Palmer in 1824; and the Bank of Bengal, a quasi-official bank founded in 1809. Inasmuch as the three private agency-house banks were little more than cashiers for their houses, those firms without banks were at a disadvantage. The quasi-official Bank of Bengal, largest and wealthiest, was little more than the government treasury and during the Burmese War of 1824 diverted all its capital to the war effort, leaving the merchants of Calcutta without short-term accommodation.[34]

Under these circumstances the partners of the Commercial Bank decided to found a separate bank, independent of either an agency house or the government. To preserve its independence they proposed that the number of shares held by any one individual be limited, election of directors be open, and the directorate be changed frequently.[35] At a public meeting held in May 1829, regulations were drawn up and elections were held. In the last week of August, subscriptions for shares were opened, and within three weeks 181 persons had purchased 444 shares for a total of Rs. 11,00,000. The Union Bank opened for business on September 28 when 500 shares for Rs. 12,00,000 had been subscribed.[36]

34Charles Northcote Cooke, *The Rise, Progress and Present Condition of Banking in India* (Calcutta: 1863), p. 202; *Bengal Hurkaru,* 20 Oct. 1845.

35*Bengal Hurkaru,* 20 May 1829.

36*Bengal Hurkaru,* 23 June 1843; *India Gazette,* 14 Sept. and 25 June 1829; *Government Gazette* 28 Sept., 6 July, and 15 Oct. 1829. The latter are excerpts in KNT Collection.

The fifteen new directors were drawn primarily from the big houses but included a few independent merchants. Three Indians were elected directors—Hari Mohun Tagore, Radhamadub Bannerjee, and Raj Chunder Doss. Ashutosh Day was chosen as one of the three trustees. In July, William Carr, an independent merchant, was elected Secretary. Interestingly, there were complaints among the Indian shareholders that they were underrepresented in the directorate, which may indicate that they had subscribed to more than three-fifteenths of the shares. Dwarkanath himself, still a public official, remained in the background, but his power was demonstrated in the election of his brother, Ramanath, as Treasurer after a vigorous canvass for votes. Although ten votes was the maximum number any single shareholder could exercise, Dwarkanath had a large constituency among the shareholders. Some were his dependents, some his debtors, and others his friends and relatives, and some shares had been bought by Dwarkanath in the name of others.[37] In the course of the ensuing twenty years the bank's capital would double in size many times over, it would come under the domination of a few large houses, including Carr, Tagore and Company, enter intrepidly upon risky ventures, and with a resounding crash in 1848 pull down the entire commercial community in its wake. But meanwhile, during the lifetime of Dwarkanath Tagore, the Union Bank was the keystone of the commercial structure of Calcutta.

Only three months elapsed between the opening of the Union Bank and the closing of John Palmer and Company, whose bankruptcy inaugurated the devastating commercial crisis of 1830–33. The atmosphere of confidence and expansiveness evaporated overnight. Alexander and Company closed its doors in December 1832 and Mackintosh in January 1833.[38] By January 1834 no major house had survived and the entire system had to be rebuilt. During this period, Dwarkanath stood firm as a rock. He was the only solvent partner in the now diminished Commercial Bank, and as soon as Mackintosh failed he issued a notice that he would pay all outstanding claims against the Commercial Bank and receive sums due to it.[39] He did the same with the Oriental Life Assurance

---

37 Palmer Papers, Engl. Lett. c 115, Palmer to Ruggooram Gosain, 30 Aug. 1830.

38 For a list of debits and credits of Mackintosh and Company, see *Bengal Hurkaru*, 4 Jan. 1833.

39 *India Gazette*, 7 Jan. 1833.

Society, owned by himself and the partners of three fallen houses-
—Fergusson and Company, Cruttenden and Company, and Mackintosh and Company. The society had been founded in 1822 to insure
the lives of agency-house partners and debtors whose liabilities could
then be met in case of death. Its assets had been used as additional
trading capital by the proprietors, and when their houses failed,
Dwarkanath Tagore, the only solvent partner, assumed the assets and
agreed to meet demands on the company. In 1834 he formed the New
Oriental Life Assurance Company with a new set of partners to carry
out the engagements of the old company.[40]

Dwarkanath emerged from the commercial crisis of 1830–33 as the
dominant figure in the Calcutta business world. He was one of the
few Calcutta businessmen who had sources of wealth that were
untouched directly by the commercial crisis. A little hard money
would go a long way in that period, and it was thanks to his sagacious
business operations as a moderately wealthy man who was able to
take the field when the giants had stumbled and fallen that he
emerged as one of the leading commercial men in the period
1834–46—if not *the* leading one. The basis of Dwarkanath's solvency
was his zamindari position. From 1830 to 1834, income from his
estates must have brought him between Rs. 65,000 and 1,10,000 per
year.[41] In addition, he was able to raise money on the security of his
land. Compared to the incomes of the great zamindars of Bengal this
was a relatively modest sum, but among the destitute European
merchants of Calcutta he was a solid man among figures of straw.
Nevertheless, under the barrage of requests for help his resources were
stretched to the limit. John Palmer, who spent the last few years of
his life trying to salvage the constituents for whose poverty he felt
responsible, was constantly writing to his friend "Dwarky" for small
loans. But, as he wrote to a widowed constituent who was in
desperate straits, "Dwarkanath has full employment for all he
possesses or can raise; or else there would be no strict limit to his
Liberality." And again: "I fancy he borrows to lend and to carry on
his own concerns."[42]

Once, early in 1832, Dwarkanath was so hard pressed that he could

40Dwarkanath Tagore vs. Assignees of late firm of Fergusson and Company,
Calcutta Supreme Court, Plea Side, 1837; *Calcutta Monthly Journal,* March 1837, pp.
211–13.

41See table of Patrimonial Zamindaris, above.

42Palmer Papers, Engl. Lett. c 119, Palmer to Smith, 5 Dec. and 21 Dec. 1831.

not raise Rs. 1,000, [43] and later that year asked the Board of Customs, Salt, and Opium to release the collateral security of Rs. 50,000 he had deposited on taking office in 1828. He argued that he could invest the money, then drawing 4 percent, at 8 or 9 percent, "an advantage which, with advertance to the amount of my salary in this office, I am persuaded the Board would not consider it equitable to deprive me of." The board accepted a personal security in Mackintosh and Company and returned his Rs. 50,000. [44]

Of the Rs. 50,000 he loaned Rs. 10,000 to John Palmer on behalf of his brother William Palmer and Sir William Rumbold of Hyderabad fame. Rumbold was in need of Rs. 45,000 to pay his bankers the interest on the loans taken out in previous years and lent in turn to the Nizam of Hyderabad. He was awaiting a decision from the Court of Directors on the validity of the Hyderabad loans, which had totaled over four million rupees. Rumbold estimated that he would be awarded at least a 10 percent recovery, and he was not to be disappointed. John Palmer raised the funds needed by Rumbold in a tight money market—Rs. 25,000 from his old banian, Raggoram Gossain; Rs. 10,000 from his Persian translator, Hurrochunder Lahory; and Rs. 10,000 from Dwarkanath Tagore. Dwarkanath brought in his relative, Ladly Mohun Tagore, as co-lender. [45]

Dwarkanath hinted at another source of his funds in this period. When Mackintosh and Company failed in January 1833, he assumed among its obligations the payment of the taxes on Mandleghat, a huge estate held in trust by the firm. Dwarkanath paid the tax of Rs. 1,50,000 and suggested where he obtained the money: "In 1833 money was very scarce. Being pressed for money on Mackintosh's failure, I got a loan on mortgage from my personal friends." [46] Those of his personal friends who were European were far more hard pressed than was Dwarkanath. He could only have meant his Indian

43 Palmer Papers, Engl. Lett. c 120, Palmer to Dwarkanath Tagore, 27 Feb. 1832.

44 WBSA, Customs, Salt and Opium, Salt Proceedings, 17 July (22–23) 1832.

45 Palmer Papers, Engl. Lett. c 121, Palmer to William Rumbold, 25 May 1832 and Engl. Lett. c 124, John Palmer to William Palmer, 13 July 1834. Among the lesser favors Palmer asked of Dwarkanath was to purchase some Rs. 2,400 of Danish lottery tickets which he had pledged to sell on behalf of the Serampore government and for aid to one Wakeel Lutfet'l who had been imprisoned. Palmer Papers, Engl. Lett. c 124, Palmer to Dwarkanath, 24 and 25 Sep. and 19 Oct. 1833; Engl. Lett. c 123, Palmer to Wakeel Lutfet'l, 14 Mar. 1833.

46 Hurlal Tagore vs. Ashutosh Day, *Bengal Hurkaru,* 25 Apr. 1836.

friends, access to whom, along with his own properties, provided him with the financial resiliency to survive 1833 and flourish in 1834.

Now, at the age of forty, Dwarkanath took his place as the leading businessman of Calcutta. Business, however, never engrossed his full attention; it was, rather, a means to support himself in a role he considered equally important—that of Calcutta's civic leader. His contemporaries saw him as, above all, an enlightened, modern Hindu prince and the paradigm of his race. In his physical appearance, however, there was little to indicate his strength of will and his worldly power. He was of medium height, "his limbs are beautifully molded, his hand being the most delicate we have ever seen belonging to one of the male sex; his countenance, in a state of repose, bears an aspect of peculiar thoughtfulness, but when lighted up, is one of great expression and striking beauty." [47] His health was as delicate as his appearance, and he was often indisposed. [48] He received scant affection from his immediate family, and with his wife, Digambari, he had little in common. Six children were born to them, of whom four, all males, survived infancy: Debendranath, 1817–1905; Girindranath, 1820–54; Bhupendranath, 1826–39; and Nagendranath, 1829–58. [49] Digambari herself died in January 1839, two days after the death of their thirteen-year-old son, Bhupendranath. [50] As soon as Dwarkanath had begun to cultivate the friendship of Europeans and to join with them while they dined, Digambari and the other female relatives who lived at Jorasanko had expelled him from the family house. He was obliged to live in a separate building, and there, in his *baithak khana*, to receive his impure visitors. [51] Banished from Jorasanko, Dwarkanath established another seat for his princely role, Belgatchia. This was a villa four miles from Dum Dum, north of Calcutta, which he purchased in the mid-1820s for about Rs. 5,00,000. [52]

In its gaudy decor and eclectic furnishings, Belgatchia was typical of the great nineteenth-century bhadralok mansions. The house was

47*Fisher's Colonial Magazine*, August-December 1842, I, 393–99.

48*Bengal Hurkaru*, 6 Feb. 1838; Palmer Papers, Engl. Lett. c 120, Palmer to Dwarkanath Tagore, 24 Jan. and 25 Feb. 1832.

49*The House of the Tagores* (Calcutta, 1963), p. 29.

50Brajendra Nath Bandopadhyaya, ed., *Sambadpetrey Sekaler Katha 1818–1840*, 2 vols. (Calcutta: 1949–50), II, 450.

51Satischandra Chakarvarty, ed., *Shrimanmaharshi Devendranath Thakurer Atmajibani*, pp. 310–11.

52*Bengal Hurkaru*, 14 Sept. 1848.

approached on an entrance road, brilliantly illuminated at night, and entered through a marble hall. On the right of the foyer was an elegant staircase adorned with statues of Cornelia and the Gracchi, the Venus Baigneuse, and Psyche. At the top of the stairs was a central hall, of Terpsichore, whose walls were hung with fine paintings and whose floor was adorned with statues of a reading Nymph, and a recumbent Venus embowered in roses. On the left of the hall was a spacious verandah, decorated to resemble a Mongol tent, with leafy walls and garlands of flowers, in the center of which was a throne of crimson velvet and gold embroidery, with pillars of solid silver chased and inlaid with gold. On the right was the music room, filled with oil paintings, marble furniture, orange damask curtains, porcelain vases, and alabaster clocks. Other rooms adjoining this one held paintings, engravings, and ivory miniatures. The subjects of the paintings included Venus and Mars, portraits of Indians, and scenes from a nautch. The south verandah was carpeted and adorned with white and crimson muslin, and its pillars were festooned with flowers.

Outside was a spacious lawn surrounded by a meandering stream over which passed four rustic bridges. In the center was a fountain, and beyond it a life-sized statue of the huntsman Meleager and his hound. In the distance a life-sized Venus could be seen rising from an artificial lake. On one side was a small island on which stood a Japanese temple, in the center an Ionic temple containing copies of the celebrated group by Canova, and at the far end a Chinese pagoda covered with lights of every shape and color and further illuminated by brilliant stars rising from the water's edge. Around the edge of the lake were rows of pillars topped by flames, and lamps were placed everywhere at random.[53]

Dwarkanath used Belgatchia as an occasional residence, but his real purpose in maintaining the house was to shower hospitality on the social elite of Calcutta, both European and Indian. When he served dinners to Europeans, he included all meats except beef, sat with his guests and, though he did not touch the food, joined in drinking wine. He invited hundreds of people to his parties, including the highest ranking officials, who rubbed elbows with their Hindu subjects. Large groups were entertained with fireworks,

[53]*Bengal Hurkaru,* 30 Nov. 1836; Letter from George W. Ives, landscape architect, to Dwarkanath Tagore, 16 Dec. 1826, in "Our Family Correspondence," Tagore Family Archives, Rabindra Sadana.

elephant rides, and musical performances; for small gatherings he devised unusual games in which the guests participated. Invitations to Belgatchia were highly coveted. [54]

In 1835, the government recognized Dwarkanath's influence by appointing him a justice of the peace, an honorary position newly opened to Indians. To balance his appointment the government selected as a second justice of the peace the social leader of orthodox Hindu society, Radha Kanta Deb. [55] Dwarkanath took an increasing interest in civic activities. In 1834 he was appointed chairman of a committee to establish a sanitary food and meat bazaar at Dhurrumtollah. [56] But perhaps because of his own poor health, medical philanthropies were his special concern. In 1833 he was elected a member of the committee of the Leprosy Society[57] and in 1835 he supported the establishment of the Calcutta Medical College by contributing scholarships of Rs. 2,000 per year for three years. In April 1835 he joined with Motilal Seal and Rajah Protab Chandra Singh to plan the establishment of a fever hospital for the poor in the Indian section of the city. [58]

Dwarkanath's philanthropic activities were not without political purpose and he used the occasion of an anti-sati meeting in 1832 to badger his orthodox opponents. A famine was raging in the Cuttack district of Orissa and, as he called on those present to donate to an emergency fund for its victims, he referred to the agent employed by the Dharma Sabha to carry their pro-sati appeal to Parliament:

Certainly if some of our countrymen could collect by subscription nearly 30,000 rupees to send an Englishman to England to gain the burning of living women, no one can imagine, think, or say, that to spend a few rupees to preserve the lives of all those people [in Orissa] would be extravagance. Please to observe how much money and labour English Gentlemen are devoting to the relief and preservation of our countrymen. But how melancholy it is, that we find our own countrymen so slack in this business. 59

54Emma Roberts, *Scenes and Characteristics of Hindostan with Sketches of Anglo-Indian Society,* 2 vols. (London: 1835), III, 299–301: Emily Eden, *Letters from India,* 2 vols. (London: 1872), I, 215–16.

55*Asiatic Journal,* vol. 28 (December 1835), p. 211.

56*Calcutta Monthly Journal,* November–December 1834, pp. 553, 790.

57Brajendra Nath Bandopadhyaya, ed., *Sambadpetrey Sekaler Katha 1818–1840,* 2 vols. (Calcutta: 1949–50), II, 315.

58Kissory Chand Mittra, *Memoir,* pp. 26–27, 64.

59J.K. Majumdar, ed., *Raja Rammohun Roy,* p. 204. In fairness to the Dharma Sabha, it should be noted that some members of that organization had subscribed to the fund. Ibid., p. 214.

Still another of Dwarkanath's manifold civic activities was his patronage of the Calcutta press. In 1829 he joined Robert Montgomery Martin, Prasanna Kumar Tagore, Rammohun Roy, Nil Rutten Holdar, and Rajkissin Singh in publishing the *Bengal Herald,* a bilingual weekly. [60] He purchased the daily *India Gazette* in 1834 and by combining it with the *Bengal Hurkaru,* owned by Samuel Smith, gained part interest in the most important daily in Calcutta. [61] He undoubtedly helped to finance the weekly, *Reformer,* owned by Prasanna Kumar. Finally, he supplied the capital for the establishment of the second most important daily in Calcutta, the *Englishman. John Bull,* a venerable Tory newspaper catering mainly to the military service, went up for sale when its owners, the agency house of Cruttenden, McKillop, crashed in 1834. With the help of Dwarkanath, a young journalist, J.H. Stocqueler, bought the press for Rs. 18,000, changed the name to *Englishman* and the politics to "liberal." By the time he left India in 1843, Stocqueler was able to dispose of the newspaper for Rs. 1,30,000. [62]

Dwarkanath also made a special point of patronizing the Calcutta European theater. Among his dearest friends was H.M. Parker, who as member of the Board of Customs, Salt, and Opium, was his supervisor and supporter. "One of the cleverest people" in Calcutta, [63] Parker directed the amateur group that performed in the old Chowringhee Theater. His mother had been a ballerina at Covent Garden, where Parker, as a youth, played violin. Appointed to his lucrative Indian post by Lord Moira, Parker, as musician, actor, poet, and playwright, more than any single man raised the level of European cultural life in Calcutta. Under Parker's influence Dwarkanath became the major patron of the Chowringhee Theater and developed a life-long interest in European music, opera, and drama. Thus, on the threshold of his most important entrepreneurial undertaking, Dwarkanath projected not so much the image of speculator, moneylender, and rent-collector as that of renaissance prince.

60 Ibid., p. 327.
61 *Bengal Hurkaru* 3 Mar. 1836.
62 J.H. Stocqueler, *Memoirs of a Journalist* (Bombay and Calcutta: 1873).
63 Emily Eden, *Letters from India,* 2 vols. (London: 1872), I, 215–16.

Chapter III

SPECTER ON THE GANGES[1]

Dwarkanath Tagore entered the full tide of his business career at an
opportune period in the history of Calcutta. By 1834 the city had
grown from an enclave port on the edge of a vast, relatively
inaccessible subcontinent to become the nerve center of an empire
stretching from the Arakan in Burma to the Sutlej River in the
Punjab. Calcutta was a young, vital city full of incongruities, partly
Indian, partly European, no longer a frontier town, not yet a
metropolis. Like London, it was both trade emporium and administrative capital. As the terminal port of the sea routes between Europe
and the Ganges Valley, the most productive and populous area of the
subcontinent, Calcutta handled roughly half the international trade
of British India. Alongside wharfs laden with produce were bathing
ghats where naked yogis performed ritual ablutions. Smoke from
funeral pyres mingled with steam from paddlewheelers in the river,
and half-cremated bodies floated among the hulls of sailing ships that
flew flags from all parts of the world. As steam–powered industries
spread north and south along both sides of the river, the manufacturing interests of Britain saw in Calcutta "the spectre of a second
Lancashire on the bank of the Ganges, which could beat the original
with cheap Indian labour and raw material." [2]

Calcutta proper stretched for four miles along the sacred river and
extended inland two miles to the east. The southern section of the
city, which included the European neighborhoods of Chowringhee as
well as Fort William and the green maidan, was inhabited by
Europeans, their servants, and the various castes that served their
domestic needs. Northern Calcutta was the "native" quarter, whose

1Part of this chapter appeared in Rachel van M. Baumer, ed., *Aspects of Bengali
History and Society* (Honolulu: 1975). I am grateful to the University Press of Hawaii
for permission to use that material in this book.

2Quoted in Amales Tripathi, *Trade and Finance in the Bengal Presidency, 1793–1833*
(Bombay: 1956), p. 228.

crowded streets were lined with ramshackle huts and mildewed tenements. Hidden among them were large colonnaded mansions opening onto inner courtyards, and these were the homes of wealthy Indian families,including the Tagores of Jorasanko and Pathuria-ghatta. Connecting the two sections of the city was the business and administrative center—Government House; Tank Square, with many business firms; Clive Street, the address of a score of agency houses; and, near the river bank, the Customs House and Mint. Adjacent to the Western business district was the center of Indian trade and finance, the Burrahbazar, heaped with the goods of north India and Great Britain, the headquarters of the Marwari, Hindustani, and Bengali money changers. Beyond Calcutta to the east was the Salt Water Lake, to the south the suburbs of Alipore and Kidderpore, and to the north Barrackpore. Across the Hooghly were Howrah, Sulkea, and Gooshree, already assuming the form of industrial suburbs.

Compared with the great capital cities of Europe, Calcutta was far from splendid. It was a primitive, unpleasant town; European intellectual life was mediocre, and modern Bengali culture as yet unborn. Sharply contrasting with the pretentious government buildings, the streets were unpaved, their deep ruts filled with mud during the monsoons and dust in the dry weather. By day they were deserted; only in the early evening did the city come to life, with Europeans promenading and driving carriages along Strand Road and Indians jostling in the crowded bazaars. At night, packs of howling scavenger jackals roamed the deserted town. But each year brought evidence of encroaching civilization—a new hospital, theater, school, library, shop. Committees of citizens and officials were formed to improve sanitation, water the streets, and raise money for cultural and educational institutions. Communications with Europe had recently been shortened from six months to two by the Red Sea route, and the effect of closer ties with Britain was beginning to be felt.[3]

3 For contemporary descriptions of Calcutta, see J.H. Stocqueler, *The Handbook of India* (2d ed., London: 1845), pp. 242–365; Emma Roberts, *Scenes and Characteristics of Hindustan with Sketches of Anglo-Indian Society,* 3 vols. (London: 1835), III, 290 ff.; Fanny Parks, *Wanderings of a Pilgrim in Search of the Picturesque during Four and Twenty Years in the East, etc.,* 2 vols. (London, 1850), II, 100 ff.; [James Hume], *Letters to Friends at Home by an Idler from June 1843 to May 1844* (Calcutta: 1844); George W. Johnson, *The Stranger in India,* 2 vols. (London: 1843); and contemporary newspapers.

TABLE 1. CALCUTTA CENSUS OF 1837

Category		Males	Females
Bengali Hindus	1,20,318 ⎫		
		85,145	52,506
Western Hindus	17,333 ⎭		
Bengali Muslims	45,067 ⎫		
		38,934	19,810
Western Muslims	13,677 ⎭		
Low castes		12,074	7,010
Eurasians		2,950	1,796
English		1,953	1,185
Portuguese		1,715	1,475
Armenians		465	171
Mugs		450	233
Moguls		314	195
Arabs		272	79
Chinese		243	119
Jews		185	122
French		101	59
Parsees		32	8
Madrassies		30	25
Native Christians		30	19
Totals		1,44,893	84,812
Total population		2,29,705	

Suburban population	
Thana	
Sulkeah	73,446
Chitpore	22,650
Manicktulah	54,935
Tauzeeraut	43,950
Nowhazaree	22,212
Total	2,17,193

Since the day of its founding, Calcutta had attracted ambitious and energetic people from all parts of Asia. A census taken in 1837[4] placed its population at 229,704, divided as shown in table 1.

The various communities lived in separate neighborhoods, spoke their own languages, and, whenever possible, followed their traditional occupations. Bengali Hindus,·who formed the largest single community, encompassed the full range of class and caste levels from upper-caste Brahmins, Kayasthas, and Baidyas to middle-level

4W.H. Sykes, F.R.S., "On the Population and Mortality of Calcutta," *Journal of the Statistical Society of London,* vol. 1, 1845, pp. 50–51; C. Finch, "Vital Statistics of Calcutta," *J.S.S.L.,* VOL. 13, 1850, p. 168.

merchant and artisan castes, to depressed castes who worked as laborers, agriculturists, and fishermen. In the 1830s and 1840s the western Hindus were either traders from Rajasthan or laborers from Bihar, Oudh, and the upper Ganges Valley. Western Muslims were either descendants of Muslim landed families or laborers from north India, whereas Bengali Muslims were shopkeepers, craftsmen, or skilled workers.[5]

As the high ratio of males to females attests, the city was then, as now, a place of employment for outsiders who saved their wages and planned to return to their villages as soon as possible. Calcutta also drew its manpower from the large population in the adjacent suburbs, and so crowded did it appear during working hours that in 1834 the statistician R.M. Martin mistakenly estimated its population at one and a half million.[6] Perhaps half of the 200,000 Hindu and Muslim inhabitants were employed by Europeans and Armenians as domestic servants, clerks, and messengers. Most of the remainder were coolies, bearers, and porters who worked on the river or streets of the city. A relatively small number earned their living as dealers in grain, oil, and cloth, as boatmen, or as skilled workmen. As for the Eurasians, many of whom were indigent, most of them served in minor clerical jobs, though the government began in 1825 to train a few as engineers, pilots, and engine drivers on its steamboats.[7]

Ultimately, the entire economy of the city depended on the trade of the port of Calcutta. From 1817 to 1840, the value of Calcutta's commodity exports annually averaged twice that of its imports—Rs. $2\frac{1}{2}$ crores of imports against Rs. 5 crores of exports. During the 1840s, both imports and exports increased to almost double their previous value. The chief trading partner of Calcutta was Britain; Calcutta's chief export to Britain was indigo, and its leading imports were textiles and yarn. Other exports to Europe and America included sugar, raw silk, silk piece goods, hides, saltpeter, and food grains. China was second to Britain as an importer of goods from the port of Calcutta; its principal import was opium.[8] Calcutta's large

5N.K. Bose, *Calcutta; 1964, A Social Survey* (Bombay: 1968), pp. 27–40.

6R.M. Martin, *History of the British Colonies,* 5 vols. (London: 1834), I, 5.

7Stocqueler, *Handbook of India,* pp. 264–66. A.C. Das Gupta, ed., *The Days of John Company. Selections from Calcutta Gazette, 1824–1832* (Calcutta: 1959), p. 234; Henry T. Bernstein, *Steamboats on the Ganges* (Bombay: 1960), pp. 142 ff.

8K.N. Chaudhuri, "India's Foreign Trade and the Cessation of the East India Company's Trading Activities, 1828–40," *Economic History Review,* second Series, vol. XIX, no. 2 (August 1966).

merchandise export surplus formed part of a total export of capital from India that exceeded imports by five to six million pounds sterling annually. Of this, 3.5 million was remitted on behalf of the East India Company, mainly to meet its home charges, and the balance represented remittances by private British subjects.

Because it tapped a hinterland rich in exportable commodities, Calcutta carried the greater burden of the commodity-export trade of India. True, the demand for indigo, opium, sugar, silk, and other products stimulated commercial activity in the city, but the unilateral transfer of funds had severe repercussions on the economy of Bengal. When commodity exports failed to meet remittance demands, bullion was exported and, in the absence of a paper currency, this resulted in a contraction of the money supply and lower prices. Because the land-revenue demand was constant, many zamindars could not meet their taxes. The most acute instance of this occurred during the commercial crisis of 1830–33 when landed estates, sold in default of taxes, glutted the market. The transfer problem also encouraged the diversion of capital from other sectors of the economy into export industries, which resulted in an unbalanced economic structure.[9]

Foreign trade and private investment in Calcutta was carried on by a group of firms, almost all British, known as agency houses. The first of these had been formed in the 1780s by enterprising Britishers who left the company's service to try their luck in private trade. As agents for the investment and remittance of private savings of civilian and military servants of the East India Company, the agency houses used the money of their constituents to finance the import and export trade, especially the country trade, and the production of indigo and other country products. Gradually competition forced them to expand their activities. They built and operated ships, served as bill brokers, formed banks and insurance companies, and lent their support to ventures in mining, manufacturing, and plantation industries.[10] The number of agency houses steadily increased over the years. In 1790 there were 15; in 1828, 27; in 1835, 61; and by 1846, 93. But of these, only a half-dozen at any one time were "great" houses; the majority were limited in their activities and operated with small sums of capital.

9K.N. Chaudhuri, ed., *The Economic Development of India under the East India Company, 1814–58* (Cambridge: 1971), pp. 41–43.

10S.B. Singh, *European Agency Houses in Bengal (1783–1833)* (Calcutta: 1966), pp. 1–35.

The history of the agency houses falls into three periods. From 1783 to 1813 the houses were few in number and their partners were closely associated with company officials who were also their constituents. Their shipment of country goods to Europe was confined to the "privilege trade"; i.e., space purchased in the holds of the company's East Indiamen. Most of their energies were directed toward the China trade, where they shipped opium, purchased at government auction in Calcutta. They were a smaller monopoly within the larger monopoly of the East India Company, free to range the Indian Ocean between the Cape of Good Hope and the South China Sea.

The second phase began after the opening of India to private trade in 1813, when a large number of new houses were formed by adventurers from Britain. Competition forced the major houses to find new outlets for investment, and the field that offered the best prospect was indigo. Demand for the blue dye was rising in Britain, and Bengal had the natural endowments to produce the finest indigo in the world. In addition, indigo proved an immediate solution to Bengal's balance-of-payments problem, which intensified in the 1820s with the increasing importation of British cotton yarn and textiles.

From Dacca to Delhi over one million acres were put under indigo, producing annually a crop valued at two to three million pounds sterling. But indigo production and export created more problems for the houses than it solved. The market for indigo fluctuated with European trade cycles and the supply with the Indian monsoon. Its production rose not in reponse to any real demand in Britain but in response to the need for an item for remittance. Even if the trade had been "spontaneous" rather than "induced," indigo would have presented problems. Seed had to be distributed and advances given to cultivators two years before the indigo was to be marketed in Britain. Its suitability for remittance purposes forced up its price in Calcutta independently of its price in London, resulting in overproduction and a glut on the London market. As often as not, indigo planters, capitalized by the agency houses of Calcutta, went bankrupt. In these cases the entire investment was lost, because the fields on which indigo was cultivated belonged to Indian zamindars and the expensive processing equipment was useless unless worked.[11]

11 Benoy Chowdhury, *Growth of Commercial Agriculture in Bengal (1757–1900)*, vol. I (Calcutta: 1964), pp. 83 ff.; Blair B. Kling, *The Blue Mutiny* (Philadelphia: 1966), pp. 15 ff.

By the mid-1820s, with so much of their capital tied up in indigo production, the agency houses began to experience a number of difficulties. The government drained Bengal of fluid capital by floating loans to support the Burmese War and further aggravated the financial situation by transferring the company's debt to England. In 1825 a commercial slump in England depressed the demand for indigo, and, to compensate for lower prices, still more indigo was produced and exported. Bullion imports fell off, thus causing a contraction of the money supply in Bengal. A number of agency-house partners sold off their enormous Indian assets and retired home. Between 1830 and 1833 the entire edifice crumbled, and the old houses, some of which had been in existence from the beginning of the century, failed. [12]

The third phase of agency-house history began in 1834 and lasted until the commercial crisis of 1847. The new houses fell into two separate groups, those that emphasized exporting and those whose main business was importing. The exporting houses, among which was Carr, Tagore and Company, were involved principally in the production and export of country products such as indigo, sugar and silk. As the funnel for capital to indigo planters and other European producers, they were the debtor houses. In one important respect they differed from their predecessors: they no longer had access to a major source of local capital, the earnings of civil and military employees of the government, who had by then lost their confidence in the agency houses. [13] For their working capital the new export houses depended on their Indian banians, government advances, and funds supplied by the importing houses. The importing houses were formed by British manufacturers to serve as agents for the sale and distribution of yarn and textiles sent on consignment from Britain. They accumulated capital from the sale of their goods and remitted the proceeds to England through bills hypothecated to indigo and other exports.

Indian businessmen were intimately involved in the commercial operations of both the importing and exporting houses. The importing houses depended for operating capital primarily on Hindustani (Marwari) moneychangers and merchant-bankers of the Burrahbazar in Calcutta, who remained outside British commercial institutions

12Tripathi, *Trade and Finance,* pp. 211 ff.

13John Crawfurd, *A Sketch of the Commercial Resources and Monetary and Mercantile System of British India* (1837), in Chaudhuri, ed., *Economic Development,* p. 276.

and maintained their traditional upcountry networks along with their traditional "bania" way of life. They advanced money to the dealers in cloth and were the middlemen for the distribution of British imports to northwestern India. They also speculated heavily in opium, and so many were wiped out by the Opium War that they could no longer finance cotton-textile imports. Thereafter the financial center for inland trade shifted from Calcutta to the northwestern provinces.[14]

Those Indians associated particularly with the exporting houses were known as banians. Banians, valued for their knowledge of internal markets and sources of supply, had served the East India Company before the advent of agency houses. The model early-nineteenth-century banian was Ramdulal Day, who acquired a fortune as a factor for the American traders. As the British learned more about India they had less need for the banian to market imports or collect products for export. But in the 1820s, with the influx of a new set of adventurers from Britain who came with little capital of their own, the banian again became important, now as a source of finance. His importance continued to increase when the crash of 1830–33 caused timidity among local British investors. By the 1840s some banians had become agency-house partners in name and many in fact.

The banians were English-speaking Bengalis from Brahmin, Kayastha, and Banik castes. Among the twenty-five to thirty listed in the directories of the 1840s, the most eminent were Motilal Seal (1792–1854) and Ram Gopal Ghosh (1815–68). Ghosh was educated at Hindu College and took a prominent role in city politics; Seal was an enlightened philanthropist and patron of western education. Perhaps with these two proud men in mind one observer noted that Europeans were employed "as agents of native capital,"[15] and another that the new banians had "assumed airs which their more wealthy predecessors had never taken on themselves; they treated their European connections not only with contemptuous disregard, but often with much insolence. The Hindoo star was in the

14Kissen Mohun Mullick, *Brief History of Bengal Commerce* from *the Year 1814 to 1870* (Calcutta: 1871), pp. 16–21. For the effect of the Opium War, see BM, *Additional Manuscripts* 37691, Auckland Private Letterbook III, Auckland to J.C. Melville, 6 Aug. 1837. Auckland describes the Hindustani bankers as "desperate gamblers . . . habitually speculating beyond their means."

15George Campbell, *Modern India* (London: 1852), p. 204.

ascendant, and these men made the most of it."[16] In the mid-fifties British capital began to move increasingly into India, and the banian, again losing much of his usefulness, was demoted or discarded altogether.

All the major Calcutta houses, but particularly the exporting houses and their Indian associates, worked together to oppose metropolitan control over local enterprises. Conflicts between Calcuttan and metropolitan interests occurred on a number of issues. Three of these—the conflict between the Calcutta and London boards of both the Assam Tea Company and the India General Steam Navigation Company, and the opposition of the Calcutta houses to British-domiciled banking—will be taken up in later chapters. Two other examples will be considered here.

The earliest and most protracted struggle of the Calcutta merchants against metropolitan encroachment was over control of a steamship line between India and Britain. In 1823 the Calcutta merchants formed a committee to raise money for à line via the Cape of Good Hope, and when that route proved impractical adopted the overland route via the Isthmus of Suez. A more serious effort began with the founding of the new Bengal Steam Fund in 1833. It was chaired by H.M. Parker and included among its directors T.E.M. Turton, Dwarkanath Tagore, and his business associate, William Prinsep. C.B. Greenlaw served as Secretary. The group subscribed Rs. 1,78,631 to finance a lobbyist in Britain.[17] In 1838 the Calcutta group joined a strong London group led by Timothy A. Curtis, Governor of the Bank of England, to press for a so-called comprehensive plan. Its objective was to form a single large company that would float enough steamers to link Britain separately with all three ports via the Isthmus of Suez. Significantly, the Calcutta group agreed to remit funds to London only on condition that the headquarters of the projected company be located in Calcutta.[18]

Meanwhile, the government began to operate its own mail service between Bombay and Suez. In 1839 a government steamer left Bombay without waiting for the arrival of the Calcutta mail. To the merchants this was the last straw, and they called a mass meeting on

16John Capper, *The Three Presidencies of India* (London: 1853), pp. 381–82. For biographical sketches of Seal and Ghosh, see Nirmal Sinha, ed., *Freedom Movement in Bengal, 1818–1904, Who's Who* (Calcutta: 1968), pp. 36, 107.

17*Bengal Directory and Annual Register for 1841* (Calcutta: 1841), pt. III, p. 178.

18H.L. Hoskins, *British Routes to India* (Philadelphia: 1928), p. 249 n.

October 5, 1839, to press for the immediate adoption of the comprehensive plan. But just before the meeting, T.E.M. Turton, with the support of Dwarkanath Tagore, formed a dissident group whose plan, called the "precursor scheme," was to raise money to send one vessel regularly from Calcutta to Suez. Turton and his followers remained a minority in Calcutta, and though pledged to become part of the larger comprehensive plan, they failed to get the approval of Curtis in London, who claimed that they divided and weakened the entire cause. The East India Company took advantage of the disagreement between Turton and Curtis to negotiate with a British firm, the Peninsular Steam Navigation Company, then operating a line between England and Spain. The British company was awarded the government mail contract, changed its name to the Peninsular and Oriental, and adopted the comprehensive plan. Though both Curtis and Turton tried to form rival companies, the battle ended when the P. & O. obtained a royal charter giving it limited liability.[19] The Calcutta merchants were now dependent for their communications on a giant British corporation whose Calcutta agent, Captain Engledue, was to wield enormous power in the city and in time direct it against Carr, Tagore and Company itself.

A second conflict between local and metropolitan interests concerned the role of the government in the export trade. The Charter Act of 1833 had excluded the government from commercial activity, and it was obliged to meet the home charges either by remitting bullion from India, selling bills on India in London, or revitalizing the hypothecation system. The government preferred the latter, whereby it, and not the private bill broker, would benefit from the difference in the rate of exchange between the rupee and the shilling, frequently amounting to 10 percent of the value of a shipment.

In 1834 the export warehouse keeper gave notice that he would advance rupees to holders of indigo, silk, and saltpeter up to two-thirds the value of the goods at an exchange rate of 2s 2d per rupee at six months sight. The goods would be consigned to the East India Company in London and released to a private agent designated by the shipper when the advance was repaid.[20] In subsequent years the terms were modified—the exchange rate was lowered to encourage shippers and raised to discourage them, the amount of advance

19 Daniel Thorner, *Investment in Empire* (Philadelphia: 1950), pp. 23–29.
20 WBSA, Board of Trade, Commercial, 5 Nov. (5) 1834.

was varied, the list of staples was expanded or contracted, and the terms of bills were extended. From 1834 to 1847, £12,701,670 was realized through advances on hypothecation. The trade continued into the 1850s, after which a new means was found for remitting funds to England, namely, through capital deposited in the home treasury by companies formed to construct railways in India. [21]

During the same period, 1834 to 1847, more than twice the amount remitted by hypothecation was raised by the government through the sale of bills on India. This method was preferred by mercantile interests in Britain, who wanted the government to remit its funds exclusively through the sale of bills. Throughout the period, the exporters of Liverpool and Manchester and their dependent houses in Calcutta subjected the hypothecation system to attack. The system was defended by Calcutta exporting houses, who favored government advances as an alternative source of short-term accommodation. When, under the pressure of British mercantile interests and the logic of laissez-faire doctrine, the government began to scale down the amounts advanced to Calcutta exporters, the exporting houses rose to defend the trade. On June 6, 1846, a group of eight Calcutta exporting houses, including Carr, Tagore and Company, petitioned the government to increase advances on consignments to England on grounds of the unprecedented shortage of money in Calcutta. In a second petition, in which they were joined by twenty-seven additional firms, they pointed out that the government itself had been responsible for the shortage of funds, draining the city of silver to meet the costs of war in the Punjab. [22]

On June 15 an opposing group of twenty-three Calcutta houses submitted a counter petition calling for the abolition of the system because of its unnatural effect on exchange and because it encouraged reckless speculation. The exporting houses, however, won the battle of petitions and persuaded the government to continue the system for a few years. For one reason, their arguments were supported by the eminent economist, James Wilson, who believed that to discontinue the system would cause great hardship to the

[21] Great Britain, *Parliamentary Papers,* 1899, vol. 31, (c. 9390), Indian Currency Committee of 1898, app. 10.

[22] IO, Financial Letters from India and Bengal, with Enclosures, 1846, vol. 93, apps. 1 and 2.

producers and exporters of Bengal, [23] perhaps because an influx of
bills representing demands on rupees would result in tight money
and paralyze Indian commerce. [24] Furthermore, because the government, unlike the private merchants, had no choice but to remit its
funds regularly, it was obliged to come to terms with the exporters.
To Dwarkanath Tagore and the other exporters, government advances were an important source of operating capital and freed their
resources for other investments.

Nevertheless, the Calcutta exporters may have been short-sighted
in their opposition to an influx of private bills. British bill holders
may have preferred immediate returns by remittance through indigo,
but if the competition for remittance forced up the price of indigo
beyond its market value in London, they might have been willing to
put their rupees into long-term investments. Long-term investment
capital managed by local agency houses might have provided the
financial basis for substantial industrial development. When, during
the railway age, British investment capital finally did find its way to
India, it came on terms favorable to Britain and controlled by
British domiciled management.

Because British investment in Bengal before 1850 was insignificant,
economic development was left to the meager resources of the local
houses. The merchants of Calcutta, with Dwarkanath Tagore prominent among them, cooperated in a series of joint undertakings to
build a commercial infrastructure. Among the earliest of these,
dating from the eighteenth century, were marine and life-insurance
schemes. The first life-insurance companies were temporary laudable
societies, but in 1822 the merchants founded one as a joint-stock
commercial venture, the Oriental Life Insurance Company. Its
prospectus stated that its proprietors would include all the principal
agency houses of Calcutta, Bombay and Madras. In addition to its
primary purpose of insuring the lives of parties in debt to agency

23Ibid. See also IO, *Home Miscellaneous 845,* Broughton Papers, H. St. George
Tucker to Hobhouse, 15 Jan., 1848; Chowdhury, *Commercial Agriculture, vol. I,* pp.
109–11; and Arthur Redford, *Manchester Merchants and Foreign Trade, 1794–1858*
(Manchester: 1934), pp. 122 ff. James Wilson pointed out the weakness of this
argument. The East India Company, which held the goods in its London warehouses
until the bills were satisfied, was presumably more rigid in extending credit than
private merchants might have been. Great Britain, *Parliamentary Papers* 1847–48, vol.
8, pt. I, Q. 7843 ff.

24BM, *Additional Manuscripts* 37691, Auckland Private Letterbook II, Auckland to
W.S. Clarke, 15 June 1837.

houses, the company provided short-term loans to various firms. Gradually it fell under the control of a few houses, and when its secretaries, Mackintosh and Company, went bankrupt, became the exclusive possession of Dwarkanath Tagore. In 1834 he reorganized the company as the New Oriental Life Assurance Society to carry on its business. [25]

Another joint venture, the Bengal Bonded Warehouse Association, was promoted by the agency houses in cooperation with the government to provide safe and convenient storage for commodities, particularly those awaiting customs clearance under the hypothecation system. The houses provided the capital, and the government gave the association an official charter to prevent the formation of any rival companies so long as it "provided sufficient accommodation at reasonable rates." [26] Incorporated in 1838, it was, with the exception of the Bank of Bengal, the only local joint-stock enterprise with limited liability. The association was capitalized at Rs. 1 million, divided into 2,000 shares of Rs. 500 each. Of the 171 shareholders, 45, or over one-fourth, were Indians. Dwarkanath held 50 shares and chaired the fourth half-yearly meeting in November 1839. [27]

Dockyards were another of the subsidiary industries supported by the agency houses. The first dockyards had been engaged chiefly in shipbuilding, Calcutta's first major industry. From the time the first ship was built in 1769, 272 ships had been built by the peak year of 1821. Thereafter, because of the influx of cheaper vessels from England, shipbuilding declined, and only 5 ships were built between 1827 and 1839. [28] By the early 1830s, two major dockyards in Calcutta were employed in repairing ships and outfitting paddle-wheelers. [29] One of these, the Kidderpore Yards, had been built in the late eighteenth century and operated by James Kyd, master shipbuilder of Calcutta, until his death in 1836. [30] The other major drydock was the Howrah Yard, located across the Hooghly River opposite the center of the city.

25*India Gazette,* 1 June 1833, and *Calcutta Monthly Journal,* March 1837, pp. 211–13.

26IO, Revenue Despatches to Bengal, 28 Apr. 1841.

27R.S. Rungta, *The Rise of Business Corporations in India, 1851–1900* (Cambridge: 1970), p. 25; *Bengal Hurkaru,* 8 Jan. 1838, and *Calcutta Monthly Journal,* November 1839, p. 527.

28John Phipps, *Ship Building in India* (Calcutta: 1840), pp. xi–xiii.

29Stocqueler, *Handbook of India,* p. 344.

30C.E. Buckland, *Dictionary of Indian Biography* (London: 1906), pp. 239–40.

In December 1836 the Calcutta Docking Company was formed to purchase both the Kidderpore and Howrah yards. Most active among the promoters and early directors were the Parsi entrepreneur, Rustomjee Cowasjee, who acted as secretary, Dwarkanath Tagore and his partner, William Prinsep, and William Bruce. They called for a capital of six lakhs to be divided into 600 shares of Rs. 1,000 each. The company purchased the Kidderpore and the Upper Howrah Docks and leased the Lower Howrah Docks from Carr, Tagore and Company. [31] Heavy capital expenditures made necessary a high volume of repairs and shipbuilding. In the first few years this was possible and, despite an annual-interest expense of Rs. 50,000 on loans, the Calcutta Docking Company earned a profit of 18 to 20 percent. In 1838–39, forty-six ships were repaired, but the company lost money on government contracts, as well as on its contracts with Carr, Tagore and Company, and began to divest itself of its excess capacity. It leased part of the Kidderpore Yard to Carr, Tagore for a coal depot and in 1837 sold the eastern end of the yard to the government steam department for its workshops. The company weathered the commercial crisis of 1847 and survived until late in the century. [32]

Ironically, the one attempt at cooperation that failed required no capital investment. In April 1834 the agency houses established the Calcutta Chamber of Commerce, the first such body in India. Its purpose was to arbitrate disputes between businessmen and to collect and publish each year an aggregate statement of the stocks on hand of imported piece goods, metals, and cotton twists. Originally, seventy-nine individuals representing almost every firm in Calcutta joined, but only ten to fifteen members attended meetings. After the first few years the number dropped still lower and the chamber faded away, to be reestablished on a new footing in 1853 as the Bengal Chamber of Commerce. According to a later report, the chamber failed "from the total want of interest and cooperation . . . in its proceedings." [33]

31Carr, Tagore and Company had purchased the Lower Howrah Docks from the estate of Barretto and Sons and operated them as the New Howrah Dock Company. Valued at Rs. 2,00,000, they were leased to the Calcutta Docking Company for Rs. 1,565 per month. *Bengal Hurkaru,* 8 Mar. 1839 and 16 Sept. 1841.

32Ibid. and WBSA, Marine Department, 20 Apr. (7) 1842, *Bengal Directory and Annual Register for 1851* (Calcutta: 1851), p. 324.

33Bengal Chamber of Commerce, *Half-Yearly Report of the Committee,* November, 1853; Geoffrey W. Tyson, *The Bengal Chamber of Commerce and Industry, 1853-1953, A Centenary Survey* (Calcutta; 1953), pp. 12–18, 179–182.

Despite the paucity of capital, the local business community embarked upon a broad range of steam-powered industries. For a time Calcutta appeared to be on the threshold of a small-scale industrial revolution, and in 1844 one observer noted that "on approaching Calcutta, the smoking chimneys of steam-engines are now seen in every direction, on either side of the river, presenting the gratifying appearance of a seat of numerous extensive manufactories, vying with many British cities."[34]

These industries were undertaken by agency houses, which provided the financial backing, in cooperation with another type of entrepreneur, the artisan-mechanic. Under conditions of great hardship, these remarkable men, the forerunners of the professional engineer, tried to adapt the industrial technology of Britain to India. Their prototype was William Jones, who had come to India in 1800 as a "mechanic" and by 1810 had started a factory at the Albion Ghat in Howrah for the manufacture of canvas from indigenous hemp. The canvas works were still operating in 1835 and yielding good returns.[35] In 1811 Jones established a factory to manufacture cartridge paper, in short supply during the Java expedition, but it closed down soon after the war. The Court of Directors discouraged its production on the ground that Jones was competing with paper manufacturers in England.[36] Jones also established an ironworks and in 1815 discovered coal in Burdwan, which, backed by Alexander and Company, he attempted to mine. He died in 1821 while engaged as architect and contractor of the first gothic building in India, Bishop's College.[37]

Most of the mechanics were masters of that new wonder of the age, the steam engine. In the early nineteenth century the application of steam power was the measure of a nation's industrial standing, and India led all the colonies and dependencies of Great Britain in the use of steam power.[38] The first steam engine had been shipped out to

34 Stocqueler, *Handbook of India,* p. 348.

35 But, wrote Phipps, by 1840 "like almost every other manufacture in this country, it has passed into the hands of natives, and wanting the benefit of European superintendance and honesty, has lost its repute; and the hopes which were once entertained of its superceeding European canvas, have disappeared." Phipps, *Ship Building in India,* p. 479.

36 Ibid., pp. 480 ff.

37 *Bengal District Gazetter, Howrah,* by L.S.S. O'Malley (Calcutta: 1909), p. 108; "Notes on the Right Bank of the Hooghly," *Calcutta Review,* vol. IV, July–December 1845, p. 476.

38 G.A. Prinsep, *An Account of Steam Vessels and of Proceedings Connected with Steam Navigation in British India* (Calcutta: 1830), p. 1.

Calcutta from Birmingham in 1817 or 1818. It was purchased by the government, fitted with buckets, and used to dredge the Hooghly. In 1823 a group of Calcutta merchants bought a pair of sixteen-horsepower engines from a British merchant at Canton. The engines were fitted into a vessel built by James Kyd and launched as the *Diana* in 1823. The *Diana* proved too small for tugging and, though hired out for pleasure cruises on the river, was a commercial failure. [39]

A few enterprising engineers built their own steam engines at Calcutta. In the 1820s a man named Toulmin made a high-pressure engine for a soda-water factory, and the engineering firm of Jessop and Company built two condensing engines at their Phoenix foundry. The first Calcutta-made boat engine, a single four-horsepower high-pressure engine, was built in 1828 by Mr. Macnaught for James Scott and Company at Fort Gloster. A year later Macnaught constructed a six-horsepower engine that would build up a pressure of 45 pounds per square inch. [40] But with these few exceptions, all of the steam engines employed in Bengal were imported from Britain. The number of engines in use in the Bengal Presidency rose from 65 (totaling 1,800 horsepower) in 1837 to 150 (5,986 horsepower) in 1845. They were employed as shown in table 2.

TABLE 2. STEAM ENGINES IN USE IN BENGAL PRESIDENCY, 1845

Location	Engines	Horsepower
Sugar mills and refineries	28	291
Docks	8	111
Collieries	8	80
Flour and rice mills	6	158
Paper factories	4	46
Government departments (Mint, etc.)	8	168
Sea steamers (government)	20	1,030
Inland steamers (government, 20; Assam Co., 2)	22	770
Packets (owned by agency houses)	10	1,980
Tugs and pleasure boats	21	1,114
Miscellaneous	15	238
Totals	150	5,986

Source: *Bengal Hurkaru*, 29 Nov, 1845

The largest single industrial complex utilizing the steam engine was located at Fort Gloster, fifteen miles south of Calcutta. In 1840

39 Bernstein, *Steamboats on the Ganges*, pp. 28 ff.
40 Prinsep, *An Account of Steam Vessels*, p. 21.

the complex included a factory for making cotton twist, a rum distillery, an iron foundry, an oil-seed mill and a paper mill, all powered by five steam engines. The cotton mill was the oldest in India and may have been set up as early as 1817. Initially a group of English girls had been brought out to teach Indians to operate the machinery, and some years later, when the mill closed temporarily, the girls were abandoned to prostitution and many died of typhoid. [41] The site was purchased by the agency house of James Scott and Company in 1829. They built a steam-powered mill to produce cotton twist, planned to erect a foundary to supply the government with ordinance, and experimented with the manufacture of steam engines. But the commercial crisis of 1830 forced them to retrench, and they sold the complex to Fergusson and Company. Fergusson and Company invested Rs. 20,00,000 in the property, adding 100 power looms to the twist mill. According to a contemporary report the quality of the twist "was daily rising in the estimation of the natives and . . . the labour of men initiated in the art of weaving is now almost double of what was performed at the commencement of the undertaking." [42]

When Fergusson and Company itself went bankrupt in 1833, the property was purchased from the estate by a joint-stock company for the bargain price of Rs. 6,00,000. Most of the shareholders, including the largest, Henry Gouger, were old India hands resident in England, but Dwarkanath Tagore held seventy-five shares, one-twelfth of the total. [43] Gouger's company discontinued the power looms so that all available steam power could be used to manufacture the more profitable twist. By 1840 the mill was producing 700,000 pounds of yarn annually from high-quality Amrautee cotton purchased at

41 Great Britain, *Parliamentary Papers,* 1840, vol. 1, pp. 116–23, testimony of Henry Gouger before Select Committee on East India Produce; *Bengal District Gazetteers, Howrah,* p. 110; Daniel H. Buchanan, *The Development of Capitalist Enterprise in India* (New York: 1934), p. 128; H.D.G. Humphreys, "History of the Bengal Coal Company," ms. in archives of Andrew Yule and Company, Calcutta. The exportation of machinery and artisans was prohibited by act of Parliament from 1774. It was freed partially in 1825 and fully in 1843. See Bernard Semmel, *The Rise of Free Trade Imperialism* (Cambridge: 1970), pp. 181 ff.

42 S.D. Mehta, *The Cotton Mills of India, 1854–1954* (Bombay: 1954), pp. 5–7; Singh, *European Agency Houses,* p. 28; *Asiatic Journal,* new series, vol. 13 (January 1834), p. 6.

43 Tagore later pledged these on loans from the Union Bank. See *Bengal Hurkaru,* 22 May 1848. In 1852 the value of a share was Rs. 600 and shares were selling at par. Thus, if the total capitalization had been Rs. 6,00,000, Dwarkanath owned one-twelfth. *Bengal Hurkaru,* 27 Mar. 1852.

Mirzapore. The lower numbers sold in Calcutta better than imported yarn and the larger numbers on a par with imports. [44] With the exception of one European superintendent, the labor force was recruited from Orissa and Bengal, was paid by the task, and worked eleven hours per day. Gouger supplied coal for the steam engines from his own mine, the Naraincoory in Burdwan, at half the price of imported English coal. The mill was making a profit, but Gouger claimed that this was only because his capital investment had been small and that Fergusson, having invested too heavily, would have lost money. In his opinion, the need for a large capital investment would preclude the establishment of any new cotton mills in India. [45]

Before the middle of the nineteenth century, manufacturing activity had spread northward along the right bank of the Hooghly River into the suburbs of Hooghly, Howrah, Sibpur, and Sulkea, called by one writer "the Southwark of Calcutta." [46] There were sugar factories, rum distilleries, cotton presses, a biscuit factory, flour mills, a mustard-oil mill, and a paper factory. In and near Calcutta itself were a number of steam-operated iron foundries. The largest of the engineering firms operating foundries, Jessop and Company, established in the eighteenth century, repaired steamboats, manufactured tools and simple machinery, and in 1825 offered to build a railway from Calcutta to Diamond Harbor. [47] After 1834 the government itself operated the most extensive foundry. From a modern plant at Cossipore, four miles north of Calcutta, the foundry supplied brass ordnance to the whole of India. The Court of Directors had sent out twelve boring and turning lathes, some lighter lathes, and two small steam engines to power the works. Adjacent to the foundry was a casting and smelting house with cupola blast

44In the same period, some nine million pounds of cotton yarn were imported annually into Calcutta, chiefly from Britain. See E. Wilkinson, *Commercial Annual of the External Commerce of Bengal during the Years 1841–42 and 1842–43* (Calcutta: 1843), p. 1.

45Great Britain, *Parliamentary Papers,* 1840, vol. 8, pp. 116–23, Testimony of H. Gouger. Another cotton mill was established at Pondicherry between 1826 and 1828 by the French Government. At first it was government-subsidized, but later it was converted into a joint-stock company with a nominal capital of five million francs. In 1830 it employed 2,000 workers and operated 22,800 spindles and 454 looms by steam. See Mehta, *Cotton Mills of India,* pp. 5–7.

46"Notes on the Right Bank of the Hooghly," *Calcutta Review,* p. 481.

47WBSA, Bengal Revenue Proceedings, 12 May (18) 1825 and 9 June (12–19) 1825.

furnaces for smelting iron and large reverberatory furnaces for smelting gun metal. [48]

A large, docile, talented labor force was available to operate the factories and mills. The leading employer was the Government Steam Department, which hired Indian and Eurasian labor as mechanics, shipwrights, millwrights, plumbers, and boilermakers. Elsewhere in the city, skilled workmen, recruited from Hindu artisan castes and from the Chinese community, worked as carpenters, painters, blacksmiths, locksmiths, and jewelers, some under European master-craftsmen. Workmen were hired in gangs under contract with a chief *mistry,* an Indian master-craftsman, who received the wages for the entire gang and distributed them as he wished. [49] Although there were mixed reports on the quality of Indian labor, those employed in the mint were said to handle the machinery, including the steam engine, with facility, and the workmen at Fort Gloster cotton mill were considered quite expert in their machinery duties. [50] Still, Asians were paid less than their European counterparts on the ground that they lacked the stamina of Europeans, and the British believed that Indian skilled labor was only one-fourth as productive as British. Indian cabinetmakers earned between 35 and 60 rupees per year, but the Chinese, who were considered superior craftsmen, earned four to six times as much, and European master-craftsmen about Rs. 1,000 per year. [51]

The agency houses were responsible for the financing and promotion of Calcutta's industrialization, but they fell short of their entrepreneurial potential. In part the blame was theirs. They spread their limited resources, both capital and managerial, too thin; their partners drained off too much capital for personal consumption and remittance home; and they set their sights on unrealistic and overly ambitious undertakings. To some extent, however, they were victims of circumstances. Capital was short; Indians invested in landed estates and salaried Europeans remitted capital home; banking was

48H.A. Young, *The East India Company's Arsenals and Manufactories* (Oxford: 1937), pp. 142–43; Stocqueler, *Handbook of India,* pp. 341 ff.

49Bernstein, *Steamboats on the Ganges,* pp. 143–53.

50Johnson, *Stranger in India,* I, 54; Great Britain, *Parliamentary Papers,* 1840, vol. 8, pp. 116–23.

51Crawfurd, *Sketch of Commercial Resources,* p. 52. Dwarkanath Tagore noted that in 1830 there was a scarcity of workmen in Calcutta. He also observed that wages had doubled between 1820 and 1830 but that during the same period the price of rice had risen fourfold. Martin, *British Colonies,* I, 341.

rudimentary, and the only chartered bank devoted itself to serving the needs of government rather than private enterprise; and support from British investors at home was disappointing. Britain's overwhelming technological superiority hampered attempts to develop indigenous manufacturing. The British free-trade movement, on which so many local merchants had pinned their hopes, proved a deceptive ally, promoting metropolitan over colonial interests whenever the two conflicted. Finally, though the government encouraged industrialization, its deeds did not match its words, and where it might have filled the breach with timely aid to floundering enterprises, proved vacillating and in the final analysis subservient to economic interests at home.

Before the mid-nineteenth century the Government of India expressed support for economic development, including industrialization, even when it conflicted with home interests. The governors-general—Bentinck, Auckland, Ellenborough, and Hardinge—were expected to balance the budget and remit the home charges in the face of rising expenses and the prevailing poverty of the peasantry, and the obvious answer was to find new sources of revenue. After leaving office Bentinck testified that he had supported steam communication with India because he believed that it would facilitate the education of Indian students in England, from which they would return with technological knowledge, the key to progress in India. It would also facilitate the influx of British businessmen who had done so much for Indian economic development. And along with plantation industries he unabashedly cited with approval the Gloster Mills, the iron foundries, and the coal mines, all of which competed with British products. [52]

Lord Auckland (1836–42) was even stronger in his conviction that India must industrialize. He favored both the revival of Heath's modern steel mill in Madras and the promotion of cast-iron manufacturing among the primitive hill tribes of Assam. Auckland directed the Cossipore foundry to supply the government's needs for suspension bridges and iron boats and instructed the coal committee to locate the best ores and fluxes available in India as the foundation for a local steel industry. He promoted experiments for the improvement of cotton, the processing of hemp, the manufacture of pottery and porcelain, and the growing of nutmeg, pepper plants, and

[52]Great Britain, *Parliamentary Papers,* 1837, vol. 7, pp. 186 ff.

cochineal insects, and he looked forward to the development of
Assam, "a country of vast promise," by the application of both
European and Indian capital.[53]

His successors, Ellenborough (1842–44) and Hardinge (1844–48),
were too involved in military affairs to devote time to internal
development, but their sentiments were not essentially different from
those of Bentinck and Auckland. In 1828, as president of the Board of
Control, Ellenborough had encouraged, in the face of strong opposition from private trade interests in the Court of Directors, a policy of
import substitution to save the Indian government money.[54] As
governor-general he strove to develop public works and establish
experimental cotton farms, but was thwarted because of a shortage of
funds.[55]   Hardinge endorsed the early planning of railway building.
"Our rule," he wrote Hobhouse on the subject of railways, "has been
distinguished by building large Prisons; and the contrast with the
Mogul Emperors, in the respect of public works, is not to our
advantage."[56] At a ceremony awarding prizes to college students in
Calcutta for their recitation of Shakespeare, he concluded his address
"by giving his hearers a practical account of the magic powers of
steam and electricity."[57]

Among the British publicists of the period, some were willing to
admit that India possessed an industrial potential and others were
not. George W. Johnson, an attorney who spent three years in
Calcutta in the early forties, minced no words on the subject:

Doubtless, it is of high importance for the increase of India's wealth to
improve her cotton growth, and to establish extensively on her soil the
cultivation of the tea-plant, but these are only some of the first steps towards
the desired object . . . . It is now shown that the mineral wealth of India fits
her for a higher destiny; and that she, like America, may be at first
agricultural, but gradually may become, also, a manufacturing country.[58]

53 BM, Auckland Papers, *Additional Manuscripts* 37689, Auckland Private Letter-
book I, letter dated 5 Aug. 1836; ibid., 7 Jan. 1837; 37693, Auckland Private
Letterbook V, 5 July 1838; ibid., 37711, Auckland's Minute Books, Minute on
Cossipore Foundry, 2 June 1839, pp. 124–27; ibid., 37698, Auckland Private
Letterbook X, 19 Apr. 1840.

54 C.H. Philips, *The East India Company, 1784–1834* (Manchester: 1940), pp.
262–63.

55 Albert H. Imlah, *Lord Ellenborough* (Cambridge: 1939), pp. 176 ff.

56 IO, *Home Miscellaneous* 853, Broughton Papers, Letter from Hardinge to
Hobhouse, 3 Jan. 1847, p. 303.

57 Viscount Hardinge, *Viscount Hardinge and the Advance of British Dominion into the
Punjab. Rulers of India Series* (Oxford: 1891), p. 64.

58 Johnson, *Stranger in India*, II, 218–19.

A Madras civil servant, I. Everett, after a visit to Fort Gloster, predicted that abundant raw cotton and cheap labor would enable the local textile mill to supply "a great part, if not the whole, of the Eastern world, to the exclusion of the European manufacture." He deplored British opposition to the export of cotton-mill machinery and asked whether "the manufactures of Bengal have not as good a claim to the protection of the sovereign as those of Lancashire. . . . . But India," he concluded, "has never yet been regarded as part of the empire. It goes by the unhappy name of colony, a place . . . made expressly to be plundered by the Mother-country." [59]

On the other hand, far more influential publicists such as Robert M. Martin and John Crawfurd, who were trying to promote British investment in India, emphasized the potential of India as a producer of raw cotton and plantation products. Crawfurd considered that any "attempt to introduce the complex manufactures of Europe into India, [would be] . . . a signal commercial blunder." [60] In the same vein, R.M. Martin wrote of the ideal relationship of mother country and colony: "*the one* [Britain] teeming with a hardy, industrious and ingenious population, two-thirds of whom are engaged in manipulating and vending the produce of more genial climes . . . *the other* [India] rich to overflowing with bounty with which nature has enriched the earth, and peculiarly so in those agricultural products necessary to the manufactures, comforts, and luxuries of the more civilized nation." [61] His racial arrogance turned to doubt by 1860 when he became aware of the industrial potential of the Indian textile industry that had developed in Bombay. "Even the present generation," he warned, "may witness the Lancashire manufacturer beaten by his Hindu competitor." [62]

Indians, noting the effects of both machine-made imports and Fort Gloster yarn on the rural weavers and spinners, were at first less certain of the efficacy of industrialization. [63] A Hindu traveler who visited Fort Gloster Mill in 1830 reported that the local people

59 I. Everett, *Observations on India by a Resident There of Many Years* (London: 1853), p. 58.

60 John Crawfurd, *Sketch of the Commercial Resources,* pp. 226–27.

61 Martin, *British Colonies,* I, 205.

62 Quoted in Morris D. Morris, *The Emergence of an Industrial Labor Force in India* (Berkeley: 1965), p. 25.

63 *Reformer,* 3 April 1835, reprinted in *Asiatic Journal,* new series, vol. 18 (October 1835), p. 92.

considered industrialization a mixed blessing. As consumers they benefited from cheaper cloth, but some, who had learned from English friends about the results of the industrial revolution in cities like Glasgow and Manchester, were fearful of the long-term effects of industrialization on human life. [64] Other westernized intelligentsia made no distinction between commerce and industry and called on the youth of the country to turn from the study of English literature to such practical subjects as science and commerce. [65] Gradually, however, Indian writers recognized the importance of industrial development. An editorial written in 1847, probably by Iswar Chundra Gupta, lamented the closing down of the Calcutta Mechanics Institute because of a lack of public interest and noted that industry and technical skills were essential for a nation's progress. [66]

The issue may never have occurred to the leading entrepreneur of the day, Dwarkanath Tagore. He saw immediate profit in the production of staples and plantation products, and though he may have believed that India would eventually produce its own steam engines and iron and steel, he was content for the time being to import superior British engines at reasonable prices. Dwarkanath cast his lot with the free traders and joined in their attack upon the restrictive policies of the East India Company. He believed that the end of the company's business operations would stimulate the import of British capital and skill, hasten the economic development of India, and lead to the rise of a strong, independent, and reform-minded Indian middle class. It was natural for an enlightened and politically astute Indian like Tagore to associate himself with the party of progress in Britain. But he closed his eyes to the full implications of a movement grounded in the concept of an industrialized England supported by agricultural colonies. It was, in fact, free-trade imperialism that would frustrate the industrial development that he and his British partners were to promote with such vigor in the thirties and forties. [67]

64Quoted from *Banga Doot* in *Samachar Darpan,* 8 May 1830, in Brajendra Nath Bandopadhyaya, ed., *Sambadpetrey Sekaler Katha 1818–1840,* 2 vols. (Calcutta: 1949–50), II, 326.

65*Reformer,* 18 Mar. 1833.

66*Sambad Prabhakar,* 8 June 1847, in Benoy Ghosh, ed., *Samayek-Patre Banglar Samaj-Chitra 1840–1905,* 3 vols. (Calcutta: 1963), I, 50.

67See speech by Dwarkanath Tagore of 18 June 1836, reprinted in K.C. Mittra, *Memoir of Dwarkanath Tagore* (Calcutta: 1870), pp. 53–57. On "'free-trade imperialism," see Bernard Semmel, *The Rise of Free Trade Imperialism* (Cambridge: 1970).

Chapter IV

CARR, TAGORE AND COMPANY

The most vigorous of the new agency houses established after the crisis of 1830–33 was Carr, Tagore and Company. During its thirteen-year history the firm led its rivals in the promotion of transportation, mining, and plantation industries, in the commercial application of steam power, and in the shaping of new forms of business organization. Soon after he launched the firm on 1 August 1834, Dwarkanath wrote the governor-general, Lord Bentinck, predicting that his house would be an instrument of national regeneration and a model to be emulated by his countrymen. He denied "merely selfish and private ambition," and wrote that "my fortune, by inheritance and successful industry, places me above any necessity for applying myself to the labour and cares of common life." Instead, the new partnership was "calculated to introduce the natives of India generally to more immediate participation in the objects of European enterprises." His house would be "upon a par with, if not in advance of, the first houses of Calcutta . . . combining . . . the advantages . . . of European and native integrity, wealth and experience" and devoted to "unfolding the productive energies of the country."[1]

This unusual letter from a businessman justifying his motives to the sovereign of British India served a number of purposes. First, Tagore wanted the governor-general to know that he had resigned his office as dewan not to escape the slander of his enemies, but to embark upon a more important and productive career. Furthermore, he wished to impress upon Bentinck the political significance of his act. Indians had now come of age and were ready to associate in public life as equals with Europeans. Finally, by stressing the social dimensions of his venture, he hoped for favorable consideration when

1Dwarkanath Tagore to Lord William Bentinck, 20 Aug. 1834, in Bentinck Papers, Portland Collection, Nottingham University Library, Ref. no. PW JF 2091.

applying for concessions from the government. Implicit in the letter was Dwarkanath's faith in British intentions and his confidence that the government would do its utmost to encourage indigenous enterprise.

Dwarkanath had good reason for confidence in the government. His words reflected the well-known sentiments of the governor-general, who, for all his ethnocentric intolerance of Indian culture, was a zealous exponent of Indian economic and political development. By opening the lower echelons of government to Indians, Bentinck raised hopes of greater Indian participation in the future, and his sympathy for the new middle class created a sense of imperial loyalty among the educated Indian community of Calcutta. On his departure the community eulogized him as the governor-general who "first taught us to forget the distinction between conquerors and conquered, and to become, in heart and mind, in hopes and aspiration, one with Englishmen."[2]

In the Indian community, as in government circles, the climate of opinion was ripe for Dwarkanath's move. Ever since the commercial crisis of 1830, the idea of Bengalis launching modern business firms had been under discussion in the vernacular press. Many Indians resented that in 1830 banians had taken heavy losses in European-managed enterprises, whereas on the eve of the crash several of the agency-house partners had retired home with fortunes. All shades of Bengali opinion joined in a crusade that anticipated by fifty years the *swadeshi* movement of the late nineteenth century. The conservative *Samachar Chandrika* urged the zamindars to purchase and operate the European-owned indigo factories left idle by the crisis, mainly to forestall the colonization of the countryside by Europeans.[3] The moderate *Reformer,* published by Prasanna Kumar Tagore and representing views close to those of Dwarkanath, called on the Bengalis to "compete with the nations of Europe and America, not only in English literature, but in the arts, Sciences and commerce." The editor pointed out that Hindus could no longer blame their religion for entrepreneurial backwardness because there were now "enough enlightened Hindoos who can lead the way."[4] Furthermore,

2*Asiatic Journal,* new series, vol. 17 (August 1835), p. 218. Lord Bentinck's views are treated in George D. Bearce, *British Attitudes Towards India, 1784–1858* (Oxford: 1961), pp. 156 ff., and in David Kopf, *British Orientalism and the Bengal Renaissance* (Berkeley: 1969).

3Brajendra Nath Bandopadhyaya, ed., *Sambadpetrey Sekaler Katha 1818–1840,* 2 vols. (Calcutta: 1919–50), II, 338.

4*Reformer,* 18 Mar. 1833.

the British now knew the country well enough to procure their own goods and no longer needed Indian banians, hence the natives, in self-defence, must trade on their own account.[5] Radical "Young Bengal," voicing their opinions in the journal *Jnananeshan,* urged their countrymen to cast off their "natural idleness and lethargy, and armed with the weapons of business, commerce, and industry, triumph over the enemies of their prosperity."[6] When Tagore launched his firm, "Young Bengal" had found a hero: "Foreigners come here and in a short time earn enough to live in comfort back home, and our country is being pumped dry in the process. Perhaps things will now change. Down-trodden Hindustan will now compete with other trading countries. May others follow the path shown by the Tagores and engage in similar ventures, which are beneficial and bold and deserve praise, and thus help remove the bad name of the Hindus as idle and ignorant."[7]

In founding his own agency house, Tagore was only the most prominent of many Bengalis who between 1830 and 1850 embarked on careers in western-style business. Most notable among the others were Motilal Seal and Ram Gopal Ghosh, both of whom followed the example of Dwarkanath and founded biracial agency houses. Many of the western-educated graduates of Hindu College turned to trade, and other Bengalis combined trade with silk and indigo production. Ocean shipping was a major area of investment, and by 1850, 45 percent of the ships registered in Calcutta belonged to Indians, primarily Bengali Muslims. In the 1840s, Indians were moving into enterprises formerly reserved for Europeans—pharmacy, hotel operation, and stablekeeping. In 1850, three Bengali firms were among the eight that tendered bids to build the first forty miles of railway in Bengal.[8]

But no other Indian businessman so strikingly captured the public

5 Ibid., 24 Mar. 1833.

6 *Jnananeshan,* 14 Dec. 1833, in *Sambadpetrey Sekaler Katha 1818–1840,* II, 331–32.

7 *Jnananeshan,* 9 Aug. 1834, ibid., II, 339.

8 Kissory Chand Mittra, *Mutty Lall Seal* (Calcutta: 1869); Ram Gopal Sanyal, *Bengal Celebrities,* 2 vols. (Calcutta: 1889), I, 179–80, on Ram Gopal Ghosh; traders and producers are named in N.K. Sinha, ed., *The History of Bengal (1757–1905)* (Calcutta: 1967), p. 361; see also WBSA, Board of Customs, Salt and Opium, Commercial, 16 Nov. (8) 1835, 19 Nov. (18) 1835, 2 Nov. (25) 1835, 8 Oct. (76) 1835, and Board of Trade, Commercial, 19 Mar. (39) 1835. Tradesmen and shipowners are listed in *Bengal Directory and Annual Register* and *Bengal and Agra Directory and Annual Register* (Calcutta: 1840 to 1850). Railway bidders are named in IO, Home Department, Railways, L/PWD/3, nos. 19–25, Agent of East India Railway Company forwards tenders received, 6 Aug. 1850.

imagination as did Tagore. His activities were closely followed in the press, and his sense of the dramatic enlivened the city's otherwise dreary public life. At the outset he defied the racial conventions of Calcutta's European society by forming an alliance with a Britisher on the basis of equality. Ten years earlier a Parsi, Rustomjee Cowasjee, had founded an interracial firm, but Parsis were classified as a Near Eastern community. A Bengali Hindu, on the other hand, was considered far beyond the pale of western civilization, enmeshed in a web of exotic vices and superstitions.[9] Except for a few enlightened individuals, most of the Britishers cited cultural differences to justify racial discrimination. Only recently had wealthy banians been permitted to enter agency-house offices wearing shoes, Indians were still not allowed to promenade around Tank Square in the evenings, and society was scandalized when Bengalis first began to attend the Chowringhee Theatre. Life in the mufassal was even more segregated, and Indians of high status were expected to dismount from their palanquins when passing a lowly British subaltern.[10]

Again disregarding convention, Dwarkanath, rather than assuming the designation "banian," styled himself "merchant," a term customarily reserved for Europeans. Perhaps this was intended less as a challenge to racial snobbery than as a desire to be identified with a class of men he greatly admired. "Twenty years ago," he had said at a public meeting, "the Company treated us as slaves. Who first raised us from this state, but the merchant of Calcutta? And the first among them was the late much lamented John Palmer. . . . It was to the merchants, agents and other independent English settlers, that the natives of Calcutta were indebted for the superiority they possess over their countrymen in the Mofussil."[11] By 1834 the merchants of Calcutta, once considered "interlopers" in the Company's dominions, had become proud burghers, a branch of the British middle class which, in the Reform Act of 1832, had won political power

9*Bengal Hurkaru* 10 to 14 Sept. 1835; J.C. Stocqueler, *The Handbook of India,* 2d ed. (London: 1845), pp. 34 ff. The firm of Rustomjee, Turner and Company included Rustomjee and Byramjee Cowasjee, Richard Turner, and J.D. Smith. See *Bengal Directory and General Register* (Calcutta: 1825 to 1828).

10John Capper, *The Three Presidencies of India* (London: 1853), pp. 381 ff.; *Bengal Hurkaru,* 6 and 9 Apr. 1835, 30 July and 1 Aug. 1844; Emily Eden, *Letters from India,* 2 vols. (London: 1872), I, 91, II, 252; *Asiatic Journal,* new series, vol. 13 (January 1834), pp. 6–7.

11Kissory Chand Mittra, *Memoir of Dwarkanath Tagore* (Calcutta: 1870), pp. 53–54.

commensurate with their economic strength. To Dwarkanath the merchants were the "second estate" of the British Indian empire, a closely knit group of enlightened men who had led the fight against officialdom for a free press, for jury trial, against the stamp tax, and against the coolie trade. [12] It was their tradition of enlightened laissez faire, political independence, and economic progress that Dwarkanath wanted to emulate and carry forward.

With another bold stroke Tagore propelled his firm into the first rank of agency houses. At the time of the signing of the deed of copartnership on 1 August 1834, Dwarkanath loaned the firm one million rupees. The loan was registered as a debt owed him by the firm on which Carr, Tagore and Company was to pay 8 percent interest, or Rs. 80,000, annually. It was kept in an account separate from his own personal account for dividends and profits and was not withdrawn during his lifetime. [13]

The source of this one million rupees requires explanation. In December 1831 John Palmer had written of Dwarkanath: "I fancy he borrows to lend and to carry on his own concerns," [14] and by Dwarkanath's own testimony, "in 1833 money was very scarce. Being pressed for money on MacIntosh's failure, I got a loan on mortgage from my personal friends." [15] Yet Dwarkanath claimed in his will that the one million rupees loaned his firm in 1834 was "unborrowed" capital. His words can only be understood if we assume that most of the one million rupees deposited with the firm was not in the form of cash but in negotiable notes pledged against future revenues from his landed estates, the gross income of which was Rs. 1,30,000 per year. Like other export houses, the firm depended for its working capital on loans and advances from the government and from banians. But unlike many of the others its credit was unquestioned. It rested on the value of Dwarkanath's landed estates, and thus his zamindaris laid the foundation for his commercial and industrial enterprises.

Tagore not only provided the firm's capital but selected the partners, directed the investment strategy, and, throughout his lifetime, actively guided the house. Carr, Tagore and Company was, in fact, more a patriarchy than a partnership. Tagore gave his

12*Bengal Hurkaru,* 17 Jan. 1833.
13KNT Collection, Will and Codicil filed 24 Sept. 1846, Supreme Court, Ecclesiastical Side.
14Palmer Papers, Engl. Lett. c. 119, Palmer to Smith, 21 Dec. 1831.
15Hurlal Tagore vs. Ashootosh Day, reported in *Bengal Hurkaru,* 25 Apr. 1836.

partners both the freedom and the means to plan and innovate. They were encouraged to hold directorships in the many joint-stock enterprises promoted by the firm and were so ubiquitous in their activities that Carr, Tagore and Company became a byword for jobbery, monopoly, and cliquism in the business world of Calcutta. In 1841, for example, William Prinsep was involved in the management of a dozen separate enterprises, Dwarkanath in six others and D.M. Gordon in two. The pattern continued as new partners inherited directorships from those who departed for home. [16]

TABLE 3. PARTNERS OF CARR, TAGORE AND COMPANY, 1834–48

Partner	Years
Dwarkanath Tagore	1834–46
William Carr	1834–41
William Prinsep	1836–42
Thomas J. Taylor	March-December 1839
Donald McLeod Gordon	1840–48
Henry Barclay Henderson	1841–48
W.C.M. Plowden	1842–43
John Deans Campbell	1843–48
George Gordon MacPherson	1842–48
James Stuart	1847–48

Tagore selected his partners from varied backgrounds. William Carr was a seasoned merchant who had come to India in 1824 and joined John Palmer and Company, first as an assistant, then as a partner. In 1829 Carr was appointed secretary of the Union Bank and, from the fall of Palmer to the launching of Carr, Tagore, worked as an independent indigo broker. Tagore described him as a "gentleman who has for some years been favorably known to the commercial circles of Calcutta as joining, in his person, talents of the highest order and most varied description, with unblemished integrity, long experience in business, and a complete knowledge of mercantile affairs." [17]

16Bengal Directory and Annual Register and Bengal and Agra Directory and Annual Register for relevant years.

17Dwarkanath Tagore to Lord Bentinck, 20 Aug. 1834. References to William Carr are found in IO, Despatches to Bengal, vol. 96, p. 1039, Commercial Department, 21 July 1824, par. 12 granting William Carr Free Merchant's indentures. Also Bengal Directory and General Register (Calcutta: 1827); Bengal Past and Present, vol. 24 (1922), p. 124, Kissory Chand Mittra, Memoir, p. 84. Carr may not have been Tagore's first choice. He had been considering R.C. Jenkins, who subsequently joined Fergusson and Company, leaving "Carr and Dwarkanath adrift." Palmer Papers, Engl. Lett. c. 124, Palmer to C.B. Palmer, 2 May 1834 and c 125, Palmer to James Caulfield, 15 Sept. 1834.

When Carr joined Tagore in 1834 he insisted that a place be found for his friend William Prinsep. 18 Prinsep worked as an assistant in the firm for two years and became a partner in 1836 when Carr departed for Europe. He was both an experienced merchant and a creative entrepreneur who generated many of the ideas adopted by the firm. A gift for innovation was his birthright: his father, John Prinsep (1746–1831), had been the leading entrepreneur of Bengal in the late eighteenth century, the first Englishman to manufacture indigo, and a promoter of cotton-textile manufacturing, shipbuilding, and the minting of copper coins. Upon his retirement to England, John Prinsep became an M.P. and a director of the Sierra Leone Company. Before his death he had made and lost two fortunes and had bequeathed seven of his sons to service in India. 19

John Prinsep's fourth son, William, arrived in Calcutta in 1817 at the age of 23, joined Palmer and Company as an assistant and soon became a partner. Palmer found William, and his elder brother George who later joined the firm, too "restless and speculative" and blamed them for the ruin of his house. George in particular "plunged into every new project occurring to himself or suggested to him by others." 20 After the fall of Palmer and Company, William Prinsep worked as an indigo broker and as agent for a large silk company established by his wealthy brother-in-law, George Haldimand. 21 As a member of Carr, Tagore and Company, William Prinsep was given the scope to exercise his creative powers. The most important and lasting of his many ventures was the establishment of the Indian tea

18 Palmer Papers, Engl. Lett. c 125, Palmer to James Caulifield, 15 Sept. 1834.

19 These sons were: (1) Charles Robert, 1790–1864, advocate general of Bengal, also translator of J.B. Say's *Treatise on Political Economy*. Say was the economist who first defined the concept of the entrepreneur. (2) George, 1791–1839, merchant, promoter of the Bengal Salt Company and other novel enterprises, author of *Remarks on the External Commerce and Exchanges of Bengal*. (3) Henry Thoby 1792–1878, B.C.S., Secy. to Govt. of India. (4) William, 1794–1874, Tagore's partner and projector of the Assam Company. (5) James, 1799–1840, assay master at Calcutta Mint, archeologist, engineer, scientist, and decipherer of Ashoka's Edicts. (6) Thomas, surveyor of Sunderbunds. (7) Augustus, B.C.S., discoverer of Palamau coal fields. An account of the family is given in Henry Thoby Prinsep, "Four Generations in India 1770–1904," IO Mss. Eur C. 97.

20 Palmer Papers, Engl. Lett. d 107, Palmer to Mary Palmer, 5 Apr. 1833.

21 Great Britain, *Parliamentary Papers*, 1840, vol. 8, pp. 302 ff., testimony of A. Rogers before Select Committee on East Indian Produce. Haldimand had married John Prinsep's eldest daughter, generously supported his widowed mother-in-law, and helped other members of the family. See H.G. Rawlinson, ed., Augusta Becher, *Personal Reminiscences in India and Europe, 1830–1888* (London: 1930).

industry on a commercial basis. In 1842 he retired to England, and until his death in 1874 served on the London Board of the Assam Company. [22]

Because of Prinsep's extensive promotional activities, Tagore undoubtedly felt the need for a new partner who would devote his full time to mercantile affairs. He selected Donald McLeod Gordon, a relative of his old friend from Mackintosh days, George James Gordon. The Gordons had worked together in the opium trade backed by Dwarkanath, and in 1836 Donald McLeod Gordon was hired as an assistant in Carr, Tagore and Company. He became a full partner of the firm on May 1, 1840. [23]

On the eve of Prinsep's departure, his place was taken by another man of unconventional talents, Major Henry Barclay Henderson. Henderson had come to Calcutta in 1824 as an accountant and had worked his way up to the second-ranking position in the Auditor General's Department. The major was a man of literary pretensions, who alluded in one of his sketches of Calcutta life to a distaste for what he called "haggling, bartering, gain seeking calculating trade." But he reconciled himself to a career in business when the ghost of John Palmer appeared to him in a dream and impressed upon him that "even the painter, and the poet achieved his immortality only, when the sun of commerce shed its beams and blessings upon his labours." [24]

In the final years of the firm, Tagore brought in John Deans Campbell, a merchant-promoter, and George Gordon MacPherson, a civil surgeon and amateur scientist who had served most of his life in the mufassal. James Stuart, the last British member, became a partner in 1847 after the death of Dwarkanath. Stuart, first hired as

22Augusta Becher describes her uncle William in retirement as "jolly, noisy, merry," and at family gatherings "the center of all fun." Ibid., pp. 27, 28, 55. For Prinsep and the Assam Company, see H.A. Antrobus, *A History of the Assam Company, 1839–1953* (Edinburgh: 1957), p. 166, and Assam Company, London Board Minute Book 9924, vol. 10, Meeting of 21 Feb. 1874.

23WBSA, Board of Customs, Salt and Opium, Commercial Proceedings, 2 June (40–41) 1836. See also Jardine Matheson Archives, Unbound Incoming Letters, Calcutta 2252, Letter from D.M. Gordon to Jardine Matheson and Company, 8 Jan. 1836, Canton and Jardine Matheson Archives, India Letterbooks, vol. 17; letter from Jardine Matheson and Company to G.J. Gordon, care of D.M. Gordon, Indigo Mart, 3 Mar. 1834, and letter from Jardine Matheson Company to D.M. Gordon, 23 Feb. 1836, India Letterbooks, vol. 20.

24H.B. Henderson, *The Bengalee,* 2 vols. (Calcutta: 1829, 1836), II, 191–211.

Dwarkanath's personal secretary, was in time acknowledged by his fellow merchants to be one of the most able accountants in the city.

Two of Tagore's partners were with the firm only briefly and would hardly deserve mention except for what their selection reveals about Dwarkanath himself. The first, Captain Thomas J. Taylor (1804–1839) of the Madras Cavalry, had been raised by his actress mother, a granddaughter of William Pitt, in London theatrical circles. Taylor cut a dashing figure in Madras society until Bentinck brought him to Calcutta to serve on a committee to prepare new regulations for the Indian postal system. In March 1839 he resigned the service and accepted a partnership in Carr, Tagore and Company, but died prematurely the following December. His selection may well reflect Tagore's enchantment with the theater and those associated with it. [25] The second was Charles Metcalf Plowden (1820–60), who joined the firm in 1843. Young Plowden had no particular qualifications, but his father, Trevor John Chicheley Plowden, had been one of Dwarkanath's first British friends and patrons. When Trevor failed to obtain a writership for his son, Tagore felt obligated to take in the young man. But Charles, unsettled and distraught, ran off to Abyssinia while enroute to England and severed his connection with the firm. [26]

Next in rank below the partners was Alexander Garrcock Mackenzie, a self-styled engineer who directed the technical operations of the house in steamshipping and coal mining. The firm employed a large number of assistants, some of whom were Indians, supervised by the long-term head assistant Francis Pinto, an Indo-Portuguese. At various times Dwarkanath's relatives worked for the firm—his cousin Prasanna Kumar, his nephews Chunder Mohun Chatterjee and Nabin Chandra Mukherji, and his sons Debendranath and Girindranath. The firm also employed Indian banians engaged in purchasing and sales on commission. [27]

25 *Friend of India,* 19 Dec. 1839, p. 805.

26 Walter F.C. Chicheley Plowden, *Records of the Chicheley Plowdens, AD 1590–1913* (London: 1914), p. 182.

27 One of these was Tacoor Lall Mullick, who began working for the firm in 1843 or 1844. One of his jobs was to accept bills for Carr, Tagore and Company. Although he took these in his own name, they were in reality loans to the firm. All went well until the firm closed its doors in 1848, leaving Tacoor Lall Mullick with heavy debts. The *Delhi Gazette* editorialized on the case, brought before the Insolvency Court, as an illustration of the commercial immorality of Calcutta. "Why, to what a miserable peddling concern would he reduce the Firm!" Quoted in *Bengal Hurkaru,* 31 Oct. 1849.

Within the firm there was some formal attempt at a division of labor. In a commercial directory of 1841, Prinsep was assigned "Correspondence and Export" and Gordon, "Imports." [28] When the coal company was organized, one partner was designated to head the "Coal Department" and act as managing director of the company. Coal sales were handled by another partner, and Dwarkanath himself managed personnel and legal matters. But it was more usual for assignments to be rotated, and the norm was generalization rather than specialization. Each partner was expected to participate in all of the multiple activities of the firm—the import-export trade, mufassal industries, estate management, and ocean shipping—and finally, to serve as directors or managers of the many joint stock enterprises promoted by the firm.

Of the nine Europeans associated at one time or another as partners, three—Carr, Gordon and Campbell—were sound commercial men. Two others, Henderson and Stuart, were accountants of obvious value to the firm, and one, MacPherson, was a "man of science." Taylor's career was cut short and Plowden contributed nothing. To none of these men can be attributed the prodigious entrepreneurial achievements of the firm. Credit for them must go to William Prinsep and Dwarkanath Tagore, the only two partners who evidenced the imaginative flair characteristic of the creative entrepreneur. Prinsep appears to have been the initiator of the Bengal Tea Company and the Bengal Coal Company and the energetic promoter of many lesser enterprises. Some of his schemes were financial disasters, and Dwarkanath, like John Palmer before him, may have regretted the association. Nevertheless, Prinsep retired to England on friendly terms with Dwarkanath, and there is no evidence of any hard feelings between them. After accounting for all the contributions to the firm made by his British partners, Dwarkanath Tagore himself stands out as the force behind its entrepreneurial activity. He had shown evidence of entrepreneurial imagination long before acquiring partners, and, through year after year of innovative activity, he was the only continuing member of the firm.

The "bread and butter" business of the firm was its export trade in raw silk, silk piece goods, indigo, sugar, rum, saltpeter, hides, timber, and rice. [29] Until 1842, shipments to Britain were consigned to a

28*Bengal and Agra Annual Guide,* 2 vols. (Calcutta: 1841), I, 207.

29See advertisements in *Bengal Hurkaru,* 22 Jan. 1838, 28 Aug. 1840, 17 July 1844 and 6 Feb. 1845. Also WBSA, Board of Customs, Salt and Opium, Customs, 4 Aug. (17A) 1837; 5 Oct. (84) 1842, and 13 Mar. (53–54) 1845.

corresponding house in the city of London, Rickards, Little and Company, and thereafter, to Roberts, Mitchell and Company. The firm also shipped to continental ports. In France, goods were consigned to Robin and Company of La Havre.[30] Unfortunately, figures for the total volume of exports are lost, and only records of exports hypothecated to the East India Company survive. During the four years 1835 through 1838, Carr, Tagore and Company exported goods under the hypothecation system valued at C.R. 14,04,003. Included were raw silk, silk piece goods and sugar, valued at C.R. 11,00,082; indigo at C.R. 2,13,262; hides at C.R. 13,938; and saltpeter at C.R. 13,000. The gross sales of these goods in England were about £35,000 per year. If one were to calculate roughly a profit of 10 percent, Carr, Tagore and Company would have netted £3,500 profit annually from its hypothecation trade alone.[31]

One of Tagore's objectives was to achieve as much vertical integration as possible—to control the production, processing, and shipping of the goods exported and sold by his firm. In this strategy he followed the lead of the old agency houses such as Palmer and

30WBSA, Board of Customs, Salt and Opium, Commercial, 9 May (10) 1836, 27 June (1) 1836, 7 July (8) 1836, and 26 May (69) 1842. NAI, Financial, India, 17 Nov. (25) 1841 and 24 Nov. (19) 1841.

31Compiled from WBSA, Board of Customs, Salt and Opium, Commercial, 1835–38. During the period 1835 to 1840, the value of exports from Bengal increased 86.76 percent—the largest increase during any five-year period from 1830 to 1905. See *Journal of the Statistical Society of London,* vol. 19 (June 1856), p. 108, and N.K. Sinha, ed., *The History of Bengal, 1757–1905* (Calcutta: 1967), p. 334, which gives the figure of 61.5 percent increase. K.N. Chaudhuri in "India's Foreign Trade and the Cessation of the East India Company's Trading Activities, 1828–40," *Economic History Review,* Second series, vol. XIX, no. 2 (August 1966) gives the index numbers for value and volume increase of these three commodities for India as a whole:

Exports: Index Number of Selected Commodities, 1828 = 100 (for India as a whole)

	1835–36	1836–37	1837–38	1838–39	1839–40
Raw silk:					
Value	57	95	48	82	79
Volume	68	100	62	85	77
Sugar:					
Value	61	113	185	179	185
Volume	78	120	218	197	181
Indigo:					
Value	70	60	63	70	104
Volume	132	86	90	88	120

Company and Alexander and Company, which had combined trade with control over extensive mufassal properties. The larger of the new houses, such as Cockerell and Company and Gilmore and Company, also owned extensive indigo and sugar factories.[32] But Tagore was more deliberate in his strategy and may have been the only Indian zamindar to integrate his landed estates directly into his commercial schemes. He exploited his ancestral estate of Berhampore, for example, as the chief source of the indigo, sugar, and silk exported by his house.

An opportunity to enter raw-silk production came in 1835. The East India Company, which produced four-fifths of India's exportable raw silk, was called upon by the Charter Act of 1833 to give up its commercial operations in India and dispose of its silk factories at auction. In November 1835, Tagore purchased Jungypore filatures, one of the East India Company's eight important silk-producing centers in Bengal, for Rs. 47,300.[33] At the same time he entered a bid on the Commercolly filatures, the finest of the company's silk factories, located in the midst of his ancestral zamindari, Berhampore.

The Commercolly silk works consisted of four filatures, extending over a radius of forty-three miles. Each filature was a large, lofty building housing copper basins for steeping cocoons and machines for winding the silk. After winding, the skeins of raw silk were baled and shipped to Britain, where they were washed, thrown, and spun into thread for weaving.[34] The sixty-thousand maunds of cocoons needed each year were purchased from growers in the neighborhood, who in turn fed their worms on mulberry leaves bought from other peasants, all of whom were tenants of Dwarkanath Tagore. Commercolly's four filatures employed at least 5,000 workers, who operated the reeling machines, carried cocoons and fuel, collected and packed the skeins, cleaned the building, and supervised operations. They produced 150,000 lb. of silk annually, which sold on the British market for

32D. Morier Evans, *The Commercial Crisis, 1847–1848,* 2d ed. (London: 1849), app., p. xii.

33WBSA, Board of Customs, Salt and Opium, Commercial, 23 Nov. (15–16) 1835. It was purchased in the name of M. Laurleta. Jungypore was located in Murshidabad District, twenty-five miles north of Murshidabad city. For a history of the silk industry in Bengal, see H.R. Ghosal, *Economic Transition in the Bengal Presidency, 1793–1833* (Patna: 1950), pp. 46 ff.

34For a description of the process of silk manufacturing, see Rev. Dionysius Lardner, *A Treatise on Silk Manufacture* (Philadelphia: 1832).

£ 75,000 to £ 150,000.   Without precise data on the price of cocoons, the wages of workers, or the cost of shipment to Europe, Tagore's profits must remain unknown.[35]

Although the Board of Trade set the value of the four Commercolly filatures at Rs. 1,75,000,[36] Tagore brazenly offered Rs. 60,000. He referred to his "entire or partial control" of the properties encircling Commercolly and in guarded terms warned that this control would "so much reduce the value of the Commercolly filatures to any other persons whatever . . . we should have but little competition to fear under a much less favorable offer." The indignant export warehouse keeper refused to forward his offer to the government.[37] Other potential buyers declined to bid against Tagore, and the governor-general turned down an offer to reserve the Commercolly works for a silk company formed in England. Not only would any rival depend on Tagore's cooperation as landlord of the mulberry and cocoon growers, but, as Auckland pointed out, the Commercolly complex would require £150,000 of ready capital to operate.[38]

After almost two years of haggling, Carr, Tagore and Company purchased Commercolly and its outfactories in late August 1837 for Rs. 84,500.[39] No sooner had they taken possession of Commercolly than a struggle ensued between the firm and the East India Company's commercial resident, R. Richardson. It took the form of minor disputes over some firewood and over the refusal of Richardson to vacate his residence before Carr, Tagore and Company had paid in full for the property. But Richardson's feelings ran deeper. He and his predecessors had devoted years of hard work to developing the

35Concerning the price of silk, see Great Britain, *Parliamentary Papers*, 1830, vol. VI, p. 310, and R.M. Martin, *Statistics of the Colonies of the British Empire* (London: 1839), p. 390 C. As to production at Commercolly, see WBSA, Board of Customs, Salt and Opium, Commercial, 3 Dec. (37) 1835.

36N.A.I., Board of Trade, 5 Mar. (1) 1835.

37WBSA, Board of Customs, Salt and Opium, Commercial, 9 Nov. (7 and 8) 1835.

38WBSA, Board of Customs, Salt and Opium, Commercial, 14 Jan. (5) 1836; BM, Auckland Papers, *Additional Manuscripts* 37689, Auckland Private Letterbooks, vol. I, letter from Auckland to J.R. Carnac, 5 Aug. 1836.

39The Court of Directors noted with some annoyance the wide differences between the original valuation placed on the property and the final sale price. IO, Despatches to India and Bengal, vol. XX, pp. 1145–46, 24 July (23) 1839. The factories were purchased in the name of David Andrew, Jr. WBSA, Board of Customs, Salt and Opium, Commercial, 31 August (14) 1837. Dwarkanath and his partners sued Andrew in 1843 for repayment of a bond executed for Rs. 3,00,000, and won the judgment.

Commercolly factory and he felt that Carr, Tagore had purchased it too cheaply. "Too much indulgence has already been shown the firm," he wrote his superiors. "I have been upwards of forty years in the country and never dealt with such screws before."[40] When Richardson finally departed, there was no one to restrain the employees of the firm from tyrannizing over local villagers. Their complaints reached the joint magistrate of Pabna, who wrote his superiors that the *chaprassis* of the company, wearing badges with the initials "C T & Co", went about the neighboring districts seizing cocoons from the growers. "The Servants of the Commercolly factory are not the quietist people in my district. They entertain a mistaken though very prevalent notion that their masters in purchasing the Commercolly factories have purchased with them some peculiar privileges of trade."[41]

Indigo, Tagore's second major export, was the leading mufassal plantation industry of Bengal. Tagore was a large producer even before he founded his firm. He started his first indigo factory, Syllidah in Pabna, in 1821, and claimed that in consequence, the income from Berhampore, once insufficient to meet the government assessment, began to show a "handsome profit."[42] Five of the seven indigo concerns eventually owned by Tagore and his firm were situated in the Pabna–Nadia area on his Berhampore and Shahazadpur estates. Two others were in Murshidabad district, at Burra Jungypore and Chota Jungypore, where he also produced silk.[43]

40WBSA, Board of Customs, Salt and Opium, Commercial, 25 Jan. (31 and 33) 1838 and 8 Feb. (32) 1838. Indeed, he had dealt with Dwarkanath Tagore once before. In 1824, as President of the Embankment Committee of Jessore District, Richardson had battled Tagore over the construction of embankments opposed by Dwarkanath on the ground that their construction would have flooded hundreds of bigahs of his land. WBSA, Territorial Revenue Department, 28 May (10–12) 1824 and 9 Apr. (23–24) 1824.

41WBSA, Judicial Department, Criminal, 16 June (44–47) 1840.

42*Alexander's East India Magazine,* vol. I, no. 3 (February 1831), pp. 211–12; Syllidah remained in the family and Debendranath Tagore was listed as its owner in 1861. *New Calcutta Directory* (Calcutta: 1861).

43The five in Pabna and Nadia were Syllidah, Rynuggur, Meerpore, Dobracole, and Comidpore. See *Bengal Hurkaru,* 23 June 1834 and *Bengal Directory and Annual Register* (Calcutta: 1827, 1831 and 1835) listing Samuel Shuttleworth, who, along with D.E. Shuttleworth, was in Tagore's employment as indigo planter at Rynuggur Concern, Commercolly. See also testimony of Alexander Forbes, *Report of the Indigo Commission,* pt. 3, pp. 60 ff. The *New Calcutta Directory* (Calcutta: 1858) lists Gordon, Stuart and Company, successors to Carr, Tagore and Company, as owners or agents of Jungypore Concerns. The Union Bank loaned Carr, Tagore and Company 18

Tagore cultivated indigo under the *raiyati* system, whereby the ryots themselves purchased the seed and owned the implements. But whereas most of the European planters obtained their indigo plant from ryots who were tenants of neighboring zamindars, Tagore was landlord of the ryots who grew his plant, and as a result his labor force was more docile and his supply of indigo more secure.[44] His seven concerns were all of moderate size, but taken together may have produced 1,600 maunds of indigo per year, which would have brought Tagore Rs. 2,00,000 in Calcutta, thus making him one of the larger indigo producers of Bengal.[45]

Tagore's sugar operations were not as successful. Cane sugar production in India had a checkered history, typified by Tagore's own experience. The peasants produced a crude product called *gur,* adequate for domestic consumption, but not saleable on the international market. Those interested in exporting sugar could either refine gur purchased from the peasants or buy raw sugar cane and refine it with modern machinery on the West Indian model. In the late eighteenth century, the East India Company tried to promote sugar as an export staple and encouraged a large number of experienced West Indian planters to take up production in all parts of British India. Almost all of these failed, with heavy losses. The industry languished until the period from 1830 to 1860 when another wave of experiments ensued, partly given impetus by the equalization of West and East Indian sugar duties in 1836.[46] Unfortunately, these experiments also failed, and attempts to develop an Indian sugar industry were not renewed until the twentieth century.[47]

Dwarkanath entered the sugar business during its second phase, and, evidently unaware of eighteenth-century attempts, claimed to

---

lakhs, secured in part on nine indigo factories, but seven of these cannot be identified. Inasmuch as each concern included a number of factories, the seven were probably included in the concerns listed above. *Bengal Hurkaru,* 22 May 1848.

44 *Report of the Indigo Commission,* pt. 3, pp. 60 ff.

45 Production figures compiled from *Report of the Indigo Commission.* Although figures are for production ten to twenty years later, it is probable that there were no radical changes during the interval.

46 In 1836 Tagore received exemption from the duty for a shipment of sugar underway before equalization. IO, Revenue Letters from Bengal and India, Board's Copies, vol. 30, Oct. 1838 to Mar. 1839. Also WBSA, Separate Revenue, Customs Proceedings, 17 Oct. (6–7) 1838 and Separate Revenue Proceedings, 7 Dec. (11–12) 1836.

47 George Watt, *A Dictionary of Economic Products of India,* 7 vols. (London: 1885–96), VI, pt. 2, 94.

be "the first person who commenced cultivating sugar-cane by the European process, and under European superintendence, in India."[48] In about 1830 he hired T.F. Henley to supervise his sugar factory in Barripore in the southern part of the 24–Pargannas.[49] There Tagore planted 600 *bigahs* of land with Otaheite cane and set up horizontal sugar mills operated by a steam engine, but was able to produce only a few *seers* of sugar. After experimenting with other varieties of cane, he sent Henley to Mauritius to study sugar production, and on Henley's return tried a third time, but could not produce enough sugar to cover the cost of his original investment. After losing Rs. 2,00,000 by the experiment in Barripore, he tried similar experiments in Ghazepore district near Benares and at Syllidah in Pabna district, also under European superintendence. Tagore had high hopes for success and wrote his manager at Syllidah, S.F. Rice, that "if economy be observed in every department of the Sugar Factory, I am still of opinion that it will succeed."[50] But after three seasons of failure, he gave up the experiment. He continued to manufacture sugar, but instead of processing his own cane, bought gur from the peasants at one-fourth the cost.[51] By 1838 only the Syllidah factory remained in operation, as perhaps the only sugar mill managed by a European in Bengal.[52]

Tagore, along with other planters who tried the West Indian method of refining, failed for a number of reasons. At Barripore the soil was unsuitable and the Otaheite cane was susceptible to destruction by white ants. But even with suitable soil and cane, the experiments failed because of the raiyati system of cultivation. The plant was cultivated by peasants scattered over a wide area, and by the time the cane was brought to the factory it had lost much of its moisture. Later commentators suggested that the West Indian

48Great Britain, *Parliamentary Papers,* vol. 45, 1841, quoted in N.C. Sinha, *Studies in Indo-British Economy Hundred Years Ago* (Calcutta: 1946), p. 84. In fact, a European planter opened a sugar refinery in Burdwan at the same time that Tagore began his experiments in the 24–Pargannas. Watt, *Economic Products,* VI, 2, 100.

49Ibid., p. 101. Interestingly, Watt does not mention Tagore as the promoter, but credits Henley with starting the experiment.

50KNT ms., letter from Dwarkanath Tagore to S.F. Rice, Syllidah via Commercolly, 22 Dec. 1835.

51N.C. Sinha, *Indo-British Economy,* p. 84.

52Great Britain, *Parliamentary Papers,* vol. 16, 1841, p. 70, testimony of W.F. Fergusson.

method would succeed only if the factory was centrally located close to the cane fields. [53]

As a by-product of sugar manufacture, Tagore produced rum for export. The rum distillery was located at Rynuggur, presumably in the neighborhood of his indigo plantation, and was also under the superintendence of S.F. Rice. Rum was sent to Calcutta in casks for export to Britain. If it met the standards of strength called "London proof" it was exempted from export duty, but if it fell below that, it was assessed eight annas per gallon as "country liquor." Tagore manufactured about 5,000 gallons of rum each year and sold it in Calcutta for twelve annas to one rupee per gallon. [54]

Tagore was not the only zamindar to produce export staples, nor was his house the only one that held plantations and factories in the mufassal. But he appears to have surpassed his contemporaries in developing his zamindaris as an adjunct of his export trade. Thus, his zamindari holdings served a dual purpose—to enable his firm to obtain superior financial credit and to give it control over the production and supply of goods exported.

Among the other activities carried on by Carr, Tagore and Company, in common with other large agency houses, was estate management. Here again Tagore tried to bridge old and new systems. The government followed principles of revenue collection inherited from the Mughal Empire, and, at least for the estates under his management, Tagore tried to rationalize an archaic and cumbersome system. In 1839 his firm requested permission from the accountant general to make a single payment each month into the general treasury at Calcutta on behalf of all the estates it managed, instead of presenting a separate payment for each estate at a local district office. The firm, which paid revenues totaling Rs. 1,00,000 per month, wanted to facilitate the transfer of funds and eliminate the fee collected on each separate payment, but the government refused to allow the concession. [55]

This massive revenue payment accounts for the claim that the extent of Tagore's dominions was second only to those of the Raja of

53 Watt, *Economic Products*, VI, 2, 97 ff.

54 WBSA, Board of Customs, Salt and Opium, Customs Proceedings, 3 Feb. (63–65) 1837, 10 Feb. (35–37) 1837, 14 July (2) 1837. For price of rum, see Watt, *Economic Products*, VI, 2, 98–99.

55 N.A.I., Finance, India, Index for 1839, reference to Consultation 3 Apr. (8 and 9) 1839.

Burdwan.[56] Under the firm's management were three classes of estates: first, Dwarkanath's personal estates (Berhampore, Kaligram, Pandua, and Shahazadpur), later placed in trust for his sons; second, those of the Tagore family, which, combined with his own, paid one-fifteenth of the total land revenue of the Lower Provinces of Bengal;[57] and third, estates purchased for speculation and investment. Among the latter was Mandleghat, a large and valuable property located in Howrah district, on three-fourths of which Carr, Tagore and Company held a lien and paid a revenue of Rs. 2,33,000 annually.[58] Although Mandleghat was clearly a speculation involving the firm as a whole, some of the estates acquired for speculation were his personal property. These included, among others, three zamindaris in Pergunna Khashpore, 24-Pargannas, acquired around 1830;[59] Swarupur in Rangpur district, acquired from Prasanna Kumar Tagore in 1834;[60] four estates in Mohungunj, near Patna;[61] and three estates in Jessore District. One of the last-mentioned, Dwarbansini, yielded Rs. 30,000 to 40,000 profit per year and was put up for sale for Rs. 2,50,000 by Dwarkanath in 1846.[62] Whether the estates were his own, his family's, or the firm's, all of his zamindari affairs were conducted from his office at Carr, Tagore and Company.

Finally, the firm engaged in another traditional agency-house activity, ocean shipping. Dwarkanath himself owned major shares in at least six ships and the firm acted as agents for five others. Tagore's pride and joy was his clipper barque *Waterwitch*, 363 tons, built to order at the Kidderpore dockyards in 1831. He owned half the ship, and ownership of the other half was divided between William Storm and the ship's commander, Captain Andrew Henderson.[63] The *Waterwitch* was the third clipper built at Calcutta, after the *Red Rover* in 1829 and the *Sylph*, built in 1831 at Howrah Dockyards for the Parsi merchant Rustomjee Cowasjee. During the 1830s, when opium shipments increased three-fold, clippers had an advantage over

56*Bengal Hurkaru,* 19 Sept. 1846.

57WBSA, Criminal Department, 15 Dec. (1–3) 1840.

58WBSA, Revenue Proceedings, Government of Bengal, 29 Mar. (112) 1848.

59WBSA, Territorial Revenue Proceedings, 8 July (10) 1833 and 15 Jan. (17) 1834.

60KNT ms., p. 59. Kissory Chand Mittra, "The Territorial Aristocracy of Bengal. The Rajas of Rajshahi," *The Calcutta Review,* vol. 56, No. 111 (1873).

61KNT ms., Dwarkanath Tagore to Marquez, 1835.

62KNT ms., Dwarkanath Tagore to Debendranath Tagore, 22 May 1846.

63Basil Lubbock, *The Opium Clippers* (Glasgow: 1933), pp. 93–94.

conventional ships because they could sail into the northeast monsoon and reach China in the winter months when prices were at their peak. [64] The populace of Calcutta laid their wagers and watched with excitement as Rustomjee and Dwarkanath raced their barques to and from Canton. In 1838 the *Waterwitch* proved her superiority by beating out all rivals on a voyage from Canton to Calcutta in the record time of twenty-five days. [65]

Her finest hour, however, came during the Opium War. Tagore had joined with other leading merchants to request a government mail charter from Calcutta to Suez, bypassing Bombay, but, until the war made rapid communications urgent, their request was denied. Finally the government agreed to accept Tagore's offer on condition that the *Waterwitch* complete the voyage in forty days, and, though the odds were against success, Tagore accepted the challenge. His ship left Calcutta on July 1, 1839, with a cargo of mail and coal and reached Aden in thirty-eight days, three less than customary on the much shorter Bombay-Aden voyage. Although her topsail sprung at Aden, the mails were carried on another ship to Suez in time for the steamer to Britain, a triumph for Tagore and the merchants of Calcutta. The government paid Tagore Rs. 8,000 for the charter, one-sixth of her usual freight for carrying opium. [66]

Dwarkanath owned two other opium clippers, the 371-ton *Ariel*, built at Kidderpore in 1837, and the 112-ton *Mavis*, built at Akyab in 1833. The *Ariel* was one of the clippers forced to surrender her cargo to Commissioner Lin, and during the war she was chartered by the government to carry the mails from China to Aden. The *Mavis* was destroyed by lightening in 1842. [67] Two other sailing ships owned by the firm, the *Lord Amherst* and the *Sophia*, were engaged in the country trade. Tagore's largest ship was the 510-ton *Zenobia*, built at Calcutta in 1815 for the Indo-British trade. Tagore purchased her for Rs. 55,000 from the estate of James Calder after the failure of Mackintosh and Company. [68] The firm served as agents for, and

64Ibid., pp. 71–72; Michael Greenberg, *British Trade and the Opening of China, 1800–1842* (Cambridge: 1951), p. 10.

65Besil Lubbock, *The Opium Clippers* (Glosgow: 1933), pp. 140–41.

66Ibid., pp. 166–67. N.A.I. Marine Proceedings, 15 May (17 and 18), 22 May (10 and 11), 5 June (6 and 7), 12 June (15–17), 26 June (14–16), 17 July (1 and 2) 1839. Tagore and his heirs retained half-ownership in the *Water Witch* until 1848, when the ship was purchased by the Canton firm of Lancelot and John Dent. Lubbock, *The Opium Clippers*, p. 94.

67Ibid., pp. 160, 264. National Library of India, *List of Merchant Ships, 1834–35*. 68*India Gazette*, 20 May 1833.

possibly owned shares in, the *Imam of Muscat,* the *Theresa,* the *Christopher Dawson,* the steamer *Tudor,* and the *Emerald Isle,* large ships engaged in the Indo-British trade. [69]

Thus, Tagore had been a ship-owner, indigo planter, and zamindari agent for some years before he founded his house, and after the liberal charter of 1833 he anticipated expansion into new areas. By establishing Carr, Tagore and Company he acquired a base of operations for his activities and a staff of managerial associates and clerical assistants to facilitate his business. His long-term plan of travel to Europe made the institutionalization of his business affairs urgent. From his office at the firm's headquarters at Colvin's Ghat, off Hastings Street, Dwarkanath directed both his own investments and the business of the house indiscriminately. He worked hard, put in long hours, and, according to James Stuart, wrote a "most excellent letter," spoke English well and was "a good man of business." He also knew how to win the loyalty of his employees. When he presented Stuart with a fine horse, valued at Rs. 1,200, the secretary wrote his parents: "It is not the amount of the present that pleased me, as I consider that my services are worth more than that above my salary . . . but it was the kind manner in which Dwarkanath did it that I was better pleased than if twice the amount had been given me. The more I see of Dwarkanath the more I like him." [70]

Dwarkanath enjoyed his work. Possibly to compensate for the earnest and purposeful way in which he pursued his pleasures, his approach to the game of business was playful and high spirited. At once hard-headed businessman and good-humored friend, he wrote chatty and entertaining letters to his mufassal constituents. Writing, for example, to a young army officer whose investments he handled, Dwarkanath quickly dispensed with business and related the local gossip, with particular attention to the young ladies of Calcutta's European society. Along with frivolous advice that the young man keep his "health and red cheeks" by marrying a "Begum of 95 years with her fortune," Dwarkanath counseled his friend to stay abreast of

69In 1837 the *Emerald Isle* was chartered by the Australian Association of Bengal and fitted by Carr, Tagore and Company with provisions to take a large group of settlers to Australia, but according to the irate passengers the provisions were inadequate and inedible. *Englishman,* 16 June 1838. For agency see *Bengal Hurkaru,* 6, 21 Jan., 17 Feb. 1841. See also lists of ships registered in the Port of Calcutta in various issues of *Bengal and Agra Directory and Annual Register.*

70KNT ms., letters from James Stuart to his family dated January 1841, April 1844, and August 1844.

politics by reading the *Merut Observer* and the *Universal Magazine*. In a postscript alluding to Prasanna Kumar Tagore, he noted that "the Reformer is sitting beside me and begs to be remembered to you."[71]

Tagore's congeniality, his intimacy with the British, and their high regard for him were of incalculable value to the firm. His personal qualities no less than his material assets help to account for the primacy of his house in the business world of Calcutta. In its early years, however, the firm was not unlike its contemporaries. Only in 1836, two years after its founding, did Carr, Tagore and Company begin its metamorphosis from a typical agency house into the leading entrepreneurial organization of its day in India.

[71]KNT ms., letter from Dwarkanath Tagore to Lt. J. Cameron, Ghazeepore, Merrut, 20 Nov. 1835.

Chapter V

RANIGANJ

The heart of Dwarkanath Tagore's business empire lay not in Calcutta but 130 miles to the northwest in the wilderness of Burdwan district. There, at Raniganj, was the coal mine, purchased by Tagore in 1836, that gave him virtual control over the supply of fuel in the Bengal presidency. In 1836 Raniganj was the oldest, largest, and richest coal mine in India. British prospectors had known since 1774 that there was coal in the area, but it was not until 1815 that serious mining began. In that year the government advanced the celebrated entrepreneur William Jones Rs. 40,000 at 6 percent, secured by Alexander and Company, to start a mine in Burdwan. Jones obtained a lease for 99 bigahs of land from the Rani of Burdwan, and operated the mine at a loss until his death in 1821. Alexander and Company paid off Jones's debts and sold the mine on mortgage to one Captain Stewart who worked it for a few years, again without commercial success.

In 1824 Alexander and Company foreclosed on Stewart and began to operate the mine on their own account, with startling success. Annual production increased from 4,000 bazaar maunds in 1824 to 2,07,000 in 1827 and, when Alexander and Company failed in December 1832, production had reached 4,00,000 maunds, or about 15,000 tons. The creditors of the firm considered the mine the "best and safest property held by the house" and continued to operate it at a profit of Rs. 70,000 per year. In July 1834 and again in February 1835 the trustees of Alexander and Company offered to sell the mine. Dwarkanath showed no interest in it at the time, but when it was offered a third time, on July 2, 1836, he purchased it for Rs. 70,000. [1]

1For the early history of the mine, see "Notes on the Right Bank of the Hooghly," *Calcutta Review,* IV (July-December 1845), pp. 478–81; H.D.G. Humphreys, "History of the Bengal Coal Company, 1843–1861," ms. in archives of Andrew Yule and Company, Calcutta; L.J. Barraclough, "A Further Contribution to the History of

The purchase of Raniganj was the most important single transaction of Dwarkanath's business career. Operation of the mine provided a focus for the diverse activities of Carr, Tagore and Company and transformed a loose partnership into an effective managerial team. The firm had all the requirements for success—managerial and technical skills, a distribution system and sales experience, legal talent, influence with both the government and local magnates, and capital resources. All of these helped the firm take advantage of the expanding demand for coal and the exploitation of newly discovered coal seams in the Raniganj area.

But from the viewpoint of C.B. Taylor, Tagore's manager at the mine site, conditions appeared far from optimum. Taylor had come out to the jungles of eastern Burdwan as a prospector in 1830, and for a mere Rs. 300 per month lived with his family in the isolated wilderness, struggling against great odds to mine and ship coal for his employers. As Tagore's manager he faced enormous problems —floods, fires, engine breakdowns, cash shortages, labor strikes, and desperate struggles in the fields and lawcourts against rival operators over mine labor, riverside wharves, and mining leases. In 1843, after six trying years at Raniganj, Taylor, with Tagore's support, left to work his own mine at Rajharrah, an even more desolate area 200 miles west of Raniganj. When this venture failed, he worked for a short time at the firm's Amta coal depot and then found employment with W. Theobald, who had formed a rival company, the Indian Coal, Coke and Mining Company. Taylor, one of the many self-trained "engineers" whose extraordinary feats laid the foundations for Indian industrial development, had little to show for twenty years of toil and sacrifice. [2]

When Taylor left for Rajharrah his place was taken by Thomas Watkins, who was less vigorous but more even-tempered and emotionally balanced than Taylor. Watkins had been superintendent of the government tea plantations in Assam where, in addition to tea planting, he had mined coal on his own account. After four years at Raniganj, Watkins was replaced by one Mr. Biddle and joined Taylor in Theobald's firm. [3]

the Development of the Coal Mining Industry in India," Presidential Address, Mining, Geological and Metallurgical Institute of India, *Transactions,* vol. 47 (April 1951), pp. 2–22.

2A vivid portrait of Taylor emerges from his letters in the Bengal Coal Company Papers, 1840–45.

3H.A. Antrobus, *A History of the Assam Company* (Edinburgh: 1957), pp. 266–67;

From their headquarters at Raniganj, Taylor, and later Watkins, directed all the mining operations of Carr, Tagore and Company. In addition to Raniganj these included a number of small mines and quarries, the most important of which was Chinakuri, twenty miles west of Raniganj, purchased by Tagore in 1837. Under the local superintendence of Mr. DaCosta, Chinakuri was a relatively deep mine and produced coal as fine as that of Raniganj, though only one-sixth the quantity.

Taylor's chief talent was engineering. When Dwarkanath purchased Raniganj the mine had fifteen shafts, each about 100 feet deep, to work a seam of coal nine feet wide. Coal was mined according to the pillar-and-stall method, 50 percent of the coal being left in place as pillars to support the roof. In 1840 Taylor decided to depillar the mine and substitute props of brick or wood for the coal. Inexperienced in this difficult and dangerous task, he relied on mining manuals for guidance, and although the operation was only partly successful, it was a remarkable engineering feat. After depillaring, the mine caved in and a fire caused by spontaneous combustion smoldered for many years. Although the old mine was abandoned in 1842, a new mine adjacent to it was available, and production was not affected.[4]

Another of Taylor's technical problems was the accumulation of water in the pits during monsoons. Although not deep by British standards, Raniganj required regular pumping by a huge, antiquated steam engine of 4 to 5 horsepower. The engine, constantly in need of repair and new parts, was tended by a full-time engineer, Mr. Cearns, who, for a monthly salary of Rs. 150, also attended the engine at Chinakuri. By 1847 the old engine had been replaced by a 20-horsepower Fawcett Preston.[5]

Recruiting, training, and keeping a skilled mining force was one of Taylor's perennial problems. As evidence of his recruiting ability, the number of miners employed at Raniganj rose from 150 in 1840 to 586 in 1845. The miners were tribals from the surrounding villages—Santals for Raniganj and Bauris for Chinakuri. The Santals, originally instructed in mining by William Jones, mined with crowbars and

Bengal and Agra Annual Gazette (Calcutta: 1841), pt. II, p. 175; Guildhall ms. 9925, Assam Company, Calcutta Minute Book I meeting of 4 Apr. 1840; *Bengal Hurkaru,* 5 July, 8 Nov., 1848.

4Humphreys, MS., "History"; p. 24; Bengal Coal Company, Taylor to Carr, Tagore, 11 Mar. 1840, and 10 Aug. 1842.

5*Bengal Hurkaru,* 22 May 1847.

wedges; the Bauris, instructed by the former owner of Chinakuri, Betts, used picks. The pick was the superior implement; the crowbar left more waste in broken and crushed pieces of coal. On one occasion the Chinakuri miners were brought to Raniganj to teach the Santals to use the pick, but were driven out by the Santals and their houses burnt down. [6]

The miners of Raniganj, using crowbars, chipped out small hollows near the bottom of the face of the coal and brought down the coal from above with wedges and hammers. Then they removed the coal from the sides of the face. When the pick was used, miners made a deep groove near the bottom of the face and then knocked out the top. Deep in the pit, young boys scurried about carrying chunks of coal to large buckets at the bottom of the shafts. Each bucket held about 500 pounds of coal, and a miner, paid by the amount he mined, filled about two buckets of coal per day. [7] The buckets were attached to ropes and raised by "gins" to the pit heads. A "gin," derived from the word "engine," was situated at each pit head and consisted of a large circular wooden drum with a rope wound around it and four arms attached on a vertical axis. The "gins" were covered by shelters to protect them from rain. On each of the four arms, six to nine women or girls, chanting as they worked, pushed the arm around and wound up the rope, raising one bucket and lowering another simultaneously. The coal was removed from the bucket by a gin coolie and transferred into bullock carts for transport to mounds at the mine or riverside. [8] Gin *sircars* kept count of the number of buckets, [9] *gariwalas* drove the bullock carts, boat coolies loaded the boats at the ghats, and boatmen carried the coal down the river. Taylor presided over the entire operation as well as over an office staff.

Despite the primitive conditions and the hazardous nature of the work, there were few serious accidents. Taylor was zealous about mine safety and would not permit miners to enter the pits if there was

[6]William T. Blanford, "On the Geological Structure and Relations of the Raniganj Coal Fields, Bengal," *Memoirs of the Geological Survey of India,* vol. III, pt. I (Calcutta: 1861), pp. 165 ff. Blanford attributes this to the extreme conservatism of the Santals "as if the innovation interfered with their religious ceremonies." Ibid., p. 166n. Coal picks and hammers were manufactured and supplied by Jessop and Company of Calcutta. Bengal Coal Company, Taylor to Carr, Tagore, 25 Feb. 1840.

[7]Bengal Coal Company, Taylor to Carr, Tagore, 20 Apr. 1842.

[8]Blanford, "On the Geological Structure," describes the procedure.

[9]Bengal Coal Company, Taylor to Carr, Tagore, 25 Nov. 1842.

the slightest danger of flooding. For years he pleaded in vain with his employers to send him a doctor, and was even willing to contribute, along with Da Costa and Cearns, to the doctor's salary. As a further incentive he pointed out that, if conversant with chemistry, the doctor could be of use in testing ores. In 1843, after a personal appeal to Dwarkanath, a doctor was sent, at a salary of Rs. 150 per month. [10]

For Taylor, mining the coal was less a problem than getting it transported to Amta en route to Calcutta. All shipping was done during a ten-day period in the rainy season when the Damodar was high enough to support the boats. Hundreds of boats were tied to the ghats of Carr, Tagore and Company; each was loaded with 200 to 600 maunds of coal and sent downstream to Amta in western Howrah District. The coal was piled at the Amta Depot, under the supervision of Mr. Martin, and in time transshipped to coal depots near Calcutta. Meanwhile the boatmen returned to Raniganj for another load, the average boat carrying three to four loads per season. The boatmen, a temperamental lot who frequently went on strike, were paid by the load but were given advances to keep them available for the dash. If the river was too low, they would dump coal overboard along the way, and invariably less arrived at Amta than left Raniganj. Dwarkanath estimated the cost of conveying coals from Raniganj to Calcutta at Rs. 10 per 100 maunds. [11]

The coal was taken from the Amta depot by boat down the Damodar to the Hooghly and thence up to Howrah and Calcutta. It was stored in the Howrah Yard, the Kidderpore Depot, or on floating rafts anchored in the river. Some was also stored near steam engines such as those of the New Mint, the Cossipore Mills, and, at times, at Sibpore for the many users there. A perusal of surviving coal orders received by the firm gives some notion of the central importance of Tagore's coal to the nascent industry of Bengal. Rubble was ordered by the Calders for their Cossipore foundary, by Haworth Harman and Company for the Cossipore Mills, by Sherrif and Company for their brickworks, by the Assam Company for their steamer and sawmill, by W.E. Jenkins for the Fort Gloster Mills, and by many small upcountry agents for distribution to local indigo, silk, sugar, and rice mills. [12]

10Ibid., Taylor to Carr, Tagore, 13 Feb. 1842; Watkins to Dwarkanath Tagore, 17 July 1844, and Watkins to Macpherson, 1 Apr. 1845.

11Humphreys ms., "History"; John Bourne, *Railways in India by an Engineer,* I.O. Tract 479 (London: 1847), p. 57.

12Bengal Coal Company, Samuel Smith to Carr, Tagore, 9 April 1840; J.H.

Steamboats were the major customers. Private steamers numbered five in 1840, three of these controlled by Carr, Tagore and Company. By 1849 there were fifteen privately owned steamers, three of which were thousand-ton P. & O. liners. [13] Not all used coal from Burdwan; some used English coal, and occasionally wood was burnt. But the Calcutta Steam Tug Association and the India General Steam Navigation Company, established in 1844, were both managed by Carr, Tagore and Company and used Tagore's coal. During twelve years of operation, from 1836 to 1848, the Steam Tug Association consumed twenty lakhs of Burdwan coal. [14]

The firm's most important customer was the government, which in 1840 had nine steam vessels, four of them Ganges boats, with a total horsepower of 600. The low-pressure Maudlin engines consumed ten pounds of Burdwan coal per horsepower per hour. [15] If the average boat was in operation fifty hours a week, the annual consumption of this flotilla would have been 7,500 tons per year, or more than two lakhs of the total Raniganj output of seven lakhs. By 1849 the government had nine seagoing steamers and ten riverboats. Coal selected for the use of river steamers belonging to the government, the Assam Company, and the India General Steam Navigation Company was transported from Calcutta to river coal depots belonging to Carr, Tagore and Company. These included Rajmahal, Cutwa, Berhampore, Coolna, Commercolly, Surdha, Colgon, Monghyr, Dinapore, Ghazipir, Mirzapur, and Allahabad. [16] Some of the coal destined for Dinapore, the river depot near Patna, and for other depots on the Ganges above Patna, was shipped directly from the Rajharra mines up the Koel and Son rivers. [17]

A Ganges steamer could carry no more than a quarter of the fuel it needed for the trip from Calcutta to Benares and therefore made frequent refueling stops along the way. In the late 1840s the Bengal Coal Company defined four coal-distribution regions: [18]

Stocqueler, *The Handbook of India*, 2d ed. (London: 1845), p. 341; Bengal Coal Company, "Coal Orders."

13 *Bengal and Agra Directory and Annual Register* (Calcutta: 1840, 1847).

14 *Bengal Hurkaru*, 19 May 1848.

15 Henry T. Bernstein, *Steamboats on the Ganges* (Bombay: 1960), p. 85.

16 Ibid, p. 84.

17 Bengal Coal Company, Taylor to Carr, Tagore, 11 Dec. and 26 Dec. 1842.

18 WBSA, Marine Proceedings, 18 Mar. (56) 1852. Prices were about one anna less in the mid-forties.

Region	*Price of coal per maund*
	(annas)
1. Calcutta	7
2. Lower Bengal, Dacca, Commercolly, etc.	8.8
3. Patna	13.76
4. Patna to Benares	15.36

When the government advertised for "Best Burdwan," only Carr, Tagore and Company or their agents could supply it. The prices charged—between six and twelve annas per maund—varied with the quality, quantity purchased, and place of delivery. Within this range a limit was set by the price of imported English coal, which, delivered at Calcutta, usually sold for a few annas more than the Burdwan. The earliest reports on Burdwan coal stated that the user would require twice as much coal to do the same work as he would with English coal. But by the 1840s, Best Burdwan was tested to average as high as 90 percent as good as English coal for use in steam engines.[19]

Nevertheless, the firm's records are filled with complaints from the government and other users concerning inferior coal supplied by Carr, Tagore and Company.[20] The reason for the discrepancy between the samples tested and the coal marketed was that Burdwan coal lay in mounds at the various coaling depots, exposed to the elements for twelve to eighteen months before distribution. English coal, on the other hand, was mined, immediately transported in enclosed shipholds, and arrived in Calcutta free from the ravages of weather.[21]

Although Taylor's responsibility ended when the coal reached Amta, his job was the most arduous of the entire undertaking. Problems of mining and transport were compounded by the presence of rival coal-mining operators in the area. His most immediate rival was Jeremiah Homfray, manager and part owner of Naraincoory, a

19 S.G. Tollemache Heatly, "Contributions towards a History of the Development of the Mineral Resources of India," *Journal of the Asiatic Society of Bengal,* vol. XI (1842). The test was made in 1775. Bengal Coal Company, "Report of J.H. Johnston, Controller, Government Steamers, 12 February 1842." One long-term user reported that Best Burdwan was 75–80 percent as good as English coal and that average Burdwan was 60–65 percent. See "An Account of Coal Working in the Damodar Valley," *Bengal Hurkaru,* 22 May 1847.

20 See, for example, Bengal Coal Company, Johnston to Carr, Tagore, 29 Aug. 1844 and I.O., Financial Department, Letters and Enclosures Received from Bengal, vol. 91, 2 Apr. 1844, letter from M.N. Forbes, Mintmaster, to P. Melville, 21 Mar. 1844.

21 Homfray pamphlet cited in *Bengal Hurkaru,* 29 July 1847.

large mine only a mile southeast of Raniganj. Naraincoory had been mined since 1830, at first by Homfray in partnership with George Jessop of the Calcutta engineering firm. After Jessop sold his share to Gilmore and Company in 1836, Homfray and Gilmore worked as partners until their failure in 1842. Thereafter, for about a year, the mine was held by a London group called the "Naraincoory Proprietors," creditors of Gilmore and Company. In 1843 they joined with Carr, Tagore and Company to form a joint-stock association, the Bengal Coal Company, which remained under the management of Carr, Tagore and Company.

From 1836 until the amalgamation of the two mines in 1843, Jeremiah Homfray and C.B. Taylor were bitter rivals for supremacy in the area. Fighting most of their battles in the courts, each tried to drive his rival from the area, take away his land under one pretext or another, prevent him from obtaining laborers, block his roads to the ghats, fight him for possession of the riverfront, and destroy the confidence of his employers. Because Taylor had the superior mine and facilities, Homfray was more often the instigator of trouble. In fact, so inferior was Naraincoory coal that the first action of the Bengal Coal Company was to close down the mine. Even though Carr, Tagore and Company was a far stronger firm than Gilmore, Taylor was a mere employee, whereas Homfray was a partner who could not be dismissed. Homfray barraged Gilmore and Company with various false charges against Taylor to be taken up by Gilmore with Carr, Tagore and Company. In Calcutta the two agency houses were on good terms and easily reached agreements over labor and ghats, but these were always violated in the field. [22]

Taylor's second important rivals were the Erskine brothers, not as exasperating as Homfray, but potentially more dangerous. His major dispute with the Erskines involved a bed of good coal called Munglepore, situated $3\frac{1}{2}$ miles northeast of Raniganj, over which the Erskines successfully fought Taylor in the courts as well as with *lathiyals*. Though they remained in the coal mining business into the latter half of the nineteenth century, the Erskines were principally indigo producers, and Taylor was eager for his firm to retaliate and manufacture indigo at Raniganj. Soon after the Erskines began

[22]Bengal Coal Company, Taylor to Carr, Tagore, various letters during this period.

dabbling in coal, Taylor planted indigo and gave advances to ryots near one of Erskine's factories. [23]

Between suits and countersuits involving Homfray, the Erskines, and a number of local Indian landholders, Taylor and Watkins found themselves in court much of the time. Taylor once wrote his employers that only one of their many estates was not then involved in a lawsuit either as plaintiff or defendant. [24] No contestant was squeamish in the use of forged documents, bribes, coaching of witnesses, and establishing dubious counterclaims. But Homfray, for one, was somewhat more ruthless than Taylor, as would be expected of the underdog in a contest for mastery of the coalfields. Against the Erskine brothers, Taylor and Watkins had other disadvantages. They were employees with little social standing whereas the Erskines, as resident indigo planters with vast estates, were prominent members of local European society. Consequently, Carr, Tagore and Company lost many more suits than they won.

Taylor filled his letters with complaints against the local political agents, magistrates, and judges, who were especially friendly to the Erskines. The Erskines were permitted to mine coal on property attached by the courts pending appeal; the testimony of their false witnesses was accepted by the courts; and they were permitted to trespass freely on the property of Carr, Tagore and Company. Prasanna Kumar Tagore appealed at least one decision to the deputy governor of Bengal in council. Watkins, though less intemperate than Taylor, wrote his employers about one official: "Mr. Cardew's open and undisguised advocacy of the Erskines has given rise to a belief in this part of the country that he has a share in their coal business. Be this as it may, there appears to be good reason for suspecting that all their aggressions upon this property has (sic) been counselled and directed by that officer." [25]

23 Bengal Coal Company, Taylor to Carr, Tagore, 12 Feb. and 21 May 1842. Also, see *Decisions of the Sudder Dewanny Adawlut, Recorded in Conformity to Act XII of 1843, in 1849* (Calcutta: 1850), pp. 366–70. This was an appeal by Carr, Tagore and Company from an earlier decision against them in regard to Munglepore. The point orginally at issue was whether their patta or that of Erskine was the legitimate one. Carr, Tagore claimed to have received theirs from the Talukdars of Munglepore and the Erskines from a gomasta named Soor Singh. Carr, Tagore also had claimed that Alexander and Company, their predecessors, had received a patta from the Talukdars as early as 1830, but the court ruled this patta a forgery.

24 Bengal Coal Company, Taylor to Carr, Tagore, 2 Mar. 1840.

25 Ibid., Watkins to Macpherson, 8 Apr. 1845. For Taylor's complaints, see letters of 14 Sept. 1840, 30 Mar. 1842, 4 April, 15 May, 4 and 28 Nov. 1842. For Watkins,

Whether deliberately or not, the action of local officials was directed toward opening up the industry and encouraging competition. A letter from A.G. Mackenzie to Woomesh Chunder Roy, the Bengal Coal Company's local attorney, reveals the grand strategy of Carr, Tagore and Company. The company tried to destroy every rival and to become the sole supplier of country coal in eastern India. All the other coal producers in the Raniganj area were at their mercy. The small mine at Munglepore, over which they contested with the Erskines, was too far from the river and of little commercial value, but Carr, Tagore and Company was determined to prevent anyone else from mining it. The Erskines' old ghat ten miles south of Raniganj was silting up, and, desperately trying to establish a new ghat, they were encroaching on the riverfront near Raniganj. Mackenzie wrote Woomesh: "We have been for some time in possession of all the riverfront occupying that distance . . . and they must be defeated by any means." He urged Woomesh to get documents and witnesses ready for a court fight and explained: "Our object is to secure all the lines of ghats for ten to twelve miles below Naraincoory to prevent parties in the interior from getting their coals shipped out there."[26]

As part of his feud with the Erskines, Taylor began in January 1842 to build vats and boilers for the manufacture of indigo. He advanced Rs. 5,000 to the neighboring ryots to induce them to plant indigo and by July had erected five indigo factories, one adjacent to an indigo factory of the Erskines. Taylor asked his employers to send him a watch, essential for timing the steeping process. He had given his own to the Raja of Pachete along with a music box, to influence the Raja to expel a prospector who was trying to open a coal mine in the Raja's territory.[27] Because of inundations, the first year of indigo planting ended with a loss,[28] but the company continued to manufacture indigo until 1845, when Watkins, asserting it was not worth his time, persuaded the company to sell the works to one Mr. Savigny. Watkins wanted them sold, even at loss, rather than abandoned completely because some of the employees were involved

see also his letter to T.C. Lock, Magistrate of Birbhum, 7 Apr. 1845, and to Macpherson, 25 Apr. 1845.

26 Bengal Coal Company, "Information regarding Colliery Matters for Woomesh Chunder Roy's perusal on his visit to all collieries, 31 March 1845."

27 Ibid., Taylor to Carr, Tagore, 31 Jan., 12 Feb., and 12 and 17 July 1842.

28 Ibid., Taylor to Carr, Tagore, 12 July 1842.

in the firm's lawsuits and might have gone over to its opponents if dismissed.[29]

Taylor and Watkins tried to interest the company in exploring other new enterprises—Taylor in timber[30] and Watkins in iron. In 1845, Watkins noted that the new railway companies were anticipating expenditures of 1,000 lakhs of rupees for iron and felt that "the time has arrived when the splendid iron ore of this district might be turned to very profitable advantage."[31] He sent Macpherson a sample of metalliferous sand found in great abundance near Raniganj and predicted that extensive ore deposits would be found in the neighboring hills. The land from which the sand was taken belonged to one of the hill rajas from whom mining rights could easily be obtained.[32] When two agents of the railway company on a search for building materials stopped at Raniganj, Watkins informed them that he could supply them with any quantity of building stone from the firm's quarry at Charulene. He reported this to Macpherson and added, "If you take up the project of an iron company in earnest we should also be able to supply them with any quantity of that article."[33] Iron mining, he wrote his employers, "offers the most alluring opportunities for the profitable investment of capital which has (sic) occurred in our time."[34]

There is no evidence that the home office ever acted upon Watkins's suggestion. Coal itself could absorb all of the capital, their own or borrowed, that Carr, Tagore and Company cared to invest. Tagore and his partners could look back with satisfaction over a decade of continual expansion in both the production and consumption of coal. From 1836 to 1846, production in the Burdwan fields had doubled, and Carr, Tagore and Company had maintained their share of 60 to 70 percent of the total and almost 100 percent of the better-quality coal produced in India. (See table 4).

The decade ahead looked even more promising. New railways, including one promoted by the firm itself, meant undreamed-of

29 Ibid., Watkins to Macpherson, 24 Nov. 1845.
30 Ibid., Taylor to H.B. Henderson, 3 Jan. 1842.
31 Ibid., Watkins to Macpherson, 20 Aug. 1845.
32 Ibid., Watkins to Macpherson, 17 Oct. 1845.
33 Ibid., Watkins to Macpherson, 25 Oct. 1845.
34 Ibid., Watkins to Carr, Tagore, 17 Oct. 1845. The ironstone shales of the Raniganj coalfield have reserves of 400 million tons of lower-grade ore, 35–40 percent Fe., according to O.H.K. Spate, *India and Pakistan: A General and Regional Geography,* 2d ed. (London: 1957), p. 264.

TABLE 4. COAL PRODUCTION, 1836–46

Total Burdwan production		Carr, Tagore or Bengal Coal Company production	
Date	Maunds	Date	Maunds
1836–39	10,00,000	1837	7,27,531
		1839	8,00,000
1840	12,25,000	1840	7,00,273
1841	14,50,000		
1842	16,75,000	1842	10,00,000
1843	16,50,000		
1844	17,50,000	1844	13,79,813
1845	20,50,000	1845	14,01,170
1846	25,00,000	1846	15,47,360
		1847	17,00,000

Source of data: Bengal Coal Company Papers; *Bengal Hurkaru*, 29 July and 16 Nov, 1847.

expansion in demand as well as the possibility of opening new fields and facilitating the transport of coal from Burdwan to Calcutta. Raniganj alone could absorb all the capital the firm could raise. The mine was far from exhausted, and existing operations could be expanded.

In the early forties, the cost of producing a maund of coal was 3 pice; in the later forties, under Watkins, about $2\frac{1}{2}$ pice.[35] To produce ten lakhs of coal in the later years of C.B. Taylor the annual expenditure was roughly as shown in table 5.[36] If Carr, Tagore and Company sold eight of the ten lakhs of coal at an average price of 5 annas per maund their gross income would have been Rs. 2,50,000. If their expenditures were Rs. 1,75,000 they would earn a net profit of over 40 percent on capital invested.[37] Notwithstanding these profits, the mining operation was always short of cash. Receipts from coal sales went into the general treasury of the firm, to be used for commercial and other purposes. C.B. Taylor continually complained about the shortage of cash and at one point threatened to resign if the

35 Three pice are equal to 0.047 rupee. Bengal Coal Company, Taylor to Carr, Tagore, 7 Nov., 1 Mar. 1842.

36 Ibid., and *Bengal Hurkaru*, 16 Nov. 1847.

37 In 1833, Alexander and Company reported that Raniganj alone had yielded a profit of Rs. 70,000, hence the figure of Rs. 75,000 is a low estimate. The prospectus of the Bengal Coal Company, drawn up in 1843, estimated income from the combined Carr, Tagore and Naraincoory mines at between Rs. 80,000 and 1,20,000 per annum. Quoted in L.J. Barraclough, "A Further Contribution," p. 7.

TABLE 5. ANNUAL EXPENDITURE OF CARR, TAGORE AND COMPANY
ON COAL PRODUCTION, 1842

Operation	Rupees
Indian labor	50,000
European salaries at mines	6,000
Legal expenses	4,000
Rents and land taxes	10,000
Transport, boat hire, storage at depots	1,00,000
Miscellaneous	5,000
Total annual expenditure	1,75,000

firm did not send him money to meet his monthly expenses of
Rs. 4,000 to 5,000. Under Watkins and the Bengal Coal Company the
situation did not change materially.

Important as Taylor and Watkins were, the offices of Carr, Tagore
and Company in Calcutta maintained tight control over the operation. The correspondence indicates that the smallest decisions were
referred to headquarters, perhaps more so in the case of Taylor than
of Watkins. Taylor wrote almost every day, sometimes twice in one
day, usually addressing his letters to "Carr, Tagore and Company,"
but sometimes to a specific member of the firm. The letters reached
Calcutta within two days and were opened by the head clerk, Francis
Pinto, who summarized their contents and forwarded summary and
letter to the "Coal Department." William Prinsep was the first
partner to serve as head of the coal department. He visited Raniganj
in November 1836 to arrange compromises of the firm's lawsuits with
Gilmore and Company, [38] and while there first conceived of uniting
Raniganj, Chinakuri and Naraincoory into one mining company. In
1837, Carr, Tagore and Company took the first step in that direction
by buying Chinakuri from Betts, but it was not until 1843, when the
firm assumed control of Naraincoory as managing agent of the
Bengal Coal Company, that Prinsep's dream became reality. [39]

The second partner to head the coal department was Captain T.J.
Taylor, who joined the firm in March 1839. He was a personal friend
of C.B. Taylor's arch foe, Jeremiah Homfray, and on a visit to the
mines in October 1839 to settle disputes with Homfray agreed to let
Naraincoory share part of the ghat belonging to Raniganj and to a
division of villages between the two mines as sources for the

38 Bengal Coal Company, Taylor to William Carr, 23 Mar. 1840.
39 Ibid., Taylor to Carr. Tagore, 6 Apr. 1842.

recruitment of labor. Both agreements were to the disadvantage of Carr, Tagore and Company and caused the firm endless trouble until the unification of the mines. [40]

After Captain Taylor's death in December 1839, William Carr, who had returned from England for a short period, took charge of the coal department, [41] but by September 1840 he had passed the job on to Donald McLeod Gordon. [42] From January 1842 to September 1843, H.B. Henderson, who in 1837 had been a member of the government's Committee for Investigating the Coal and Mineral Resources of India, [43] took charge. The coal department was next headed by Captain A.G. Mackenzie, who relinquished it to G.G. Macpherson, first Managing Director of the Bengal Coal Company.

Various other members of the firm were involved in special aspects of the coal business. D.M. Gordon gathered evidence for lawsuits and prepared documents for the merger operation. [44] Taylor often wrote directly to A.G. Mackenzie on matters relating to the steam engines and implements, Prasanna Kumar Tagore planned the legal strategy, [45] and William Carr and his brother John were involved chiefly in sales. Overall coordination was the job of Dwarkanath Tagore. His special functions included personnel decisions, relations with government, finance and merger negotiations, and legal problems relating to the purchase and leasing of land.

Carr, Tagore and Company held Raniganj under two separate *pattas* or deeds of lease from the Burdwan Raj. The first had passed down to the firm from William Jones, who in 1812 had received from the Rani of Burdwan a patta for the mine itself, 133 bigahs of land on which the buildings had been erected and the shafts sunk. The second patta had been acquired by the firm from Alexander and Company, a patta received in 1826 from the Raja of Burdwan for three villages comprised in the Raniganj Talook—Raniganj, Hurradhanga and Sibgung. These villages, originally dedicated to religious purposes, had been exempt from government tax and assigned to a

40 Ibid., Taylor to D.M. Gordon, 12 Sept. 1840; to Carr, Tagore, 14 Sept. 1840, 26 Apr. 1842.

41 Ibid., Taylor to William Carr, 23 Mar. 1840.

42 Ibid., Taylor to D.M. Gordon, 26 Sept. 1840.

43 *Report of a Committee for Investigating the Coal and Mineral Resources of India* (Calcutta: 1838), I.O., Record Department (26) 708/1.

44 Bengal Coal Company, Taylor to D.M. Gordon, 26 Feb. 1842.

45 Ibid., Taylor to Henderson, 28 Nov. 1842, and "Information for Woomesh Chunder Roy, 31 Mar. 1845."

particular individual during whose lifetime the rent could not be raised.[46]

In March 1840 the deputy collector of Burdwan measured and assessed the *taluk,* preparatory to abolishing its revenue-free status. Taylor considered this beneficial to the company: so long as the government tax was paid, the company's tenure would be secure and free from arbitrary enhancement or cancellation by the Raja of Burdwan. For additional security the new patta could be made out in the name of Carr, Tagore and Company rather in the name of Dwarkanath Tagore.[47] In April 1842 Taylor went to the Raja's court to open negotiations to change the lease from revenue-exempt to taxable, but the Burdwan officials, including the Raja and his father Parun, saw an opportunity for extortion and threatened to auction the property if Taylor did not come forward at once with at least Rs. 2,500. Taylor held his ground, knowing that the firm's undertenure, the original William Jones patta, was secure and offered the Raja a few hundred rupees for a new lease.[48] Despite months of haggling and several visits to the court, Taylor failed to accomplish his mission.[49]

Taylor would have been saved considerable trouble if Dwarkanath had been at home instead of in Europe during 1842. Tagore returned to Calcutta on January 5, 1843, and on January 17, together with his friend Longueville Clarke, one of the leading barristers of Calcutta, he wrote a letter to the Raja of Burdwan that settled the matter once and for all. The Raja, Mahtab Chand, replied with a courteous letter to Dwarkanath and Clarke on February 9 stating that he would have his amlas "make ready the papers of Raneegunge" and that as soon as they were ready he would notify Tagore's attorneys.[50] The agreement was executed on 13 September 1842, giving Dwarkanath Tagore as agent of the Bengal Coal Company a patta for Raniganj, Shibgunj, and Harodangah.[51]

46Ibid., Taylor to Carr, Tagore, 11 Oct. 1838, and 2 Mar. 1840; Barraclough, "A Further Contribution," p. 3. For definitions of terms, see A.C. Ganguli and N.D. Basu, eds., *A Glossary of Judicial and Revenue Terms of British India by H.H. Wilson* (Calcutta: 1940), and C.D. Field, *Introduction to the Regulations of the Bengal Code* (Calcutta: 1897), pp. 49–50.

47Bengal Coal Company, Taylor to Carr, Tagore, 27 Mar. 1840.

48Ibid., 11 Apr. 1842.

49Ibid., 16 Apr., 10 Aug., 24 Aug., and 4 Sept. 1842.

50Ibid., Maharajah Mahatub Chund Bahadoor, Burdwan, to Dwarkanath Tagore, 9 Feb. 1842.

51Ibid., indenture dated 1 Dec. 1862 between Debendranath Tagore and the

In addition to heeding some strong words from Longueville Clarke, it could well be that the Raja was reminded of the important part Dwarkanath had played in saving his throne. In 1834 there appeared a *sanyassi* who claimed to be Protab Chand, the natural son of the former Raja, Tej Chandra. Protab had died in 1821, but the sanyassi claimed he was Protab, had never died, but had been wandering as an ascetic for fourteen years and now returned to claim his inheritance. In a great lawsuit that ensued, all of Bengali society took the part of one side or the other. Dwarkanath sided with Mahtab and testified that Protab, who had been a friend of Rammohun Roy and Gopi Mohun Tagore, had often visited Calcutta. This sanyassi, he claimed, bore no resemblance to the young Protab, and his testimony had much to do with the final decision of the judges in denying the claim of the sanyassi.[52]

Taylor also wrote Dwarkanath directly for help in negotiations with a zamindar of Chota Nagpur, Kissenauth Roy. The zamindar owned more than forty villages in the vicinity of Raniganj, covering an extensive coal field and containing scores of villagers who could be persuaded to work in the collieries. Similarly Taylor informed Dwarkanath of the latest status of various lawsuits, a sign that legal problems were one of Dwarkanath's particular areas of competence and interest.[53]

Personnel matters were another province that engaged Dwarkanath's attention. Once, in a letter defending the integrity of his accountants, and his clerks, Taylor warned the supervisor of the coal department that they had been appointed by Dwarkanath Tagore, "and of course you must use your discretion in removing them all immediately."[54] Taylor also appealed to Dwarkanath for improvement in the terms of his own employment. In 1840 he wrote complaining that he was no better off than when he had come to "these jungles" ten years before, but when approached by other mining companies had refused to change employment out of loyalty to Carr, Tagore and Company. He asked Tagore specifically for some shares in one or two of the small collieries he had opened for the firm that year and said he would be happy "to start his own colliery right under Homfray's nose."[55]

Bengal Coal Company, Ltd.

52*Bengal Hurkaru*, 22 Sept. 1838. An account of the trial is given in Sumbhoo Chunder Dey. *Hooghly Past and Present* (Calcutta: 1906), pp. 192–234.

53Bengal Coal Company, Taylor to Dwarkanath Tagore, 16 and 25 Feb. 1840.

54Ibid.,Taylor to Carr,Tagore,19 May1842.Dwarkanathwas in Europe at the time.

55Ibid., 30 Oct. 1840.

Notwithstanding Taylor's extraordinary contribution to the firm, Tagore's settlement with him was peculiarly ungenerous. They arranged for Taylor to open and operate a mine at Rajharrah in Palamau District, 200 miles west of Raniganj. In exchange for Taylor's meager property in Howrah and a mortgage on the new mine, the firm was to advance him Rs. 500 per month for three years. Taylor left Raniganj with his family on February 1, 1843, and struggled for three years with little success. Steam captains refused to use his slow-burning, smokeless, flameless coal which turned to powder on exposure to air. Eventually the Bengal Coal Company took over the mine and sold its coal as low-grade domestic fuel.[56]

Among Tagore's most important assignments was negotiation with the government, the firm's largest customer. In these negotiations the firm held the upper hand, and Tagore put this to every possible advantage. Although the government tried to free itself from dependence by encouraging British imports and developing new fields, Tagore was usually able to corner the market. At the same time, he reacted to the slightest rumor of government negotiations with other possible suppliers by reminding the government of its professed intention to encourage the development of an Indian coal industry. Tagore skillfully outmaneuvered the government by alternately exploiting his near-monopoly of the coal industry and sanctimoniously appealing to broader principles of state policy.

The contest between Tagore and the government began months before his firm had actually become legal owners of Raniganj. Carr, Tagore and Company inherited Alexander and Company's contracts to supply coal to government vessels, and when the Marine Board advertised for tenders for a new three-year contract, to begin on 1 June 1836, Tagore won the award. But in April there was a severe drought, the Damodar was shallow, and it was impossible to float coal down the river to fulfill Alexander's old contract. When Tagore asked for indulgence, the board had no alternative but to agree, not

56Augustus Prinsep, then district officer of Palamau, first brought the government's attention to the coal deposits in that area. Ironically, Homfray, in his testimony before the Committee for Investigating the Coal and Mineral Resources of India, made extravagant claims for Rajharrah coal and these misled Taylor, who was ruined by his faith in Rajharrah. See *Report* of above committee, p. 64. See also Barraclough, pp. 11–14; Bengal Coal Company, Taylor to Carr, Tagore, 23 Dec. 1842, Taylor to D.M. Gordon, 13 Dec. 1842, and Taylor to Carr, Tagore, 1 Oct. 1842. For complaints about the coal from users, see Guildhall ms. 9925, Assam Company, Calcutta Minute Book III, 30 Aug. 1844, and Bengal Coal Company, J.H. Johnston to Carr, Tagore, 29 Aug. 1844.

only because no one else could supply the coal, but because no other firm could have fulfilled the three-year contract that was to begin in June. Nor was it to Tagore's disadvantage that one of the members of the Marine Board was his old friend, H.M. Parker. [57]

A year later, Tagore, with the help of Parker and the Marine Board, won a second round against the government. The Board of Revenue had ordered that tolls be equalized all along Tolly's Nullah, an inlet from the Hooghly. Tagore's Kidderpore Coal Depot was located near the entrance and, despite Tagore's argument that his boats should pay a smaller toll than boats traveling far up the channel, the Board refused to concede a differential toll rate. Under the urging of the Marine Board, however, it did permit Carr, Tagore and Company to raise the price of their coal to be supplied to the government under the three-year contract, as compensation for the increased toll. [58]

Nevertheless, the government was determined to free itself from Tagore's stranglehold, and in January 1837 Lord Auckland established a Committee for Investigating the Coal and Mineral Resources of India. [59] C.B. Taylor, who had just gone to work for Tagore, was not consulted, but the committee relied for expert advice on Homfray and the Erskines. Homfray was paid to investigate Rajharrah, and his report, made on the basis of a few surface scratchings, was a fraud. [60]

The committee reserved most of its enthusiasm for Assamese coal, causing the distinguished geologist, William Blanford, who reviewed the report in a paper delivered in 1861, to remark: "It is singular to find that the Committee, who would seem almost systematically to have exaggerated all accounts of distant coal fields, should have so much neglected the far more valuable deposits in the neighborhood of Calcutta." [61] He attributed this to the difficulty of transporting coal from Raniganj to Calcutta, but a more likely reason for the neglect of Raniganj was the government's desire to build up a rival to Carr, Tagore and Company. [62]

57 WBSA, Marine Proceedings, General, 13 July (14) 1836.

58 WBSA, Misc. Revenue Proceedings, 7 Mar. (5–8) 1837.

59 The members were W. Carcroft, James H. Johnston, H.B. Henderson, W.N. Forbes, James Prinsep, and J. McClelland.

60 Taylor to Carr, Tagore, 1 Mar. 1841, quoted in Barraclough, p. 12.

61 Blanford, "On the Geological Structure."

62 In 1847 D.H. Williams, a government geologist, explored the Burdwan region and issued a *Geological Report on the Damoodah Valley* (London: 1850, Calcutta: 1853).

Notwithstanding Auckland's entreaties,[63] no action was taken on the coal committee's report, and the pending expiration of Tagore's three-year contract with the government lent urgency to the governor-general's search for an alternative supply. His secretary wrote Captain Johnston, Controller of Steam Vessels, that Auckland wanted Sylhet and other coal tested before renewal of the contract became necessary.[64] "Can nothing be made out of the Cheera Poonjee and other coal beds? Lord A. has been desirous that before July next when we shall be thrown if unprepared on the mercy of the present." Auckland suggested that it might be wise to renew Tagore's contract for only one year and to try during the next rainy season to ship Cheera coal by boat to Calcutta.[65] But the outbreak of the Opium War in November 1839 threw the government almost completely into the hands of Dwarkanath. In March 1842, Captain Johnston listed a dozen steam vessels employed or about to be employed in the China seas. They had a total horsepower of 2,050 and a daily coal consumption of 193 tons.[66] If they steamed every day they would have consumed about 13 lakhs of coal per year, more than the annual output of Tagore's mines at the time. In addition, the riverboat, tugboat, and industrial demands for coal had to be met.

In their search for coal supplies other than those from Burdwan, the government turned to England, but this too involved dealing with Dwarkanath. In April 1840, Carr, Tagore and Company sold the government 1,300 maunds of English coal for 12 annas per maund. Upon delivery it was found to be so poor in quality that the Marine Board, through its secretary, C.B. Greenlaw, refused to pay more than 6 annas. After a prolonged controversy, in which the firm refused to accept less than 10 annas per maund, the issue was referred for arbitration to T.E.M. Turton, the acting advocate general. Turton ruled in favor of Carr, Tagore and Company, and the

His report, alluding to the superior coking coal of Burdwan, was hailed by the friends of the Bengal Coal Company, including the editor of the *Bengal Hurkaru*. See *Bengal Hurkaru* editorial, 25 May 1847.

63B.M. *Additional Manuscripts* 37693, Auckland Private Letterbook V, J.R. Colvin at Simla to J. McClelland, Calcutta, 3 July 1838.

64B.M. *Additional Manuscripts* 37694, Auckland Private Letterbook VI, Colvin to McClelland, 10 Aug. 1838.

65Ibid., Colvin to Johnston, 24 Oct. 1838. The Shillong plateau in Assam is indeed the site of a large and rich coal field, but because of transportation problems the field was still undeveloped as late as 1957. See Spate, *India and Pakistan*, p. 557.

66PRO 30/12/53, Ellenborough Papers, Memorandum of 14 Mar. 1842.

government was obliged to pay the firm at the rate of 10 annas per maund.[67] Significantly, the dispute coincided with the struggle between Greenlaw and Turton for support in the Calcutta community for their rival schemes for a steam route from Calcutta to Europe, and Tagore and his partners were among the leading supporters of Turton and his "Precursor" scheme.

Severe floods in Burdwan in 1840 exacerbated the shortage of coal, and the contractors were raising their prices. Auckland appealed to the East India Company to offer a bounty to ships from Newcastle, Glasgow, Liverpool, and Bristol that would carry coal to India in ballast.[68] The government agreed to guarantee to take any good steam coals brought to Calcutta for 8 annas per maund. But there was nothing to prevent the shippers from selling coal on the open market in Calcutta, and the first two shipments sold for 9 annas per maund, forcing the government to compete with other buyers for coal.[69] Carr, Tagore and Company was among the buyers and had 90,000 maunds of English coal to sell in 1842. After fulfilling its contract and supplying the government with 3,00,000 maunds of Burdwan coal at 6 annas per maund, Tagore sold the remainder of his Burdwan at 8 annas and his English at 9 annas.[70]

In the closing months of the Opium War, prices had risen to over 12 annas per maund. The government ordered 6,000 tons (1,62,000 maunds) directly from Carr, Tagore and Company, and Greenlaw planned to buy "quietly" another 6,000 tons on the Calcutta market to prevent Carr, Tagore and Company from conering the supply.[71] The British coal industry was no less avaricious than the Indian and, unlike Dwarkanath, dealt with a sympathetic government. When prices reached 13 annas per maund, the East India Company shipped 8,000 tons to Calcutta, a windfall for British producers.[72] As Greenlaw wrote, the Marine Board "have read with attention and

67Bengal Coal Company, correspondence between Carr, Tagore and Company, C.B. Greenlaw, and J.H. Johnston, April through July 1840.

68B.M. *Additional Manuscripts* 37701, Auckland Private Letterbook XIII, Auckland to W.B. Bayley, 18 Sept. 1840.

69Ibid., 37705, Auckland Private Letterbook XVII, Auckland to James C. Melville, 9 June 1841.

70Bengal Coal Company, Johnston to William Prinsep, 9 Sept. and 10 Oct. 1840; WBSA, Marine Proceedings, 4 May (14) 1842.

71PRO 30/12/53, Ellenborough Papers, letter from C.B. Greenlaw, Secretary, Marine Board, to Ellenborough, 18 Mar. 1842.

72PRO 30/12/53, Ellenborough Papers, letter from East India House, 29 Mar. 1842, and PRO 30/12/53, C.B. Greenlaw to Ellenborough, 30 Apr. 1842.

consideration" of "the evident desire and intention of Her Majesty's Government rather to keep up the supply [of coal] from England than from India." [73]

When prices returned to normal after the war, and India was no longer attractive to British coal producers, the Marine Board had no alternative but to fall back on Carr, Tagore and Company. The board was chastised by the Court of Directors in January 1844 for entering into a new contract with Carr, Tagore and Company three months before the old one had expired, for not having taken security for the performance of the engagement, and for not demanding repayment of a balance due to the government under the old contract. The board begged off in part by arguing that "in dealing with firms so respectable as that of Messrs. Carr, Tagore and Company it has not been usual to take any other security than that of the parties themselves." [74]

Whenever an actual threat appeared to shake Tagore's monopoly, he eloquently appealed to the higher principles of free enterprise and the government's duty to develop the resources of India. In 1844 a report circulated that the government had entered into an agreement with someone in Calcutta to supply three lakhs of coal from the Cheera Poonji mines at cost price only to have the opportunity to work the Assamese mines which belonged to the government. Dwarkanath Tagore, as managing director of the newly established Bengal Coal Company, wrote the government that a joint-stock company had just been established to work the "most eligible collieries in Burdwan," that some seventy "respectable gentlemen" had invested eleven lakhs of rupees in the collieries and expected to bring to Calcutta twenty lakhs of maunds annually. The company, he pointed out, employed over 5,000 persons at the mines and 1,500 boats with crews totaling 9,000 men to bring the coal to Calcutta. All the company wanted, he explained, was a fair chance to compete on the open market for government contracts and to earn a fair profit on their investment. The government replied that there was no substance to the rumor and that it would continue to contract for the best and cheapest coal on the market. [75]

73Ibid., Greenlaw to Ellenborough, 17 May 1842.

74I.O., Despatches to India and Bengal, vol. 42, pp. 846–48; Bengal Marine Department, 3 Jan. (2) 1845, ref. Bengal Marine Department, 17 Jan. (2) 1844.

75WBSA, Marine Proceedings, 27 Aug. (25–26) 1844, letter from Dwarkanath Tagore to Secretary, Government of Bengal, 15 Aug. 1844, and reply, 27 Aug. 1844.

Again, when the Marine Department advertised in March 1846 for wood to use in government steamers, Tagore expressed surprise that a government that had always been "desirous of encouraging the mining of coal" and "the development of this as well as the other mineral resources of the country" would permit the use of wood in its steamers. The government replied that it advertised for wood only because the price of coal was 13 annas per maund and the Marine Department could, by using wood, save Rs. 60,000 per year. [76]

The government's dependency on the Bengal Coal Company continued until the railway age stimulated the growth of the industry. By 1860, fifty collieries were at work in the Raniganj field and were producing 99 percent of Indian coal. [77] The Bengal Coal Company maintained its leadership and is still the largest producer of coal in the private sector. [78]

Dwarkanath Tagore's final contribution to the coal industry was his role in the formation of the Bengal Coal Company. Although the idea of uniting the two largest producers, Raniganj and Naraincoory, had been voiced by William Prinsep as early as 1836, Homfray, who was part owner of Naraincoory, opposed the merger. [79] After the failure of Gilmore and Company in 1842, in which Homfray had also lost his share in the mine, there was a new interest in unification. Ownership of Naraincoory reverted to a group of creditors of Gilmore and Company who called themselves the "Naraincoory Proprietors." They were represented by William F. Fergusson of Fergusson and Company, a leading Calcutta agency house, and he and Dwarkanath were the principal negotiators.

By the terms of the agreement, the capital stock of the company was placed at Rs. 11,00,000, divided into 1,100 shares of Rs. 1,000 each. The Naraincoory proprietors received 400 of these and Carr, Tagore and Company 700. Thus, on paper at least, an investment of Rs. 70,000 made in 1836 had grown in value to Rs. 7,00,000 by 1843. On the other hand, the Naraincoory proprietors contributed somewhat less than 4/11 of the total assets of the Bengal Coal Company. Homfray himself admitted that the Naraincoory mine was exhausted of good coal, and their Barakar mines, though potentially rich, were

76WBSA, Marine Proceedings, 11 Mar. (39) 1846, and 25 Mar. (24–25) 1846.
77Daniel H. Buchanan, *The Development of Capitalist Enterprise in India* (New York: 1934), p. 257.
78*Andrew Yule and Company, 1863–1963* (Calcutta: 1963), p. 12.
79Bengal Coal Company, Taylor to Carr, Tagore, 6 Apr. 1842.

TABLE 6. RANIGANJ PROPRIETORS[a]

Dwarkanath Tagore[b]	Radhamadub Bannerjee, banian
H. B. Henderson[b]	Gopylall Tagore, cousin of Dwarkanath
J. Deans Campbell [b]	Bissonauth Motiloll
D.M. Gordon[b]	Prassanna Kumar Tagore,[b] attorney
William Storm, merchant	Horrischunder Laheery
Debendranath Tagore[b]	Joychund Paul Choudry, zamindar
Rustomjee Cowasjee, merchant	Oomeshchunder Roy, zamindar and indigo planter, Nadia

NARAINCOORY PROPRIETORS	
Antonio Pereira	139 shares
Alexander Rogers	90 shares
R.S. Cahill	60 shares
William Sloan	33 shares
James Fergusson	25 shares
William F. Fergusson	20 shares
H. Gouger	16 shares
J.D. Dove	16 shares
Total Shares	400 shares

[a]Source of Data: Bengal Coal Company, W.F. Fergusson to J. Deans Campbell, Managing Director, Bengal Coal Company, 21 Apr. 1844.
[b]Member or associate of Carr, Tagore and Company.

situated too far from the Damodar to be economical.[80] Aside from the mines, the Naraincoory proprietors contributed only their ghats on the river and their recruiting rights in nearby villages.

It appears, then, that Dwarkanath gave away more than he gained by the merger. As an individual, however, he made substantial gains. By creating a joint-stock company with marketable shares, he was able to dispose of his ownership at a large profit. At the same time, under the terms of the agreement, Carr, Tagore and Company was vested with the management of the company in perpetuity.[81] In addition, the nominal value of the stock, assigned to it by the shareholders themselves, was highly inflated.[82] It was stipulated in the agreement that before any of the Naraincoory proprietors could sell any of their 400 shares, 300 shares belonging to Carr, Tagore and Company had to be sold at par. These 300 shares were deposited with

80Ibid., Homfray to Fergusson, 4 June 1844; Watkins to Macpherson, 7 June and 26 Oct. 1845.
81*Bengal Hurkaru,* 17 Apr. 1848.
82Humphreys, ms., "History of the Bengal Coal Company."

the Union Bank as security for a loan of Rs. 2,00,000 to be liquidated as the shares were sold off.[83] On 19 July 1844, Fergusson, in order to establish the liquidity of the 400 Naraincoory shares, offered to buy all of the 300 shares still unsold.[84] Thus, Tagore sold out at par, Fergusson slightly below. By 1852, shares had declined more than 40 percent in value, and the actual victims were those who had bought shares at par and held onto them.[85]

The first five years of the company were the most difficult. When organizing the company and assessing its capital position, the founders had neglected to provide for operating expenses. These amounted to Rs. 1,00,000 annually to mine the coal and Rs. 2,00,000 to transport it to Amta, all of which had to be disbursed before any coal could be delivered. In fact, twelve to eighteen months were required from the time coal was mined until it reached the customer.[86] The effects of this shortage of operating expenses were acutely felt at the mine. In January 1845, Watkins wrote Mackenzie: "Do, for heavens sake, my dear Mackenzie, take pity on our poor people who are literally starving for want of food and clothing." He enclosed a statement showing that Rs. 26,823 were needed to clear the firm's immediate debts. At the end of the year he warned Macpherson that if they did not pay the wages due they would lose their miners to Erskine.[87]

Initially, Tagore and Fergusson had provided for a cash credit of Rs. 1,00,000 to 1,50,000 from the Union Bank on the security of the company and the collateral security of 16,00,000 to 18,00,000 maunds of coal. This was to be liquidated on a monthly basis as the coal stocks on hand, amounting to Rs. 2,17,592, the outstanding bills of Rs. 35,744, and the outstanding advances to boatmen of Rs. 38,113 were received by the firm.[88]

Yet, perhaps on orders from Dwarkanath to maintain the market price of the shares, the management, instead of reserving operating

83 See "Prospectus of Bengal Coal Company" in Barraclough, "Further Contribution," pp. 6–7.

84 Bengal Coal Company, W.F. Fergusson to Dwarkanath Tagore, 19 and 23 July 1844.

85 *Bengal Hurkaru*, 27 Mar. 1852. By 1849, the largest shareholder was R.C. Jenkins, with 161 shares. Homfray had become a shareholder, as had Digambar Mitra. Ibid., 12 Nov. 1849.

86 Ibid., 16 and 22 Nov. 1847.

87 Bengal Coal Company, Watkins to Mackenzie, 21 Jan. 1845 and Watkins to Macpherson, 3 Nov. 1845.

88 Barraclough, "A Further Contribution," pp. 6–7.

funds from income, divided the whole of the profits among the shareholders. At the first annual meeting of shareholders in November 1844, a 9-percent dividend was declared, and at the second annual meeting, one of 12 percent.[89] Only gradually, and under the pressure of higher interest rates, did the firm begin to reserve some of the profits for working expenses. In 1846 the management again reported a 12-percent profit, but recommended that some of the dividend be returned to the company by issuing new shares and giving each shareholder an option to buy one-quarter new share for every share owned.[90] But the shareholders failed to exercise their options and only 30$\frac{1}{4}$ new shares were issued out of 275. At the next annual meeting the management went a step further. Profits had risen to 16 percent, but that amount was to be paid only to shareholders who had taken up the new shares. The others were to receive 8 percent, and the remaining 8 percent was credited to each shareholder's account, bearing an interest of 10 percent per annum.[91] Finally, in 1848, the management admitted their previous mistake in paying cash dividends, and, in order to pay off part of its enormous debt of Rs. 2,70,000 and to reserve the total needed for working capital, they declared no dividend at all. By 1850 the company had paid off its entire debt, and by 1853 it had a working capital of Rs. 3,00,000.[92]

The history of dividend payments illustrates the gradual development of a new and sounder attitude on the part of shareholders and management alike. Those companies fortunate enough to escape the ravages of the commercial crisis of 1847–48 emerged into a new era of responsible management and patient investors. Another indication of this new attitude on the part of shareholders was open criticism of management. Management responded by publishing fairly complete financial reports in the newspapers prior to the annual meeting, in place of the customary cursory statement designed to screen their activities. The first of these was dated September 30, 1847.[93]

When Gordon, Stuart and Company, the successors of Carr, Tagore and Company as managing agents of the Bengal Coal Company, assumed management they were attacked by shareholders

89*Bengal Hurkaru*, 22 Nov. 1844 and 8 Nov. 1845.
90Ibid., 10 Nov. and 5 Dec. 1846.
91Ibid., 16 Nov. 1847.
92Humphreys, ms., "History of the Bengal Coal Company," p. 52.
93*Bengal Hurkaru*, 16 Nov. 1847.

CHART 3. BENGAL COAL COMPANY
STATEMENT OF ACCOUNTS (A)

Assets

Cr.			Dr.		
BLOCK			**CAPITAL ACCOUNT**		
Amount of Block as per deeds			Amount of original		
of conveyance from the Proprietor			subscribed Capital 11,00,000	0	0
of the Ranneegunge and			Amount paid of increased		
Naraincooree Collieries to the			Capital	30,250 0	0
Trustees of the					
Bengal Coal Company 11,00,000	0	0		11,30,250 0	0
CASH			**CASH**		
at Union Bank			Loans on Interest 3,49,335	14	8
9,019 11 9			**COALS**		
In hand			Government advance		
9,430 0 0			1,17,624 0 0		
Outstanding bills in			India General SN Co.		
course of realization			7,437 5 3	1,25,061 5	3
56,425 8 2	74,875 3	11	**SHAREHOLDERS**		
COALS			Unclaimed dividends		
Moocheecollah 2,00,000			1,680 5 4		
mds. at 4½ as per md.			Undivided profit of 1846		
56,250 0 0			1,463 3 9	3,143 9	1
Omptah 13,00,000 mds.					
at 3½ as per md.				16,07,790 13	0
2,84,375 0 0			Net amount of profit		
Coals delivered in September			Co. Rs. equal to		
41,275 14 11			16–4–1 per cent	1,81,614 15	5
Do. at upcountry stations					
on the way			Co. Rs.	17,89,405 12	5
1,56,224 8 5					
Do. delivered from the					
stations to the steamers—			E.E.		
receipts in hand			H.B. Henderson,		
41,665 1 2	5,89,790 8	6	Managing Director		
Advances already					
made on account					
of next season	24,740 0	0			
Co. Rs. 17,89,405 12	5				
Calcutta, 30 September, 1847					

who called for their dismissal and the appointment of new
managers.[94] They were defended by Fergusson and other large
shareholders and won reappointment.[95] But thereafter they were
careful to subordinate their steamship operations to those of the coal

94*Ibid.*, 16 Nov. 1847, 28 Nov. 1848 and 12 Nov. 1849.
95Ibid., 17 Apr. 1848 and 13 Nov. 1849.

CHART 4. BENGAL COAL COMPANY
STATEMENT OF ACCOUNTS (B)

Abstract Statement of Colliery operations for 1846–47 From Oct. 1846 to Sept. 1847.

Place	Coal mined (maunds)
Raneegunge	13,70,061
Chinacoory	2,27,227
Doomarconda (Barakar)	69,010
Apprentice mines	5,787
Realized from Colleries	8,041
Total coal mined	17,10,126
Total maunds despatched to Omptah.........	17,10,126
Remaining surplus up to 30 Sept.	1,37,781
Total maunds of coal mined...............	18,44,907

Calcutta, 30 Sept. 1847

H.B. Henderson,
Managing Director

Statement of Sale of Coals for last Season and of Coals on Hand on 1st Oct. 1847
Cash realized for sale of Coals from 1st Oct. 1846 to

30 September 1847	4,55,782	14	11
Bills under Realization	56,425	8	2
Deliveries in Sept. 1847 for which receipts are in hand	41,275	8	2
	5,53,483	15	3

Stock of Coals on Hand 1st October 1847—mds.

Mines	1,34,781
Omptah	13,00,759
Moocheecollah...........	2,00,000
Upcountry depots	1,25,453
In progress on the River to ditto	1,00,000
Total Maunds	18,60,993

Calcutta, 30 Sept. 1847   E.E.

H.B. Henderson,
Managing Director

company. Gordon, Stuart and Company remained in control until 1859, when the shareholders again grew dissatisfied with the company's neglect of mining operations in favor of their commercial interests. They were limited to clerical functions until they retired from business in 1867. The proprietors operated the company through a superintendent until 1908, when the Bengal Coal Company was returned to its original form of management by the appointment of Andrew Yule and Company as managing agents. [96]

96Humphreys, ms., "History of the Bengal Coal Company."

The coal company was Dwarkanath's first major enterprise. Yet he almost destroyed his own creation and certainly took little interest in it after the formation of the Bengal Coal Company. One reason was his need for cash to preserve and continue his style of life. He was ambivalent about his role. Was he merchant or prince? Was his first priority entrepreneurship or public activity? Another factor was his lack of sustained interest in an enterprise after it had become established and after British merchants whom he considered able, such as William F. Fergusson, R.C. Jenkins, and William Storm, began to take an active interest in the enterprise. Instead of devoting himself to established enterprises, he was always on the search for new directions and new opportunities. He was the entrepreneur, the founder, the initiator, the promoter, but not the routine manager. It is a characteristic that reappears again and again in the histories of the joint-stock companies born or nourished under his wing.

CHART 5. IMPROVED POSITION OF BENGAL COAL COMPANY
OPERATING POSITION (END OF YEAR)

End of Year—1847		1848	1849
Assets		*Assets*	*Assets*
Coal on hand valued at	6,33,118	5,39,134	5,82,000
Liabilities		*Liabilities*	*Liabilities* (as of Nov. 12)
Loans on interest at 12%	3,51,016	2,71,283	1,08,445
Increased capital and reserved fund and unclaimed div.	30,250	1,20,516	4,13,755
Profit on Sales	2,51,852	1,47,335	59,800
(16% div. rec. 8% going to reserved fund unless shareholder had bought additional shares)	6,33,118	(no. div. paid) 5,39,134	(dispensed as dividend of 5%) 5,82,000

Chapter VI

TEA, SALT AND TUGBOATS

After 1834, the vehicle for economic development in eastern India was the joint-stock company. The form was as old and time-honored as the East India Company itself; more recently, in eighteenth-century Calcutta, it had been applied to commercial, banking, and insurance companies.[1] After the fall of the old agency houses and the decentralization of the capital market, however, there was a renewed interest in the joint-stock form to mobilize the large sums of capital needed to implement technologically advanced business ventures.

On the other hand, the development of company law lagged behind commercial requirements and inhibited the growth of joint-stock companies. Until the passage of limited-liability acts in the 1850s, each shareholder in an unincorporated company was individually responsible for the company's entire debt. The only exceptions were companies specifically chartered by the government, usually such enterprises as the Bank of Bengal or the Bonded Warehouse Association, in which the state was a patron or share-holder. Unchartered joint-stock companies were considered risky speculations and investors subscribed for their shares with some misgivings.

Among the local capitalists, Dwarkanath Tagore seemed more willing than most to take the risk. He adopted the form as the medium for many of his own entrepreneurial schemes, and during his prime he or his partners were involved in the promotion and

1R.S. Rungta, *The Rise, of Business Corporations in India, 1851–1900* (Cambridge; Cambridge University Press, 1970), pp. 10–12. The joint-stock form had been applied in Calcutta to a trading company in 1756, a bank in 1786, and the development of an agricultural estate on Sagar Island in 1818. The "Saugor Island Society" was promoted by John Palmer, James Young, Hurrymohun Tagore, Ramdulal Day, and Gopeemohun Deb. Indians held about a quarter of the shares. The society was abandoned during the commercial crisis of 1830. George Prinsep, *Sketch of the Proceedings and the Present Position of the Saugor Island Society* (I.O. Tract 146, Calcutta: 1831).

direction of almost every joint-stock company formed in Calcutta. His first joint-stock venture was the Union Bank, and he was active in the promotion and direction of the Bonded Warehouse Association and the Calcutta Docking Company. More to the point, his firm acted as "secretary" or managing agent for six others—the Calcutta Steam Tug Association, the Bengal Salt Company, the Steam Ferry Bridge Company, the Bengal Tea Association, the Bengal Coal Company, and the India General Steam Navigation Company.

Aside from the obvious advantage of employing the capital of others for his own schemes and of spreading the risk of new ventures, Dwarkanath may have found the form appealing on philosophical grounds. To the small, cohesive group of civic-minded Calcutta businessmen, a thin line separated service-oriented business ventures from public works, and in the age of laissez faire, public-spirited citizens often undertook projects that later generations left to government. Dwarkanath may have persuaded the business leaders of Calcutta to invest in a tugging service not only because it might be profitable, but because their own commercial business and that of the whole city would benefit from its facilities. The Steam Ferry Bridge Company was another obvious case where notions of civic responsibility coincided with expectations of profit. To a man with Dwarkanath Tagore's highly developed sense of citizenship, the joint-stock company was one way of increasing not only the capital but also the personal participation of the citizenry in the development of the country.

Tagore and his partners were innovative and energetic in promoting joint-stock companies. As managers of these companies, however, they engaged in subterfuge, were overly ambitious, and were inattentive to costs and technological details. As for the shareholders, they were courageous in their willingness to take risks, but neglectful of their responsibility to subject projects and management to hard scrutiny. In addition, the government vacillated between its desire to encourage investment in economic development and an overscrupulous commitment to doctrines of laissez faire. The result was a weak industrial beginning, easily shattered by the commercial crisis of 1847. An opportunity was lost to establish biracial local control of industries in the twilight period before investment was monopolized by British managing agents with their bias for export industries.

The first of Tagore's new joint-stock enterprises was the Calcutta Steam Tug Association. Its purpose was to provide tugging service from Calcutta to the mouth of the Hooghly River, 100 miles southward, a dangerous stretch of waterway replete with shallows and sandbars. Sailing ships took fifteen days to make the voyage that a tugboat could accomplish in two.[2] Beginning in 1823 the merchants had tried to provide a regular tugging service but had failed and were forced to rely on the uncertain availability of government steamers. The last attempt by an agency house to provide a tugging service was made by Mackintosh and Company in 1829. The firm launched the paddlewheeler *Forbes,* built of teak in the New Howrah Dockyards and fitted with two 60–horsepower Boulton and Watt engines.[3] When Mackintosh failed, the *Forbes* went on the auction block and, on 20 February 1836, was bought by Dwarkanath Tagore. A month earlier he had purchased the Raniganj coal mine for Rs. 70,000. Now he paid Rs. 1,10,000 for a single steamboat.

Dwarkanath invited a group of businessmen to his office, and on February 26 they founded the Calcutta Steam Tug Association. The deed, modeled after those of joint-stock insurance companies, provided for an association that would, unless renewed, dissolve after a period of five years. Two hundred shares valued at Rs. 1,000 each were issued and, once they were purchased, shareholders were not permitted to transfer them without the sanction of the majority of the shareholders resident in Calcutta. The capital was to be invested in the purchase of the *Forbes* and a second vessel for Rs. 90,000 to be built locally and fitted with engines taken from an old steamer, the *Emulous.* Every six months the proprietors were to meet to pass on accounts, declare dividends and approve expenditures of over Rs. 10,000. At meetings, shareholders were to have 1 vote for 1 share, 2 for 5 shares, 3 for 10 shares, and 4 for 20 or more shares. Finally, a committee of five directors, elected annually, was to appoint a secretary to conduct the day-to-day operations of the company. After the terms were agreed upon, the directors appointed Carr, Tagore and Company as secretaries, and at a later meeting agreed to pay the secretaries a commission of 5 percent on the net earnings of the steamers for their services.[4] Some of the provisions reflect the shareholders' apprehensions concerning the obligations of unlimited liability. Thus, shares could be traded only subject to the will of the

2*Bengal Hurkaru,* 13 Aug. 1829.

3H.T. Bernstein, *Steamboats on the Ganges* (Bombay: 1960), pp. 28 ff.; W.H. Coates, *The Old Country Trade of the East Indies* (London: 1911), pp. 113–16.

4*Bengal Hurkaru,* 5 Mar. 1836 and 10 Oct. 1839.

majority of the shareholders in Calcutta. Presumably men of some substance, who could share the burden of debt, would be acceptable, and local residents were favored because they were within reach of the law for the execution of debts. The five-year limitation of the deed would enable the proprietors to dissolve their obligations at that time if they so desired. In fact, the deed was renewed, and the company was not dissolved until after 1858.

The new association was a landmark in the development of business organization in India. As a joint-stock company managed by a single agency house, the arrangement contained all the essential features of the managing-agency system. Tagore's contribution was to adapt a form of management that had been confined to insurance companies and apply it to a productive, joint-stock enterprise. The Steam Tug Association, unlike an insurance company, invested its equity in capital equipment, utilized modern technology, employed labor on a large scale, and required the regular purchasing of fuel and spare parts. By combining the joint-stock form with agency-house management Tagore spread the risks of the enterprise while maintaining managerial control. The managing-agency system was soon adopted by other agency houses and, because it was particularly well suited to the modern sector of business in India, spread throughout the country in the second half of the century. In the absence of investment banking, the system facilitated capital formation and the promotion of new enterprises and allowed scarce managerial skills to be used more efficiently. At the same time, the system was easily abused and in later years was known as much for its corruption as for its entrepreneurial contributions.[5]

The first general meeting of the Steam Tug Association, held on 2 March 1836, was attended by representatives from a wide range of agency houses as well as by seven leading Indian banians. By the time of the second meeting in March 1837, two of the leading agency houses—Cockerell and Company and Colville, Gilmore and Company—had dropped out, and the holdings of the Carr, Tagore "clique" had considerably expanded. The "clique," in addition to Dwarka-

5Useful descriptions are found in P.S. Lokanathan, *Industrial Organization in India* (London: 1935); Raj K. Nigam, *Managing Agencies in India* (Delhi: 1957); S.K. Basu, *The Managing Agency System* (Calcutta: 1958). For a defense of the system, see Geoffery Tyson, *Managing Agency* (Calcutta: n. d.), and *Achievements of the Managing Agency System* (Calcutta: 1954). See Rungta, *Rise of Business Corporations*, pp. 219 ff., for an historical view. For a critique of my views on the role of Dwarkanath Tagore, see Rungta, pp. 253–55.

nath and William Carr, included Prasanna Kumar Tagore, William Prinsep, and George Prinsep. Friends of Tagore, such as James Young and D.M. Gordon, stayed on, as did partners of Gilmore and Company, Bruce Shand and Company, and Mackillop, Stewart and Company. Only one of the seven banians, Raychunder Mookerjee, attended the second meeting. The other six may have retained their shares, but they lost interest in the proceedings. Rustomjee Cowasjee and M.M. Manuk, an Armenian merchant, were present. In sum, the Tagore group had increased its hold on the association. Although resentment over Tagore's high-handed assumption of control may have caused the defections, the *Bengal Hurkaru,* ever friendly to Dwarkanath, attributed them to "evidence of jealousy—the bane of all attempts at cooperation among the merchants."[6]

The association began business in 1836 with a capital of Rs. 2,00,000. In 1838 it doubled its capital to Rs. 4,00,000 by adding another 200 shares, and in 1842 raised another Rs. 1,00,000 by the further sale of shares. Thus, by May 1848, after twelve years of operation, the company had a capitalization of Rs. 5,00,000. The secretaries (Gordon, Stuart and Company, who had succeeded Carr, Tagore in 1848) reported that in the course of twelve years the association had acquired steamers and machinery worth Rs. 7,54,000, including docking facilities owned by the association at Howrah Yard. In addition, the company had paid annual dividends averaging $13\frac{1}{4}$ percent on the capital.[7]

During the commercial crisis of 1848, the shareholders appointed an independent committee to review the records of the Steam Tug Association. They took issue with the secretaries' report and charged that Carr, Tagore and Company had been lax in its accounting procedures and deceptive in its annual reports to shareholders. The committee found that the Steam Tug Association's assets were Rs. 3,00,000 rather than Rs. 7,54,000. Consequently, an original subscriber who had invested Rs. 1,000 for a share in 1836 would now, twelve years later, find that his share represented only Rs. 600 in equity. On the other hand, the same subscriber would have received Rs. 1,390 per share in dividends.[8] Accumulated dividends and equity

6*Bengal Hurkaru,* 7 June 1836.

7*Bengal Hurkaru,* 28 Mar. 1848. Reports of half-yearly meetings are found in *Bengal Hurkaru,* 21 Mar. 1837, 19 Sept. 1837, 9 Jan. 1838, 10 Oct. 1839, 4 Nov. 1841, 8 Apr. 1842, 12 June 1843, and 20 May 1844.

8Ibid., 28 Mar. and 19 May 1848.

together would, after twelve years, total about Rs. 2,000, a gain of about 8 percent per year. This was approximately the local rate of return for lending money on the collateral of real estate. Those who had invested in the additional subscriptions of 1838 and 1842 would have earned considerably less.

Why had the Steam Tug Association not earned more during its first twelve years of operation when, aside from some government competition, it had, until 1845, a monopoly of tugging? One reason was the high rate of depreciation on the hulls and machinery, besides the high initial cost of construction and engines. 9 (See table 7.)

TABLE 7. COST AND 1848 VALUE OF TUGBOATS OWNED BY THE
CALCUTTA STEAM TUG ASSOCIATION

Tug	Date put into service	Original cost (rupees)	Major repairs (rupees) *	Value in 1848 (rupees)
"Forbes"	1836	1,20,000	30,000	68,800
"Seetakoond"	1837	80,000	15,507	(nil)
"A. Henderson"	1839	1,57,100	none	57,000
"Dwarkanath"	1840	1,75,000	none	70,000
"F. Gordon"	1844	1,00,000	none	82,000
Total investment in boats during 12 years (including repairs):				Rs. 7,02,607
Total value of boats in 1848:				Rs. 2,77,800

* Minor repairs had cost about Rs. 50 per month per tug, amounting to an additional Rs. 25,000.
Source: *Bengal Hurkaru,* 10 Oct. 1839, 19 May 1848.

Depreciation amounted to at least 65 percent during the twelve years, or over 5 percent per year. Considering the primitive technology, the high cost of imported parts, and the destructive effect of the climate on the hulls and machinery, this figure does not seem unreasonable. Coal was the largest single item of operating expense. The secretaries took advantage of their position to supply the tugs with Raniganj coal and charged one anna per maund more than the market price. Inasmuch as the tugs consumed a total of 20,00,000 maunds of coal during the twelve years of operation, the overpayment would have cost the association about Rs. 1,25,000. Further-

9 PRO/30/12/53, Ellenborough Papers, C.B. Greenlaw to Ellenborough, 28 Mar. 1842.

more, there was some suspicion that the coal company had delivered 25 percent less coal than the association paid for. In addition to outright extortion, the secretaries engaged in the more common offense of misrepresenting to the shareholders the true state of the company's affairs. Although aware of the heavy depreciation costs, they neglected to set aside a reserve fund and instead paid for repairs with new stock flotations. They even borrowed to maintain the level of dividend payments, and by 1841 they owed Rs. 1,56,000 to the Union and Agra Banks.[10]

One solution would have been to raise the rates for tugging services. From 1836 to 1845 the association had charged Rs. 400 per day for tugging and Rs. 250 per day for return hire; from 1845 on, it charged Rs. 300 per day for tugging and Rs. 150 per day return. The pre-1845 rates were set to compete with government rates; after 1845, rates were set to meet private competition. After repeated complaints that the government was engaged in unfair competition with private enterprise and violating the Charter Act of 1833, the government gradually withdrew from competition. Receipts from freight and passage from government river-steamer and tugboat hire declined from Rs. 1,39,577 in 1836–37 to Rs. 3,600 in 1841–42.[11] For a few years the Steam Tug Association had the Hooghly all to itself. But in December 1844, following Tagore's precedent, Allan, Deffell and Company promoted the Hooghly Steam Tug Company and acted as its managing agent. The new company forced the Steam Tug Association to lower its rates to Rs. 300.[12] In the following year the prospectus of another venture, the Bengal Steam Tug Company, arrived from England. It posed the threat of a heavily financed rival with an imported capital of £150,000, three times that of the Calcutta Steam Tug Association. To justify placing six powerful new tugs on the Hooghly, the Bengal Steam Tug Company pointed out that the number of ships using the port of Calcutta had almost doubled between 1837 and 1844.[13]

The *Englishman* cheered on the new company,[14] but the *Bengal Hurkaru* published a detailed analysis of the economics of tugging and concluded that there were too many tugs then or soon to be in

10*Bengal Hurkaru*, 28 Mar. 1848.

11PRO/30/12/31–15, Ellenborough Papers, Report of Bengal Finance Committee, 1 June 1844.

12*Calcutta Star*, 9 Jan. 1845.

13*Bengal Hurkaru*, 9 Mar. 1846.

14*Englishman*, 7 Mar. 1846.

TABLE 8. TUGS IN OPERATION AT CALCUTTA, 1846

Owner	Tug	Horsepower
Calcutta Steam Tug Association	"Forbes"	120
	"A. Henderson"	110
	"Dwarkanath"	150
	"F. Gordon"	130
Hooghly Steam Tug Company	"Lion"	100
	"Unicorn"	100
Motilal Seal	"Banian"	90
Assam Company	"Assam"	100
Apcar and Company	"Union"	120
	"Rattler"	150
	(unnamed)	150
Total	11 vessels	1320 h.p.

operation to make the effort economical as shown in table 8. The *Bengal Hurkaru* calculated that an influx of six new tugboats would reduce everyone's profit to a paltry Rs. 40 per month per boat.[15] In any event, the Bengal Steam Tug Company never materialized; it was abandoned in the commercial crisis of 1847.

On balance, Tagore's first venture in managing agency can be considered a qualified success. Given the high rate of failure of new joint-stock companies in early nineteenth-century Calcutta, the Calcutta Steam Tug Association showed remarkable powers of survival. As late as 1858, the association, under the management of Gordon, Stuart and Company, operated eight tugs and was capitalized at Rs. 7,50,000.[16] Even with the manipulation of its accounts by Carr, Tagore and Company, the association showed an average profit of 8 percent, which, considering the technological problems involved, was quite respectable.

For better or worse, Carr, Tagore and Company, in its management of the Steam Tug Association, exhibited most of the characteristics of the mature managing agent. It acted as the entrepreneur in promoting the company, provided the initial capital, and then opened its shares to the public. It maintained control of the

15In his list of expenditures the editor estimated that coal would account for Rs. 2,200 out of Rs. 5,550 per month per tug. *Bengal Hurkaru,* 30 Mar. 1846.

16*New Calcutta Directory* (Calcutta: A.G. Roussac, 1858), p. 95.

joint-stock company by purchasing as many shares as necessary, and negotiated a managing-agency contract with the directors of the company. It integrated the association into its other business interests and saw to it that the Steam Tug Association purchased its coal and made use of, and later purchased outright, the docking and repair facilities owned by Carr, Tagore and Company. By favoring the shareholders of one company under its management over those of another, Carr, Tagore and Company, as the first managing agent, was also the first to introduce the abuses that later brought the system into disrepute. Yet, for all their faults, managing agents in the British period were, according to one observer, "the real entrepreneurs in India . . . responsible for the introduction of new products, new methods of production, and new sources of raw materials; they have discovered and exploited new markets and have usually undertaken whatever reorganization Indian industry has experienced." [17]

The second joint-stock enterprise managed by Carr, Tagore and Company was the Bengal Salt Company. It originated not with Dwarkanath Tagore but with George Prinsep and had all the earmarks of a Prinsep scheme, being bold, grandiose, and ingenious. Prinsep proposed to manufacture, on a large scale and by modern technological processes, a salt that would be cheaper, cleaner, and superior to that manufactured by molunghees. In contrast to the products of Bengal's other "modern" industries—indigo, sugar, and silk—salt would be destined for the domestic mass market. Prinsep had found a commodity eminently suitable for local manufacture; abundant raw materials were at hand, and the commodity was a necessity of life, inexpensive, and universally consumed. To succeed, all Prinsep needed was to perfect the technology and obtain government cooperation to rationalize the revenue and distribution systems.

Prinsep launched his project in 1828 when he received from the government a lease of fifty bighas of land at Balliaghat on the Salt Water Lake, with a license to manufacture salt both on that site and on Palmer's estate on Sagar Island. The salt was to be manufactured by solar evaporation and precipitation into large, shallow, glazed-brick tanks. To support his experiment, the government advanced

17Andrew F. Brimmer, "The Setting of Entrepreneurship in India," *Quarterly Journal of Economics,* vol. LXIX (November 1955), p. 555.

him Rs. 32,000 and agreed to purchase from him 50,000 maunds of salt per year for three years at the price paid for Madras solar-evaporated salt. By 1831 it was apparent that for technical reasons the experiment had failed. Prinsep abandoned the works on Sagar Island, and at Balliaghat supplemented the solar-evaporation process with artificial heat. By 1834 he was producing not the 50,000 maunds promised but 17,200 maunds per year. [18]

Undaunted by his failure, George Prinsep built a larger salt factory at Narainpore, east of the Salt Water Lake, and in 1836 received a government contract to supply salt for six years. In January 1839 he proposed further expansion and requested permission to set up a new salt works at Gordah in the 24-Pargannas, sixteen miles south of Calcutta. [19] To finance the Gordah works, Prinsep organized a joint-stock company. On February 6, 1839, he gathered a "private meeting of friends to the scheme of a Bengal Salt Company" and told them of the vast potential of Gordah, located in the midst of salt-rich *jhils* or shallow lakes and capable of producing 2,00,000 maunds of salt annually. The new company would buy, construct, and operate the works. Narainpore, Balliaghat, and still another factory, Beontah, recently built near Narainpore, would remain the private property of George Prinsep. To develop Gordah, the Bengal Salt Company was to raise a capital of Rs. 30,00,000, divided into 3,000 shares of Rs. 1,000 each. [20]

18WBSA, Board of Customs, Salt and Opium, Salt Proceedings, 15 July (64–66) 1828, and WBSA, General Department, (1 Aug. 28–29) 1828. Salt manufacture and distribution is discussed in Tarasankar Banerjee, *Internal Market of India (1834–1900)* (Calcutta: 1966), pp. 214–48. IO, Despatches to India and Bengal, vol. I, pp. 375–76, Separate Department, 12 Feb. (1) 1834, Collection No. 16, "Relative to Mr. G.A. Prinsep's contract to manufacture salt by solar evaporation," 13 Sept. (96–97) 1831. Also, Palmer Papers, Engl. Lett. c 118, Palmer to Elliot Macnaughton, 7 and 18 Sept. 1831; and WBSA, Board of Customs, Salt and Opium, Salt Proceedings, 13 June (8–10) 1834.

19WBSA, Board of Customs, Salt and Opium, Salt Proceedings, 23 Nov. (1–3) 1846; *Bengal Hurkaru,* 7 May 1839.

20The audacity of this figure of thirty lakhs is obvious when compared to the capitalization proposed by other joint-stock ventures:

Company	*Nominal Capitalization*	
Calcutta Steam Tug Association	Rs.	2,00,000
Bengal Tea Company		10,00,000
Steam Ferry Bridge Company		2,00,000
Bengal Coal Company		11,00,000
India General Steam Navigation Company		18,00,000

Prinsep was both overoptimistic and overambitious. He spread his efforts among four separate factories instead of concentrating on the one most likely to produce salt. And, instead of forming the Bengal Salt Company around the most successful of his existing factories, he led his friends into a new and untried area. Gordah would never succeed. Nevertheless, he started with hopeful reports, and a provisional committee, that included Dwarkanath Tagore, was appointed to determine how much would be called for in the first assessment to construct the works at Gordah. Prinsep estimated that it would require less than 5 percent of the total capital of the company to produce two-lakhs of maunds of salt annually. [21]

Copies of the prospectus were sent to England and the 1,000 shares were placed with Tagore's correspondent, Rickards, Little and Company. Prinsep made sure in his prospectus to note that all rights and control in the management were reserved for the directors and officers appointed in Calcutta. John Deans Campbell tried to promote sales in England, but without success. He did note, however, that the merchants of Glasgow, contemplating their own schemes, had met on January 15 to attack the government salt monopoly and to call on the government to permit the establishment of private enterprise in salt manufacture. [22]

George Prinsep died on 26 March 1839, in his forty-eighth year. William took charge of his brother's affairs and found himself by necessity the provisional secretary of the Bengal Salt Company. At once there was opposition. A shareholder complained in a letter to the *Bengal Hurkaru* that, though a capable man, William Prinsep, as a member of Carr, Tagore and Company, had competing interests. "It will never do to allow the management of the Company's matters to pass into the hands of an *agency house*. Their magnitude and importance require the undivided attention of an active, intelligent and steady man, otherwise they will never prosper." [23] Alluding to the criticism at his first meeting with the shareholders on May 4, William Princep admitted he could not give the salt company his full attention, but he pledged to do his best and apparently satisfied the

21*Bengal Hurkaru*, 18 Feb. 1839. Thus, he contemplated producing salt at Rs. 60 per 100 maunds compared to the production cost of molunghee salt of Rs. 80 per 100 maunds. John W. Kaye, *The Administration of the East India Company* (London: 1853), p. 667.

22*Bengal Hurkaru*, 7 May 1839.

23Ibid., 20 Apr. 1839.

TABLE 9. MAJOR SHAREHOLDERS IN THE BENGAL SALT COMPANY, 1839

Shareholder	Shares
Estate of George Prinsep	500
William Prinsep	300
Theodore Dickens (attorney)	300
H. Holroyd (Fergusson and Co.)	200
Dwarkanath Tagore	200
Debendranath Tagore	120
Bissumber Doss	96
Prassanna Kumar Tagore	50
Rustomjee Cowasjee	50
Motilal Seal	50
Ramanath Tagore	20

shareholders by assuring them that he would have help from the experienced personnel who had worked for his brother.

Prinsep was optimistic about the future. Of the original 3,000 shares, 2,051 had already been taken up: 47 Europeans held 848 shares, and 55 Indians 703 shares. The major shareholders are listed in table 9. Theoretically, the Tagores had pledged to invest Rs. 3,90,000, far more than the total initial investment in Raniganj and the Steam Tug Company combined. In practice, the assessment was to be raised in small installments.

Because the government licensed the production and monopolized the wholesale distribution of salt, Prinsep regarded soliciting concessions from the government as his most important assignment. George and William Prinsep assumed that their salt would be treated on the same basis as high-quality imported salt rather than in a class with molunghee-produced salt and asked for permission to pay an excise tax at the place of manufacture equivalent to the duty charged imported salt. If this request were denied, then Prinsep wanted a contract from the government to purchase the firm's output on the best possible terms.

Within the Board of Customs, Salt and Opium there was disagreement over the viability of the Bengal Salt Company. H.M. Parker, Tagore's steadfast friend, tried to help the company; his junior colleague, John Trotter, tried to discourage it. Trotter was backed by W.P. Palmer, Salt Agent of the 24-Pargannas, who voiced two objections to the company: First, he had watched George Prinsep fail in one after another of his experiments and now opposed the introduction of modern salt-making technology "as not calculated for the country," unlikely to be profitable or to provide a regular supply of salt. Secondly, he thought that the principal responsibility of government was to the molunghees, and that all allotments should be reserved for them. [24]

In July the Supreme Council had agreed with Trotter and Palmer; by September the council changed its mind. No doubt, they wrote, competition would bring distress to the molunghees, but the substitution of manufactured salt would be gradual and, in the long run, in the best interests of the country. [25] Prinsep attributed the change of heart to his detailed explanation of the case, [26] but some years later one of the shareholders, D.C. Alwyn, ascribed it to the influence exercised on the Supreme Council by William Prinsep's brother, Henry Thoby Prinsep, a temporary member of the council after 1835 and a regular member from 1840 to 1843. [27]

Whatever the reason, the Supreme Council now strongly recommended to the Court of Directors that the Bengal Salt Company be permitted to sell salt to the government on payment of an excise tax at the site of manufacture at the same rate as the duty levied on imported salt, Rs. 3, as. 4 per maund. [28] The council added that if the excise-tax plan was disallowed by the Court of Directors, they had already committed the government to buy the salt on a par with molunghee salt at 12 annas per maund. If this were disallowed, the Council had pledged to take over the works at cost. [29] The Court of Directors agreed to the contract but not to the excise plan. Fearing the additional expense of setting up excise-tax-collection establishments the Court was "not disposed to sanction any change in the system under which the salt revenue is at present administered."

24I.O., Revenue Letter Received from Bengal and India, Board's Copies, vol. 31, April–August 1839, pp. 463–73; WBSA, Board of Customs, Salt and Opium, Salt Proceedings, 23 Nov. (1–3) 1846.

25I.O., Revenue Letters Received from Bengal and India, Board's Copies, vol. 32, September–December 1839, p. 246.

26Bengal Hurkaru, 30 Sept. 1839.

27Great Britain, Parliamentary Papers, 1852–53, vol. 28, pp. 337–38.

28This was still not sale on the open market. Both Prinsep's salt and imported salt was distributed wholesale by the government from golahs at fixed prices. H.R. Ghosal, Economic Transition in the Bengal Presidency, 1793–1833 (Patna: 1950), p. 118.

29I.O., Revenue Letters Received from Bengal and India, Board's Copies, vol. 32, September–December 1839, pp. 244–49.

Perhaps if there had been only one such factory instead of four, the Court might have agreed. [30]

In the spring of 1840, nature and man conspired against the success of Gordah. The works were almost completed when they were severely damaged by a gale that delayed production by at least another year. Meanwhile, Prinsep, distracted by his coal, tea, and commercial activities, mismanaged the construction operation. In May he published a list of expenditures, a poorly drafted statement classifying items under so many ambiguous, redundant, and mystifying headings that a large group of shareholders rose to challenge his management. Among the questionable items was a payment of Rs. 300 to the estate of George Prinsep, payments for "labor" under half-a-dozen separate headings, and large unexplained sums for stocks and stores. One shareholder complained that the company retained both a surveyor at Rs. 150 per month and an engineer at Rs. 500 per month who did little but copy George Prinsep's obsolete plans. [31] When, in January 1841, Prinsep reported the works still unfinished and asked for a new assessment of Rs. 20 per share, a group of shareholders called for his resignation. [32]

A stormy shareholders' meeting was held in July 1841. The company had spent Rs. 1,90,000, the Gordah works were still unfinished, and the process of solar evaporation had failed. When Prinsep recommended conversion to a new process based on the principle of graduation, [33] T.E.M. Turton rose to oppose further experimentation and demanded his money back. "Carr, Tagore and Company," he declared, "exercised a dictatorial power over the Salt Company which was not creditable either to the proprietors or the directors," and he proposed that the company take a separate office for its secretary, unconnected with any agency house. Longueville Clarke, Tagore's old friend, rallied the shareholders and defeated Turton's motion. [34]

30I.O., Despatches to India and Bengal, vol. 24, pp. 471–73; Revenue Letters from Bengal, Board's Copies, vol. 30, October 1838–March 1839, pp. 722–28; Despatches to India, Separate Revenue Department, Salt, 15 July (3) 1840; and Despatches from Court of Directors to Governor General, 15 July 1840.

31*Bengal Hurkaru*, 21 and 23 May, 1 and 8 June 1840.

32Ibid., 1 Feb. 1841.

33For a description of the graduation process see U.S., Congress, Senate, 35th Cong., 1st sess., *Report of the Commissioner of Patents for the year 1857, Agriculture* (Washington, D.C.: 1858), pp. 143 ff.

34*Bengal Hurkaru*, 12 July 1841.

A few months later, Prinsep, about to leave for England, resigned. The new acting secretary, John Kelly, proceeded with conversion to the graduation principle and in May 1842 reported to the proprietors, now sobered and starved for any good news, that Gordah had at last produced salt—18,000 maunds by solar evaporation. It had brought the highest price of any salt on the market, Rs. 431 per 100 maunds. A new engine, purchased by Prinsep in England, had arrived to pump brine for the graduation process; the jungles had been cleared; and the health of the workers, a serious problem, had much improved. [35]

With William Prinsep in England, A.G. Mackenzie and Major Henderson joined the direction to ensure that control of the Bengal Salt Company should remain with Carr, Tagore and Company. The firm also acted as Prinsep's agent in the management of Narainpore, Balliaghat, and Beontah, and, in correspondence with the government, applied for contracts and other concessions for both the Bengal Salt Company and the private works simultaneously. In June 1843 John Kelly resigned and A.G. Mackenzie took over to manage the Bengal Salt Company in its final years. [36] At the peak of their production the Gordah works produced 10,000 to 15,000 maunds per year, not enough to cover expenses. In the fall of 1844 the proprietors voted to liquidate the company, first leasing, then selling the works to Dr. C.D. Mitchell. Thus ended the Bengal Salt Company. It had been nominally capitalized at thirty lakhs, had spent three lakhs of shareholders' money, and was finally sold for Rs. 20,000. [37]

While Gordah floundered for a few years under Dr. Mitchell, Balliaghat and Beontah were closed in 1844. By 1846 Narainpore was the only factory producing salt in Bengal. Carr, Tagore and Company managed it on behalf of William Prinsep, and although the operation was well supervised by Mr. Curey, an energetic and experienced former officer of the Salt Agency, production did not meet expenses. Salt making in Bengal was coming to an end, and W.P. Palmer strongly opposed renewal of the Narainpore contract.

35 Ibid., 8 Oct. 1841, 9 May 1842.

36 WBSA, Board of Customs, Salt and Opium, Salt Proceedings, 15 May (35–37) 1843, 31 Jan. (10) 1842.

37 WBSA, Board of Customs, Salt and Opium, Salt Proceedings, 23 Nov. (1–3) 1846; I.O., Revenue Letters to Bengal, vol. 1846, pp. 441–42; *Bengal Hurkaru,* 24 Sept. and 8 Oct. 1846; IO, July 1844 and 5 Apr. 1847.

He had been ordered to reduce his allotment to the molunghees and gradually to abolish his agency. All remaining contracts, he felt should be reserved for the molunghees, "who are poor and have subsisted with their families upon the profits of salt trade for half a century, whose necessities are greater and who have made and sold millions of rupees worth of salt . . . Humanity and justice dictate the propriety of my noticing the claim of the molunghees before those of Carr, Tagore and Company." [38]

In a long report on the history of the four English factories, Palmer blamed their failure on technical problems that were never overcome, experiments that failed, and the wear and tear of weather and climate on costly and extensive works that devoured what little profit could be derived from the produce. "Shareholders of the Salt Company," he wrote, "have since informed me that had they been aware of the correspondence that had passed between the Board, myself, and the late G. Prinsep, they would never have embarked in an enterprise according to my views so unpromising, and I must confess in reference to what had then transpired, that no society ever expended capital in a scheme more visionary." [39] Finally, on 30 September 1847, the *Friend of India,* referring to Narainpore, editorialized: "We regret to announce that the last of the salt works established by private capital, the most extensive and best managed, has been brought to a close." [40]

The unanswered question is whether the technical problems referred to by Palmer could have been solved by better management. If the salt company had received the full attention of its managers, the experiment might possibly have succeeded. Tagore and the Prinseps, however, preferred to devote their energies elsewhere, yet prevented others from taking over the management. As a result, when the government salt monopoly ended in 1863 [41] no industry existed in Bengal to take advantage of it, and molunghee salt was replaced not by the product of a modern indigenous industry but by a flood of English salt.

Calcutta's most skeptical investor would have predicted success for Tagore's next project, the Steam Ferry Bridge Company. The

38 WBSA, Board of Customs, Salt and Opium, Salt Proceedings, 23 Nov. (1–3) 1846.

39 Ibid.

40 Quoted in *Bengal Hurkaru,* 1 Oct. 1847.

41 Tarasankar Banerjee, *Internal Market of India (1834–1900),* (Calcutta: 1966), p. 248.

company was established to build and operate a floating bridge to convey passengers and freight to Howrah across the Hooghly River. More than 10,000 people crossed the river each day at Calcutta in small dinghies, and every year at least 150 lost their lives when the boats capsized. Not only was crossing by dinghy slow and dangerous, but the need to load and unload goods from the small boats prevented the proper development of the economy of Howrah.

The idea for a steam-ferry bridge was first suggested publicly by the editor of the *Bengal Hurkaru*. He had come across an account of a ferry that had been operating successfully for over four years at Hamoaze near Plymouth in England.[42] Designed by James M. Rendel, the ferry was both guided and propelled by chains laid across the channel. The editor wrote that even if a similar bridge could not be built profitably at Calcutta, the government should build it on grounds of humanity alone.[43]

So quickly did Carr, Tagore and Company act on the suggestion that the article could well have been planted to publicize the scheme. Tagore assigned his new partner, Captain Thomas J. Taylor,[44] to promote the project. On September 7 Captain Taylor petitioned the government for the exclusive privilege of operating a ferry for twenty-one years within the city of Calcutta near the present Howrah Bridge. While the application was under review,[45] Taylor placed advertisements in the local newspapers requesting captains of vessels using the port of Calcutta to provide him with information on the strength of the tide.[46]

Before he could form his joint-stock company, Captain Taylor, age 35, died on December 15, 1839.[47] The project was taken over by his

42 James M. Rendel, "Particulars of the construction of the Floating Bridge lately established across the Hamoaze. . ." *Transactions of the Institution of Civil Engineers*, vol. II, (London: 1838), pp. 213–77.

43 *Bengal Hurkaru*, 26 Aug. 1839.

44 Taylor was born in 1804. His mother was the daughter of the Earl of Stanhope and the granddaughter of the Elder Pitt. Taylor attended Eton and Haileybury, but because of a boyish prank was denied a writership and appointed instead to the Madras Cavalry in 1823. He became a lion of Madras society and manager of the Madras Post Office. But promotion was slow and Taylor was restless. Lord Bentinck brought him to Calcutta in 1834 to serve as secretary to the Committee on Customs and Post Offices, and he helped H.T. Prinsep prepare new all-India postal regulations. He resigned from the service in March 1839 and joined Carr, Tagore and Company. *Calcutta Monthly Journal*, Apr. 1, 1839, pp. 37–44; H.T. Prinsep II, "Three Generations in India," I.O. Mss. Eur. C 97/1, vol. II, p. 229,

45 *Bengal Hurkaru*, 8 July 1840.

46 Ibid., 13 and 14 Sept. 1839.

47 Ibid., 16 Dec. 1839.

ubiquitous partner, William Prinsep, who called the first meeting of the Steam Ferry Bridge Company in the Town Hall on 7 July 1840. Prinsep assured the score of investors who attended that the government soon would approve the plan with minor alterations. Following Rendel's plans, he described the equipment: a floating iron bridge, 90 by 90 feet, pulled back and forth across the Hooghly by two giant chains passing over cast iron sprocket wheels. The chains would be laid under the river, attached to both shores, and operated by a forty-horsepower steam engine. The ferry would cross in seven minutes and carry 1,100 passengers. A second ferry would be ordered as a spare and eventually placed at another point on the river. The company would purchase a small steamer to tug ships that might need help sailing across the chains. [48]

Prinsep estimated that the initial investment would total Rs. 1,77,000, almost double the amount spent by Rendel at Hamoaze, a figure that appeared more than adequate. To operate the ferry would cost about Rs. 24,000 annually, and receipts from fares would bring in about Rs. 60,000, a net profit of Rs. 36,000 per year. Potential users would include 12,000 daily foot passengers (at $\frac{1}{2}$ pice each), cabin passengers, palanquins, carts, bullocks, buggies, carriages, horses, and dak peons. The company was capitalized at Rs. 2,00,000, divided into 2,000 shares of Rs. 100 each. As their English agent, the seven directors, headed by Prinsep, appointed Captain Andrew Henderson, former commander of the *Waterwitch;* with the advice of James Rendel, he was to order the bridges, engines, and chains and arrange for their shipment to Calcutta. Henderson was to receive a commission of $2\frac{1}{2}$ percent on the gross expenditure. Five thousand pounds were sent to Tagore's London correspondent, Rickards, Little and Company, for Henderson's use, the remainder to be remitted when the contracts and dates of completion were furnished by the supplier, Acraman, Morgan and Company. [49] By the end of the year the Steam Ferry Bridge Company received from the government the exclusive privilege Taylor had requested, and the company was launched. The undertaking appeared to be carefully planned, technologically sound, and certain of success.

48*Bengal and Agra Annual Guide and Gazetter* (Calcutta: 1841), pt. III, p. 175; and *Calcutta Monthly Journal,* June 1841, p. 369.
49*Bengal Hurkaru,* 8 July 1840.

Prinsep sounded the first ominous note at the shareholders' meeting of 2 June 1841. He reported that although the original issue of shares—and more—had been taken up, expenditures paid or pledged already totaled Rs. 2,10,000, and additional expenditures of Rs. 70,000 were anticipated before operations could begin. Captain Henderson, James Rendel, and Rickards, Little and Company had exceeded their budget and had made commitments on which the company could not renege. The bill for equipment was up from £12,000 to £18,550; insurance and freight would be more than double the original estimate, and the agents had helped themselves to an astonishing £2,840 in commissions and fees.[50] With the prospect of so large an extra expenditure, Prinsep asked the shareholders for further instructions. It was decided that existing contracts had to be honored and both ferry bridges and tug must be purchased, but that as soon as the second boat was completed, it would be sold in England at, it was hoped, not more than 10–percent discount. The company would continue and would operate with one ferry bridge.[51] Basically, Captain Andrew Henderson had been a poor choice. He had an exaggerated opinion of his own talents as a designer and builder of boats and, in all likelihood, interfered with Rendel and "improved upon" Prinsep's modest specifications. [52]

A year later the situation had further deteriorated. William Prinsep had departed, and Carr, Tagore and Company served with no compensation as acting secretaries. Major H.B. Henderson, the partner delegated to manage the company, met with fourteen shareholders on 15 June 1842, and presented a dismal report. The small tug, which had cost £2,200 rather than £1,200, had been damaged soon after arrival and was being repaired. More serious, the Calcutta Docking Company had protested that the chains would interfere with their northern dock and lower its value, and the original site for the Calcutta terminus had to be moved. Some work had already been done on a second site, but now it appeared that the Howrah terminus would also be opposed by the Docking Company, and an entirely new site would have to be found.[53] An engineer, Mr.

50 See table 10.

51 *Bengal Hurkaru,* 4 June 1841.

52 H.A. Antrobus, *A History of the Assam Company, 1839–1953* (Edinburgh: 1957), pp. 142–43, discusses A. Henderson's unpopularity as a director of the Assam Company.

53 *Bengal Hurkaru,* 4 June 1841.

TABLE 10. EXPENDITURES FOR CAPITAL INVESTMENT,
STEAM FERRY BRIDGE COMPANY
(in pounds sterling)

	Rendel's Hamoaze ferry [a]	Prinsep's first estimate [b]	Expenditures, June 1841 [c]	Greaves's estimate [c]
Two bridges, Engines, and chains	6,538	12,000	18,550	18,550
Commission and fees	1,000	400	2,840	Extras 1,587
Insurance, freight	—	1,000	2,260	3,597
Assembling in Calcutta	—	800	2,000	3,835
Contingencies	—	800	740	—
Walls and approaches	1,530	1,500	2,000	14,146 [d]
Small tug	—	1,200	1,300	2,133
Totals	£ 9,068	£ 17,700	£ 29,690	£ 43,848

aRendel, "Floating Bridge...", *Trans. Inst. Civil Engineers*, vol. II (London, 1838), pp. 213–27.
b*Bengal Hurkaru*, 8 July 1840.
cIbid., 4 June 1841.
dIncludes assembling.

Greaves, had arrived from England, was surveying the river for a new site, and would supervise the erection of the bridges. His estimate of the amount necessary to complete the work exceeded Prinsep's by £14,146.[54]

The shareholders now debated whether to continue the project. Calcutta was in the midst of a commercial slump, many of the original investors were bankrupt or had departed, and the company owed Rs. 79,807. In order to continue, each subscriber would have to pledge to pay up an additional Rs. 100 per share. Though the company had applied for limited liability, this had never been granted, and now the anxious shareholders decided to liquidate the company as soon as possible. Hope was expressed that another group would be formed from among the present shareholders and that new investors would purchase the equipment and complete the system. Captain Vint and Ramcomul Sen joined in a resolution calling for a meeting on August 1, 1842, to close the partnership and sell the stock.[55]

In July the two ferry bridges arrived by different ships. One reached Calcutta in good condition, but the second, sent aboard a leaky vessel, arrived with its machinery rusted. They were hypothecated to houses whose London correspondents had been drawn upon by Captain Henderson. Rickards, Little refused to honor the bills, hence Carr, Tagore paid off the notes and took the bridges in lien.[56]

Carr, Tagore and Company, intimating that they were planning to continue with the project, wrote the government requesting a remission of customs duty on the bridges on grounds that "the only chance of our carrying through the object of the undertaking must depend on the Company being put to no further outlay" and reminding the government of "the public benefit of a Bridge of Communication across the Hooghly and the blessing of such a work to the community at large." The government granted their request.[57]

That, however, was the full extent of government help. The newspapers and the public pleaded for government assistance, and

54Ibid., 17 June 1842; see also table 10.

55*Bengal Hurkaru,* 17 June 1842.

56Ibid., 3 Aug. 1842. Acraman and Company had sent the second bridge because it was of no use to them, and they hoped eventually to receive their money from Calcutta. *Friend of India,* 21 Apr. 1842.

57WBSA, Separate Revenue, Customs Proceedings, 13 July (16) and 27 July (11) 1842.

the *Friend of India* pointed to the millions government spent on wars.[58] But the government, under Lord Ellenborough, replied to a special plea from Carr, Tagore and Company with the enigmatic statement that "although the Governor General can hold forth no grant or loan of money, the good feeling and patronage evidently extended to this, and similar public works, form a subject of congratulation."[59]

The meeting of August 1 confirmed the resolution of June 15 that the stock be put up for sale—the sound bridge for Rs. 50,000, the damaged one to the highest bidder, and the small steamer for Rs. 20,000. When that meeting ended, W.F. Fergusson took the chair and called for a committee to consider purchasing the stock and carrying on the project, but failed to arouse any new enthusiasm, and the two bridges were sold to speculators for Rs. 80,000.[60]

The Steam Ferry Bridge Company, in the words of one irate shareholder, was "the last in a long series of unfortunate undertakings, all of which had failed through jobbery and bad management, causing ruin to many and loss to all who had supported them." He alluded to the "directors-class" that had repeatedly shown poor judgment and incompetence.[61] Indeed, the directors had shown poor judgment on two counts: the appointment of Captain Andrew Henderson as agent and the failure to make a thorough study of the costs involved in building the walls, ghats, and landing sites. But in this case the government must be allotted the major share of responsibility for the failure. Aside from outright subsidy, a charter of limited liability might well have been sufficient to encourage adequate capitalization. The people of Calcutta had to wait until 1874 for their bridge. In that year the government built a pontoon bridge at a cost of £220,000, and in 1943 replaced it with the present cantilever-type Howrah Bridge.[62]

Finally, after years of trial and error, William Prinsep took part in an enterprise that survived—the Assam Company. In 1823 a British adventurer confirmed, as had long been suspected, that tea grew naturally in the hills of Assam, and in 1834 Lord Bentinck appointed

58*Bengal Hurkaru,* 29 June and 18 Oct. 1842; *Friend of India,* 23 June 1842.
59*Bengal Hurkaru,* 3 Aug. 1842.
60Ibid., also Basil Lubbock, *The Opium Clippers* (Glasgow: 1933), p. 133.
61*Calcutta Star,* 20 July 1844.
62C.E. Buckland, *Bengal under the Lieutenant-Governors* 2 vols., 2d ed. (Calcutta: 1902), II, 622.

a committee to investigate the possibilities of introducing into India a new plantation industry. The Tea Committee consisted of a group of distinguished officials and included Radhakanta Deb and Ramcomul Sen. George James Gordon served as secretary. The committee, reporting that tea could be grown in Assam on a commercial basis, wrote, "We have no hesitation in declaring this discovery . . . to be by far the most important and valuable that has ever been made in matters connected with the agricultural or commercial resources of this empire."[63]

In June 1834, the committee sent Gordon, who had opium-trade connections with Jardine Matheson of Canton, to China on the *Waterwitch* to obtain information about the cultivation of tea and to bring back seeds, plants, and tea makers. The government set up the first experimental tea garden in 1837, gradually substituted Chinese plants for indigenous ones, and in 1838 sent the first shipment of tea to London.[64] At the end of 1838 the Tea Committee reported to the government that operations in Assam were no longer mere experiments and recommended that they should be turned over at the earliest possible date to "the enterprise and energies of individual capitalists."[65]

At least four separate groups, three in London and one in Calcutta, approached the government in February 1839 for information or for permission to form companies to cultivate tea in Assam. Small, Colquhoun and Company and Daniel, Tullock and Company of London asked the Court of Directors for information on 4 February 1839. Their requests were forwarded to the Government of India.[66] The third group, formed on February 12, consisted of merchants with East India commercial interests, led by G.G. de Hochepied Larpent. Larpent himself had been a partner of the Calcutta firm of Cockerell and Company and was now head of their London correspondent, Cockerell, Larpent and Company, the largest of all houses in the East India trade.[67] After receiving encouragement from the chairman of

63Quoted in Percival Griffiths, *The British Impact on India*, 2d ed., (Hamden, Conn.: 1965), p. 436.

64Antrobus, *Assam Company*, pp. 1–34.

65WBSA, Revenue Department, Tea Committee, Official Consultation 7 Jan. (26) 1839.

66I.O., Despatches to India and Bengal, vol. 19, pp. 1146–55, India Revenue Department, 20 Mar. (5) 1839, PC 2379, Tea Cultivation in Assam.

67See D. Morier Evans, *The Commercial Crisis 1847–1848* (London: 1849), app., pp. v–xxi. On Larpent, see Daniel Thorner, *Investment in Empire* (Philadelphia: 1950), pp. 41–42.

the Court of Directors, the London merchants formed the Assam Company. It was to be capitalized at £500,000, divided into 10,000 shares of £50 each, of which 8,000 were to be sold in Great Britain and 2,000 reserved for India. On February 16, Larpent wrote to Cockerell and Company and Boyd and Company in Calcutta to negotiate with the Government of India for the transfer of their tea plantations and for the services of their superintendent in Assam. [68]

The directors of the Assam Company learned from Cockerell and Company on May 3 that a local company had already been formed, with a projected capital of Rs. 10,00,000, one-fifth the capital projected by the Assam Company. The local company had proposed to the government to take over the tea tracts and the services of the superintendent and his experienced Chinese labor. "This has been all done so quietly that we are indebted to chance alone for the discovery." Cockerell and Company had already discussed the matter of a coalition with the Calcutta company, and they were in favor of it. If the Assam Company agreed, it could place with them the 2,000 shares earmarked for India. [69]

The Calcutta group, which called itself the Bengal Tea Association, was a joint-stock company organized by the partners of Carr, Tagore and Company. William Prinsep had called a meeting of "capitalists" to form the association early in February 1839. It is likely that Carr, Tagore and Company learned of the government's intention to turn over their experimental plantations to private enterprise through George James Gordon, an old friend of Dwarkanath's. He had been a member of Rammohun Roy's Calcutta Unitarian Committee in 1827, a partner in Mackintosh and Company, and, after its fall, a dealer in opium in association with Donald McLeod Gordon. In 1836, D.M. Gordon worked as an assistant in Carr, Tagore and Company and helped finance some of G.J. Gordon's opium shipments to Canton with loans from William Carr. On 1 May 1840, D.M. Gordon was admitted as a partner to the firm of Carr, Tagore and Company. [70] Hence, Tagore and Prinsep were

68Antrobus, *Assam Company*, pp. 35–37.

69Guildhall, Prideaux Mss. 8797/2.

70WBSA, Board of Customs, Salt and Opium, Commercial Proceedings, 2 June (40–41) 1836; Jardine Matheson Archives, Unbound Incoming Letters, Calcutta 2252, Letter from D.M. Gordon to Jardine Matheson, Canton, 8 Jan. 1836; *and* India Letterbooks, vol. 26, Letter from Jardine Matheson, Macao, to Carr, Tagore and Company, 30 June 1840.

ready to move as soon as the government indicated that the experimental stage was ending.

Prinsep met with his group of merchants during the first week of February and immediately wrote to Lord Auckland, who was in Delhi at the time. The *dak* took at least a week to reach Delhi from Calcutta, and the governor-general replied to Prinsep's request in a minute dated 16 February 1839. Auckland was willing to give Prinsep's company "all reasonable encouragement" but could not agree to any terms until he had more exact proposals from the promoters. If the company were sound and appeared to have a good chance of success, he would have no difficulty in transferring to it all the buildings, implements, and staff belonging to the government. But he was opposed in principle to the extensive holding of lands by corporate bodies and would not consider making large grants of land to the company.[71]

After a delay caused by "unavoidable circumstances,"[72] Prinsep wrote on May 1 to J.P. Grant, officiating secretary to the Government of India, asking him to lay before the president of council the more exact proposal Auckland had requested. The association, Prinsep wrote, wanted to learn as soon as possible on what terms the government would make over to it "the gardens already laid out with all their nurseries, means and appurtenances, their contracts with Chinese gardeners and artificiers, etc., and their permission to avail themselves of the Services of Mr. Bruce, and any other uncovenanted Servants now employed upon this cultivation in Assam." Apprised of interest from London, Prinsep added that his plan was "well calculated to allow of a further capital to be hereafter raised by a corresponding association in England."[73] Auckland forwarded Prinsep's letter to Captain J.P. Jenkins, the commissioner in Assam, with a recommendation that the government retain part of its gardens and carry on its cultivation simultaneously with that of the private company.[74]

71 BM, *Additional Manuscripts* 37711, Auckland Minute Books, pp. 82–84, Minute by the Governor-General on Manufacture of Tea in Assam, dated Delhi, 16 Feb. 1839.

72 *Bengal Hurkaru*, 31 May 1839; Prinsep is undoubtedly referring to the death of his brother, George.

73 I.O., Bengal Revenue Consultations, General, No. 15, enclosed in letter dated 16 May (14) 1839.

74 I.O., Bengal Revenue Consultations, General, 15 June (14) 1839, letter from Government of India to Government of Bengal dated 6 May 1839; Bengal Revenue Consultations, General, 15 June (19) 1839.

Only a few days after Prinsep's letter of May 1, Cockerell and Company and Boyd and Company received their letters from the Assam Company in England, and immediately approached Prinsep to arrange a "junction of interests."[75] The agents accepted Prinsep's conditions that the direction in Calcutta be independent of London and that preference on the London Board be given to returning members from Calcutta. In exchange, the Bengal Tea Association agreed to call itself the Assam Company. On May 30, 1839, Prinsep called the first general meeting of subscribers to the Bengal Branch, Assam Company, held at the office of Carr, Tagore and Company. Sixty-three subscribers were present, with Theodore Dickens in the chair.

Prinsep's major concern was to "define the nature of the existence of the Indian company" and "whether the junction of the two bodies formed in London and in Calcutta, is a perfect one or depending upon after measures from the London proprietors." By "perfect" Prinsep meant "perfect equality," in which, though the Calcutta constituency represented only one-fifth of the capital, it would have equal voice in the operations. But Prinsep's resolution that the Calcutta branch "retain their separate existence and independent management" was defeated by a group of shareholders who felt more secure in being directed from London. Finally, H.M. Parker moved a compromise resolution that carried by a large majority: "That we, the subscribers to the Bengal Tea Association, do form a junction with the London Company, on condition that the Local Management be conducted by a Committee of Directors to be elected exclusively in this country."[76] In an era of experimentation with corporate forms, this was perhaps one of the most interesting—a double-headed company with two boards of directors.

Nine directors, representing various houses, were elected for the ensuing year and Prinsep was chosen honorary and provisional secretary. Seventy-eight shareholders subscribed for the 2,000 shares. Of these, 280 shares were held by Indians, including 100 each by Motilal Seal and Dwarkanath Tagore. Altogether the Carr, Tagore "clique" held about 500, or one-quarter of the shares.[77]

75*Bengal Hurkaru*, 31 May 1839.
76Ibid.
77In addition to Dwarkanath's 100 were William Carr, 100; William Prinsep, 100; T.J. Taylor, 100; Prasanna Kumar Tagore, 30; Ramanath Tagore, 20; and John Carr and D.M. Gordon, 25 each. Guildhall, Assam Company Manuscripts, Calcutta Minute Books, 9925/1, p. 9.

Although Carr, Tagore and Company had been the initial promoters of the Bengal Tea Association, after the merger their major link was through William Prinsep. As secretary during the first year of the company and as chairman during his last sixteen months in India, Prinsep played a key role in the establishment of the tea industry in India. He was also responsible in part for the precarious position of the company not only during its first two years, but until 1848 when the operation was finally placed on a firm foundation. As with steam ferries and salt manufacturing, Prinsep's major shortcoming was his incompetent handling of technical problems. Again, his most valuable contribution was liaison with government officials. Both in Calcutta and in Assam he worked out complex details concerning legal position, production facilities, and land-tenure rights, and skillfully guided the new company through the shoals of official red tape.[78]

Soon after his encouraging minute, Auckland began to have second thoughts about permitting a private company to operate on the turbulent northeast frontier.[79] Sensing his hesitation, the Supreme Council passed a resolution on 15 June 1839, calling for a detailed land survey and withholding all grants until "a regular system for the arrangement of such leases or grants has been laid down and published for general information."[80] In effect, depending on the thoroughness of the survey, this would have postponed grants of land for an indefinite period. T.C. Robertson, president of council, warned that the resolution would retard the progress of tea operations for years. But the majority, led by W.W. Bird, asserted that "even if some little delay" should take place it would be better than premature and hasty undertakings. Not only would it be ruinous to permit a private European company to go into tribal lands on this turbulent frontier, but the government in its present ignorance of frontiers and boundaries could by mistake create a monopoly of tea production for the Assam Company. The Court of Directors agreed with the majority of council.

78Antrobus (*Assam Company*, p. 43) writes of the government's "prevarication" in making over the land to the Assam Company.

79BM, *Additional Manuscripts* 37696, Auckland Private Letter Book, vol. VIII, Auckland to H.T. Prinsep, 31 May 1839.

80I.O., Revenue Letters to Bengal, Board's Copies, vol. 17, 1840–41, pp. 43–57, Court of Directors to Governor General, 19 Feb. (2) 1840.

On July 8 the secretary to the government reaffirmed the council's orders and added that the government was determined to continue indefinitely in possession of the tea tracts and all means of processing tea.[81] But Auckland broke the impasse, and on July 19 wrote a minute taking the side of Robertson against Bird on the ground that the preliminary operations of survey would "depress and discourage the spirit of speculation now ready to come in aid of the views of Government."[82]

The government's policy now appeared favorable; only the details remained to be worked out with local officials in Assam. Fortunately for the company, Captain Jenkins did everything he could to help them along. He recommended specific sites and urged them to apply quickly for lands because other speculators were exploring in Assam. When his district officer, Lt. Brodie, held back, Jenkins urged the company to apply directly to himself.[83] On November 18 Grant approved the company's taking possession of tea wastes and other tracts recommended by Jenkins.[84] The Assam Company received far fewer developed government tracts than they had anticipated, but enough land to begin operations.

The next step, at least as crucial to the company as acquiring land, was obtaining supervisors and laborers. William Prinsep interviewed Robertson, who agreed in principle to transfer Bruce and the laborers to the Assam Company, but wanted to refer the final decision to the Tea Committee, the local authorities, and the Supreme Council. To Prinsep this again looked like procrastination, and he wrote the London board "pointing out the tardy encouragement received by our Company."[85]

Meanwhile, Walter Prideaux, secretary of the Assam Company in London, had contacted Hobhouse (Lord Broughton, president of the Board of Control) and the Court of Directors complaining of a breach of faith in the refusal of the Government of India to make

81 Guildhall, Assam Company Manuscripts, Calcutta Committee Minutes, 9925 1, 23 July 1839.

82 I.O., Revenue Letters to Bengal, Board's Copies, vol. 17, 1840–41, pp. 43 ff.

83 Guildhall, Assam Company Manuscripts, Calcutta Committee Minutes, 9925/1, 23 July 1839.

82 I.O., Revenue Letters to Bengal, Board's Copies, vol. 17, 1840–41, pp. 43 ff.

83 Guildhall, Assam Company Manuscripts, Calcutta Committee Minutes, 9925/1, 12 Nov. 1839.

84 Ibid., 26 Nov. 1839.

85 Ibid.

over the tea plantations and staff to the Assam Company.[86] But London could do very little; the key to favorable treatment was Lord Auckland. Prinsep managed to obtain an interview with Lord Auckland for February 18, a few days before which Auckland wrote Hobhouse, "I expect on Tuesday a deputation from the Assam Tea Company, and hope also to put that body into activity but it is not very easy to give them all that they require without giving the power also of interfering with other speculators, or at least without crippling our means of giving assistance." [87] Prinsep and the delegation asked Auckland for the services of C.A. Bruce, a portion, at least, of his "means, appurtenances and nurseries," and permission to erect a station on the banks of the Tingri Nullah in Matak country. This was a tribal area within which grew wild tea collected by local chiefs and sold to the government. By establishing a post on the edge of the Matak country, the Assam Company hoped to tap this natural supply of tea. Although local officials urged caution in intruding into tribal areas, Auckland replied favourably and soon afterward published a minute which confirmed what he had told Prinsep. [88] The governor-general agreed to turn over two-thirds of the government's laborers and artificers to the company, including Mr. Bruce, a large number of Chinese, and Dr. Lum Qua, the Chinese manager and interpreter. He would give the company permission to gather tea in the Matak area and lease to them two-thirds of the government tea tracts with the provision that one-half of that could be reclaimed within five years and that for ten years all their cultivation would be open to inspection. The company was to reimburse the government for expenses and for items received. He concluded by ordering the Tea Committee disbanded. [89]

A month later Auckland wrote Hobhouse justifying his action: "I hold it to be of immense importance that an impulse should be given to the employment of English capital in this country and it can scarcely be so with a better prospect of success then in the objects of this Company." [90] When the chairman of the East India Company, W.B. Bayley, complained that Auckland had given away too much to

86 Ibid., 1 Feb. 1840, reporting letter from Prideaux dated 4 Dec. 1839.

87 BM *Additional Manuscripts* 37698, Auckland Private Letter Book, vol. X., 16 Feb. 1840.

88 Guildhall, Assam Company Manuscripts, Calcutta Committee Minutes 9925/1, 18 Feb. 1840.

89 BM *Additional Manuscripts* 37712, Auckland Minute Book, vol. IV, pp. 202–19.

90 BM *Additional Manuscripts* 37968, Auckland Private Letter Book, vol. X., 20 Mar. 1840.

the Assam Company, the governor-general replied that he hoped the government would soon withdraw from all interference, "and it seems to me to be of immense importance that we should attach wherever we can British capital to our sail."[91]

A period of interpretation and implementation followed upon the governor-general's minute. The Assam Company came up against a new opponent in another of Jenkins' assistants, Captain Vetch, who was authorized to divide lands and implements between company and government. Prinsep complained that Vetch assigned the company inferior lands, kept company employees away from the Matak border, retained for the government all the plantings of Chinese tea, and made an unfair division of implements. Vetch, he added, would not even provide an elephant for the company's superintendent, C.A. Bruce, who was moving through the jungles at the risk of his life.[92]

Gradually, after another session between Auckland and Prinsep,[93] local problems were resolved, and in February 1841, along with the secretary, F.R. Hampton, Prinsep became the first director to tour the company's tea estates in Assam. He returned at the end of April, apparently pleased by what he saw.[94] At the first general meeting held on August 11, 1841, the shareholders were cheerful and confident. Dwarkanath Tagore moved that the proprietors express their "most cordial concurrence" with the activities of the directors as well as their confidence "that the Prosperity of the Assam Company will always be identified with the leading national interests."[95]

Prinsep resigned from the Calcutta board at the meeting of November 26, 1841. In his long resignation speech he urged his fellow directors to take a "deep interest" in the company's affairs and warned of the dangers of "lukewarmness" which had so often been the cause of business failure in India. As his successor he recommended H.B. Henderson, a man "who will not scruple at some personal sacrifice of his time and convenience to devote his attention to *all* that passes." Henry Chapman, replying for the directors, noted Prinsep's services in the formation of the company and the progress made under his chairmanship. He referred in particular to "the advantage

91Ibid., 37700, Auckland Private Letter Book, vol. XII, 11 July 1840.

92Guildhall, Assam Company Manuscripts, Calcutta Committee Minutes 9925/1, 13 June and 4 July 1840.

93Ibid., 28 May 1841.

94Antrobus, *Assam Company*, pp. 342–44.

95Guildhall, Assam Company Manuscripts, Calcutta Committee Minutes 9925/1, General Meeting, 11 Aug. 1841.

the Company has derived from the free interchange of communications to which the governor general has invited you" and of the "friendship existing between yourself and the local authorities" that "obviated many difficulties which might have been encountered by our superintendants." But the directors disregarded Prinsep's recommendation of Henderson and chose Larpent as his successor.[96] On his return home, Prinsep was elected a member of the London board of the Assam Company and remained a member until his death in 1874 at the age of eighty. Of his original 100 shares he held 70 when he died. Thirty had been transferred to James Stuart of Carr, Tagore and Company in 1844.[97]

Prinsep's departure ended Tagore's personal influence in the affairs of the Assam Company. His partners continued to represent the firm on the Calcutta board—H.B. Henderson in 1842–43 and John Deans Campbell until 1844—and both later served on the London board.[98] Prasanna Kumar Tagore provided some services for the company: his estate in Mymensingh, halfway between Calcutta and Assam, became a staging place for the supply of goods and boats for Assam,[99] and he also recommended a friend as chief of the native establishment at the plantations.[100] Tagore's docking facilities were used to outfit the Assam Company's ill-starred steamer and to construct its equally unfortunate saw-mill, both at a cost of Rs. 15,000. In addition, the Assam Company paid Carr, Tagore about Rs. 35,000 during a five-year period for the supply of coals.[101] But none of these gave Carr, Tagore and Company much voice in the policies of the Assam Company.

96Ibid., 26 Nov. 1841.

97Ibid., 9925/2, 5 July 1844. In 1874 the shares were worth about £40 on the London Exchange, which made his Assam Company investment worth about £2,800 out of a total estate valued under £4,000. Principal Probate Registry, Somerset House, London, *Index* for 3 Mar. 1874 and "Last Will and Testament of William Prinsep of Wonersh near Guildford in County of Surrey." Prinsep's five sons each had an Indian career. Charles Prinsep, the oldest, ended his career as Statistical Reporter and Keeper of the Records for the Government of India; James Hunter, a judge at Kanpur; Edward Augustus, Settlement Commissioner in the Punjab; Henry Auriol and Frederick Bruce, both majors in the Indian Army. Indian Army and Civil List, July 1873; Frederic Boase, *Modern English Biography* (London: 1965), II, 1646.

98Antrobus, *Assam Company*, pp. 399, 401.

99Guildhall, Assam Company Manuscripts, Calcutta Committee Minutes 9925/1, 29 June 1839.

100Antrobus, *Assam Company*, p. 343.

101Compiled from Assam Company, Calcutta Committee Minutes.

An incident that occurred in August 1843 completed Tagore's break with the Assam Company. He hired the company's steamer for a voyage to Allahabad, and, while he and his party traveled in the steamer itself, a flat towed behind carried fuel and freight. Shortly after leaving Calcutta the steamer had difficulties with the towing apparatus—incidentally, constructed in Tagore's dockyards—and Dwarkanath ordered the flat cast off. The directors were furious and instituted a lawsuit against Dwarkanath, who sued them in return. Sitting among the directors, an embarrassed John Deans Campbell remained silent. Eventually the parties compromised.[102]

This was only the outward sign of an inevitable course of events. With one-quarter of the shares, Carr, Tagore and Company would have been able to direct the affairs of the Bengal Tea Association, but merger with the Assam Company dwarfed their power, and control of events shifted to London. Prinsep had tried to forestall the inevitable by providing for a merger deed of "perfect equality," and Theodore Dickens, the second Calcutta chairman, had resigned on 1 August 1840, because he could not "act cordially" under a deed which gave control of all affairs to the London board.[103] Their case was hopeless, however, because the tea industry could never have succeeded without imported capital, and outside capital led to outside control.

The years of crisis, 1842 to 1846, were ones of continual tension and disagreement between the two boards. In November 1842 the London board decided to send an agent to Calcutta to inspect and report directly to them on the affairs of the company. The Calcutta directors had drawn heavily on London, but had shown no results. Prideaux attributed the problem to the fact that the Calcutta directors were men of business "whose hands are so full of other duties and whose time is so much occupied with their own affairs that it is impossible for them to give proper attention to the business of the Company."[104] Indeed, there was a shortage of directors—in 1843 six of the nine resigned and only four new directors, all without experience, could be found to replace them. Prinsep had called for a devoted successor, but he was replaced in rapid order by four

102Ibid., 9925/2, 1 Aug.–15 Sept. 1843; 9925/3, 4 Oct. 1844.

103Ibid., 9925/1, 1 Aug. 1840. See also letter from William Prinsep to R.H. Cockerell, 8 May 1839, in Guildhall, Prideaux Manuscripts 8797/2, in which Prinsep insisted on local management and direction by the Calcutta board.

104Guildhall, Prideaux Manuscripts 8802, Draft Minute on Present State of the Management of the Assam Company in India, n.d. See also Guildhall, Assam Company Manuscripts, 9924/3, London Committee Minutes, 4 Nov. 1842.

chairmen in four years. It was not until Henry Burkinyoung became managing director, a new post created for him, in 1845, that Prinsep found a worthy successor. [105]

Another problem was the inexperience of the directors and the officers in Assam in the technology of tea-making. Inasmuch as the art was new, their ignorance could have been excused, but, as Burkinyoung later pointed out, no one even attempted to master the technical problems, so that "the whole capital . . . was expended with comparatively little or no results, not even that which is ordinarily gained under failure, practical experience." [106] One flagrant error, made on the recommendation of Bruce in November 1841, was to send all the raw leaves down to Calcutta for picking, drying, and packing. The tea was shipped in open baskets and arrived damp, moldy, and unuseable. Only half the crop could be sold at all. [107]

In general terms, the Calcutta directors were more inclined than those in London to regard the mission of the company to be the development of Assam. They viewed Assam as a rich, unexploited frontier and, using the company's capital, promoted experiments in all directions at once—coal mining, iron-making, a sawmill, a steamboat, flax cultivation, and so on. The London board chided the Calcutta board and urged it to forget the ancillary industries and concentrate on producing good tea. In the short run, London's view was more sound, but in 1846, when Henry Burkinyoung realized that operations had begun to improve and that the time had come to expand the tea gardens, London was still thinking in terms of contraction. There was even talk of dissolving the company, and one reason it survived at all was that in 1845 it received from the Government of India a charter granting the shareholders limited liability. [108] The Calcutta board, sometimes with good reason and sometimes without, was more optimistic, more imaginative and more venturesome, the London board more careful and conservative. Conflict between the two boards continued until 1866. In that year London succeeded in abolishing the Calcutta board and in the following year appointed a managing-agency firm, Schoene, Kilburne and Company as their Calcutta agents. [109]

105 Antrobus, *Assam Company*, p. 56.

106 Ibid., pp. 477–48.

107 Ibid., pp. 272 ff.; Guildhall, Assam Company Manuscripts, Calcutta Committee Minutes, 9925/1, 26 Nov. 1841.

108 Antrobus, *Assam Company*, pp. 61–62.

109 Ibid., p. 154.

Of the four early joint-stock companies promoted by Carr, Tagore and Company, two failed and two survived. All four, however, were burdened with overwhelming technological problems, poor management, shortages of capital, and governmental obstruction—though not to the same extent. The Tug Association had fewer technological problems because its captains and engineers were able to benefit from ten years of experience with paddlewheelers on the Hooghly River. The Assam Company muddled through its infancy because it could draw on the London board for its funds. On the other hand, the Salt Company was the neglected orphan among Carr, Tagore's joint-stock enterprises. Its management was neglectful and its technical problems all but insuperable. The Ferry Bridge Company was the victim of a series of misfortunes, some of which were beyond the control of its managers. One was the premature death of Captain T.J. Taylor; another, the commercial slump of 1842; and a third, the unfortunate choice of Andrew Henderson as London agent. Only the government could have saved the company, but it refused. In view of the failure of Carr, Tagore and Company to give these enterprises the management they required, the managing-agency system was discredited at the very time of its origin. Only with the establishment of a new set of British managing-agency firms in Calcutta later in the century did the system win the confidence of investors. Unfortunately, however, these new managing agents were content, for the most part, to expand old primary industries rather than to explore new industries that would compete with those in Britain. The only notable exception was the jute-mill industry. Otherwise, until the twentieth century, managing agents in eastern India introduced few undertakings that Carr, Tagore and Company and its contemporaries had not already attempted—coal mining, tea planting, steam shipping, dockyards, sugar refining, and railways. The want of creative entrepreneurship by British managing agents has been attributed to their reluctance to defy the industrial establishment of Great Britain and thereby to jeopardize their relationships with business friends back home.[110] It can also be ascribed to their perception that India was destined always to be a producer of agricultural and primary products and an economic satellite of the industrially advanced nations of the West.

110A.K. Sen, "The Pattern of British Enterprise in India, 1854–1914: A Causal Analysis," in Baljit Singh and V.B. Singh, *Social and Economic Change* (Bombay: 1967).

Chapter VII

PRINCE DWARKANATH AT COURT

By 1841 Dwarkanath Tagore stood at the summit of his business career. During the seven previous years he had built his agency house into a firm that led all rivals in the promotion and management of new industrial enterprises, developed the country's largest coal mine, acquired a fleet of ships, and augmented his vast, productive landed estates. Now the time had come to put business temporarily aside, to leave the management of his affairs to his partners and to realize his old dream of following the path of Rammohun Roy to Europe. In the remaining five years of his life, civic and public duties would take priority over business. He became the leading public man of his city, and Calcutta's nearest approximation to a lord mayor. Lavish expenditures on philanthropy, patronage of the arts and social leadership earned him the nickname "Prince Dwarkanath."

Of all his public activities his philanthropy made the strongest impression on his contemporaries.[1] Charity was traditionally the most important moral obligation of the wealthy Hindu and the amount donated was one measure of a man's social status. The great families of Calcutta competed in spending vast sums on festivals, sraddhas, food for the poor, gifts for Brahmins, and support for temples. Dwarkanath did not neglect these traditional charities. He donated liberally to Brahmins and continued to perform the costly Durga Puja in his home.[2] But his reputation as philanthropist came from his donations to western-style charities. Here he adapted a traditional duty to a modern purpose. If donations to Brahmins enhanced a Hindu's status in the traditional context, donations to western-style charities would, he assumed, enhance his status among the British. He regularly donated fifty or one-hundred rupees more

1 See the testimonial to him on the eve of his departure for Europe in Kissory Chand Mittra, *Memoir of Dwarkanath Tagore* (Calcutta: 1870), app. B, p. xlii–xlvii.
2 Ibid., p. 36; *Bengal Hurkaru*, 23 Jan. 1841; *Calcutta Courier*, 12 Oct. 1839.

than the next man to any public subscription. Interracial and international causes, such as funds for Afghan War widows or victims of famine in Ireland or of cholera in France, were his special concern.[3] In these donations Dwarkanath appeared at least as interested in enhancing the status of his countrymen as in promoting his own personal reputation. By donating to western causes, by helping the Europeans in their time of need, he asserted the moral and social parity of Indians with Britishers.

Dwarkanath led his countrymen, many of whom were no less generous than he, in channeling philanthropy into modern agencies. When, on the occasion of his father's sraddha, he donated Rs. 2,000 to the District Charitable Society, the editor of *Jnananeshan* held him up for emulation and called on other wealthy Hindus to divert their lavish expenditures from nautches to schools and other useful causes.[4] Among the rich Hindus the sraddha was customarily the occasion for the most lavish expenditure. Dwarkanath followed this tradition by making his mother's sraddha the occasion for the most spectacular donation of his career. In 1838 he donated Rs. 1,00,000 to establish the "Dwarkanath Fund for the Needy Blind," which helped hundreds of unfortunate Hindus and Muslims with pensions adequate to live in dignity. On the same occasion, however, he did not neglect his traditional duties, and distributed Rs. 50,000 to the Brahmins.[5]

Besides serving as an example, he prodded and cajoled his wealthy Indian friends into modernizing their charitable activities. He urged them to help the poor in an organized, rational way rather than by the haphazard distribution of alms to beggars. As head of the "Native Committee" of the government-sponsored District Charitable Society, he worked to place the entire system of poor relief on a basis of dignity and self-respect. He campaigned to outlaw begging, organized support for a public alms house and devised a plan to enlist the participation of wealthy Indians to help identify the needy and distribute relief.[6] Medicine was his special interest. Concerned

3*Friend of India*, 25 Aug. 1842.

4*Jnananeshan*, 15 Oct. 1833, reprinted in *Englishman*, 16 Oct. 1833.

5S.N. Mukherjee, "Class, Caste and Politics in Calcutta 1815–1838," in E. Leach and S.N. Mukherjee, eds., *Elites in South Asia* (Cambridge: 1970), pp. 33–78; *Bengal Hurkaru*, 13 Mar. 1838.

6*Bengal Hurkaru*, 3 and 13 Mar. 1838; *Calcutta Courier*, 3 Sept. 1833 and 5 Mar. 1838; *Bengal Annual Directories* for 1837 and 1841; *Samachar Durpan*, 11 May 1833, in KNT Collection; K.C. Mittra, *Memoir*, p. 37.

that the poor as well as the rich should have access to modern
scientific medicine, he pressed his wealthy countrymen into supporting the Native Fever Hospital. [7] When the high-caste Hindu youth
studying at the Calcutta Medical College refused to dissect corpses,
he donated prize money and assured the principal that "no induce-
ment to native exertion is so strong as that of pecuniary reward." But
he also set a personal example by joining his rival *dalapati,* Radha
Kanta Deb, in frequent visits to the dissection laboratory. [8]

Of all the Hindu leaders, Dwarkanath was the most "European-
minded." [9] At the same time, he had a precocious sense of identification with his countrymen and seemed to feel personally responsible
for the reputation of his people in the eyes of the world. If he was
ostentatious in his philanthropy and hospitality, it was rather for the
sake of the good name of his countrymen than to satisfy his own
vanity. When Indians were disparaged, he was embarrassed and
defensive. In England, for example, he confronted Captain Madden
of the Bengal Artillery, who had accused the sepoys of cowardly
behavior in the Afghan War. According to the report, Dwarkanath
denied the captain's allegation and stood up "manfully in defense of
his countrymen." [10]

Dwarkanath lost no opportunity to assert his social position as the
indigenous counterpart of the governor-general. Guests who attended
a soiree at Government House in 1837, for example, noticed upon
entering the hall two massive trophies to be awarded the winners of
the Calcutta sweepstakes. One was the Auckland Cup; the other, "in
the excess of bad taste, and such as only a Baboo would have
approved," was the Tagore Cup. [11]

Tagore developed his suburban estate, Belgatchia, into a second
Government House, and when Lord Auckland paid his first visit to
Belgatchia he came with a train of retainers as though calling on a
maharaja. [12] Dwarkanath's parties were second only to those of the
governor-general as the major social events of the city. The governor-
general and his niece, Emily Eden, first dined at Belgatchia on 28

7*Bengal Hurkaru,* 19 June 1835.

8K.C. Mittra; *Memoir,* p. 26.

9Brougham Papers, Col. James Young to Lord Brougham, 14 (?) June 1842.

10*Bengal Hurkaru,* 25 Aug. 1842.

11Quotation is from Fanny Parks, *Wanderings of a Pilgrim in Search of the Picturesque
during Four and Twenty Years in the East, etc.* 2 vols. (London: 1850), II, 104. Also,
Calcutta Courier, 4 January 1837.

12Emily Eden, *Letters from India,* 2 vols. (London: 1872), I, 215–16.

November 1836, together with three hundred other guests, including Calcutta's leading European actors, singers, and musicians, the chief justice, one or two generals, Thomas Babington Macaulay, and "most of the female beauty and fashion in Calcutta." The guests danced the waltz, quadrille, and galop, and, in the evening, "multitudes of natives assembled for the fireworks."[13] Still more prized were invitations to his small parties, where guests entertained themselves with unusual and interesting games. Dwarkanath, wrote Miss Eden, "is the only man in the country who gives pleasant parties."[14]

As self-appointed local potentate, Dwarkanath felt obligated to entertain important foreign visitors to his city. Among these were a young prince of Holland on duty with the Royal Navy; a Russian prince, Alexis Soltykoff; and Captain Leopold von Orlich of Germany. Some were treated to elephant rides, juggling exhibitions, and fireworks, others to nautches and recitals of western music.[15] Von Orlich was shocked by the nautch-girls, whose "movements became so offensive, that we requested that the dance might be concluded. The notions of morality and decorum entertained by the Indians, even when they have acquired that degree of refinement which our host undoubtedly possessed, are still so different from ours, that they are quite insensible to that impropriety which so much shocked us."[16]

In February 1840, Dwarkanath gave another splendid dinner party to which, as usual, Indians were invited only to view the fireworks. One of the Bengali newspapers chided: "In the Belgatchia Garden knives and forks clatter. What pleasure is there in eating—do we know? No. Only Tagore Company knows."[17] Consequently, a few evenings later Dwarkanath invited the bhadralok to a party featuring every nautch-girl of talent in the city. Thereafter he regularly mixed his guests and, to a grand ball in honor of the wife of the deputy

13*Bengal Hurkaru*, 30 Nov. 1836.

14Eden, *Letters from India*, I, 234–35.

15*Calcutta Monthly Journal*, December 1837, p. 847; Prince Alexis Soltykoff, "Bombay and Calcutta in 1841," trans. and ed. by H.L.O. Garett, *Journal of the Punjab Historical Society*, vol. 2, April 1933, p. 82.

16Captain Leopold von Orlich, *Travels in India*, 2 vols., (London: 1845), II, 187.

17From *Prabashi*, quoted in Satischandra Chakravarty, ed., *Shrimanmaharshi Debendranath Thakurer Atmajibani* (Calcutta: 1927), p. 310.

governor, invited not only the wealthy but some "humble folk" to mingle with the Europeans. [18]

The civic activity he most enjoyed was patronage of the theater. In 1835 Tagore bought the lively Chowringhee Theatre for Rs. 30,000 and made it over to a newly formed dramatic society. He delighted in the role of impresario and in the company of those who shared his enchantment with the stage—Parker, Stocqueler, Plowden, James Hume, and T.J. Taylor. The playhouse also presented a setting for social intercourse between the races, and Emma Roberts describes "parties of Hindostannee gentlemen beautifully clad in white muslin . . . . sitting as near the stage as possible." Because they preferred tragedy, the management obliged them with frequent performances of *Macbeth* and *Othello*. [19] The major attraction was the actress, Esther Leach, self-trained but "far above the average talent of the best [London] stage." [20] She played at the Chowringhee until it burnt down in May 1839, then raised funds for a new theater, the Sans Souci, and performed there until the tragic evening of November 22, 1843, when her dress caught fire and she died of burns at the age of thirty-five. The theater closed, and Dwarkanath, who had been a close and, some said, affectionate friend of Mrs. Leach, did not have the will to reopen it. [21]

In politics, as in business, philanthropy, and the arts, Dwarkanath was instrumental in forging alliances between the races. The European non-official community, consisting of merchants, lawyers, artisans, and planters, had been the first people in the city to agitate on political questions. They favored free trade, a free press, security of property, and the right to settle in the mufassal; in sum, the rights of Englishmen. They saw as their political adversary the East India Company and as their allies, the free traders of Great Britain. Rammohun Roy and Dwarkanath Tagore joined forces with them on a number of issues—against the Stamp Act and the coolie trade, and,

18*Bengal Herald,* 4 Feb. 1843. The host wore "a rich dress of velvet Tartan" which he had brought from Edinburgh, and a gold medal presented him by Queen Victoria. KNT ms., letter written by James Stuart, n.d.

19Emma Roberts, *Scenes and Characteristics of Hindostan with Sketches of Anglo-Indian Society,* 3 vols. (London: 1835), III, 87–88.

20[James Hume,] *Letters to Friends at Home by an Idler from June 1843 to May 1844* (Calcutta: 1844), p. 116.

21KNT ms., Dwarkanath Tagore to W. Dampier, 12 Dec. 1835; Amal Mitra, "Dwarkanath Tagore, Patron of the English Stage in Calcutta," *Amrita Bazar Patrika,* 16 Jan. 1955; H.N. Das Gupta, *The Indian Stage* 4 vol., (Calcutta: 1935–46), I, 253–54, 268, 273.

above all, against censorship of the press. When Rammohun left for Europe, Dwarkanath, the leading press magnate of Calcutta and, as a "native," immune from transportation for political opposition, took his place as chief spokesman of the movement for a free press. [22]

To Dwarkanath, freedom of the press was an article of faith. Those who favored censorship could justify it only on the ground that India was a vanquished land, won by force and held by force. Censorship was imposed in 1823 because the rulers of India believed that among a hostile population a press critical of the government would promote "insubordination, insurrection and anarchy." [23] But Dwarkanath Tagore had devoted his life and fortune to making India into an integral part of the British realm and believed that through western education the creation of a new British-Indian nationality was already in process. "Education . . . is rapidly expanding its powerful influence, a gulph is no longer placed between the enlightened Englishman and the benighted Native; they are gradually mingling into one people." [24] Thus, when in 1835 Lord Metcalfe, in the face of opposition from the Court of Directors, courageously repealed the censorship law, Dwarkanath called his act "one of the most valuable ever attempted by the Indian Government. It strengthens their own hands and ears, and eyes, in ruling this vast region, and it is also a guarantee to the people that their rulers mean to govern with justice since they are not afraid to let their subjects judge their acts." [25] Of course, the press would be critical of the government, but it would be the criticism of a loyal opposition interested not in overthrowing but in improving and strengthening British rule in India.

As a leader of that amorphous party of the loyal opposition, Dwarkanath's first objective was to bring more Indians into the political arena. Because the Hindu elite were proud and sensitive, his most difficult problem was to prevent racial animosity from destroying the coalition of nonofficial Europeans and politically conscious Indians. Among the Europeans, color prejudice was compounded by Christian intolerance toward Indian culture and religion. Those who did sympathize with Indian culture, the "orientalists," were more likely to be officials. Political distrust was still another factor, though

22A.F.S. Ahmed, *Social Ideas and Social Change in Bengal, 1818–1835* (Leiden: 1965) pp. 66 ff.; Kissory Chand Mittra, *Memoir*, p. 45.
23Sir Thomas Munro, quoted in Ahmed, *Social Ideas*, p. 58n.
24*Englishman*, 7 Dec. 1838.
25Kissory Chand Mittra, *Memoir*, p. 47.

in Calcutta Europeans feared insurrection from the Indians of Agra, Oudh, and beyond, rather than from those of the city. The Indians held similar feelings about the Europeans, ranging from disgust at their unclean habits to resentment against alien rule and Christian bigotry. Yet, in spite of the difficulties, Rammohun Roy, Dwarkanath Tagore, Prasanna Kumar Tagore and their friends identified their political interests with those of the nonofficial Europeans. To sustain this alliance they had to overlook racial insults and religious aspersions and to emphasize those interests the two races held in common.

Dwarkanath was very quick to avert any possible explosion over race. The Indian community had been upset when, in a thoughtlessly provocative editorial, Stocqueler of the *Englishman* had called for limiting freedom of the press to journals with "European proprietors and editors."[26] Dwarkanath referred to the editorial at a public banquet celebrating the end of press censorship. A toast had been proposed to the merchants of Calcutta for their support of the movement, and, while the band played "Money in Both Pockets," Dwarkanath rose to reply on behalf of his fellow merchants. He used the opportunity to congratulate his countrymen "that no distinction had been made in the recent act between native and European, and made light of the *Englishman's* editorial, attributing it rather to "a little selfishness [between newspaper editors] than . . . any fear of political danger." The crowd responded with laughter, and the tension relaxed.[27] His disarming humor contrasted with the strong words of the young editor of *Jnananeshan,* Rasik Krisha Mallick, who spoke of "the ungenerous attack on the native press."[28]

To further the development of his interracial coalition, Dwarkanath took what some have considered a proracist position against an enlightened act to deny Europeans special legal privileges in India. Labeled the "Black Act" by Europeans, it was framed by Thomas Babington Macaulay. He had come to India in 1834 as law member of the Supreme Council and was assigned the job of codifying the laws and rationalizing the judicial system of British India. Macaulay found two parallel judicial systems in operation: one, the Supreme Court at Calcutta, a King's Court staffed by British justices who dispensed British Law; the other, the courts of the East India

26*Englishman*, 3 Jan. 1835.
27*Bengal Hurkaru*, 19 Sept. 1835.
28*Calcutta Monthly Journal*, 1835, pp. 170–71.

Company. The company's courts were staffed by civil servants with no formal legal training, and included some Indians at the lower levels. They dispensed a jumble of British, Mughal, Hindu, customary, and equity law. In 1836, as part of his new scheme to rationalize the judicial system, Macaulay proposed to place British subjects in the mufassal under the civil jurisdiction of the company's courts. Except in criminal suits, he would deprive Europeans of their old privilege of direct access to the Supreme Court in Calcutta. Tagore's party joined with the non-official Europeans and attacked Macaulay vociferously. Macaulay, in turn, denounced the opposition for attempting to form a racial oligarchy.[29]

Dwarkanath and his friends tried to ignore the racial implications inherent in the position of their European allies. But at the meeting of 18 June 1836, to protest the act, one Mr. Wyborn embarrassed the leadership by daring to raise the question in the most lurid terms. "Are the Hindoos now in a fit state to sit in judgment over their conquerers of a different religion?" Wyborn asked. He graphically described "one of their hideous and disgusting festivals" and pointed out that a Hindu *sadhu*, a "revolting creature . . . may . . . secure the bench of the Sudder Dewanny Adawlut and [rule] in a suit between a Gentoo and an Englishman. . . . This nation is now considered fit to decide upon the destinies of civilized Christian Europeans." R.H. Cockerell, the sheriff, interrupted him and warned him not to say anything more that would "give pain to any class."[30] When Wyborn began again in the same vein, Cockerell stopped him and told him to apologize to the Indians who were present. The audience had mixed reactions: some wanted to hear more from Wyborn, others wanted him muzzled.[31]

With racial feelings scarcely hidden beneath the surface, Tagore called on his fellow Indians to support the British on grounds that to deprive any group of its privileges was a bad precedent for all.[32] By July, 118 Indians from the whole of northern India had joined with 582 Europeans in a petition to the Court of Directors. In Calcutta, Dwarkanath and Prasanna Kumar were joined by Dakshinaranjan Mukherjee and by Rasamay Datta, a politically active orthodox Hindu of the older generation.[33] Although only a handful of Indians

29 C.D. Dharker, *Lord Macaulay's Legislative Minutes* (Madras: 1946), pp. 272 ff.
30 *Bengal Hurkaru*, 21 June 1836.
31 Ibid., 22 June 1836.
32 *The Reformer*, 15 May 1836, reprinted in *Bengal Hurkaru*, 16 May 1836.
33 *Bengal Hurkaru*, 30 June and 11 July 1836.

joined with Tagore, even fewer were outspoken in defense of Macaulay's liberal act. It was Tagore's special campaign, and perhaps he saw in it, as Gandhi saw in the Khilafat movement, an opportunity to unite in a common cause two segregated communities.

At the public meeting of 18 June 1836, to protest the act, Tagore made one of the most passionate speeches of his public career. The government, he said, wanted to "equalize Englishmen with the Natives. But what equalization do they put in practice. The natives have hitherto been slaves; are the Englishmen therefore to be made slaves also? This is the kind of equality the government are seeking to establish. They have taken all which the Natives possessed; their lives, liberty, property and all were held at the mercy of Government and now they wish to bring the English inhabitants of the country to the same state! They will not raise the Natives to the condition of the Europeans, but they degrade the Europeans by lowering them to the state of the Natives." The Court of Directors, said Dwarkanath, were "desirous of exercising absolute and despotic power in this coun-try."[34] His opposition was not only theoretical. He was continually involved in lawsuits and could compare both sets of courts. The mufassal courts were manned by "college boys without any experi-ence" who were led around by corrupt amlas. Bribes amounted to twenty times authorized fees, and the courts were so inefficient that Dwarkanath claimed to have four lakhs of long-standing decrees unrealized. He concluded his speech by calling on all present, Indians and British, to "defend those rights and to preserve us from the threatened despotism" of the Court of Directors, who "desire . . . to rule India with absolute power."[35]

The fundamental difference between Macaulay and Tagore lay in their conception of the East India Company. Macaulay had been employed by the company and sent to India to help convert it into a legitimate civilian government dedicated to the well-being of all its subjects. Dwarkanath, on the other hand, looked upon the company as a relic of mercantilism and a played-out engine of conquest still maintaining a garrison state. Its courts were derivative and illegiti-mate. It was a second-class government reducing those it ruled to second-class citizenship. Why should British subjects in England be under the rule of common law and Parliament whereas those who happened to live in an Asian province were under the laws and

34 Kissory Chand Mittra, *Memoir*, p. 54.
35 Ibid., p. 57.

government of an anachronistic mercantile company? Ideally, Dwarkanath would favor abolishing the inferior judicial system of the East India Company and placing all subjects under King's Courts. Macaulay, on the other hand, would upgrade the company's courts and place Europeans under their jurisdiction.

A year later, Dwarkanath testified on conditions in the mufassal before the Committee on Improvement of the Mofussil Police. He described district society as divided into two classes; those who bribed and those who received bribes, and he freely admitted that, like every other zamindar, he bribed local Indian officials. But he suggested a solution: the appointment of respectable English-educated young men—Indians, Eurasians, or British—as deputy magistrates in place of the present ignorant daroghas and sheristadars. His suggestion was, in fact, taken up by the government, and qualified young graduates of Hindu College were appointed deputy collectors and magistrates in subsequent years.[36]

Dwarkanath's criticisms of company courts led Abercrombie Dick, Judge of Midnapore and Hidjlee, to write a letter to the *Englishman* defending the integrity of the amlas and questioning the patriotism of a man who cast aspersions on the character of his own countrymen. In his reply, Tagore admitted that it had been "painful" to "point out the errors of my countrymen." But "the regeneration of my countrymen," he asserted, could be accomplished only by "candid and fearless exposure." He attributed their "want of truth ... integrity ... and independence" to "the loss of liberty and national degradation" following the Muslim conquest. When the people could not protect their lives by arms they "fell into the opposite extremes of abject submission, deceit and fraud." The East India Company, instead of introducing English laws and institutions, was carrying on "the whole of the Mahomedan Revenue and Judicial system, and even made it more corrupt by means of their *alterations!*"[37]

Significantly, Dwarkanath refrained from attributing India's moral decadence to the caste system, Kulinism, or idolatry. Unlike Rammohun Roy, he always took care to maintain good relations and avoid conflict with orthodox Hindu leadership. Moreover, he must have felt that the time was ripe to bring the Hindu leaders more fully into political activities. They had already joined together in 1828 to

36 Bengal, *Committee on Improvement of Mofussil Police, Report and Appendices* (Calcutta: 1838), pp. 35 ff.; Peary Chand Mittra, *A Biographical Sketch of David Hare* (Calcutta: 1877), pp. 30–33.

37 K.C. Mittra, *Memoir,* pp. 59–62.

petition against religious discrimination in the Jury Act, and in 1829 petitioned against resumption of rent-free tenures.[38] In 1831 they formed the Dharma Sabha to defend the institution of sati, but as that controversy cooled, the Dharma Sabha had degenerated into "an Indian court of inquisition [and] spiritual tyranny."[39] On the urging of the orientalist scholar, H.H. Wilson, strongly supported by Ramcomul Sen, the leaders of the Dharma Sabha agreed in April 1836 to drop religious questions in favor of political concerns. Within a year, the Dharma Sabha leadership joined with Theodore Dickens, who represented the European nonofficial community, and Prasanna Kumar Tagore to form a new organization, the Landholders' Society. The first political organization of modern India, the Landholders' Society soon became the focus of the "loyal opposition." Its first executive committee of twelve included Dwarkanath and Prasanna Kumar Tagore, George Prinsep, and five leaders from the Dharma Sabha.[40] Dwarkanath and Theodore Dickens became the most active members of the society.

Its major purpose was to fight with petitions and a parliamentary lobby the resumption of rent-free tenures. The *Friend of India,* organ of the Baptist mission, attacked the Landholders' Society for its selfish concentration on the rights of zamindars and charged that it "represents but one local interest; and that the interest of the strong and not the weak." Dwarkanath was particularly sensitive to this criticism and he tried to answer the missionary attack by emphasizing the work of the society for the welfare of the people at large. But he could find little of consequence to say. He spoke of the society's advocating the use of vernacular languages in the courts, the distribution of maintenance allowances to poor witnesses at trials, and the reduction of the stamp duty on official documents—all of which would be of more benefit to the poor than the rich.[41]

Clearly there was room for a political organization more sympathetic to the peasantry, and Dwarkanath was to be instrumental in organizing one. One of the main activities of the Landholders'

38Ahmed, *Social Ideas,* app. 104, 126–27.

39*Reformer,* 30 Apr. 1836, reprinted in *Asiatic Journal,* n.s., vol. 21, October 1836, p. 68.

40S.N. Mukherjee, "Class, Caste and Politics in Calcutta."

41K.C. Mittra, *Memoir,* app., pp. xxiii ff.; for a history of the Landholders' Society, see S.R. Mehrotra, "The Landholders' Society, 1838–44," *Indian Economic and Social History Review,* vol. 3, no. 4, December 1966, pp. 358–75; and B.B. Majumdar, *Indian Political Associations and Reform of Legislature (1818–1917)* (Calcutta: 1965), pp. 23–26.

Society had been to establish contact with the British India Society, a coalition of Manchester manufacturers and humanitarian Quakers formed in Britain to encourage the development of India as a source of non-slave-grown cotton.[42] On his visit to Britain, Tagore, as an emissary of the Landholders' Society, contacted the leaders of the British India Society and brought one of them, George Thompson, back to Calcutta. Thompson would not only infuse new life into the Landholders' Society but would mobilize "Young Bengal" into forming a radical political organization sympathetic to the peasantry.[43]

Despite his leadership of the loyal opposition and his impassioned criticism of the administration, the Government of India encouraged Dwarkanath's civic activities and accorded him special honors. For one reason, British rule over the subcontinent was still incomplete. The Marathas had only recently been conquered, the Sikhs were strong and independent and the Russians were threatening the vulnerable northwestern frontier. Bengal, led by its loyal, reliable zamindars, was, in this period, the pillar of the Raj.[44] Dwarkanath, the representative zamindar, might criticize the government, but he did so as an insider, a confidant of governors-general, a man whose social position and fortune depended on the British. At the same time, his good will was important to the East India Company and the Government of India. In the age of evangelical humanitarianism it was necessary to clothe colonial activities with morality and to justify the East India Company as an agent of civilization. Dwarkanath was the symbol of the success of the company's government. Here was a "native" who had risen out of a milieu of benighted superstition, who spoke and wrote English eloquently, admired British customs and institutions, and dedicated himself to the welfare of his country and the empire. He must be encouraged in every way, held up for emulation as a man who would lead his people in the paths of westernization and loyalty. Some talked of a knighthood for Dwarkanath, and others of conferring on him and his reformer friends "full British citizenship" on the Roman model to compensate them for loss of caste.[45] Although none of these honors materialized, Dwarkanath

42S. Maccoby, *English Radicalism, 1853–1886* (London: 1938), pp. 16–17, 364.

43*Bengal Hurkaru,* 27 Mar. 1843.

44For a contemporary review of the British position in India, see *Calcutta Review,* vol. XV, January-June 1851, pp. 202 ff.

45IO, Home Miscellaneous, vol. 853, Broughton Papers, Letter from Henry Seton to J.C. Hobhouse, 6 Sept. 1846.

was soon to be more lionized and honored by the British than any Indian before or since.

During the latter part of 1841, Dwarkanath prepared for his long-awaited trip to England. He had been out of Bengal twice before, in 1835 and 1838, on trips in the upper provinces. The earlier one had been an extended tour encompassing Agra, Brindaban, and Benares; the later one, taken to regain his health, was interrupted by the death of his mother.[46] His comings and goings were always public events. On the occasion of his departure for England, his friends, both European and Indian, celebrated with an elaborate meeting and eulogistic speeches. They presented him with a formal address in which, with an unintentionally frank admission of British prejudice, they rejoiced that the people of England would have an opportunity to meet "one who is calculated to raise the estimate which some in England may heretofore have been disposed to entertain of the native gentlemen in India."[47]

He embarked for Suez on his own steamer, the *India*, on 9 January 1842, accompanied by his physician, Dr. MacGowan, his nephew, Chunder Mohun Chatterjee, his aide-de-camp, Purmanund Moitra, three Hindu servants, and his Muslim cook. The other passengers included H.M. Parker and Sir Edward Ryan, the Chief Justice of Bengal.[48] The next six months were relaxed and happy ones during which the forty-eight-year-old tourist exulted with the wide-eyed enthusiasm of a youth in the scenic splendors, the historic landmarks, and the exotic customs of foreign lands. In long travel accounts written to friends at home, he noted every detail of flora, fauna, and topography, art, history, and society from the fertile plantations of Ceylon to the pyramids of Egypt, the tombs and churches of Malta, the mountains and palaces of Italy, and the towns and fields of Germany and Belgium. He was armed with letters of introduction to governors, merchants, and noblemen and took every opportunity to attend musical events and state functions. He noted the prices and quality of goods and compared everything he saw with its counterpart at home. In Rome, the high point of the trip, he called on the Pope and gloried in the art. "If a man has money," he wrote, "this is the place to get rid of it, in the fine arts, statues, paintings, mosaics, etc. but I pay great attention to ———'s advise and keep myself from

46K.C. Mittra, *Memoir*, pp. 35–36; *Calcutta Courier*, 12 Feb. 1838.
47K.C. Mittra, *Memoir*, p. 76.
48Ibid., p. 79.

making purchases, although the temptation is very great." In Naples he had his first view of a railway—"think what was my sensation when it passed near my carriage." He crossed the Channel at Calais, arrived in Dover, passed the night at Canterbury, and on the morning of June 16 first "made my appearance in this blessed city of London." [49]

From the moment he arrived in London, the tranquil stage of his trip ended. The next four months were crowded with activity, including meetings with political leaders, dinners, parties, speeches, and sightseeing. A reporter noted that he was "so feasted and plagued by the curious and officious, that he declares himself to be a slave in the land of liberty; his hotel morning, noon and night is so beset with visitors of varied character and complexion it is the greatest difficulty for any one to obtain a quiet half hour's converse with him on matters that pertain to business, and he has some weighty calls just now in that way." [50]

Soon after his arrival, he met the Prime Minister, Robert Peel; and a few days later Lord Fitzgerald, president of the Board of Control, introduced him to the Duke of Wellington, Prince Albert, the Duchess of Kent, and Queen Victoria. "'How long have you been in this country?' asked the Queen, holding out her hand. 'Only a few days,' replied Dwarkanath. 'I have overcome the prejudices of myself and all my friends and relations. I have travelled some thousands of miles under trial and privation to see your Majesty—Queen of this great nation. Now if I went back tomorrow, I am amply repaid.' The Queen smiled; he kissed her hand, and passed on" [51] He was to see more of the royal family. He spent June 23 with the Queen, reviewing troops, and on July 8 was invited to dinner at the palace. He conversed with Victoria and Albert on India and played whist with the Duchess of Kent. [52] The Queen noted in her diary, "The

49 Letters from Dwarkanath Tagore in *Friend of India*, Sept. 1, 8, and 15, 1842.

50 *Friend of India*, 25 Aug. 1842. Dwarkanath was not the only Indian of distinction to visit England during this period. In 1839 the Indian notables then in London included Nawab Eckbaloo Dowlah, Prince of Oudh; Prince Jama-ood-Deen, son of the late Tippoo Sultan; Meer Afzul Ali and Meer Kurreem Ali, agents of the Rajah of Sattara; Ishanger Naorodjee and Hirjeebhoy Merwanjee, young Parsis studying ship building; and Dorabjee Maucherjee, merchant of Bombay. John Hyslop Bell, *British Folks and British India Fifty Years Ago: Joseph Pease and his Contemporaries* (London: n.d.), p. 65. The two young Parsis are mentioned in the *Calcutta Review*, vol. IV, July-December 1845, *Miscellaneous Notices*, p. 1.

51 *Friend of India*, 25 Aug. 1842, quoting from *Monthly Times*.

52 K.C. Mittra, *Memoir*, p. 89.

Brahmin speaks English remarkably well, and is a very intelligent, interesting man." [53] With her secretary, Charles A. Murray, he struck up an intimate friendship, and they discussed Indian politics with an air of familiarity. [54]

On June 22 Tagore attended a meeting of the Court of Directors, heard a debate on Indian indentured labor in Mauritius, and that evening was entertained by the directors with a dinner at London Tavern. [55] Similarly, he was honored with a banquet by the Lord Mayor of London at Mansion House, where, overwhelmed by the flattery and warmth of his reception, he replied to a toast in his usual ardent style with words that would plague him for years. He expressed his gratitude for the hospitality and friendship he had received in England and then, presuming to speak on behalf of his countrymen, expressed their gratitude for British rule. "It was England who sent out Clive and Cornwallis to benefit India by their counsels and arms. It was England that sent out . . . the great man who had introduced a proper and permanent order of things in the East. It was the country . . . that . . . protected his countrymen from the tyranny and villainy of the Mahometans, and the no less frightful oppression of the Russians. And all this was done—not in the expectation of a requital—not in the hope of anything whatever in return, but from the mere love of doing good . . . . It was impossible for his countrymen to treat the English with ingratitude." [56] When the speech reached India, many of his friends were bewildered. In England it brought an immediate response from Charles Forbes and Joseph Pease of the British India Society, who felt that the speech exalted "military exploits over humane statesmanship." [57] Dwarkanath, in reply to Pease, explained that it had been his intention, "however imperfectly I was enabled to fulfill it—to state that, all things considered, my nation has been benefited by its deliverance from the yoke of the Mohammedans, etc." But the Quaker "was not convinced." [58]

[53] Royal Archives, *Queen Victoria's Journal,* July 8, 1842. Quoted with the gracious permission of Her Majesty Queen Elizabeth II.

[54] Letter from C.A. Murray to Dwarkanath Tagore, 3 Aug. 1844, copy in Tagore Family Archives, Rabindra Sadhana.

[55] K.C. Mittra, *Memoir,* p. 57.

[56] *London Mail,* 4 Aug. 1842, reprinted in *Friend of India,* 22 Sept. 1842.

[57] Bell, *British Folks,* p. 141.

[58] Ibid., pp. 141–42.

Among British leaders, he established his strongest ties with the Radical, Lord Brougham, who had been a founder of the British Indian Society. He was introduced to Brougham by Colonel James Young, formerly head of Alexander and Company in Calcutta and an old Benthamite. Young called Dwarkanath "my own very particular and old friend, at the head of everything liberal in India . . . and stands in the shoes of Rammohun Roy . . . . But he is not a scholar like the other—a man of the world, of excellent natural parts, and master of English to a wonderful degree. He has long set the example of discarding all nonsense about *caste* and eating and drinking and so fourth—altogether he is the most remarkable man of his day in India."[59] Dwarkanath discussed with Brougham the promotion of education in India, and on his departure the Society for the Diffusion of Useful Knowledge, founded by Brougham, presented him with a gift. He promised "to return here again next year after a hasty visit to my own country and then to be able to take a greater part in the proceedings of your most excellent institution."[60]

Dwarkanath sought out cultural as well as political leaders. In his lavish Calcutta style, he hired a steamer for a party at Richmond on the Thames to which he invited many of the literary figures he admired. Caroline Norton, a minor Victorian poetess, helped him organize the party.[61] Among the artists he grew to know were Martin Thee and F.R. Say, and from Say he commissioned a full-length portrait.[62] Possibly an appreciation for technology led him to cultivate an acquaintance with Charles Babbage, inventor of the mechanical calculator.[63]

Dwarkanath went about the business of touring with such dutiful intensity that he might have considered himself the eyes and ears of India. Included in his exhaustive lists of places to visit were the usual art galleries and exhibitions, parks, the zoo, the silversmiths and the waxworks; but, in addition, asylums, hospitals, schools, dockyards,

59 Brougham Papers, Col. James Young to Lord Brougham, June 14, 1842.

60 Brougham Papers, Dwarkanath Tagore to Thomas C———— (?), 28 Sept. 1842; also Dwarkanath Tagore to Lord Brougham, 28 Sept. and 4 Oct. 1842.

61 Amalendu Bose, "A Note on Dwarkanath Tagore," *Visvabharati Quarterly,* vol. 31, no. 3, 1965–66, pp. 222–26.

62 The painting is described in H.E.A. Cotton, *Calcutta Old and New* (Calcutta: 1907), pp. 777 ff.

63 Letters from Dwarkanath Tagore to Charles Babbage are in BM, *Additional Manuscripts* 37200, f. 176; 37205, f. 15; and 37192, f. 214.

and factories. [64] He made special notes of going to Maudslay and Company "the best place for making steam engines upon the patent as well as the old way," to Barclay's Brewery, [65] and to Printing House Square where, as a newspaper publisher himself, he watched with wonder 20,000 copies of the *Times* being printed in a couple of hours. At Convent Garden, India for once came off better by comparison. He declared that the vegetables there "were not near so fine as those shown at the Town Hall," exhibited by the Agricultural and Horticultural Society of Bengal. [66] And, of course, the theater. In his diary he notes, "went to Drury Lane. Saw Manno Faliero or Doge of Venice and Follies of a Night." [67] He toured the nearby country-side in the company of Lord Amherst and noted the green fields, formal gardens, and country homes. [68]

The periods between tours were hardly more restful. A journalist described him at home in his London apartment: "We have seen him surrounded by a dozen persons, each directing his attention to a different subject, and have admired the facility with which he can pass from topic to topic, conveying his thoughts on all with singular fluency and equally singular terseness and emphasis. We have seen him at one and the same time dictate letters of business and letters of compliment; make engagements, answer inquiries, receive new-comers, recognize old friends, exchange jokes, strike bargains and smoke his hookah." [69]

From about mid-August to mid-September he traveled on rail-roads, "the greatest wonders of England," to the Midlands, the north of England, and Scotland. In Scotland he called on some of his old friends from India, or their relatives, and saw a march of Chartists and unemployed in Glasgow. "At present some 300,000 people are out of employ which poor devils are being roughly handled by the troops. [George Thompson] may talk of the starvation of the Hill Coolies in India, but I see around me still more distress." [70] In Liverpool he visited Fawcett's Engine Manufactory and watched four

64 Rabindra Sadhana, Tagore Family Papers, loose diary pages.
65 Ibid.
66 K.C. Mittra, *Memoir,* pp. 91–93.
67 Rabindra Sadhana, Tagore Family Papers, loose diary page, September 1842 (?).
68 Ibid., Tuesday, August 2, 1842 (?).
69 *Fisher's Colonial Magazine,* vol. I, August-December 1842, pp. 393–99.
70 Letter from Dwarkanath to Debendranath, printed in *Bengal Spectator,* 1 Nov. 1842, copy in KNT Collection.

engines on order for the Steam Tug Association being manufactured. He toured the steel works in Sheffield, and at Newcastle the owner of Raniganj visited the coal mines and wrote in his diary a minute description of the operation.[71]

In mid-September he returned to London to prepare for his homeward journey. At the end of the month Dwarkanath bade farewell to the Queen and presented her and the Prince of Wales with gifts from India. The Queen in turn promised him portraits of herself and Albert. There was some talk of a knighthood, and James Young pressed Lord Brougham, "I do wish they would make him a Baronet—the *premier* Indian Baronet." But no action was taken.[72]

Perhaps in anticipation of such an honor, Dwarkanath, with the help of his Calcutta friend, Laurent Dent, arranged to register a coat of arms at the College of Arms. The warrant describes him as "Dwarkanath Tagore of Bengal in the East Indies, Zumeendar and Merchant in the Commission of the Peace for the Town of Calcutta . . . he has held the important post of Dewan or Head Officer in several civil departments under the Government of India." IIis coat of arms included shield, crest, and motto. The shield was divided into three parts: in the bottom third was a sailing ship on waves; in the middle third, an open book between two scrolls; and in the top third, two lotus flowers. In the crest above the shield, an elephant held a lotus flower in its trunk. Behind the elephant stood a banner on which was depicted a plough. The motto beneath the shield read: "Works Will Win."[73]

He left England on October 15 to spend the remainder of the month in Paris. Louis-Philippe received him at St. Cloud on October 28, introduced him to the French royal family, and conversed with him on Indian affairs. Tagore took the opportunity for sight seeing, attending the theater, and meeting French social leaders, including members of the Rothschild family.[74]

While in Paris he received a letter from the Court of Directors of the East India Company commending him for his work in the encouragement of education, his introduction of the arts and sciences,

[71] K.C. Mittra, *Memoir,* p. 95.

[72] *Bengal Herald,* 26 Nov. 1842; Brougham Papers, James Young to Lord Brougham, 10 Oct. 1842.

[73] The coat of arms of Dwarkanath Tagore was registered at the College of Arms, Dec. 6, 1842. See also Rabindra Sadhana, Tagore Family Papers, Laurent Dent to Dwarkanath Tagore, 20 and 29 Jan. 1844.

[74] *Bengal Hurkaru,* 24 Dec. 1842; *Moniteur Universal,* 20 Oct. 1842.

and his philanthropy. The effect, wrote the directors, would be to promote "the identification of the feelings and interests of the native and European population committed to their government, and thus strengthening the bonds which unite India with Great Britain." They announced that they were preparing a gold medal for him to be awarded in India. In reply, Dwarkanath, who a few years earlier had called the directors the despotic enslavers of his people, now alluded to the "just and liberal rule of the Honorable Court" and "of the excellence of a government whose pure and benevolent intentions, whose noble solicitude for the welfare and improvement of the millions committed by providence to its charge may challenge the admiration of the world." [75]

Once again, as in his Mansion House speech, Dwarkanath appeared to have been overwhelmed by the personal kindness and courtesy of the masters of India. His reply might, indeed, indicate some change of heart toward the East India Company. It is more likely, however, that neither the diplomatic hyperbole of his recent statements nor the exaggerated language of his Calcutta speeches reflected his exact feelings. Tagore was an actor, playing the role appropriate to the moment and making the statement suit the situation. In Calcutta he was the bold and uncringing political leader trying to whip up support for political action. In England he was the urbane diplomat, emissary from the people of India, playing the "Grand Mogul," surrounded by his retainers, and exchanging gifts, courtesies, and hospitality as an equal. This role called for the language of diplomacy. At bottom, however, he believed what he had said. On the one hand, the East India Company had exploited and robbed his people. On the other, in the contemporary world the British alone could provide the best possible government for India. No other western country had the enlightened institutions and the advanced technology, and in India itself, no indigenous power could have risen to the challenge and organized an administration to keep order, dispense justice, and defend the frontiers.

On November 9 he departed from Marseille for India. At Bombay, Dwarkanath and his party were taken aboard a special steamer dispatched by the government and brought to Madras. From there another steamer brought them to Calcutta. An English lady, Elisa Reade, had joined the party at Bombay and celebrated her good

75 *London Times*, 4 Nov. 1842.

fortune. "Dwarkanath was a great acquisition—he used to amuse me very much by his description of England and the different people he met with." She described "the crowds of natives that assembled to see him land in Calcutta and Dwarky himself said he had been more stared at since his return to Calcutta than he was in London. I fancy the Brahmins, so bigoted are they, expected to see him transformed into some beast or other. We had also the celebrated Mr. George Thompson on board, he is very agreeable and very clever. Dwarkanath's nephew Chunder Mohun Chatterjee was an exceedingly gentlemanly young man in fact his manners are better than Dwarky's."[76]

They landed in Calcutta in December 1842. Dwarkanath had hoped to return to England the following October, but he was destined to postpone his next departure until March 1845. In the intervening years, simple problems grew more complex, and his second trip to England was less the fulfillment of a dream than an escape from impending difficulties.

[76]IO, Ms. Eur. 123, Letter 6 of 1842 from Mrs. Elisa Reade to her sister, Elinor.

Chapter VIII

THE PRINCE AT BAY

Dwarkanath spent the first few months of 1843 "incessantly occupied in seeing my friends, narrating my adventures, and bringing up my arrears of business."[1] Meanwhile, his companion, George Thompson, lost no time in offending the Europeans[2] and stirring up the Indian community of the city. Observers such as James Hume, editor of the *Calcutta Star,* were puzzled by the connection between Dwarkanath and Thompson. "Mr. Thompson was Dwarkanath's fellow traveler, he came here at his invitation, he knew what Dwarkanath had said [at Mansion House]. To me it is a little singular that there should have been any sympathy between them."[3] Thompson's reputation as a radical firebrand preceded him to Calcutta. He had won international fame for his eloquent oratory at antislavery meetings on both sides of the Atlantic, later campaigned against the exploitation of blacks in the West Indies, and in the past few years had devoted himself to Indian questions. In July 1839 he had helped found the British India Society of London and was one of the leaders Dwarkanath was delegated to contact while in England.

The Landholders' Society had instructed Dwarkanath to "enter into certain arrangements" to bring Thompson to India,[5] but the orator's friends tried to persuade him not to accept the invitation,

1 Brougham Papers, Dwarkanath Tagore to Lord Brougham, April 1843.

2 One of those offended was Charles Huffnagle, American merchant and later consul at Calcutta from 1843 to 1857. Thompson angered Huffnagle at a meeting of the Agricultural and Horticultural Society by his references to slavery in America. George Thompson, *Addresses Delivered at Meetings of the Native Community of Calcutta and on other Occasions* (Calcutta: 1843).

3 [James Hume,] *Letters to Friends at Home by an Idler from June 1842 to May 1843* (Calcutta: 1843), pp. 80–81.

4 S.R. Mehrotra, "The British India Society and its Bengal Branch (1839–46)," *The Indian Economic and Social History Review,* vol. IV, no. 2 (June 1967), pp. 140–41.

5 From a speech by Thompson delivered 24 Oct. 1842, reprinted in *Bengal Hurkaru,* 20 Jan. 1843.

and at first he was reluctant to go. The British India Society had recently concluded an agreement with the Anti-Corn-Law League to subordinate Indian questions to the "more important" issue of cheap bread for the British workingman, and George Thompson had been "on loan" as a lecturer for the league. Furthermore, Joseph Pease was suspicious of wealthy Indian princes who came to London, moved in "commercial and courtly circles" and forgot the "miseries of their poor countrymen." [6] But at last the effusive and tender-hearted radical surrendered to Dwarkanath's entreaties and agreed to accompany him to India. [7]

Thompson had expected to lecture in Calcutta on the evils of the Afghan War, coolie emigration to Mauritius, the opium and salt monopolies, and the oppressive land tax. These, however, proved to be the wrong issues. By the time he arrived the war was over, the government had reformed the system of indentured labor, and he soon discovered that revenue questions were too complex for platform oratory. [8] Instead, he turned his attention, first, to encouraging the Western-educated young Bengalis to form a political organization and, then, to arousing the Landholders' Society from its deep "slumbers." [9]

Thompson delivered his first speech on January 11 before the Society for the Acquisition of General Knowledge. Founded in 1838, the society numbered about 150 members, of whom more than half were alumni or students of Hindu College. They met monthly to hear papers and discuss topics of historical, social, and political interest. [10] In January, Thompson told the group that he had come to India "to rouse the intelligent natives themselves to a sense of the necessity of becoming the narrators of their own grievances, as far as

---

6 John Hyslop Bell, *British Folks and British India Fifty Years Ago: Joseph Pease and his Contemporaries* (London: n.d.), p. 40. This self-righteous attitude was quite misplaced. In their enthusiasm to develop India as a source of non-slave-grown cotton for British industry, they were willing to profit from the semi-slavery and low wages of the Indian peasant. They said nothing about developing Indian industry or raising Indian wages. In addition, within a year, they too would join in praise of the East India Company for outlawing slavery in India and recalling Lord Ellenborough. Ibid., pp. 163 ff., 181 ff.

7 Ibid., pp. 139–43. In addition, Thompson had recently lost an election to Parliament. *Bengal Hurkaru*, 18 Jan. 1843.

8 *Friend of India*, 29 Dec. 1842.

9 Ibid., 13 Apr. 1843.

10 Goutam Chattopadhyay, ed., *Awakening in Bengal in Early Nineteenth Century*, vol. I (Calcutta: 1965), pp. xi ff.

they suffered any, that were removable by legislation."[11] Inspired perhaps by Thompson's rhetoric, an incident occurred at an S.A.G.K. meeting held a few weeks later that was to have far-reaching political repercussions. Dakshinaranjan Mukherjee, a grandson of Surya Kumar Tagore, read an essay denouncing the police and courts of the Bengal mufassal as "notoriously and shamelessly corrupt." During his presentation he was interrupted by Captain D.L. Richardson, principal of Hindu College, and accused of converting the hall, which belonged to the College, into a "den of treason." Richardson was called to order by Tarachand Chakrabarti, president of the society, who scolded the principal and demanded an apology.[12] Shocked by the audacity of Tarachand, the European press, which thereafter labled the young radicals "Chuckerbutties," accused them of self-serving disloyalty.

The following month the S. A. G. K. met in a new hall, the Fouzdaree Balakhana, and it was there, on 6 April 1843, that George Thompson recommended that they form the Bengal branch of the British India Society. The new political organization, which included among its members a few Britishers, was established within a week. Its announced purpose was to collect and disseminate information on conditions in British India and to peacefully and lawfully "advance the interest of all classes of our fellow subjects."[13] In fact, the cause of deepest interest to its members was to expand opportunities for the employment of educated Indians in the administration. In some respects the Bengal British India Society and the Landholders' Society were rival organizations. The "Chuckerbutties," who inquired into such questions as the condition of the peasantry, widow remarriage, and Kulin polygamy,[14] were, after all, led by those who had followed Rammohun Roy and studied under Derozio. In contrast, the Landholders' Society drew its members, with the exception of a few such as Dwarkanath and Prasanna Kumar, from the ranks of the old Dharma Sabha.

The press noticed that Dwarkanath, though Thompson's sponsor, had not joined the British India Society; and James Hume concluded, "of course it is impossible that Dwarkanath should

11 Thompson, *Addresses,* p. 8.
12 Chattopadhyay, pp. 390–94.
13 *Friend of India,* 13 Apr. 1843.
14 Mehrotra, "The British India Society."

countenance the proceedings of the Chuckerbutties."[15] Possibly Dwarkanath would have felt out of place joining an organization whose members were at least twenty years younger than himself. He stayed with his peers, the zamindars, but his sympathies were with the young. In 1839 he had said that the youth of Bengal should "organize themselves into a compact band of patriots for the assertion or preservation of their political rights."[16] Now he took up their favorite cause, government employment, in a strong letter to his new friend, Lord Brougham. He wrote the "Great Schoolmaster" asking him to press Lord Ellenborough to cooperate more fully with the Bengal Council of Education. Dwarkanath pointed out that as a result of the support given English education by Bentinck and Auckland the schools of Bengal had already "sent into the company's service some of the most efficient subordinate agents in the administration of the civil affairs of the country, and it is to the subordinate service that we must continue to look for the very best instruments the government can employ to carry out its purposes."[17] Lord Brougham did as Dwarkanath asked and wrote Lord Ellenborough urging him to support English education. But the plea was rejected. The governor-general, soon to be recalled for his autocratic behavior, replied that English education for the lower classes—meaning the Bengali bhadralok—had been a mistake. He would rather creat a college for the nobility and a noble honor guard for the sons of native rulers.[18]

One result of the new "radical" politics was to induce the British to close ranks and to "rally round a government so ungenerously, so unjustly assailed."[19] From that position it was only a short step to the dissolution of the fragile interracial alliance forged by Dwarkanath in the 1830s. Dwarkanath found himself looked upon as a collaborator by some of the very "radicals" he helped spawn. Among a series of letters-to-the-editor written under such pseudonyms as "Mookerjee Baboo" and "Old Hindoo," was one directed against Dwarkanath for his Mansion House speech.

"Dwarkanath Tagore," the letter charged, "betrays the heartless

15[Hume,] *Letters to Friends at Home . . . June 1842 to May 1843,* p. 181; *Bengal Hurkaru,* 9 Feb. 1843.

16Quoted in N.K. Sinha, ed., *History of Bengal (1757–1905),* (Calcutta: 1967), p. 170.

17Brougham Papers, Dwarkanath Tagore to Lord Brougham, April 1843.

18Ibid., Ellenborough to Brougham, 18 July 1843.

19*Friend of India,* 13 Apr. 1843.

sycophant who has no principles to guide him and who has no honour to call up a blush." His reference to "English generosity, disinterestedness and urbanity" was so much "twaddle." Our rulers "hold our religion in contempt . . . mock our manners, laugh at the customs which ages have rendered permanent and honourable . . . grind us down to . . . slavery," and "every situation which might have attached to it something like respectibility is given away . . ᴜuropeans, although the natives of the soil are fully capable of conducting it as well or better." In Britain, Dwarkanath had an unequaled opportunity to "represent to her Majesty the deplorable state in which his countrymen are placed . . . . But it appears that it would be too much to expect such patriotism at the hands of a Baboo . . . . If he has not the heart to be manly, he ought at least to practice the negative virtue of silence." [20]

In the midst of the newly charged political atmosphere the gold medal awarded to Dwarkanath by the East India Company arrived in Calcutta. When, at a public ceremony on 10 May 1843, William Wilberforce Bird, the deputy governor, presented the medal to Dwarkanath, he took the opportunity to "exhort my Native Friends who are looking for high situation to profit by [Dwarkanath's] example, to display in the first instance the same zeal, ability, energy, and perseverance . . . and then they may rest assured that they will not fail in obtaining such advancement and such rewards as may be justly due to their merits and services." Dwarkanath, too, used the occasion for some political remarks, though they were too subtle to be grasped by the press. When abroad he had seen evidence "of a deep and growing anxiety to make that union [of Britain and India] subservient to the highest and best interests of my fellow countrymen." He considered the prize "less a compliment to myself, than . . . a pledge conveyed through me to the Natives of India, that their happiness and elevation are objects dear to their rulers." [21] Bird interpreted the gold medal as a reward for past service; Dwarkanath construed it as a pledge for the future and turned it into a solemn promise by the British government for the future advancement of the people of India.

Dwarkanath's political views, delicately balanced between collaboration with Britain and devotion to India, were so misunderstood that it was even suggested that his family had planned to excommu-

20 Reprinted in *Bengal Hurkaru*, 28 Sept. 1842.
21 Reprinted from *Calcutta Star* of 11 May 1843 in *Friend of India*, 18 May 1843.

nicate him for political reasons. A letter to the *Friend of India*, supposedly written by Hara Kumar Tagore, head of the Pathuria-ghatta family, described a meeting of the Tagore paribar at which it had been decided to excommunicate Dwarkanath because of his addresses to the Court of Directors and the Lord Mayor of London. According to the letter, his statements had been humiliating to his countrymen and detrimental to their political welfare. [22] A few days later, Upendra Mohun Tagore, who had been present at the meeting, wrote that the Hara Kumar letter was a forgery. Hara Kumar and a few other members of the family had, indeed, suggested that Dwarkanath be excommunicated. But his offense had been to cross the oceans and dine with Europeans. At the family meeting, where the majority opposed excommunication, political issues never arose. "I wish that there were such political sectarian feeling in India," wrote the young Upendra Mohun, "but alas! there has not been an instance witnessed in our shores wherein religious or social excommunication has taken place for the maintenance and change of *political opinion.*" [23]

Among the conservative Bengalis, Dwarkanath's social behavior came in for stronger criticism than did his politics. Some of the popular Bengali verses circulating in this period indicate the grounds for disapproval. Most of them referred to the wine imported by Carr, Tagore and Company and imbibed by a section of the westernized Bengalis. "What do we know of the quality of wine? Tagore Company knows. Every Saturday comes the cart with brandy and champagne." Or, "Blessed Calcutta; blessed Saturday. What beauty is there in holding the bottle." Others referred to sexual affairs: "The flag flies over the red-light district. With great celebration the hemp burns. Drunk in Mechuabazar having great fun," and "Drinking sherry and champagne, eating ham and beef. If my wife leaves me, I shall take a pretty damsel on my lap, smoke two cigars and darken

22*Bengal Hurkaru,* 21 Mar. 1843.

23Ibid., 23 Mar. 1843. Another item of unfinished business from his first trip to Europe caused the government some anxiety. Dwarkanath had assumed that the full-length royal portraits promised him by the Queen were meant for him personally. But they were painted at public expense and Peel asked Lord Hardinge to intervene with Dwarkanath and obtain his acknowledgement that they were to be placed in a public place in Calcutta. The Queen mollified Dwarkanath by sending him a miniature portrait for his personal use. BM, Peel Papers, *Additional Manuscripts* 40540 and 40474; Rabindra Sadana, "Our Family Correspondence," Murray to Dwarkanath Tagore, 3 Aug. 1844.

the room with smoke." Another: "Come dear, my dear, open the door. Thus saying, make a clamor in the whore-house."[24]

Dwarkanath's private life was a favorite subject for the scandal-mongers. Rajaram Roy, the foster son of Rammohun, could not resist including some gossip about Tagore in a letter to Janet, the daughter of David Hare. Dwarkanath's "money and influence," he wrote, "secures any lady almost he likes." He told the story of a ship captain who had married the beautiful sixteen-year-old daughter of the actress Esther Leach and had asked the owners' permission to take his new bride aboard. Dwarkanath, posing as a friend of the captain, promised he would intervene and speak to the owners on the captain's behalf; but, instead, he recommended that the ladies be required to stay ashore. He then offered to take care of both the young wife and her mother while the captain was at sea. "Dwarkanath Tagore is taking care of the late Mrs. Leach and the Captain's wife with vengeance; he has the lady brought to his house every night. This is not the first instance."[25]

Whatever the truth of this sordid affair, Dwarkanath made no attempt to conceal his liaisons. Perhaps, unconsciously, he meant to convey to the British that "partnership" must embrace all aspects of British-Indian relationships. The kind of comfortable friendships he had with European women—and with European men, for that matter—would be unthinkable in the late nineteenth century. An example was his relationship with Miss Charlotte E. Harvey. In 1837 he loaned her and Signor Pizzoni of the Italian Opera Company some money, and she in turn offered Dwarkanath singing lessons. Inviting him to her forthcoming wedding, she wrote, "I trust, however, to be able to dine with you once before I am married," and signed the letter, "Believe me always and ever to be your sincere and I dare say not further."[26] Dwarkanath kept company in England with Mrs. Caroline Norton, a minor Victorian poetess of beauty and wit, separated from her husband and the object of "whispered scandals." Mrs. Norton joined Dwarkanath in hosting a riverboat party for literary celebrities, and, in a letter inviting Charles Dickens

24 Bengal popular verses are found in KNT Collection. The author is grateful for the help of Samaren Roy in translating them.

25 Letter from Rajaram Roy to Janet Hare, 6 June 1844, in "120 Years Ago—Janet Hare with Raja Rai," *Behala,* Autumn Number, 1371 (1964), pp. 24 ff.

26 Charlotte E. Harvey to Dwarkanath Tagore, 25 Oct. 1837, in "Our Family Correspondence," Tagore Family Archives, Rabindra Sadana.

and his wife, alluded to their combined venture: "We have a little steamer of our own to go down the river." [27]

The natural companionship that characterized Dwarkanath's relations with European women would have been impossible with Bengali women of his own class. His family life was marred by the insularity and piety of his wife, Digambari Devi, and the other women of the Jorasanko household. After he had begun to dine with European guests at Belgatchia, the women of his family refused to sit with him, and if he inadvertently touched one of them they would feel obliged to purify themselves. He had built a biathak khana, a sitting room to receive guests, in the courtyard at Jorasanko. After he returned from Europe and refused to undergo the purification ritual, the women exiled him and his nephew, Chandra Mohun Chatterjee, from the main house, and the baithak khana became their residence. [28]

Such experiences turned him into a strong advocate of female education. He once wrote the Catholic Archbishop of Calcutta applauding his efforts in the education of female children and lamenting the lack of cooperation among the Indians. [29] Some years after his death, an Englishwoman, reminiscing about Dwarkanath, recalled his words to her on female education: "The day is far distant for this happiness to be conferred on my countrywomen. I would give something to see that man, among the Hindoos, who will have the courage to bring forward his wives and daughters to be instructed upon European principles of education." [30] Unfortunately, his own daughter died in infancy, and his words were never put to a test.

After the death of his wife in 1839, Dwarkanath paid little attention to the women of Jorasanko. Within his family the person who caused him the most anxiety and pain was his eldest son, Debendranath. Debendranath wrote in his autobiography that he spent his youth "plunged in a life of luxury and pleasure" [31] —the conventional "evil youth" to which every saint confesses. It is more likely that Dwarkanath, early on, saw in his son signs of the

27 Amalendu Bose, "A Note on Dwarkanath Tagore," *Visvabharati Quarterly,* vol. 31, no. 3 (1965–66), pp. 222 ff.

28 Satischandra Chakravarty, ed., *Srimanmaharshi Devendranath Thakurer Atmajibani* (Calcutta: 1927), notes, pp. 310–12, 349–51.

29 K.C. Mittra, *Memoir of Dwarkanath Tagore* (Calcutta: 1870), p. 70.

30 *Bengal Hurkaru,* 8 June 1850.

31 Satyendranath Tagore and Indira Devi, trans., *The Autobiography of Maharshi Devendranath Tagore* (Calcutta: 1909), p. 3.

intellectual power and strength of character of Debendranath's later years. Far more so than his father, Debendranath exhibited those characteristics associated with the "capitalist spirit": asceticism, the work ethic, high standards for himself and others, orderliness, scrupulous attention to detail, and a faith in the mastery of reason over nature. His own son, Rabindranath, noted these characteristics in Debendranath many years later. "My father was very particular in all his arrangements and orderings. He disliked leaving things vague or undetermined and never allowed slovenliness or make-shifts. . . . It was not so much the little less or more that he objected to, as the failure to be up to the standard." [32]

Rabindranath described how his father "had an extraordinary memory" and "the habit of keeping everything clearly before his mind, — whether figures of accounts, or ceremonial arrangements, or additions or alterations to property."[33] When Rabindranath was twelve years old Debendranath took him on a pilgrimage to the Himalyas and indoctrinated him with a large dosage of the "Protestant ethic." "To train me to a sense of responsibility . . . father placed a little small change in my charge and required me to keep an account of it."[34] "After ten o'clock came the bath in icy-cold water. . . . To give me courage my father would tell of the unbearably freezing baths he had himself been through in his younger days."[35] Debendranath himself wrote of a temple priest at Benares who asked him for money and, in a most un-Indian fashion, was told, "I shan't give you money . . . you are able to work, and earn your bread."[36]

Debendranath was engaged throughout his youth in an inner struggle to free himself from becoming enmeshed in "the world." One can imagine the boy growing up in the women's apartments of Jorasanko under the Vaisnavite influence of Aloka Sundari where the values of asceticism, simplicity, and *bhakti* prevailed. One can also image an undercurrent of whispers disapproving of Dwarkanath and his glittering, sensual life. "In the formation of his early religious impressions he was influenced not so . much by the broad and reformed views of his father as by the nursery tales and traditions

32 Rabindranath Tagore, *Reminiscences* (London: 1954), p. 78.
33 Ibid., p. 85.
34 Ibid., p. 84.
35 Ibid., p. 95.
36 *Autobiography of Maharshi Devendranath Tagore*, p. 108.

held sacred by the old ladies presiding over his father's house." [37]
Among the other formative influences was Rammohun Roy, at whose
Anglo-Hindu School Debendranath began his education; and Hindu College, where Debendranath continued his studies and learned
to respect the power of reason over superstition and the blind forces
of nature.

Debendranath records in his autobiography the final outcome of
his inner struggle—a belief in the unity of God and in the separation
of God and nature. God, he concluded, was a simple, rational,
unadorned spirit that imbued the world with intelligence and
meaning. Conversely, he developed a strong abhorrence for monism,
idolatry, and worldly goods. [38] Of all his struggles, that against wealth
was his most difficult. It was the subject of his first religious
experience, at the deathbed of his grandmother, where, after
experiencing "a strange sense of the unreality of all things . . . a
strong aversion to wealth arose within me." [39] Later, searching for a
supreme authority to support his views, he found it in his own Hindu
tradition when the torn page of a book containing a Sanskrit *sloka*
mysteriously fluttered into his hand. When translated it told him to
"preserve thyself from self-sufficiency, and entertain not a covetous
regard for property belonging to any individual." [40] Significantly,
Debendranath had to wait until he had finished his day's work at the
Union Bank before he could return home and translate the verse. [41]

After his grandmother's death, Debendranath spent all his spare
time studying the Upanishads and, joined by his brothers, began to
hold religious meetings. He refused to perform puja to the family
idols, and during such ceremonies he and his brothers would remain
standing in the rear of the room. He employed a pundit, Ramchan-
dra Vidyabagish, to instruct him in Sanskrit. "One day," he wrote in
his autobiography, "being annoyed with Vidyavagish [Dwarkanath]
had remarked, 'I always thought Vidyavagish was a good fellow, but
now I find he is spoiling Devendra with his preaching of *Brahma-
mantras*. As it is he has very little head for business; now he neglects

---

37 Pandit Sivanath Sastri, *Ramtanu Lahiri, Brahman and Reformer* (Roper Lethbridge,
ed.), (London: 1907), p. 201.

38 *Autobiography of Devendranath Tagore*, pp. 9–10, 24.

39 Ibid., p. 3.

40 Rammohun Roy's translation of the *Isa Upanishad* in Kalidas Nag and
Debajyoti Burman, eds., *The English Works of Raja Rammohun Roy*, pt. II (Calcutta:
1946), p. 53.

41 *Autobiography of Devendranath Tagore*, pp. 14–15.

business altogether; it is nothing but Brahma, Brahma the whole day.'"42

The conflict between family responsibility and religious conviction reached a climax in 1846. While Dwarkanath was in England "the task of managing his various affairs devolved upon me. But I was not able to attend to any business matters properly. My subordinates used to do all the work, I was only concerned with the Vedas, the Vedanta, religion, God, and the ultimate goal of life. . . . My spirit of renunciation became deeper under all this stress of work. I felt no inclination to become the owner of all this wealth. To renounce everything and wander about alone, this was the desire that reigned in my heart."43 He did go off on a boat trip up the Ganges, but not alone. His wife and children insisted on joining him; furthermore, a storm broke out, and, at the very moment his father was dying in London, Debendranath nearly drowned in the river.44 He returned to Calcutta to even greater burdens. "I had lost my father, then the whole day there was the worry and trouble of social duties and over and above that there was this spiritual struggle going on within me. Which would triumph, the world or religion?—one could not tell—this was what worried me."45 He was reassured when one night his dead mother appeared to him in a dream and asked him, "Hast thou really become a *brahmagnani* (one who knows Brahma)? *Kulam pavitram janani kritartha* (Sanctified is the family, fulfilled is the mother's desire.)"46

Even so, Debendranath was not free until Carr, Tagore and Company went bankrupt and closed its doors. "Things turned out just as I wanted —all our property went out of my hands. . . . What I had prayed for was now granted and realized. . . . As the moon is freed from *Rahu,* so did my soul become free from the things of the world, and feel the heaven of Brahman."47 Some twenty-five years later, however, there were still signs of ambivalence. On the journey with Rabindranath to the Himalayas, Debendranath brought along a child's life of Benjamin Franklin to read his son. "But," wrote the son, "he found out his mistake soon after we began it. Benjamin Franklin was much too business-like a person. The narrowness of his

42 Ibid., p. 25.
43 Ibid., p. 41.
44 Ibid., pp. 43–44.
45 Ibid., p. 48.
46 Ibid., p. 49.
47 Ibid., p. 65.

calculated morality disgusted my father. In some cases he would get so impatient at the worldly prudence of Franklin that he could not help using strong words of denunciation."[48]

Debendranath dedicated his considerable organizing skills to the revitalization of Hinduism. In 1839 he gathered a few friends together and formed the Tatwabodhini Sabha, whose object was to glean support for theistic principles from the Upanishads and *shastras.*[49] By energetic recruiting he built up the membership of the Tatwabodhini Sabha to 800 within a few years,[50] and, in addition, founded a newspaper, the *Tatwabodhini Patrika,* as a vehicle for his views. In 1842, he gathered his most devoted followers and with them joined the moribund Brahmo Samaj. As its leader, Debendranath brought the organization back to life, regularized its ceremonies and rules, and set its finances in order. A few years later he became alarmed at the number of Hindus being converted by the Reverend Alexander Duff of the Scottish Church Mission. Debendranath enlisted the cooperation of all sections of Hindu society, from orthodox Hindus to Brahmos, and established a system of primary free schools where children could study western subjects without the intrusion of Christian doctrine.[51] He was a prime mover, in the 1850s, in the formation of the British Indian Association, a precursor of the Indian National Congress.[52] Finally, he managed the zamindaris left him by Dwarkanath with such care and efficiency that he was able to support his large family in comfort and pass on to his descendants estates worth many times what they had been when he inherited them.[53]

Debendranath's life's work was in most respects the very antithesis of that of his father. His world was the world of pundits and Sanskrit texts, of holy places and silent retreats. For him, the West held no attraction at all and Europeans hardly existed. Even his modernist organizational activities were directed, not toward social reform as valued by the West, but toward revitalizing the inner life of the

48 Rabindranath Tagore, *Reminiscences,* p. 90.

49 *Autobiography of Devendranath Tagore,* pp. 16 ff.

50 Dilip Kumar Biswas, "Maharshi Debendranath Tagore and the Tattvabodhini Sabha," in Atulchandra Gupta, *Studies in the Bengal Renaissance* (Jadavpur: 1958), p. 35.

51 *Autobiography of Devendranath Tagore,* p. 39.

52 B.B. Majumdar, *Indian Political Associations and Reform of Legislature (1818–1917)* (Calcutta: 1965), pp. 35–37.

53 Ex parte Hitendranath Tagore, Opinion of B.M. Chakravarty, 23/4/07 in KNT Collection.

Hindu. He rejected, from the deepest recesses of his soul, any partnership with the West or the Europeans—rejected literally the partnership of Carr, Tagore and Company and figuratively partnership in the British Empire.

Yet the means for Debendranath's work, both material and moral, were provided by Dwarkanath. After the departure of Rammohun Roy, the Brahmo Samaj had languished for want of leadership. At the time, no one had the will, the resources, and the courage to defy all of Hindu society and lead the iconoclastic sect. When Debendranath was ready, he had these resources; for in spite of his glorification of poverty, his father's wealth made him independent and financially secure. Nor did he fear social ostracism; he followed his father's example of complete disdain for the petty orthodoxies and social snobberies of Bengali society. It was Dwarkanath who kept alive Rammohun's social dissent and fearless nonconformity and passed on these attitudes to his son.

In 1843 Dwarkanath may still have harbored a dim hope that his eldest son would in time follow him in the firm. His new will, signed on 16 August 1843, provided that if Debendranath so wished he could, after Dwarkanath's death, take up his father's shares in Carr, Tagore and Company. If he did not, then Girindranath was to have the same opportunity, and, on his refusal, Nagendranath. Lacking faith in the business acumen of his sons, however, Dwarkanath reaffirmed the provision made in his trust deed of 20 August 1840, that the four "ancestral" zamindari estates be held in trust for his sons. As Debendranath wrote, "his keen intelligence made it clear to him that should the management of these extensive affairs devolve upon us in the future, we would not be able to cope with them." [54]

Aside from caring for his sons, Dwarkanath's will also indicated a concern for the future of Carr, Tagore and Company. If, instead of joining the firm, his sons wished to withdraw the one million rupees Dwarkanath had lent Carr, Tagore and Company, they could do so at a rate of no more than Rs. 2,00,000 per year, and with due regard "to the commercial safety and credit of the firm." Its other provisions included providing each of his sons an inalienable share of Jorasanko. He generously provided incomes for the other members of the Jorasanko family and earmarked Rs. 1,00,000 for charity. As trustees

---

[54]*Autobiography of Devendranath Tagore*, p. 52. Actually, two of the estates were ancestral and two had been acquired by Dwarkanath.

and executors of his will Dwarkanath appointed D.M. Gordon, Prasanna Kumar Tagore, and his three sons.[55]

Soon after he had filed his will, Dwarkanath left for a trip into the mufassal to recoup his failing health. He traveled by steamboat to Allahabad and from there by dak to Agra and Delhi. Everywhere along the journey, which lasted six months, he was treated as a visiting dignitary.[56] The journey not only improved his health but also set in motion the formation of a new joint-stock venture, the India General Steam Navigation Company. Since 1834 the government had been operating a regular steamboat service between Calcutta and Allahabad under the direction of Captain James H. Johnston, controller of government steam vessels. By 1840 there were nine government steamboats in operation, four of them on the Ganges.[57] Dwarkanath found that each time he had traveled on the Ganges, the government steamboat service had deteriorated further; and the planters, merchants, and officials he met on the way urged him to establish a private steamboat service.[58]

Though there had been moves since 1837 by London business groups, as well as by the Calcutta Steam Tug Association, to promote a river-steamboat company, no one took action until January 1844 when Dwarkanath returned from his mufassal journey. He first discussed his idea of forming a steamboat company with Captain Johnston and with Rowland M. Stephenson, editor of the *Englishman*, a zealous railway enthusiast; then he took up the matter with the directors of the Calcutta Steam Tug Association.[59]

The directors moved quickly, and at the next meeting of the Steam Tug Association, on 26 January 1844, presented the shareholders with a prospectus for the "India General Steam Navigation Company." They proposed that the new company be grafted on to the Steam Tug Association and that the old company drop its name and adopt the new designation. Subscribers to the India General were to raise a capital of Rs. 20,00,000, divided into 2,000 shares of Rs. 1,000 each, and would receive dividends from the operation of the Steam Tug Association until their own boats arrived from England. A meeting of all interested was called for February 6.[60]

55 Will of Dwarkanath Tagore in KNT Collection.
56 *Bengal Herald,* 5 Aug. and 16 Dec. 1843.
57 Henry T. Bernstein, *Steamboats on the Ganges* (Bombay: 1960), pp. 82–83.
58 *Bengal Hurkaru,* 10 May 1844.
59 Ibid.
60 *Bengal Hurkaru,* 2 Feb. 1844.

The next six months witnessed an all-out struggle by a group of independent shareholders to keep the new company out of the hands of Carr, Tagore and Company and its friends. The battle began over the proposal of union with the Tug Association, continued over the constituency of the India General's board of directors, and culminated in a battle over the selection of a managing director. Carr, Tagore and Company lost the first round. At the February 6 meeting, Dwarkanath himself was challenged by a dissident shareholder who objected to union with the Steam Tug Association. Dwarkanath pointed out that this meeting had not been called to make any final decision, but to select a committee that would make a recommendation. [61]

The committee was stacked in favor of the Steam Tug Association and ordinarily would have recommended union, but was obliged to report against it. It reported on February 20 that, because of legal technicalities, junction was impossible at present, that the India General Steam Navigation Company should be established as a separate company for the present, but that at some future time union might be possible and desirable. The committee also reported a favorable interview with the deputy governor of Bengal at which the governor agreed to cooperate with the new company and, when its boats were in operation, to withdraw all government boats from competition except those necessary for military purposes. In addition, the governor would not oppose recommending that the company receive a charter of limited liability. [62]

Though Tagore's group lost the first round, they won the second. The provisional board of directors of the new company were almost all friendly to Carr, Tagore and Company. [63] Rowland Macdonald Stephenson was elected provisional managing director and A.G. Mackenzie of Carr, Tagore and Company, provisional secretary. James Hume, editor of the *Calcutta Star,* noted that two Calcutta editors—Samuel Smith of the *Bengal Hurkaru* and R.M. Stephenson of the *Englishman*—were directors. [64] Hume had always been a

61 Ibid., 7 Feb. 1844.

62 Ibid., 21 Feb. 1844.

63 Ibid. The Provisional Board of Directors consisted of A.J. de H. Larpent, chairman; Samuel Smith, vice-chairman; John Allen; Radhamadub Bannerjee; J. Deans Campbell; Rustomjee Cowasjee; Alexander Rogers; John Storm; and A. Thompson.

64 [James Hume,]*Letters to Friends at Home, by an Idler from June 1843 to May 1844* (Calcutta: 1844), pp. 180–81.

watchful critic of joint-stock-company management in the city; now, excluded from the board of directors, he wholeheartedly leapt into the battle. The other neglected newspaper, the *Friend of India,* applauded the selection of Stephenson, but considered that of Mackenzie "unfortunate." The misfortunes of so many promising speculations "in the City of Palaces," wrote the editor, "renders us peculiarly anxious that this noble undertaking . . . should steer clear of the Scylia and Charybdis on which so many useful enterprises have been wrecked." [65]

On May 8 the provisional directors supported the recommendation of the old committee that any idea of union with the Tug Association be abandoned. Dwarkanath was not pleased, and his speech showed how sensitive he had become to accusations of "jobbery" and allusions to the monopolistic domination of his firm. He denied that there had been anything sinister behind the pressure for such a union and said that, while others had only talked, the Steam Tug Association had acted and seriously taken up the Ganges project. He reminded his listeners that the Steam Tug Association was a successful company whose stock had grown since 1836 from almost nothing to a value of nine lakhs. Nevertheless, if the majority were opposed to union with such a successful company, he would go along with them. Hume, sensing he had gone too far in antagonizing Dwarkanath Tagore, placed in nomination a slate for the permanent board of directors that once again consisted of Tagore's friends. Dwarkanath, now pacified, made his own gesture of goodwill. By suggesting that the new company would benefit from the mistakes of some of the older joint-stock companies and beware of "incurring expenses in the dark," Dwarkanath intimated that the opposition had been somewhat justified. [66] The directors elected were John Storm, chairman; Samuel Smith, vice-chairman; D.M. Gordon; R.C. Jenkins; John Lyall; and Alexander Rogers. [67] The second round had ended with a board of directors partial to Carr, Tagore and Company.

On a motion by James Hume, the two executive posts of managing director and secretary were to be advertised. R.M. Stephenson was one of three candidates nominated for managing director. Five lesser candidates applied for secretary, and one candidate offered himself in

65*Friend of India,* 4 Apr. 1844, reprinted in *Bengal Hurkaru,* 5 Apr. 1844.
66*Bengal Hurkaru,* 10 May 1844.
67Ibid., 18 May 1844.

nomination for the combined position—A.G. Mackenzie.[68]

On the eve of the election meeting of July 22 an anonymous letter appeared in the *Bengal Hurkaru:* "Rumours are afloat of a Coal Coalition having been got up, by means of which certain parties, whose plans were considerably disarrayed some months back, still hope to exercise a strong influence in the management and direction of the Inland Steam Company [*sic*] as well as in the affairs of the new Steam Tug Companies."[69] At the meeting, Hume led the attack on the "Coal Coalition." He first tried to get the deed of settlement changed because under it, not the managing director, but the board of directors were accountable to the shareholders for losses that might occur. Dwarkanath and his attorney friend, William Theobold, defended the deed and defeated Hume's attempt. J.P. McKilligan of Colvin, Gilmore and Company then moved that the positions of managing director and secretary be combined and carry a salary of Rs. 600 per month. The inclusion of this salary figure was crucial because the independent candidate, R.M. Stephenson, had said the job called for a salary of Rs. 2,000.[70] Hume struggled against McKilligan's motion by calling for a board of three managing directors, but again lost. McKilligan's motion won, and with Stephenson out of the race, Mackenzie received a large majority of the votes, especially from absentee voters in the mufassal.[71]

Carr, Tagore and Company had won the third round and placed their man, A.G. Mackenzie, in the management of the India General Steam Navigation Company. Mackenzie resigned his post as manager of the Steam Tug Association, but proceeded to direct the affairs of the new company as if it were an adjunct of the old. During the next six months the directors ordered two steamboats and flats from Maudslay and Company, London. While waiting their arrival, the new company purchased the steamer *Assam* and the flat *Naga* from the Assam Company for Rs. 70,000 and an old East India Company steamer, the *Auckland,* for Rs. 25,000. These proved poor bargains—the *Naga* was sold off, the *Assam* required extensive repairs, and the *Auckland* was converted into a flat. When the steamers arrived from England, Mackenzie leased the Kidderpore Dockyard from Carr, Tagore and Company for five years at Rs. 150 per month.[72]

68 Ibid., 27 June 1844.
69 Ibid., 22 July 1844.
70 Ibid., 10 May 1844.
71 Ibid., 24 July 1844.
72 The yard had passed to William Prinsep from his brother, James Prinsep.

Finally, the I.G.S.N. Company purchased from the Steam Tug Association the machinery and plant at the dockyard for Rs. 58,000 and agreed to repair all the Tug Association boats in the future.[73] A few years later, the *Bengal Hurkaru*, discussing the desperate financial condition of the company, traced "the first cause of this unfortunate result to a large portion of the Company's money, instead of being employed in building boats and thus creating paying and useful stock; having been sunk in the expensive dead block of a work shop at Garden Reach big enough for a little navy."[74] Mackenzie had so thoroughly subordinated the new company to the interests of Carr, Tagore and Company that even at the end of the nineteenth century "all natives refer to the India General as 'Carr Company,' and letters are repeatedly addressed 'Marine Superintendent, Carr Company,' to the great mystification of the postal authorities."[75]

When the boats from London arrived, they proved unmanageable and too weak for service on the Ganges. The London committee that had been set up to arrange for their construction had changed the original design and "in the teeth of distinct orders" had built them on specifications much different from those sent out. By the end of 1847 the company had lost two lakhs, and against Rs. 40,113 in cash had Rs. 1,12,562 in liabilities.[76] At the meetings of 19 June and 19 July 1847, James Hume renewed his attack on Mackenzie. The managing director was accused of subordinating the interests of the India General to the Steam Tug Association, paying too much for purchases from the association and not getting paid for tugboat repairs, as well as for questionable expenditures on masonry, coal, timber, and stores, for presenting unaudited accounts, and for "mysterious outlays" which were not explained. Hume was joined by the attorneys J.S. Judge and William Theobald, both of whom had once supported Mackenzie. Mackenzie's only defenders were the diehard coal-company interests—D.M. Gordon, W.F. Fergusson and Longueville Clarke.[77] By the meeting of September 8 Hume had rallied his forces and was able to rout the "coal coalition" He directed his fire at the real target—Carr, Tagore and Company. "Was there anything so very startling in such a complaint of bad

73 Alfred Brame, *The India General Steam Navigation Company, Ltd.* (London: 1900), pp. 15 ff.
74 *Bengal Hurkaru*, 3 May 1847.
75 Brame, *The India General*, p. 17.
76 *Bengal Hurkaru*, 3 May 1847.
77 Ibid., 20 June and 21 July 1847.

management? Was the ruin of a company by mismanagement a thing unheard of in Calcutta? Need he mention the Salt Company, the Ferry Bridge Company, whose capitals had been all swept away?" [78]

The old directors were voted out and James Hume became chairman of the board of directors, with Captain J. Engledue, the P. & O. Company superintendent, as vice-chairman. Though the company worked at a loss for the next few years, Hume was able to put it on a solid financial basis by the time he resigned in July 1851. Mackenzie, who had leased the yard in his own name rather than that of the company's, had to be removed by litigation. When Gordon, Stuart and Company tried to regain control by appealing to the London shareholders, Hume abolished absentee voting rights and disbanded the London board. [79] In the long run, the India General, like the Bengal Coal Company and the Assam Tea Company, proved to be one of Dwarkanath Tagore's more successful ventures and still survives under a successor company. But the pattern of its early years is familiar: an enterprise well-conceived, vigorously promoted, and then mismanaged. "No concern ever commenced operation under more promising auspices than did this company," wrote the *Bengal Hurkaru*, "and we regret to say that no undertaking could well have disappointed public expectations more thoroughly." [80]

Dwarkanath Tagore's last business venture was a railway company, the Great Western of Bengal. He died just as railway promotion was getting underway; he was permitted a brief glance of the railway age, the promised land of capitalist expansion in India, but was prevented from entering it. The Great Western of Bengal was established in competition with the East India Railway Company promoted by Rowland Macdonald Stephenson. After his failure to win the post of managing director of the India General, Stephenson returned to England and published a pamphlet in which he extolled the opportunities for railway building in India and concluded with a proposal for the East India Railway Company. He had been interested in railway promotion even before coming to Calcutta, had purchased the *Englishman* to publicize his views, and had spent his time in Calcutta collecting data on the costs, engineering problems, and strength of support for railways in the local business community.

78 Ibid., 10 Sept. 1847.
79 Brame, *The India General*, pp. 16–36.
80 *Bengal Hurkaru*, 3 May 1847.

The line he proposed would travel from Howrah through the coal fields of Burdwan and, in its first stage, terminate at Mirzapur near Benares.[81]

One of the businessmen most enthusiastic about a line to Burdwan was Dwarkanath Tagore. He was reported to have been "very desirous to have a railway to the collieries and would raise one-third of the capital for this portion of the line, if undertaken immediately."[82] It is surprising then, that Dwarkanath did not endorse Stephenson's East India Railway Company, but joined a group to promote a rival company. The Great Western of Bengal proposed a line from Calcutta northward directly to the Ganges, with its terminus at Rajmahal, the port of the India General Steam Navigation Company. Presumably an east-west spur would connect it with the Burdwan coal fields. A far less bold undertaking than its rival, the Great Western of Bengal was designed to make use of existing transport facilities on the Ganges. Both companies were launched from London in the spring of 1844.

Stephenson's major rival for investment capital in the London money market was the Bombay Great Eastern Railway, a locally promoted and managed company.[83] To discredit the Bombay undertaking, Stephenson cited his experience with locally managed joint-stock enterprises in Calcutta. He had, he wrote, inquired at length into "the causes which had led to the comparative failure of so many of the speculations which for several years past have been brought forward in Calcutta," and concluded that "the single evil to which to attribute the want of success . . . is mismanagement." Therefore, "no undertaking of magnitude in which other than local capital is invested should ever be embarked in, of which the sole and irresponsible control is placed under Calcutta management." He blamed the failures not on "willfull or intentional malpractices" but on lack of "personal attention" given their management by the busy merchants of India. To avoid failure in the future he recommended that "the chief management of such important undertakings . . . be retained in England."[84] Even James Hume, his old supporter, could not go that far and noted sarcastically that Stephenson "recommends

---

81 Daniel Thorner, *Investment in Empire* (Philadelphia: 1950), pp. 44 ff.

82 Rowland M. Stephenson, *Report upon the Practicability and Advantages of the Introduction of Railways into British India* (London: 1844), p. 48.

83 Thorner, *Investment in Empire*, p. 53.

84 Stephenson, *Report*, pp. 8–10.

that all power should be lodged at home—where no companies were ever mismanaged and where bubbles are unknown."[85]

Though the Great Western of Bengal was also to be managed from London, its strong Calcutta committee guaranteed a local voice in policy decisions. Whereas the London board of the East India Railway Company consisted of "eight of the most prominent East India houses trading with Calcutta, Bombay and Madras" as well as P. & O. and London banking interests,[86] that of the Great Western of Bengal included former Indian officials, such as H.T. Prinsep; General McLeod, chief engineer of Bengal; H.B. Henderson of Carr, Tagore and Company; and W.P. Andrew, a former Indian postmaster who would one day become the foremost railway promoter of India and the Near East. Its Calcutta committee consisted of representatives from the leading local houses and included four wealthy Indians, Ramrutton Roy, Nursingchundra Roy, Brijonauth Dhur, and Rustomjee Cowasjee. The Calcutta agent for the sale of shares and for negotiations with government was Carr, Tagore and Company.[87] Those who sponsored the East India Railway were interested mainly in opening up new markets in northwestern India for the import of British textiles and the export of raw cotton, and their route was, in fact, to be more suited to the coming era of economic and military expansion into the Punjab. The Great Western of Bengal was supported by indigo and sugar planters in northern Bengal and the Ganges valley and those with faith in the future of steamboat traffic.[88] Once again metropolitan interests overcame local ones, and in April 1847 the East India Railway Company with its stronger London committee gained the support of the East India Company and absorbed the Great Western of Bengal.[89] In 1859, the East India Railway, which had opened a line to Raniganj in 1855, built a spur to Rajmahal on the Ganges.

In the meantime Dwarkanath was preparing for his longed-for return to England. It had not been an easy or pleasant two years. His health had troubled him, his eldest son had been a grave disappointment, his sanctimonious relatives had tried to excommunicate him,

85*Calcutta Star,* 12 Mar. 1845.

86Thorner, *Investment in Empire,* pp. 61, 67–68.

87*Bengal Hurkaru,* 6 Apr. 1846.

88Thorner, *Investment in Empire,* p. 79; Stephenson, *Report,* pp. 28–29. Someone referred to the G.W.B. as the "commercial line" and the E.I.R. as the "political line." Thorner, p. 134.

89Thorner, *Investment in Empire,* p. 135.

and young "patriots" had attacked him in the press for his praise of British rule. His system of interracial politics began to erode as the European newspapers assailed the "Chuckerbutties," the fruit of their own Western values, and his first-born had united Brahmos and Hindu conservatives in anti-Christian activities. Finally, there were signs of impending economic troubles. So many of the schemes in which his house had taken part had failed that shareholders had lost confidence in his firm. Whether or not he foresaw that the overexpansion of credit and the overproduction of indigo would soon lead to a devastating commercial crisis, he did feel that it was time for him to contract operations, to liquidate his peripheral assets and consolidate his holdings. But this work had to be left to Debendranath and the partners to execute, for he could no longer bear the heat of Calcutta. Soon after he steamed off for Europe on 8 March, 1845, cracks in the commercial structure began to appear. The problems of the Union Bank, keystone of the city's credit system, suddenly became the center of interest in the business world of Calcutta.

Chapter IX

THE FALL OF THE UNION BANK

1. The Tagore Era

During the period between the commercial crisis of 1830 and that of 1847, Calcutta's largest business institution was the Union Bank. As a joint-stock enterprise with hundreds of shareholders, both European and Indian, the bank reflected the commercial life of the city in all its strengths and weaknesses. The launching of the bank in 1829 had signaled the coming-of-age of the mercantile community. It gave the merchants a mechanism through which they could cooperate to mobilize capital, expand credit, engage in exchange banking, issue banknotes, and influence the production and prices of agricultural commodities. The Union Bank became a symbol of local allegiance, and when it was threatened by attempts from London to establish a rival bank, directors and shareholders rallied to defend their monopoly and preserve local control over banking. Finally, the bank gave European and Indian businessmen equal accommodation, and both races were involved in its direction.

Inevitably, however, the Union Bank labored under the same handicaps as the other commercial institutions of the city. First, almost all its assets eventually were committed to financing the production of a single export commodity—indigo. Second, the government, faithful to the doctrine of laissez faire, denied the bank any official cooperation, regulation, or surveillance. Third, the directors of the bank, like those of other joint-stock companies, were inexperienced and were distracted by the demands of personal business. They left matters in the hands of those willing to devote their time to management, men, unfortunately, of poor judgment and little integrity. As a result the bank failed, the good intentions of the founders were completely frustrated, and the Union Bank, with its vested interest in interracial cooperation, was succeeded in time by banks run exclusively for European needs and actively hostile toward Indian business.[1]

1 Michael Kidron, *Foreign Investments in India* (London: 1965), pp. 9–10.

When Dwarkanath Tagore and the partners of Mackintosh and Company unveiled their project in May 1829, they received the enthusiastic support of the mercantile community.[2] At the time the only existing bank in the city was the semiofficial Bank of Bengal, which was obliged to give priority to government requirements and to invest its funds in government paper. During the 1820s, three private agency-house banks had, to some extent, served as commercial banks; but as their constituents withdrew deposits on the eve of the crisis of 1830–33, there was need for a new source of credit for merchants, independent of both government and any single house. To fill this need, the promoters issued an attractive prospectus calling for a joint-stock bank to be capitalized at fifty lakhs divided into 2,000 shares of Rs. 2,500 each, accounts open to public scrutiny, frequent meetings of shareholders, and a limit on the number of shares any one person could hold. When, on 28 September 1829, twelve of the fifty lakhs had been paid up, the bank opened for business. Advertisements announced that the Union Bank would discount approved acceptances, bills of exchange, and short-term promissory notes and would receive deposits at 4 percent.[3]

As soon as the new bank was launched, it faced its first major crisis. The directors could not bring themselves to refuse credit to the "prince of British merchants," and, though his house was on the brink of failure, had loaned John Palmer and Company six lakhs, one-half of the bank's total resources. When Palmer failed in January 1830, the Union Bank was almost swept under with him. Thereafter, to protect the bank, the secretary, William Carr, adopted the precaution of taking landed property, including indigo factories, as security for the debts of the other agency houses. Although the deed of partnership did not permit loans secured by landed property or indigo factories, when a house in debt to the bank could not meet its obligations, such securities could be sequestered by the bank. When these houses failed, the Union Bank was able to retrieve its losses,[4] but by authorizing the bank to acquire its first indigo properties, Carr had made an ominous decision. During the commercial crisis of 1830–33 the bank paid no dividends, and the original shares, which

2An unprecedented number, 250 persons, attended the second meeting, on June 15. A.C. Das Gupta, ed., *The Days of John Company, Selections from Calcutta Gazette, 1824–1832* (Calcutta: 1959), pp. 383–85.

3*Bengal Hurkaru*, 20, 22 and 27 May, 30 July, and 1, 12 and 14 Oct. 1829.

4Speech by Dwarkanath Tagore, *Bengal Hurkaru*, 23 Jan. 1843.

had sold for Rs. 2,500, could be purchased for half that amount. Beginning in July 1833, however, affairs improved, dividends climbed from 6 percent in 1833 to over 8 percent for most of the period after 1836 and, until the commercial slump of 1842, shares sold at par or above. [5]

From the first, relations between the bank and the government were cool. When the Union Bank appealed for a charter of limited liability, the request was denied on the ground that banking was unregulated by law and if the bank were to fail, depositors and creditors would have no legal recourse for their money. Thus, in the eyes of the law the Union Bank remained a partnership; and, though under the law every shareholder-partner had to be joined in a suit, each and every proprietor was legally liable to the fullest extent of his personal resources for any debts of the bank. [6] In addition, the government refused a request from the directors that the notes of the Union Bank be accepted for the payment of revenue at the Treasury in Calcutta. [7] At first, however, Union Bank notes, amounting to a circulation of 13 lakhs, had been accepted by the Bank of Bengal, whose own note circulation was 120 lakhs. But in 1834, because funds were needed for loans to merchants, the Union Bank withdrew the government paper it had deposited as collateral with the Bank of Bengal and its banknotes were no longer accepted. Thereafter, Union Bank note circulation dropped to between 4 and 7 *lakhs* and its notes were accepted only among a limited circle in Calcutta. [8]

Despite these handicaps, the bank prospered. Toward the end of the decade, however, the directors of the bank, led by Dwarkanath Tagore, made three unwise decisions. The first was to increase the bank's capital sixfold, from Rs. 15,00,000 to Rs. 1,00,00,000. Following this, they decided to enter the exchange business on a large scale. Finally, they committed the bank to provide vast sums of credit to support the production of indigo. The combination of dealing in bills of exchange, which required high liquidity, with sinking large fixed

5 *Bengal Hurkaru,* 20 Oct. 1845.

6 R.S. Rungta, *The Rise of Business Corporations in India, 1851–1900* (Cambridge: 1970), pp. 36 ff.

7 IO, Despatches to India and Bengal, vol. 1, pp. 947–1019; Bengal Territorial Financial Department, 16 Apr. (17) 1834. Letters dated 1831 and 1832.

8 S.P. Symes Scutt, *History of the Bank of Bengal* (Calcutta: 1904), pp. 28, 36. *Bengal Hurkaru,* 16 Jan. 1835. In 1840, the Bank of Bengal offered to lend the Union Bank ten lakhs at 2½ percent if the Union Bank would withdraw all its notes, but negotiations failed. *Bengal Hurkaru,* 18 May 1840.

investments into indigo plantations stretched the resources of the bank to the breaking point.

Apparently Dwarkanath had intended from the first that the Union Bank would move gradually into the exchange business, which was divided at the time between the Calcutta agency houses and the East India Company. Dwarkanath represented those houses, less interested in the bill business than in producing indigo, who would stand to gain from a more competitive bill market. Many of the bank's constituents, however, were from houses whose major business was dealing in bills of exchange. These were opposed to competition from the Union Bank, and Dwarkanath and his friends had to implement their policy by indirection. Instead of proposing that the bank enter the bill business, they called for so large an increase in capital that the bank would have no alternative but to employ its capital in exchange operations. The directors carried through increases in the capital of the bank from 15 to 21.6 lakhs in 1836, to 32 lakhs in 1837, and to 80 in 1838. By 1839 the capital stood at one *crore*. [9]

The increase was justified by an apparent threat of competition from a new joint-stock bank, the Bank of India, promoted in London in 1836. Supporters of the new bank included such leading British merchants as Thomas Baring and G.G. de H. Larpent as well as some of Tagore's old friends, William Little of Rickards, Little and Company, Aeneas Mackintosh, and John Deans Campbell. The promoters were suspected of creating a stalking horse to forestall any serious efforts at imperial banking. [10] Their prospectus called for a bank, capitalized at £5,000,000, to be governed from London, with branches in the three presidency towns. It would absorb the Bank of Bengal, collect the government revenues, issue paper currency, handle all government remittances and, in addition, deal in private exchange and bill discounts. On no account, however, would it give advances for agricultural production. [11] So preposterously ambitious a scheme could not help but arouse united opposition from all the

9 C.N. Cooke, *The Rise, Progress and Present Condition of Banking in India* (Calcutta: 1863), pp. 177 ff.

10 *Bengal Hurkaru*, 11 Nov. 1836, 25 Feb. 1837. John Crawfurd, *A Sketch of the Commercial Resources and Monetary and Mercantile System of British India*, in K.N. Chaudhuri, ed., *The Economic Development of India Under the East India Company, 1814–58* (Cambridge: 1971), pp. 303–304.

11 *Reasons for Establishing a New Bank in India* (London: 1836).

local Calcutta interests—the Government of India, the Bank of Bengal, the Union Bank, the agency houses, and the Calcutta press.

The editor of the *Bengal Hurkaru* pointed out that, contrary to its stated intentions, the Bank of India would not be able, any more than the Union Bank, to avoid investment in agricultural production. Any bill of exchange, if not secured on signature alone, would have to be hypothecated to indigo or another commodity. Hence the only difference between the proposed bank and the Union Bank would be that the former would have a government charter, would have its notes accepted, and would be directed from London. Direction from London, according to the editor, not only would be an insult to the local mercantile community but would handicap its operations. The local businessman knows the value of goods, the prospects for future seasons and the character of applicants for credit far better than could the banker resident in London.[12] Sounding much like an Indian nationalist of fifty years later, the editor wrote that India needed not more imported capital or skill, but the free importation of Indian goods into Britain, an end to the "drain of tribute," an extension of the permanent settlement, the diversion of resources from wars to internal improvements, and the employment of the "native aristocracy" in posts of "honor and emolument."[13] In any event, the Bank of India never got beyond the proposal stage, nor did similar English schemes such as the Bank of Asia, promoted in 1841, or the East India Bank, promoted in 1842.[14]

In 1837 John Crawfurd developed a more serious argument for an imperial bank in his pamphlet, *A Sketch of the Commercial Resources and Monetary and Mercantile System of British India, with suggestions for their improvement, by means of Bank Establishment.* Crawfurd argued for the separation of commerce and indigo production from exchange

12*Bengal Hurkaru,* 11 Apr. 1837.

13Ibid., 17 Apr. 1837.

14Cooke, *Banking in India,* pp. 345–46. In time, imperial banks were established. The Delhi and London Bank was founded in 1844, but developed only after 1847. The first important imperial exchange bank was the Chartered Bank of India, Australia and China, founded in 1853. See Compton Mackenzie, *Realms of Silver* (London: 1954). It was followed by the National Bank of India, 1863; the Hong Kong and Shanghai Banking Corporation, 1864; the Mercantile Bank of India, 1893; and the Eastern Bank, 1910. Cooke, pp. 233–34. Unlike the Union Bank, none of these financed agricultural production, which was done almost exclusively by managing agents and Indian moneylenders after 1847. See J.M. Keynes, *Indian Currency and Finance* (London: 1913), pp. 206 ff; and S.K. Basu, *Industrial Finance in India* (Calcutta: 1961), pp. 99 ff.

operations and called the Calcutta agency houses that tended to monopolize all three "mere jackalls, interposed between English capitalists and Risks," who made speculative, long-term investments with money entrusted to them for remittance home. In England the exchange business was conducted by bill brokers, but in India no such class of men existed; and in order to facilitate and legitimize this highly important business, Crawfurd advocated a new type of bank that would specialize in exchange banking between Britain and India.[15]

With the defeat of the Bank of India proposal and with a crore of rupees at their disposal, the directors of the Union Bank were now ready to propose that the bank enter the exchange business. The debate divided the Calcutta mercantile community along new lines and in the process revealed some of the attitudes toward local investment and imported capital. Essentially, Dwarkanath and his friends agreed with Crawfurd that the exchange business should be conducted by a bank rather than by the agency houses, but wanted the exchange bank to be governed from Calcutta, not from London. In a minute on the subject, dated March 4, 1840, Dwarkanath argued that he had long favored the Union Bank's undertaking the exchange business. Like Crawfurd, he pointed out that London was not really foreign, that it was to Calcutta as Calcutta was to Mirzapur, and that there would be no political uncertainty involved in the transfers. By entering this field, he wrote, the Union Bank would benefit the exporter by checking government rates on advances.[16]

Another supporter of the bill business, the attorney Theodore Dickens, pointed to the abundant capital in Calcutta and argued that if there were "business enough and choice here, do not engage in exchange business with England, but it is precisely because if we do not engage in that business, we shall have other and probably worse business to seek." The bank was embarrassed with money which it could not employ with profit. So long as there was no improvement in the judicial or fiscal administration in the provinces that "would open to the application of our capital the comparatively dormant resources of the interior," he wrote, the only safe place to employ capital was within the limits of the city.[17]

15 Crawfurd's pamphlet in Chaudhuri, ed., *Economic Development*, pp. 217–316.
16 *Bengal Hurkaru*, 11 July 1840.
17 Ibid.

On the other hand, an opponent of the scheme pointed to the danger of having such bills outstanding if the price of indigo were to fall;[18] and the editor of the *Bengal Hurkaru,* taking the side of the "bill houses," wrote that by lowering the exchange rate, British capitalists, who earned their profits of 8 to 12 percent on the disparity between the rupee and the pound, would be discouraged from investing in India. If the proposed plan reduces exchange toward the level of a bullion rate, asked the editor, "will the English capitalist be satisfied to send out his money to a market to invest without profit in dear produce or dear bills of exchange?"[19] Inasmuch as European merchants in India were interested only in quick profits to remit home, and indigenous Indian capital was confined to carrying on local business, investment from Britain, he concluded, was the only hope for the development of India. The directors themselves were almost evenly divided on the issue, but when the proposal came up for a vote at the general meeting of July 18, the Tagore steamroller carried it 462 to 63. [20]

In conducting the bill business, the Union Bank earned a small profit on the rapid turnover of perhaps a third of its capital each year. [21] The bank would purchase bills in Calcutta drawn on London agency houses and remit these to its London bank, Glyn, Halifax, Mills and Company. It would then sell in Calcutta its own bills on Glyn. The bank's profit was the difference between the buying and selling price of the bills. Although it appeared to be relatively safe, the exchange business was, in fact, full of risks. The bills purchased in Calcutta were drawn at ten months' date, and though they may have reflected a good price for indigo when they were purchased, the price could drop and the house on which they were drawn may not have been able to meet its obligations ten months later. Glyn and Company would then have refused to honor drafts on them by the Union Bank. [22] If the Union Bank had had the resources to carry on the bill business through bad years as well as good, money hypothecated to indigo would eventually have been repaid. But with one crore of capital, the bank did not have the resources to facilitate the indigo exporters and carry them through unfavorable seasons.

18*Bengal Hurkaru,* 11 July 1840.
19Ibid., 11 July 1840.
20Ibid., 20 July 1840.
21Ibid., 16 Jan. 1847.
22Cooke, *Banking in India,* p. 196.

The high-handed tactics used by Tagore and his supporters in augmenting the bank's capital and pushing through the bill business created an opposition faction among the proprietors. One shareholder complained that the directorship was monopolized by a few houses and, obviously referring to Dwarkanath Tagore, noted that "one man, I do not say European or Native," held so many shares that he could carry any vote. [23] Indeed, after 1834, the directors were invariably selected from members of six agency houses—Carr, Tagore and Company; Cockerell and Company; Gilmore and Company; Hamilton and Company; Fergusson Brothers; and William Storm. [24] Until 1844, Dwarkanath controlled the policy of the bank, not only through the large number of shares he personally owned, but by soliciting those of relatives, dependents, partners, clients, and friends. The case of A.H. Sim illustrates his power. Sim, an accountant, was removed in October 1838 for some minor indiscretions, but was later reinstated by a Tagore-controlled vote of the shareholders. In May 1839 one of the Indian clerks informed Dwarkanath that Sim had doctored the accounts and had embezzled Rs. 1,20,600 from the bank. Dwarkanath conferred with William Carr, Longueville Clarke, and the chairman, James Cullen, and pledged to make up the difference if the affair were kept secret. Though Sim's embezzlement became public knowledge, Dwarkanath paid the difference and saved the bank from a run by panic-stricken depositors. [25]

To restrict Tagore's power, the dissident shareholders called for a special meeting to consider the acceptance of proxy votes. Thirty percent of the shareholders representing 40 percent of the votes were nonresident in Calcutta, and the acceptance of proxies would have radically altered the balance of power within the proprietorship (See

TABLE 11. DISTRIBUTION AND VALUE OF UNION BANK SHARES, JANUARY 1840

	Calcutta residents	Nonresidents
Number of shareholders	371 (70%)	152 (30%)
Value of shares	Rs. 60,53,000 (62%)	Rs. 35,67,964 (38%)
Votes	1,438 (60%)	819 (40%)

23 Bengal Hurkaru, 11 July 1839.
24 See Bengal and Agra Annual Directories for various years, 1834 through 1847.
25 Bengal Hurkaru, 7 Aug. 1840.

table 11).[26] Tagore rallied his forces and, by a wide margin, defeated the motion to accept proxies.

The disgruntled shareholders then moved to attack Dwarkanath through his friend, George James Gordon. Under Dwarkanath's influence, Gordon had been appointed to succeed James Young as secretary of the bank in 1840. He had been a partner of Mackintosh and Company, and, after a sojourn in England had returned to Calcutta "in painful circumstances." He needed the lucrative appointment to help recoup financial losses incurred in the crash of 1830–33. Dwarkanath had carried a motion to raise his salary from Rs. 1,600 to Rs. 2,000 per month, and the dissident shareholders now called for a special meeting to consider the raise. Once again, however, they lost the vote.[27]

Although the decisions to increase the bank's capital and to enter the bill business were openly debated by the proprietors, the decision to support indigo production was made in camera. The directors began by establishing a "new class of cash credit accounts" which, in effect, gave unlimited credit to the indigo-producing agency houses. The first intimation that this new business had been undertaken was made in a report by the directors at the meeting of 18 July 1840. Without consulting the shareholders, the directors had begun to lend money to agency houses on deposit of title deeds to indigo factories, equipment, and lands as well as on assignment of the annual produce. At the same time, the bank adopted the system prevailing in Scotland of establishing cash credits on the personal security of the borrower along with some collateral security. Unlike the Scottish system, however, money was drawn as needed and repaid as it became available. This violated the deed of the Union Bank, which prohibited loans for over four months, but it was circumvented by permitting the borrower to pay interest every three months and to renew the loan.[28]

In 1842 a commercial crisis brought down a number of firms that, under the new system, were heavily indebted to the Union Bank: Gilmore and Company, Fergusson Brothers, Boyd and Company, McLeod Fagan and Company, Bruce Shand and Company, and Cantor Low. When a group of shareholders called on the secretary for an account of the bank's losses, Gordon denied that the bank had lost

26Ibid., 29 Jan. 1840.
27Ibid., 16 and 29 Jan. 1840.
28Ibid., 20 July 1840.

much, if anything, by the failures and for a year continued to hold off their questions with vague statements.[29] The truth about the bank's leading debtor finally came to light in March 1843 when a committee of shareholders reported that the bank had lost Rs. 4,79,663 on loans to Gilmore and Company.[30] Most of this loss had been caused by the carelessness or collusion of George James Gordon. In February 1840, Gilmore had borrowed Rs. 2,71,095 from the bank on the collateral of deeds to the Naraincoory Colliery and coal stored in depots.[31] When Gilmore failed, ownership of the mine was assumed by a group of assignees. For an unexplained reason, Gordon handed over to William S. Smith, a member of Gilmore and Company and a director of the Union Bank, the title deeds kept by the bank, and Smith in turn gave these to the assignees, leaving the bank without collateral.[32] The remainder of the money had been loaned to Gilmore on goods such as cotton bales, indigo, copper, and sugar deposited by the firm in a private godown. Not only did the firm place a false value on the goods, but after their failure permitted other creditors to remove goods from the godowns.[33]

Suspicious that Gordon and the directors were misleading them, a group of shareholders, consisting of small merchants and professionals, vigorously tried to reform the operation of the Union Bank.[34] Had they succeeded, the bank might have survived the crisis of 1847, but their efforts were defeated by the partners of the big houses and a few of the leading attorneys, led by Dwarkanath Tagore. The dissidents called for an end to "cliquism" in the directorate, the dismissal of Gordon, the cessation of loans on indigo crops, and the appointment of independent auditors. "It was considered," said Patrick O'Hanlon, one of the leaders of the group, "that the fittest persons to manage the affairs of the Bank were those who had been able most successfully to appropriate its funds."[35]

At a special meeting called on 30 July 1842, the dissident

29 Ibid., 17 Jan. 1842.
30 Ibid., 13 Mar. 1843.
31 Ibid., 21 Jan. 1843; Cooke, *Banking in India,* pp. 187 ff.
32 *Bengal Hurkaru,* 24 and 26 Jan. 1843.
33 Ibid., 13 Mar. and 18 July 1843.
34 The group included P. O'Hanlon, Arthur Pittar, R.H. Mytton, F.H. Burkinyoung, R.J. Lattey, J.S. McLeod, Eneas Mackintosh, T.C. Morton, the Rev. W. Morton and James Hume.
35 Patrick O'Hanlon, *Mr. O'Hanlon's Remarks on Mr. G.J. Gordon's Publication* (Alipore: March 1843).

shareholders attempted to infuse new blood into the directorate. R.J. Lattey pointed out that partners of Gilmore had served on the directorate over a period of years during which their firm was failing, and that out of delicacy the other directors had never denied Gilmore accommodations. P. O'Hanlon and T.C. Morton proposed that partners of a retiring director should be ineligible for election for one year following their partner's retirement. D.M. Gordon of Carr, Tagore and Company, who had succeeded Dwarkanath on the directorate in January 1842, spoke against the motion, but T.E.M. Turton, who had supported the big houses in previous years, now turned against them and added his voice to the fight against cliquism. Perhaps he was piqued by the desertion of many of his friends from the ranks of the "Precursors" to those of the "Comprehensives" in the maneuvers for a steamship link with Britain. Despite the justice of their cause, the reformers lost the vote 161 to 344.[36]

A few months later, O'Hanlon launched a personal attack on G.J. Gordon as well as Dwarkanath Tagore, who, he claimed, supported Gordon with the authority of 700 shares.[37] Dwarkanath, recently returned from his first trip to Europe, and at the height of his influence in the bank, spoke in both his own and Gordon's defense. As "perhaps" the largest shareholder himself and responsible for shares belonging to friends and relatives, he argued, it would hardly be in his interest willfully to neglect the interests of the shareholders at large. He pointed out that although the bank had lost money on goods fraudulently removed from private godowns, the additional 2 percent charged on the shortage of unbonded goods had made up for much of this loss. In a slap at the prevailing mores, Dwarkanath related the story of how the bank's Indian watchman, who had dared to try to prevent a European from making off with some goods, had been kicked by the man and later reprimanded by his own employers for his impertinence. Finally, he said, Gordon had tried time after time to convince the directors that they should institute better security, but had failed.[38]

O'Hanlon was not convinced, and, when the shareholders met a

36*Bengal Hurkaru*, 30 July and 1 Aug. 1842.
37O'Hanlon held a long-standing grudge against Gordon stemming from a dispute between O'Hanlon and Mackintosh and Company over a debt. See *Mr. O'Hanlon's Remarks.*
38*Bengal Hurkaru*, 13 Mar. 1843.

few months later, observed that the directors were "going on without reform and without restoring the confidence of the public, and that it was Dwarkanath's fault." Dwarkanath, according to the report, rose with "more than usual warmth of manner" to repudiate "the insinuation made against him." He again claimed that the bank's interests were identical to his own and reminded the shareholders how he had intervened to save them in 1842 when its bills had been dishonored by Couts and Company in London. "However wrong he might have sometimes been in his judgement . . . he did claim credit for honesty and singleness of purpose." He denied that the directors of the bank had absorbed all the bank's money and said that after investigation he had found that "not one-third of the loans were given to the directors."[39]

As the number of shareholders in opposition grew, however, the directors were forced to make some token concessions. In place of the independent auditors that had been requested, the directors appointed a Committee of Finance and Accounts consisting of Dwarkanath Tagore, A.J. de H. Larpent of Cockerell and Company, James P. McKilligan of Colville, Gilmore and Company, and W.P. Grant, all of whom were heavily indebted to the bank.[40] The directors also agreed to limit advances on indigo crops to a total of 25 lakhs per season, to reject requests for renewals of short term loans, and to liquidate outstanding loans, amounting to Rs. 62,40,260, on indigo factories and sugar works. They even agreed to coopt on the directorate a representative of the dissidents, the Reverend W. Morton, who now became "a sheep among wolves."[41] Finally, the most popular reform measure was the dismissal of G.J. Gordon as secretary.

Gordon's last report, made at the meeting in July 1843, indicated that losses on the accounts of defaulting houses had been greater than anyone had anticipated. This was largely because almost all the collateral was in the form of indigo or indigo factories, which had declined in value as a result of the low price of indigo on international markets. Later it was disclosed that altogether the bank had Rs. 61,75,231 tied up in loans on indigo factories and sugar works. This included about 20 lakhs in claims on Gilmore and Fergusson for old advances, 36 lakhs in current advances to leading

39 Ibid., 17 July 1843.
40 Ibid., 31 July 1843.
41 Ibid., 17 July 1843.

houses and 7 lakhs in outlays to factories acquired by the bank itself
through default. In addition, Rs. 14,18,676 were sunk in loans on
goods in possession of the bank and Rs. 17,62,582 in private bills
discounted. Thus Rs. 93,56,489 out of the bank's capital of
Rs. 1,00,00,000 was out on loan. Although some of these loans should
have been written off as losses, all of them were still carried on the
books as assets in possession of the bank. In 1843–44, another 21
lakhs, half that of the previous year, had been loaned out to seven
large indigo-exporting houses for the current season. Furthermore,
the exchange business was being conducted with bills largely
hypothecated to indigo consigned to London. In short, the bank was
no longer a general commercial bank, but had become simply a giant
satellite of the indigo-exporting agency houses. The only useful role it
performed in the 1843–44 period was to finance the organization of
the Bengal Coal Company, a transaction on which it lost no money.
Despite the bad debts, Gordon reported a "profit" of Rs. 7,85,730 on
current operations and declared a dividend of 8 percent. In fact, the
dividend was taken not from profits, not even from paid-up capital,
long since loaned out, but from the floating deposits![42]

Gordon's successor was James Calder Stewart, who, like Gordon,
had once been a partner in Mackintosh and Company. Stewart had
been a director of the Union Bank in 1831–33 and recently had
served under Gordon as deputy secretary. A much better accountant
than Gordon, he was more reserved, less gregarious, and better suited
to the role of watchdog over the directors. His failings were timidity
and misplaced loyalty. What he saw during his tenure as secretary,
from December 1843 to the end of 1846, he kept to himself rather
than taking it before the shareholders. It was not ordinary
carelessness or poor judgment alone that he withheld from the public,
but embezzlement and dishonesty.

The beginning of his tenure brought a marked increase in public
confidence in the Union Bank. The press hailed his first report, and
the shareholders expressed their gratitude for receiving, at last, what
appeared to be a candid and full accounting. Shares rose to Rs. 280
premium. Stewart reported in January 1844 that the total losses on
insolvent estates had been ten lakhs, but that the reserve fund

42Ibid., 17 July 1843 and 16 Jan. 1847. Cooke, *Banking in India,* p. 186; A.J. de H.
Larpent, *Facts Explanatory of the Connection of the Late Firm of Cockerell and Company of
Calcutta with the Union Bank of Calcutta* (London: 1848); J.C. Stewart, *Facts and
Documents Relating to the Affairs of the Union Bank of Calcutta* (London: 1848).

contained about 2 lakhs, giving the bank a deficit of 8 lakhs, less than the annual average profit of 8 percent. No loans for indigo cultivation had been made for the current season except to carry on the bank's own properties, and, in the course of the year, outstanding loans on the security of indigo had been reduced from 62 to 27 lakhs. Although an "unprecedented influx of capital" into Calcutta had resulted in reduced interest rates and competition for bills, which made the bank's exchange business less profitable, he reported that 114 lakhs were employed in a profitable manner on valid security and in the course of early return. R.J. Lattey, who boasted that he had been the first shareholder ever to question a report, congratulated the directors on their statement. He was seconded by James Hume. The one ominous note was a report by W.P. Grant that negotiations with the government to permit civil servants to serve on the board of directors had failed. [43]

Throughout 1844 and, in fact, until the end of 1846, an aura of confidence prevailed, but there were occasional hints of subterfuge that could have been pursued. The *Friend of India,* for example, after praising the report of July 1844, made note of a few suspicious items. One was that some nine lakhs carried in January as a balance due from Fergusson and Company had been transferred to a heading listing properties owned by the bank. Another was that private acceptances had increased from 19 to 55 lakhs over the year, and the editor expressed the hope that these loans had been made on good collateral for legitimate commerce, and not for indigo speculation. [44]

Distribution of dividends was another problem that proprietors and directors alike treated by hiding their heads in the sand. Considering the losses of 1842 and the need to build up a reserve fund, the shareholders should have been willing to forgo dividends, but in 1844 and 1845 the directors recommended dividends of 7 percent. The directors were caught in a dilemma: if they reduced dividends, the shareholders might respond by selling out. For example, Holludhar Mullick threatened that if the bank were to cut its rate of interest, he and many of his countrymen who held Union Bank shares would sell out and invest their money in landed property, "which is very certain of giving a higher rate of interest without so much risk!" [45]

43 *Bengal Hurkaru,* 22 Jan. 1844.
44 *Friend of India,* 18 July 1844, quoted in *Bengal Hurkaru,* 19 July 1844.
45 Letter dated 17 Jan. 1845 in *Calcutta Star,* 18 Jan. 1845.

By 1845, Dwarkanath Tagore had sold most of his Union Bank shares. Perhaps he realized that he and his accomplices on the directorate had gone too far and that he alone could not reverse the bank's slide into disaster. More likely, he was concerned about his mortality and gradually converting his commercial holdings into zamindaris to be held in trust for his sons. Finally, he needed cash for his second trip to England. At the January 1845 meeting the Reverend Morton congratulated Dwarkanath on recovering from his "late serious illness" and added, "in reference to that gentleman's acknowledged greatness as a commercial man, that whatever might have been his former position in the Union Bank, he was, at present, by no means the great Leviathan he had been; that he was not now a greater Shareholder than many other persons, and that if he and all 'his tail' were to quit tommorow, the loss would not be much, if at all, felt by the bank."[46] Dwarkanath did not live to see the final tragic outcome of his policies.

2. The Grant Era

The leading power in the bank was now William Patrick Grant, master in equity of the Calcutta Supreme Court, who held the chairmanship of the bank's finance committee.[47] Grant was heavily involved with Cockerell and Company; the second member of the committee, John Beckwith, was a partner in Cockerell and Company and the third, W.F. Gilmore, a partner of Colville, Gilmore and Company. The other directors represented, as usual, houses most heavily in debt to the bank, and helped one another obtain loans on questionable security. While the directors continued to issue optimistic reports, the secretary, J.C. Stewart, struggled behind the scenes to restrain them. When he complained to Grant that four agency houses engrossed two-thirds of the bank's capital, and presented the finance committee with a list of reforms, Grant wrote him to "think them over before you stir matters which are somewhat of a gunpowdery nature."[48] Stewart, in desperation, quietly tried to enlist the help of

46*Bengal Hurkaru*, 20 Jan. 1845.

47Grant held the high-ranking post of Master in Equity of the Calcutta Supreme Court, which paid him the handsome salary of Rs. 4,000 per month. His father was Sir John Peter Grant (1774–1848), Puisne Judge of the Calcutta Supreme Court; and his brother, John Peter Grant (1807–93), was a rapidly rising civil servant of great ability who later served as Lt. Governor of Bengal in 1859–62 and as Governor of Jamaica in 1866–73.

48Stewart, *Facts and Documents,* pp. 54 ff.

prominent local shareholders and to arouse the shareholders in England, but without success.

From the official reports issued by the directors it appeared that the bank was gradually divesting itself of the indigo factories it had assumed on mortgage and reducing its loans to agency houses for indigo cultivation. The number of concerns owned outright by the bank dropped from eleven in 1844 to four in 1846, and the amount advanced to keep these four concerns in operation dropped from almost 8 lakhs to a little over 4 lakhs. Loans to agency houses for indigo cultivation declined from 26 lakhs in 1844–45 to 14 lakhs in 1845–46.[49] But, in fact, the bank continued to increase its support for indigo cultivation, and in the annual reports the directors disguised indigo loans under euphemistic headings (see Table 12). "Private bills discounted" and "loans on personal security," renewable indefinitely, were loans to agency houses for seasonal indigo advances. "Loans on bullion, Government paper and joint stock shares" were almost all made on joint-stock shares, the bulk of which were shares in the Union Bank itself. Finally, "post bills" were renewable short-term loans issued without collateral.[50] Almost every rupee loaned by the bank eventually found its way to an indigo plantation.

TABLE 12. DISGUISED INDIGO LOANS BY THE UNION BANK, 1846–47

	Jan. 1846	Jan. 1847	July 1847
Private bills discounted	37,52,247	38,75,654	41,69,500
Loans on personal security	4,35,635	6,99,088	11,70,900
Loans on bullion, government paper, and joint-stock shares	12,55,807	27,79,807	25,87,704
Post bills	—	13,51,757	27,72,166

Behind this policy was the increasingly desperate situation of the great indigo houses. Indigo prices had been declining since 1840.[51] The more they declined, the more capital had to be borrowed to keep them in operation; the more capital borrowed, the more indigo had to be contracted for—thus flooding the market and keeping marginal concerns in operation. The Union Bank had to participate in this

49 Ibid., pp. 74–75.
50 Bengal Hurkaru, 16 Jan. 1846, 16 Jan. 1847, and 15 July 1847.
51 Benoy Chowdhury, Growth of Commercial Agriculture in Bengal (1757–1900), (Calcutta: 1964), vol. I, pp. 115, 119.

charade because, in order to have any chance of recovering its debts, it had to keep factories operating, even at a loss. All of this was done to preserve the partners of the indigo houses from facing eventual but certain bankruptcy.[52]

Covert support for indigo production was not the only way in which the directors misused the bank's money. On grounds of facilitating resale of the largest indigo concern, the Big Union, the bank spent 18 lakhs to convert a second mortgage on the concern for $1\frac{1}{2}$ lakhs in cash and took a new mortgage on the balance. Not only had it quadrupled its equity in a losing property, but it was now responsible for an annual outlay of over 2 lakhs to keep the concern in production.[53]

At the end of 1846, Stewart decided that continued opposition from within was futile and resigned his position. Reasoning that it was too late for reform and that exposure of the bank's management would only lead to panic, he failed to take the case to the public. Nevertheless, his resignation aroused suspicion, and at the meeting of January 1847 the shareholders, led by Turton, subjected Grant to a series of hostile questions. He held off the attack with denials and lies,[54] but by the next meeting, in July, the merchants of Calcutta had become increasingly alarmed by news of a widespread commercial crisis developing in Britain and demanded a full accounting. In their report the directors alluded to the "pressure of the money market" and the consequent withdrawal of large amounts of deposits.[55] Miraculously, however, they announced that the bank had earned a net profit of Rs. 5,13,895 and recommended a dividend of 7 percent, again concealing the fact that it would be paid out of deposits. Nevertheless, all remaining confidence had evaporated, and, when Turton demanded a special meeting in August to hear a detailed report on the bank's position, he received the unanimous support of the shareholders. The August meeting produced only a half-truth—an admission that the bank had lost Rs. 24,47,852 on the production of indigo.[56]

52Cooke, *Banking in India,* p. 199.
53*Bengal Hurkaru,* 16 Jan. and 15 July 1847.
54Ibid., 18 Jan. 1847.
55Ibid., 15 July 1847.
56Ibid., 19 July and 30 Aug. 1847.

By that autumn, Britain was in the throes of a full-scale commercial crisis. The railway mania of 1845 had absorbed floating capital needed for commercial purposes into fixed, long-term investments. When the Irish potato crop failed in 1846, large wheat imports were required, and a deficiency in the American cotton crop raised the price of that commodity. Commercial money was in short supply, interest rates were high, and the Bank of England's reserves fell dangerously low. During the period of tight credit and high interest rates, British grain speculators had contracted for wheat at high prices, but in July 1847 a bumper crop of cheap wheat arrived and the speculators went broke. In August 1847, nineteen corn importers suspended business. Because they were linked to other kinds of mercantile houses, bills were dishonored right and left, and the disaster spread. In September, two of the largest London East India houses, Cockerell and Company and Lyall Brothers, were among the thirty-seven firms that fell. Both were closely connected with Calcutta houses deeply in debt to the Union Bank. By November, failures spread to Calcutta, where sixteen agency houses suspended operation.[57] "This week," wrote the editor of the *Bengal Hurkaru* at the end of November, "has been an eventful one—long to be remembered in the commercial history of this city." Credit and confidence had disappeared, business was reduced to cash transactions, no acceptances were discountable in the bazaar, and even the *shroffs* were in trouble. Trade was depressed. Sugar, rice, and silk were hardly purchased at all, opium was lower than ever, and, though jute remained in demand, indigo had dropped Rs. 18 per maund from the previous year. Union Bank shares had fallen to Rs. 200–250 per share.[58]

In October Glyn, Halifax, Mills and Company refused to honor Union Bank drafts, and the London shareholders called an emergency meeting. Present were many who had been Dwarkanath's friends, including H.M. Parker, William Prinsep, James Young, and John Carr. They called for drastic reforms and reorganization of the bank's management, but it was much too late.[59] On December 18 the Calcutta shareholders held a special meeting to hear a report on the effects of the recent failures. Grant reported that the bank had

57 James Wilson, *Capital, Currency and Banking* (London: 1847), pp. 127 ff.; D. Morier Evans, *The Commercial Crisis 1847-1848* (London: 1849), pp. 54 ff.
58 *Bengal Hurkaru*, 27 Nov. 1847.
59 Ibid., 9 Dec. 1847.

lost Rs. 17,28,500 by the failure of Cockerell and Company and Rs. 89,000 by that of Lyall, Matheson. In addition, because of the failure of houses in London, unredeemed bills amounting to Rs. 18,50,000 would be returned to the bank. Of these, only Rs. 4,50,000 were secured. Finally, Cockerell, Larpent of London had misappropriated post bills for which the Union Bank would have to provide Rs. 4,50,000. The directors promised a full report in the following month and announced that they expected to keep the bank operating on a reduced capital.

The shareholders demanded more information: How many post bills had been issued? How had Cockerell, Larpent "misappropriated" post bills? Why had the bank continued to acquire indigo factories after promising to get rid of those it had ? Grant, attempting to shift the blame to the directors of the pre-1842 period, claimed that he had always opposed advances to indigo factories, but "when they were made, there had been a large majority in the Direction, of a different opinion." One of Grant's supporters was more explicit: "There was a large party in the Direction in those days, who did exactly what they chose. They composed Dwarkanath Tagore's tail, and out-voted everybody else." Among the shareholders, Jeremiah Homfray refused to accept the excuse and angrily pointed out that Grant had greatly expanded advances to indigo planters by the issuance of post bills. While the *Englishman* now admitted that the Union Bank was insolvent, the *Bengal Hurkaru* argued that the bank still owned some of the best indigo factories in Lower Bengal and that indigo was selling at a reasonable price of Rs. 120 to 130 per maund.[60]

By the next meeting, on December 31, Grant admitted that, with one-half of the lands usually under indigo out of production, the indigo factories were less of an asset than previously reported. Turton moved to send 22,282 maunds of indigo held by the bank to London at once for sale, but Longueville Clarke asked who among the directors could be trusted with the indigo and pointed out that it would immediately be seized by Glyn and Gompany. When Turton's motion carried against Clarke's arguments, one shareholder was heard to remark, "so much for Dwarkanath's tail."[61]

Gradually the knavery of W.P. Grant was coming to light. At the next meeting, on January 10, Grant revealed under Longueville

60Ibid., 21, 23, and 25 Dec. 1847.
61Ibid., 1 Jan. 1848.

Clark's aggressive questioning what he had meant by the "misappropriation" of post bills by Cockerell, Larpent and Company. In the previous June, Grant, to raise money to pay his own debts, had drawn £40,000 against Cockerell, Larpent and Company and to get immediate acceptance had sent Cockerell, Larpent an equivalent amount in Union Bank post bills as collateral security. He then sent the bills drawn on Cockerell, Larpent to two Calcutta houses, Jardine Skinner and Company and Kelsalls and Company and again, as security, deposited with them 4½ lakhs of Union Bank post bills. In London, Cockerell, Larpent, in desperate straits itself, cashed in the post bills; and when its own bills were dishonored in Calcutta, the two Calcutta firms cashed in their post bills. Thus, to enable Grant to obtain 4 lakhs for his personal use, the Union Bank had become liable for 9 lakhs of post bills.[62] When one proprietor said he presumed that Grant was personally liable for the amount, Grant replied that he "could not see why the proprietors would be so perverse. Nobody here was to blame. It was the fault alone of the house in London which had misappropriated the bills."[63]

Further investigation now unmasked another case of misconduct, the existence of a secret "shares club." Eight proprietors—Manikjee Rustomjee, John Storm, W.R. Lackersteen, Radamadub Bannerjee, W.P. Grant, Rustomjee Cowasjee, John Lyall, and T. Holroyd—had formed a club in the fall of 1846 to support share prices by purchasing them with the bank's own capital. Grant opened for each member a credit line of four lakhs, on which the member could borrow up to Rs. 1,000 per share. Only Radamadub Bannerjee paid cash for his shares; the others used promissory notes issued by the bank, and drew 15 lakhs from the account.[64]

A third scandal involved the Commercial Bank of Bombay. On 2 November 1847, Abbott, the new secretary, received a request from the Commercial Bank to purchase Bank of Bengal notes for cash. Abbott in turn asked J.S.B. Scott of Hickey, Bailey and Company, the broker in these notes, to arrange the purchase. But on December 13, Scott, with the knowledge of Abbott and some of the directors, misappropriated the money to pay off debts owed the Union Bank by Hickey, Bailey.[65]

62 Ibid., 11 Jan. 1848; Evans, *Commercial Crisis,* pp. xix–xxi.
63 Stewart, *Facts and Documents.*
64 *Bengal Hurkaru,* 29 July and 25 Aug. 1848.
65 Ibid., 17 Jan., 29 May, 26 June, and 31 July 1848.

At last, on January 15, 1846, the proprietors voted to suspend all proceedings of the Union Bank. The suspension was forced when one of the creditors objected to the directors' paying off a debt of 14 lakhs to Jardine, Skinner and Company. Because of this undue preference the creditor called for a meeting of creditors, and T.E.M. Turton, who was now managing the bank, proposed that a committee of shareholders be appointed to wind up the affairs of the bank and meet with all the creditors. Among those nominated to serve on the committee Turton named James Stuart. This was objected to, not on grounds of any deficiency of ability or integrity, but because Stuart had belonged to Carr, Tagore and Company, a firm deeply in debt to the bank. Turton objected that to eliminate Stuart, and another debtor, W.F. Fergusson, would be to strike "out the brains of the committee. . . . There were no better men in Calcutta than Messrs. Stuart and Fergusson, and as to Carr, Tagore and Company's account, he wished all the debts due to the bank were as good." The proprietors accepted Turton's slate and elected a committee consisting of H.M. Elliot, T.C. Morton, Fergusson, J.C. Stewart, and James Stuart.[66]

On January 22 the committee reported that the bank was insolvent: its assets were Rs. 61,07,999 and liabilities Rs. 68,82,610. Although indigo properties owned by the bank had a book value of 23 lakhs, this amount could be realized only if the properties were sold off gradually. In addition, the bank also owned about rupees ten lakhs of indigo in storage and about five lakhs of joint-stock shares, two-fifths of which were shares in the Bengal Indigo Company. The committee valued at 14 lakhs private bills discounted and loans on personal security that stood in the books at 38 lakhs. Among the bank's largest liabilities were 24 lakhs of post bills and 29 lakhs of returned and dishonored bills. The committee recommended, first, an immediate assessment of Rs. 200 per share from each proprietor to meet the bank's debts, and, second, the appointment of a committee to assess each shareholder for additional money to cover the balance of the debts. The new committee would ask for the cooperation of the creditors to exempt individuals who paid their assessments from being sued in court. [67]

66Ibid., 22 Jan. 1848. Elliot was Foreign Secretary to the Government of India and co-author of *The History of India as Told by its own Historians.*
67*Bengal Hurkaru,* 22 Jan. 1848.

At the stormy January 22 meeting, all the frustrations and passions of the mercantile community came to the surface. Discussion of the report opened with an acrimonious debate between Stewart and Grant in which each thrust by Stewart against Grant brought cheers from the floor. In the course of the debate Stewart mentioned that one director had "put his hand in the till" and another "made an unsuccessful attempt." When asked for the names of these directors, Stewart replied that, soon after his appointment, W.P. Grant and Dwarkanath Tagore had gone to the cash department and had, without his knowledge, discounted a bill for Rs. 5,000 previously declined by the other directors. James Stuart leapt to his feet and asked for more particulars: "The aspersion cast is of as grave a character as it can be." D.M. Gordon then joined the debate. "As the name of Dwarkanath Tagore has been mentioned in connection with this transaction, I reluctantly come forward to explain to the meeting, more in detail than has been done, the circumstances under which it took place." He produced the bill and read that it had been drawn by Joynarian Mookerjee and sent to the Union Bank for discount. When two of the directors refused to purchase it, Joynarian went to Dwarkanath who found that a bill for Rs. 3,000 was due to Joynarian. In addition, Joynarian, a man of wealth and influence, had recently appointed Dwarkanath trustee for a fund of Rs. 3,00,000. Finally, Gordon pointed out, Ramanath Tagore, the treasurer, did not pay out any money until he had received approval from J.C. Stewart. Stewart, now on the defensive, denied that he had meant to imply dishonesty, but had wanted only to illustrate the general laxity prevailing at the time. After a number of speakers testified to the integrity and honesty of Ramanath Tagore, the arid discussion ended. No doubt Dwarkanath had been guilty of running the bank as if it were his personal business, and in their desperation the proprietors would sooner or later have conjured up his name. More striking, however, was the demonstration of loyalty by James Stuart and D.M. Gordon toward their dead partner and his family. Loyalty among ex-partners was a rare sentiment in Calcutta, especially among those whose firms were in liquidation. [68]

With illusions of solvency finally laid to rest, the 500 proprietors of the Union Bank now faced eight months of terror. A few years before, in November 1845, the Union Bank had received a concession of

68 Ibid., 24 Jan. 1848.

dubious value from the government. Under Act 23 of 1845 the bank could sue and be sued in the name of its secretary or treasurer. Though far from the desirable charter of limited liability, it was a belated recognition of the bank's corporality. It permitted the bank to realize some heavy outstanding claims that had been uncollectible because under the law of partnership all of the shareholders would have been required to file separately as plaintiffs in any lawsuit. As long as the bank was the creditor it worked to the bank's advantage; but if the bank were the debtor, the result could be disastrous. Previously any creditor of the bank would have been obliged to sue each partner separately, and, if the creditor won his case, each partner would be equally liable. The creditor could not single out any individual proprietor for prosecution. Now a creditor could sue the bank in the name of its secretary, and if he won, and the partnership did not have the funds, the execution could be issued against individual proprietors seriatim. A rich proprietor who had only one share could be made liable for the entire debt of the bank, and his only recourse for the return of his money would be to sue each of his fellow proprietors singly in equity. [69]

There was no escaping the law. Even shareholders who had sold out before the crash were liable, though their liability was secondary. The creditors met with T.C. Morton, who had assumed management of the bank's liquidation, and most, but not all, agreed not to sue any shareholder who paid the sum assessed him by a joint committee of creditors and proprietors. On this basis the creditors' committee agreed temporarily to postpone suits, but never bound themselves legally not to sue any particular shareholder, especially one who was backward in paying his assessment. [70]

Each month brought more bad news. Court decisions confirmed the validity of the bank's debts, including post bills issued secretly and fraudulently by W.P. Grant, and upheld the responsibility of the shareholders to pay every last rupee of debt unless the creditors agreed to compromise. [71] In the spring of 1848, the Union Bank still had a chance for survival and even rebirth. Its indigo holdings were substantial and would regain their value when the crisis had passed. If the small proprietors had paid their assessments and the wealthy ones had combined to underwrite the bank's current deficits, the

69 Ibid., 28 Nov. and 18 Dec. 1845.
70 Ibid., 31 Jan., 28 Feb., 1 and 8 May, 2 June, and 31 July 1848.
71 Ibid., 25 Mar. 1848.

debts could have been paid off. As it was, few would cooperate, and under pressure, especially from Glyn, Halifax, Mills and Company of London, the sheriff was forced to seize the bank's assets and sell them at auction for a fraction of their value, often for one anna on the rupee, wiping out real along with imaginary assets. [72]

The committee appointed to carry out the unpopular task of assigning the assessment due from each shareholder could do no right, and the newspapers were filled with examples of gross injustice. Some men lost all their savings whereas others, often more culpable, got off lightly. Altogether 474 shareholders (83 Indians and 391 Europeans) were assessed. [73] An incomplete list of shareholders and assessments, published on September 20, 1848, is shown in table 13. [74]

TABLE 13. INCOMPLETE LIST OF UNION BANK SHAREHOLDERS, SEPTEMBER 20, 1848

	Indian	European	Total
Number	80 (83)	353 (391)	433 (474)
Amount assessed	Rs. 13,10,000	Rs. 38,93,700	Rs. 52,03,700
Average assessment	Rs. 16,375	Rs. 11,030	

Twenty-seven of the shareholders were assessed Rs. 50,000 or more, and of these, 23 were Europeans and 4 Indians. Those assessed a lakh or more are listed in table 14. By June 1849, 23 of the 83 Indians (28 percent) and 148 of the 391 Europeans (38 percent) had paid their assessments. [75]

TABLE 14. UNION BANK SHAREHOLDERS ASSESSED A LAKH OR MORE, SEPTEMBER 20, 1848

Shareholder	Assessment (rupees)
Ashutosh Day	3,00,000
Promothanath Day	3,00,000
Rajah Nursingchundra Roy	1,50,000
James Hastie	1,00,000
Joseph Willis	1,00,000

72 Ibid., 1 May, 9 June, and 22 July 1848; 5 Mar. 1852.
73 Ibid., 21 and 23 Sept. 1848; 8 June 1849.
74 Ibid., 20 Sept. 1848.
75 Ibid., 26 June 1849. The Tagores listed were assessed as follows:

Sailendranath	Rs.	3,000
Prasanna Kumar		40,000
Ramanath		20,000

The assessments against the Day brothers were the most controversial and gave rise to bitter racial feelings. Ashutosh and Promothanath Day, the sons of the Bengali millionaire banian Ramdulal Day, who had died in 1825, were reputed to be the wealthiest men in Calcutta. Together they owned a mere thirteen shares of Union Bank stock[76] which they had sold on 19 November 1847, the day after the failure of Cockerell, Larpent and Company. But in those turbulent final months the sale went unregistered, and they were still included in the list of shareholders. The Day brothers took their case to court, and it was ruled that legally they were still shareholders.[77] They tried in every way possible to evade liability for debts they had had no part in incurring and were especially angry when the executive committee of the bank in liquidation delayed publishing the names of those who owed the bank money—men like W.P. Grant, A.J. de H. Larpent, and the Tagores.[78] It was only at the meeting of April 29 that the shareholders instructed the committee to publish the names of debtors.[79]

Until the Commercial Bank of Bombay brought suit against them along with two other wealthy proprietors, Nursingchundra Roy and Joseph Willis, the Days refused to pay any contribution. When legal proceedings began on May 16, the Days attempted to transfer many of their properties to their wives.[80] After six months of trial, the case was compromised, and the Days agreed to pay their six-lakh assessment on condition that two lakhs be reserved for the Commercial Bank of Bombay. Nursingchundra Roy also agreed to pay his assessment, but Willis continued to litigate.[81] The *Bengal Hurkaru* lamented that if the Days had only paid up at once many of the assets of the bank could have been saved, but the *Englishman* disagreed and wondered if the entire assessment scheme was not a gigantic plot by the directors to force the Days to bail them out.[82]

Mothooranath	5,000
Gopilal	20,000

Bengal Hurkaru, 20 Sept. 1848. The *Bengal Hurkaru* of 1 Jan. 1849 lists Dwarkanath, Debendranath, and Girindranath as having paid their full assessments, but no figures are given. This would explain the absence of the three Indian names from the September 20 list in the *Bengal Hurkaru.*

76 Ibid., 28 Aug. 1848.
77 Ibid., 15 Apr. 1848.
78 Ibid., 27 Mar. 1848.
79 Ibid., 29 Apr. 1848.
80 Ibid., 16 May and 6 Nov. 1848.
81 Ibid., 4 and 11 Nov., 2 and 8 Dec. 1848.
82 *Englishman,* 15 Nov. 1848, quoted in *Bengal Hurkaru,* 16 Nov. 1848.

To the Indian community, the Day case had the appearance of their own countrymen taking the consequences for European duplicity. A Bengali vernacular newspaper editorialized:

The Supreme Court, the Bengal Secretariat, and the Tax Office are in downright ferment. We hear of defalcation to the amount of two, three, four and even twelve lacs of rupees in different offices; and yet, strange to say, the sahebs in charge of these establishments suffer nothing from the circumstances. Had a Bengali been implicated in the matter, we would have had packs of police serjeants pursuing the supposed culprit and dragging him from the zenana to a criminal jail by way of a prologue to something still more fearful; we would have also had wholesale libels against Natives in general from all Christian quarters, the real saheb and the would be ones exulting ly joining in the same chorus. "Bengali lag bura chor, fanci ho ne se acha hota."[83]

The *Bengal Hurkaru* itself warned that unless a law of limited liability were passed, Indians would never again buy shares in joint-stock companies.

As to the natives, who it is so desirable to see becoming members of Joint Stock Companies, the Union Bank affair has given a death blow to their confidence in any such associations. We have heard several highly respectable natives declare that nothing would induce them to take shares in any of them and that such was the general feeling among their countrymen. Who can be surprised at such a result? No power of logic will ever persuade a native that there is any justice in a law, which, as if the loss of the capital vested by him in a Bank were not sufficient, makes him liable also for an enormous amount of debts contracted without his knowledge and in violation of every principle and role of the association.[84]

As the closing days of the liquidation process approached, Ashutosh Day wrote to T.C. Morton, chairman of the Union Bank, that since he and his brother, who had died on December 27, had contributed so much to the assessment fund, he wanted to know how the money had been disbursed. He "hoped the meeting would consider it due to him and the native community at large that the accounts should be fully and completely audited from the beginning, including the whole of the receipts, whether from assets or assessments, as well as payments of every description." J.S. Judge,

83"The Bengali is a great thief; even the threat of hanging does not deter him." Editorial in *Gyandurpan*, 11 Mar. 1848, quoted in *Bengal Hurkaru*, 16 Mar. 1848.
84*Bengal Hurkaru*, 28 Aug. 1848. In 1849 a group of Indians backed by the Maharaja of Burdwan projected a new bank in Burdwan from whose management all "Christian agency" would be excluded. Ibid., 30 Mar. 1849.

Dwarkanath's old attorney, rose to the defence of Morton and asked, "Who saved us? Was it a gentleman who then went about saying that he had nothing, that he was ready to go through the insolvent court, but neither creditors nor executive committee should get anything out of him?" No, it was Morton, Judge claimed, who had tried in vain to persuade the shareholders to unite and purchase claims on the bank. Morton, to the annoyance of the creditors, had purchased whatever claims he could at auction and salvaged some of the assets, but he could have saved much more if larger resources had been at his disposal. [85]

Sheriff Hogg held four auction sales and realized about ten of the forty lakhs of assets placed at auction. [86] At the first sale, in June 1848, there were few serious bids because of fear that titles to property would be challenged. The Union Bank building on Tank Square, valued at Rs. 60,000, went for Rs. 4,000; the indigo factories for less than one-tenth their cost; a claim of Rs. 6,60,000 on Gilmore and Company was sold for Rs. 1,700 and one of Rs. 1,76,378 against Fergusson Brothers for Rs. 220. On July 22 the sheriff sold Rs. 27,00,000 of debts due to the bank for Rs. 1,60,000. [87]

Of the total Rs. 1,29,12,108 claimed upon estates by the Union Bank, that upon Carr, Tagore and Company was Rs. 18,00,000. The 18 lakhs were secured as follows:

1. Indigo factories: Decracole and Soojanuggur, Hatoory and Noadah—Bunbar—Moisdah—Hyrampore, Hurrindah and Bispore. These factories were being carried on by third parties and were still thought to be of considerable value.

2. Zamindary estates: Mandleghat Taluk and a second mortgage of Patparah.

3. Shares:

> 71   Calcutta Docking Company
> 75   New Fort Gloster Mills Company
> 5   Bengal Indigo Company
> 94   Steam Tug Association

4. Various bills and promissory notes with other parties. The report noted that arrangements were in progress with the trustees of Carr, Tagore and Company for an adjustment of the account. [88]

85Ibid., 1 Mar. and 28 June 1852.
86Ibid., 3 Jan. 1851.
87Ibid., 9 June and 22 July 1848.
88Ibid., 22 May 1848.

In conference between the executive committee of the bank and the trustees of Carr, Tagore and Company, the 18-lakh debt was compromised to 6½ lakhs.[89] Although Carr, Tagore and Company was not insolvent and its trustees had announced that they would pay their debts in full, the debt was sold at auction and purchased by Muddun Mohun Chatterjee, probably a client of the Tagore family, for a mere Rs. 40,500.[90]

It was common practice for debtors of the bank to purchase their own debts at a discount. James Hume, editor of the *Calcutta Star* and a critic of the business establishment of Calcutta, owed the Union Bank Rs. 67,500 and at the auction purchased his own debt for Rs. 21,000. When he came to a meeting of the proprietors and now spoke as a creditor, Longueville Clarke, whom he had attacked in his newspaper, asked Hume how much the bank owed him. The reply was, "Fifteen rupees, four annas." He then asked Hume to account for the securities on the loan of Rs. 67,500. Hume defended himself, but Clarke had made him look the fool.[91] Though clever enough in the cockpit of stockholder meetings, Clarke had not been clever enough to use the legal resources at his disposal to save his fellow shareholders from ruin. One example of a lost opportunity was his failure to invoke Act 111 of 7 and 8 Victoria 1844, which specified the procedure for winding up joint-stock companies. It provided for the appointment of a receiver who had the power to compel the shareholders to contribute, and when they had done so, to release them from further liability. By July it was too late to apply this law to the Union Bank, whose assets had already fallen into the hands of the sheriff.[92]

The government itself made no attempt to see that justice was done either to the creditors or to the shareholders, who were victims of fraud. In fact, it appeared to deliberately obstruct justice. First, it prevented H.M. Elliot from serving on the new executive committee for liquidating the bank's affairs. Elliot's presence would have ensured the confidence of the creditors' committee and perhaps prevented the precipitate seizure of assets by the sheriff, which frustrated plans for an orderly liquidation. The government's position was that no official should serve as director of a trading company, but

89 Ibid., 27 Mar. 1848.
90 Ibid., 24 July 1848.
91 Ibid., 10, 12, and 14 Aug. 1848.
92 Ibid., 7 July 1848.

the Union Bank in liquidation was hardly a trading company.[93] An act to legalize the arrangements made between shareholders and creditors of the Union Bank was first drafted in October 1848 and was promulgated on February 14, 1849. The act simply provided that no consenting creditor should take legal action against any shareholder who pays his assessment.[94]

The business community was crying out for a law to limit the liability of shareholders, but such an act had little chance of passage in the disreputable atmosphere of Calcutta when it could not be passed in England. Instead, at the end of 1850, the government approved Act 43 for the regulation of joint-stock companies. It made registration optional and obligated registered companies to publish their audits and file them with the Supreme Court. Upon failure, a company would go into insolvency court, where an official assignee would determine the assessment and the priority of creditors. Assessments would be determined by the number of shares, not by the individual's reputed wealth, and the liability of ex-shareholders would cease after three years. A shareholder would also retain the power to compromise debts. True, if such an act had been on the books in 1847, it would have enabled the creditors to receive full payment and the shareholders to contribute much less than they did, but it did not provide for the most important needs of joint-stock companies—paid-up capital, official audits, and limited liability. The *Bengal Hurkaru* thought it might better have been called "an act to deter all prudent people from vesting any money in Joint Stock Associations, more especially, in Joint Stock Banks," and, along with Hume's *Calcutta Star,* the newspaper advised against anyone's investing in joint-stock companies.[95]

At the end of January 1850, the executive committee reported that the liquidation could be considered completed. The Union Bank's liabilities had originally been set at sixty lakhs; by the time the scheme began they had been reduced to fifty-four. As of January 1850, liabilities of fifteen lakhs remained. But no claims remained in hostile hands and those in litigation were being adjusted. All the shareholders who had paid their assessments were now free from the threat of lawsuits. Most of the fifteen lakhs outstanding were owed to Glyn and Company, which, well into 1851, continued to raise havoc

93 Ibid., 22 Mar. 1848.
94 Ibid., 19 and 21 Oct. 1848; 15 Feb. 1849.
95 Ibid., 2 and 8 Nov. 1849; 3 Jan. 1851.

among the London shareholders, many of whom had sold out long before the Union Bank had failed. [96]

The Reverend John Marshman summarized the events of 1847–48 in the June 1848 issue of his scholarly periodical, the *Calcutta Review*. In a scathing attack on the European commercial community of Calcutta, he blamed the fall of the Union Bank on the "folly and fraud" of its directors, and characterized the European merchants in general as men given to "systematic extravagance of living and wild gambling speculations . . . whose moral sense is depraved and whose habits are corrupted." Their ability to trade "seems to consist mainly in their consummate unscrupulousness in raising money." They come to Calcutta without capital, take up residence in opulent mansions, purchase horses and carriages, spend great sums on entertaining and "make a mock of religion, systematically despite its duties, and devote the Sabbath Day to hunting." As a result, "the character of Britain as a mercantile nation has been sullied, and the name of Christian has been dishonored in the presence of the heathen." [97]

Assuming that fundamentally the businessmen of Calcutta were neither more nor less ethical than their counterparts in Britain, what was inherent in the system that encouraged large-scale speculation on credit and extravagant personal expenditure? To begin with, a man with capital would hardly be likely to leave his home and family to live as a colonial in exile. Consequently, Calcutta attracted more than its share of men who depended on the capital of others for their speculations. Furthermore, they were determined to make their fortunes quickly and return home, a tradition that began with the first adventurers to the Indies in the seventeenth century. The early European traders borrowed from Indians and from the East India Company; the later ones used the savings of civil and military officers of the company. In the 1830s and 1840s they relied chiefly upon bills drawn at ten-months' date on correspondents at home.

If, while living in the East, they violated the Protestant ethic of frugality, modest living, and patient accumulation of capital, this too is understandable. They adopted a grandiose style of life to compensate in some measure for their loneliness and boredom. In addition, European gentlemen in Calcutta were expected to keep up with the

96 Ibid., 29 and 30 Jan. 1850; 8 July 1851.

97 [John Marshman,] "Commercial Morality and Commercial Prospects in Bengal," *The Calcutta Review*, vol. 9, January–June 1848.

social pace set by highly paid officials, and to support a score of servants who could not easily be dismissed. Because of unhealthy, crowded conditions in much of the city, they considered a mansion in Chowringhee to be as much a necessity as a luxury. Extravagant living on borrowed capital was a deeply ingrained way of life in Calcutta and could only be sustained by large-scale speculation.

Of all Indian products, indigo was most accessible to them for earning quick gains on credit. But indigo was inelastic in production, and fluctuation in demand had to be absorbed in price. To maintain stability of production the industry needed large reserves of liquid capital to tide it over periods of low prices when costs of production were higher than earnings. [98] At bottom the problem was not fraud, folly, or extravagance, but the inability of the European capitalist of Bengal, so heavily dependent on credit, to mobilize the resources to carry the indigo industry during periods of slump. Imported capital would have solved the problem, yet the agency houses sabotaged any scheme that would interfere with their jealously guarded monopoly. Like the proverbial dog in the manger, they could not do the job themselves, and would not let anyone else do it either.

Dwarkanath had been a leader in the fight of the local interests to maintain the monopoly of the Union Bank in the bill market. Although he must have known how fragile was its capital base, he believed, perhaps, that in an emergency he could mobilize new capital from the untold reserves of wealthy Indians who preferred to invest in land rather than in joint-stock companies. Had he been on the scene in 1847, he might have been able to keep the bank afloat. The Europeans who assumed leadership of the bank could not do what Dwarkanath might have done—convince wealthy Indians such as the Day brothers that it was in their interest to bail out the bank.

Two other factors contributed to the precipitate fall of the bank. One was that the overextension of credit made the bank susceptible

98Alasdair I. MacBean, *Export Instability and Economic Development* (London: 1966). MacBean's study shows that primary-product-export instability in underdeveloped countries does not significantly retard economic growth or affect national income or investment. Nevertheless, he does indicate that the short-term consequences for expatriate firms depend on the ability of the firms to sustain drops in earnings. "If the companies are satisfied to hold their operating costs and payments to government steady while letting repatriated profits vary according to good and bad years, the foreign exchange receipts of these countries, net of profits, are made relatively more stable," (P. 87.) The indigo agency houses had no opportunity to vary their repatriated profits, because these had been pledged in advance to their creditors.

to the slightest contraction in international commerce. The other was the hands-off policy of the government. If it had stepped in to restrain the creditors and organize the repayment of debts, the bank could have survived. The indigo factories held by the bank had an intrinsic value, but that value could be realized only in good times. During the commercial crisis they were worthless, and the sheriff sold them at auction for a pittance. Thus the whole was lost because the immediate demands of the creditors could not be met.

The Union Bank was replaced in time by lending institutions that had British personnel and gave preferential treatment to British borrowers. For all its faults, the Union Bank had brought together Indians and Europeans as directors and as employees and had made no racial distinctions in extending credit. If it had survived beyond mid-century, it might well have become a vested interest with a commitment to interracial business engagements. Such a commitment by the premier financial institution of the city might have helped to bridge the chasm that developed between Indian and European in the social, cultural, and political life of Calcutta after midcentury.

Chapter X.

THE LEGACY

While the Union Bank was drifting toward catastrophe, Dwarkanath was involved in preparations for his own final voyage. He had planned a second visit to Europe soon after returning from his first, and an attack of his recurrent fever in January 1845 made him eager to leave the unhealthy city as soon as possible.[1] His motives for returning to Europe, however, were more than personal. "Beyond the gratification of visiting distant lands," he told his friends, he was going not "for any selfish ends." Still troubled by their criticism of his fawning behavior in 1842, he felt called upon to assure his self-selected constituency that this time he would not gloss over their grievances. At a ceremony organized to acknowledge his gift to the city of the royal portraits, he spoke like a modern politician on his way to the capital: "There was, no doubt, difference of opinion between him and numbers of his countrymen, but he would tell one and all of them that wherever his lot might be cast, he would not lose sight of the interest of his country and theirs, nor spare the utmost within his humble power to promote that interest."[2]

On March 8, 1845, with eighty fellow passengers, he left aboard the giant P. & O. steamer *Bentinck* bound for Suez. In his own party were his youngest son, Nagendranath; his nephew, Nabin Chandra Mukherji; his secretary, Thomas R. Safe; and three servants. Among the other passengers were Dr. H.H. Goodeve and, in his charge, four Bengali medical students. Two were supported on scholarships provided by Tagore, and he had cajoled a group of Calcutta philanthropists and a reluctant government into supporting the other two.[3]

1 *Calcutta Star,* 18 Jan. 1845; *Bengal Hurkaru,* 8 and 14 Jan. 1845.
2 *Bengal Hurkaru,* 3 Mar. 1845.
3 IO Records, Despatches to India and Bengal, vol. 45, pp. 417–18; Public Department, 9 July (10) 1845. Brougham Papers, Auckland to Brougham, 1 May 1845.

When the party broke journey in Egypt, Dwarkanath was in high spirits. He conversed in Persian with Mahomet Ali about the construction of a railway from the Red Sea to the Mediterranean and appeared, wrote James Stuart, "to be playing the Great Man to a vast extent. The Pasha has been very attentive to him, much more so than he was before, and gave him a Palace to live in and his own scarlet clothed mules to ride, and young Ibrahim Pasha took him to every place that was to be seen and altogether he was, as he himself writes, 'once more an Indian Prince.'"[4] After Egypt and the quarantine stop at Malta, the party traveled to Bordeaux where they sampled wine from the winery that supplied Carr, Tagore and Company with its clarets, then spent ten days in Paris and reached London on June 21.[5]

Dwarkanath was determined that his son and nephew would use their time in England to good advantage. Nagendranath was to acquire a liberal education, studying literature, Latin, and "the manners of Europe" to "pave the way for my future advancement when I again reach my native shores."[6] Nabin Chandra, who had served as an apprentice in the Union Bank, was to be trained in business and was placed with Roberts, Mitchell and Company. "They all promise to make me a thorough merchant within the time I shall remain here," he wrote his cousin Girindranath. The company's silk broker worked with him two or three hours each day, opening silk bundles and pointing out differences in quality and price.[7] All was not drudgery, however, for Nagendranath teased him, "when I met you yesterday you were . . . impatient to throw yourself at the feet of Miss Roberts."[8] His uncle, wrote Nabin Chandra, was "exceedingly pleased" with his progress. "He often lectures me to take care not to be like Chunder Mohun [Chatterjee] who came here as a baboo and out the same without reaping any

4KNT ms., letter from James Stuart, undated. K.C. Mittra, *Memoir of Dwarkanath Tagore* (Calcutta: 1870), p. 109.

5Ibid., pp. 110 ff.

6Tagore Family Papers, Rabindra Sadhana, "Our Family Correspondence," Nagendranath Tagore to Sir James Lushington, 6 Aug. 1848. Nagendra also sent home for Hindustani dictionaries and grammars. Nagendranath to Nabin Chandra Mukherji, 6 July 1846.

7"Our Family Correspondence," Nabin Chandra to Girindranath Tagore, 6 July and 20 Nov. 1845.

8Ibid., Nagendranath Tagore to Nabin Chandra, 16 July 1846.

benefits from London. . . . He was only fond of skylarking at the ladies and nothing else." 9

The two young men attended the theater, read the latest novels, and commented intelligently on such political events as the fall of the Peel ministry and the dispute with America over the Northwest territories. The Americans, Nabin felt, would be certain to lose any war with Britain and were afraid of the English, who recently had defeated the Sikhs, reputedly the most fearless soldiers on earth. But the young men reserved their greatest enthusiasm for the lectures of Michael Faraday at the Royal Institution. Nabin Chandra took voluminous notes on electromagnetism and transmitted them in detail to Girindranath in Calcutta. 10

Even more diligent in their studies were the four Bengali medical students. When they first arrived, Suruji Kumar Chuckerbutty (later Suruji Goodeve Chuckerbutty) led his class of 600 in comparative anatomy, and at the completion of the course, Bholanath Bose, in competition with 200 English students, won two gold medals, one in comparative anatomy and one in botany. The others, Gopal Chandra Seal and Dwarkanath Bose, did almost as well, and all of them went on to productive and distinguished medical careers in India. 11

While this historic first contingent of Indian students abroad was hard at work, their patron kept a frenetic schedule of social engagements. "Baboo," observed his nephew, "goes out after breakfast, once comes in the middle of the day to take some luncheon, then goes out to dinner and dancing parties, comes back at the dead hour of $2\frac{1}{2}$ in the morning when not a soul wakes except I to get instructions for the next day's work and what is strange is though he goes to bed as late as that he rises in the morning at six as fresh as possible." 12

Presumably, he kept his promise to promote the interests of his countrymen. Soon after his arrival, Dwarkanath met with officials of the East India Company and later exchanged views with William Ewart Gladstone, then Secretary for War and Colonies, on the

9Ibid., Nabin Chandra to Girindranath Tagore, 7 Nov. 1845.

10Ibid., 20 Nov. and 19 Dec. 1845; 2, 7, and 24 Jan. and 2 June 1846.

11Ibid., 19 May 1846; *Bengal Hurkaru,* 2 and 9 May 1848; Lt. Col. D.G. Crawford, *Roll of the Indian Medical Service, 1615–1930* (London: 1930), pp. 242–43, 248; S. Goodeve Chuckerbutty, *Popular Lectures on Subjects of Indian Interest* (Calcutta: 1870).

12"Our Family Correspondence," Nabin Chandra to Girindranath Tagore, 6 July 1845.

removal of religious bars to the admission of Indians into Parliament.[13] The Queen and Prince Albert welcomed him back to the court as an old friend, asked him about Lord Hardinge, and expressed the hope that the governor-general "is doing all to improve the country." He attended a Liberal party meeting at Fishmonger's Hall where "Lord Melbourne spoke in praise of Sir Robert Peel . . . . Lord John Russell also spoke and I returned thanks for health."[14] From early August to mid-September 1845, Dwarkanath visited Ireland. After spending some time with the Protestant officialdom, he stayed for a few weeks with Daniel O'Connell. They discussed their common problems as subjects of foreign rule; but, where O'Connell saw the solution as independence, Dwarkanath looked forward to a stronger imperial union based on racial and religious equality.[15]

Cultural interaction with the British was, to Dwarkanath, as important as political and certainly more enjoyable. He hosted a dinner for Dickens, Thackeray, and other men of letters at which "the conversation sparkeled with wit of the highest order."[16] J.H. Stocqueler, former editor of the *Englishman,* who found Dwarkanath looking rather weary from "the racket of London life," arranged a dinner for him with a lively group of minor literary celebrities. "There was plenty of intelligent drollery and good-humored raillery, and as Dwarkanath 'laughed consumedly' in the intervals of the sober chat with his neighbour who was curious about the Ramayana, the Shasters, the Koran, and the Zendvesta, I saw the party was a hit. Indeed, he said to me, when we adjourned to coffee in the drawing room—'I have had a delightful evening. I have lived an hour in a galaxy of stars.'"[17]

At another party, Dwarkanath met the author "J. Dix," who had recently returned from America. "I was going to America two years ago," Dwarkanath told him, "but that Dickens book frightened me, and I did not go. Is it all true what he said, for if so, I would not like the people?" Dix replied that he had "never been better treated than in America, and that as for rudeness and incivility, I had not

13K.C. Mittra, *Memoir,* p. 116.
14Rabindra Sadhana, Tagore Family Papers, loose diary pages, dated 7 and 30 July and 2 Aug. 1845.
15K.C. Mittra, *Memoir,* pp. 115–16.
16Ibid., p. 114.
17J.H. Stocqueler, *Memoirs of a Journalist,* (Bombay and Calcutta: 1873) pp. 124, 170.

experienced any," and then asked, "Do *you* think of going to America?" "I do," replied Dwarkanath, "and next year; what you have said gives me confidence, but I shall read your book first well." Dix concluded that he had "seldom met with a man of greater energy and ability than Dwarkanath Tagore. He talked on all subjects, and evinced a depth and variety of information which was quite surprising." [18]

The London winter of 1845 was particularly dreary and cold, and by early December Dwarkanath was "very unwell." [19] To escape he went to Paris on 18 December, 1845, and stayed there until March 9, 1846; during that time his health improved, and he began to "enjoy himself just as much as ever, just as gay as in London." [20] While in Paris, Dwarkanath called on F. Max Müller, the Sanskritist, who attributed great significance to their meeting. Dwarkanath found him copying the text and commentary of the Rig Veda, and Max Müller surmised that "Debendranath heard from his father that European scholars had begun in good earnest to study the Veda, and that its halo of unapproachable sanctity would soon disappear." [21] Dwarkanath ended his visit to Paris with a massive farewell party at which, according to an exaggerated newspaper report, he gave away handfuls of gems. [22] He returned to London in good health, "so much so," wrote his nephew, "that he will be able to enjoy his English parties without the least fatigue. He almost never dines at home." [23]

Increasingly, Dwarkanath had surrendered himself to self-destructive hedonism. He behaved as if his strength and his business affairs were slipping from his control. In his frustration he alternated between excessive spending and a last-minute compulsion to keep a tight hold on his money. Girindranath, for example, had asked Nabin Chandra to send him some plates of pierglass, and Nabin replied, "If I get them cheap. . . . I rather think Baboo will not pay for these. I know he has grown economical in these respects. . . . The truth is

18Extract from J. Dix, *Pen and Ink Sketches of Authors, etc.,* courtesy of Amritamaya Mukherjee.

19"Our Family Correspondence," Nabin Chandra to Girindranath Tagore, 10 Mar. 1845, and note from Nagendranath Tagore to Nabin Chandra, undated.

20Ibid., T.R. Safe to Nabin Chandra Mukherji, 27 Dec. 1845.

21F. Max Müller, *Biographical Essays* (London: 1884), pp. 36–40.

22*Bengal Hurkaru,* 9 May 1846, excerpted from *The Court Journal* (London), 14 Mar. 1846.

23"Our Family Correspondence," Nabin Chandra to Girindranath Tagore, 10 Mar. 1846.

the money—your father will not give a single pice. Of that I am sure." Again he wrote, "I heard Mr. Safe asking for some money from the Baboo to buy something for Ramanath Tagore in which he seemed not to have any inclination to pay." [24] On the other hand, he continued to entertain at parties, shower his hosts with lavish gifts, and donate to charitable institutions. [25] To the outside world he was still a munificent prince, but to his family and intimates he had become a man preoccupied with financial security.

Whether this was justified or not, he began to worry about his business affairs at home. Nabin Chandra informed Girindranath that his uncle intended to decrease the enormous establishment in the godown department and "to get rid of the strangers from these and appoint one of the family on his return. Of course he will manage personally. In the meantime he has written to Dr. MacPherson to place Baboo Mudden as temporary in that department in lieu of Malik." [26]

In May 1845, Dwarkanath wrote Debendranath, in charge of his zamindari affairs, a letter that reflects both his economic anxieties and his disappointment with his eldest son:

I have this moment received your letter of the 8th April and quite vexed with the negligence shown both on the part of Raja Baradakant and your own Mooktears about the sale of Tallok Shahoosh. As for the former he does not care a pice about his own affairs—but how your servants can shamefully neglect to report these matters is surprising to me. All that I have hitherto heard from other quarters, as well as what Mr. Gordon has written to me about your Amlas now convinces me of the truth of their reports. It is only a source of wonder to me that all my estates are not ruined. Your time I am sure being more taken up in writing for the newspapers and in fighting with the missionaries than in watching over and protecting the important matters which you leave in the hands of your favourite Amlas—instead of attending to them yourself most vigilantly. If I was strong enough to bear the heat and climate of India, I would immediately leave London personally to superintend—as it is—my only alternative will be to write and authorize the House to get rid of the mortgaged properties and to dispose of as many of the Mofussil estates as they can as soon as possible.

24 Ibid., 8 Sept. and 7 Oct. 1845 and 6 Mar. 1846.

25 Rabindra Sadhana, Tagore Family Papers, letter from Theobald Mathew, Cork, 17 Oct. 1845. "The munificent donation which you placed at my disposal for charitable purposes, knowing your ardent zeal for education of youth, I gave to the excellent Richmond School."

26 "Our Family Correspondence," Nabin Chandra to Girindranath Tagore, 7 Feb. 1846.

I hear of nothing going right. We are losing every Lawsuit. Doorbasinee and Ramisserpore in confusion and others quickly becoming so. The mail tomorrow morning prevents my further writing on other matters quietly and at leisure. Tell Deby Roy, Greender and Ramchunder that I have received their letters and postponed answering until next mail, also Ashutosh Dey.

I hope Gordon has been able to arrange about Rani Kattawaney's before this letter reaches. Also tell Deby Roy that if he could get a purchaser of Doorbasinee I shall have no objection to sell but not under 2,50,000 Rupees—say two lacs fifty thousand rupees. It is fully worth that sum to anyone who would properly manage it and yield him 30 to 40,000 profit. The purchaser can easily get it sold through the Collector's sale which would enable him to break off all the tenures on the estates. To us the collector's sale and our purchase will always give an appearance of a Benamee transaction.

*   *   *

I see Mr. Elliot has left the Chowringhee House. Do try to sell, it always being difficult to get a tenant.

If the estate Shahhos and Mulloy have not yet been put into the charge of Mr. MacKinzie, do so without a moments delay.

With my best regards to all at home. [27]

Soon after his return from Paris, Dwarkanath's health began to fail. His last month was spent at Worthing, a seaside resort, accompanied by his secretary, a musician, and seventeen servants. Even here he played the celebrity and received visitors, including the Duchess of Cleveland, who came to see him daily. Years later, the innkeeper reported that through all his pain he had never complained but had remained cheerful, amiable, gracious, and kind to the lowest servant. Hooly, his favorite servant, slept at his doorstep and during the day sat near him on a mat "tickling the soles of his feet for hours together." On July 27, hardly conscious, he was brought back to St. Georges Hotel in London, where he died on August 1. [28] According to Stocqueler: "A terrific thunderstorm passed over the great city at the hour of his death, as if it were only natural that so truly great a man should pass away in a moment of striking

27 Rabindra Sadhana, Tagore Family Papers, Dwarkanath Tagore to Debendranath Tagore, 22 May 1845.

28 Letter from Satyendranath Tagore to Gaganendranath Tagore from Worthing, Sussex, 25 August 1862, published in *Tattvabodhini Patrika*, undated clipping, KNT Collection.

solemnity. I had never heard such peals of thunder, or saw such vivid flashes of lightening . . . as that which accompanied the divorce of the soul from all that was earthly of the noble Dwarkanath."[29] He was buried without religious rites in Kensal Green Cemetery, watched over by his son; his nephew; the medical students; and, among other friends, his former partners, Major Henderson and William Prinsep. The Queen sent four royal carriages. On his tombstone is carved the simple inscription, "Dwarkanath Tagore of Calcutta."[30]

Dwarkanath's death left his young charges helpless and unprepared for the future. Nabin Chandra returned to Calcutta and threw himself on the mercy of Debendranath and Girindranath.[31] Nagendranath, only seventeen at the time, abandoned his plan to enter Cambridge University, and spent the next few months wandering about England, losing himself in drink and sightseeing. Although he wrote Nabin Chandra, "you know I do not like the English people in general. I hate their customs and detest their mercenariness," he was reluctant to return home.[32] When, at last, he did return, he wrote in vain to Lord Auckland, Sir, James Lushington, Sir James Hogg, and T.C. Plowden for help in obtaining a government appointment.[33]

Meanwhile, Debendranath, along with his brother Girindranath, performed a cremation ceremony on the bank of the Ganges using an effigy of *kusa* grass. As they began the formal, lengthy sraddha ceremonies, they were advised by their relatives and by Radhakanta Deb not to deviate from the orthodox ritual. But Debendranath insisted on a Brahmo ceremony, and the sraddha turned into a scene of chaos and confusion, the guests walked out, and Dwarkanath's sons were ostracized from Hindu society. "This was," wrote Debendranath, "the first instance of a sraddha being performed without idolatry in accordance with the rites of Brahma-dharma," and

29 Stocqueler, *Memoirs,* p. 171.

30 According to the *Times,* Dwarkanath died of an affliction of the liver; obituary, 19 Sept. 1846. Hyslop Bell attributes his death to "auge or malarial fever." J.H. Bell, *British Folks and British India Fifty Years Ago: Joseph Pease and His Contemporaries* (London: n.d.), p. 143.

31 "Our Family Correspondence," Nabin Chandra to Girindranath Tagore, 20 Aug. 1846.

32 Ibid., Nagendranath Tagore to Nabin Chandra Mukherji, 27 Aug. and 17 Oct. 1846.

33 Ibid., Nagendranath Tagore to Lushington, 6 Aug. 1848; to Auckland, 4 Apr. 1848; Auckland to Nagendranath, 30 Nov. 1848.

Dwarkanath's death-ceremonies became a landmark in the history of religious reform in India. [34]

Early in December, the leading Europeans, joined by a large number of Indians, held their own memorial meeting in Town Hall. The European speakers emphasized his liberality to the poor, his devotion to interracial friendship, and his efforts to educate his countrymen. A Bengali speaker noted that "India has now no friend to plead for her rights and privileges, no advocate to espouse her cause," and called on his countrymen to "put their shoulders to the wheel, identify their interest with the interest of Government, come forward and support undertakings which are for the general welfare of the community." Appropriately, the meeting voted to commemorate Dwarkanath's memory with a scholarship fund to support Indian students at the University College of London, [35] but the fund fell victim to the crisis of 1847.

Between the death of Dwarkanath and the closing of Carr, Tagore and Company sixteen months later, Debendranath and Girindranath exercised majority control of the firm. Debendranath left its supervision to Girindranath, on whose advice the partnership was dissolved and the remaining British partners were paid handsome salaries to carry on the business. The house might have survived under Girindranath had it not been for the commercial crisis of 1847, but on December 31, unable to meet a demand for Rs. 30,000, the firm closed its doors. [36] Donald McLeod Gordon called a meeting with the creditors on 4 April 1848, and Robert Castle Jenkins, as chairman, read the accompanying statement of accounts. Although the firm's stated assets were adequate to cover its liabilities, immediate payment would have been impossible. Therefore, to forestall insolvency and a devastating auction, the creditors agreed to place the properties in trust, with R.C. Jenkins, F.R. Hampton, and Ramanath Tagore as trustees. The debts were to be paid off from current income and the gradual sale of property.

The meeting was pervaded by an atmosphere of amiability, tinged with sadness for the death of Dwarkanath, sympathy for his inept sons, and respect for the integrity of his former partners. Dwarkanath having left behind a large number of dependents who now

34Debendranath Tagore, *The Autobiography of Maharshi Devendranath Tagore* (Calcutta: 1909), pp. 46 ff.

35K.C. Mittra, *Memoir,* app. c., pp. xlvii-lviii.

36*Autobiography of Maharshi Devendranath Tagore,* pp. 53, 63.

CHART 6. STATEMENT OF ACCOUNTS

Assets

Pledged:

Joint stock shares	Rs. 4,19,500
Indigo blocks	2,95,000
Seebpore works (Narayanganj, Dacca)	50,000
Personal account	4,00,000
Patkharah, less first mortage	2,00,000
Sundry small home properties	50,000
Mundleghat estate	2,00,000
	Rs. 16,14,500

Unpledged:

Joint stock shares	54,450
Indigo block	1,05,000
Indigo for 1848, 21,000 *maunds* at 120 per *maund* —2,10,000, less required expenses, 80,000	1,60,000
Silk factories	1,05,000
Personal account	8,64,000
	Rs. 12,88,450

Total assets, pledged and unpledged.	Rs. 29,02,950

Liabilities

Covered:

Loans on joint stock shares	Rs. 3,45,000
Sundry security	7,70,000
Balance indigo account in Union Bank	5,20,000
	Rs. 16,35,000

Uncovered:

Union Bank including discounts	Rs. 4,25,000
Sundry floating accounts in India	70,000
Sundry floating accounts in Europe	1,76,000
Sundry fixed accounts in Europe	80,000
London exchange account	1,60,000
	Rs. 9,11,000

Total liabilities, covered and uncovered	Rs. 25,46,000

looked to his sons, W.F. Fergusson suggested that they be permitted to retain the family residence at Jorasanko. He absolved the partners from any blame for the collapse of the firm, and D.M. Gordon, "overpowered with emotion" and "even effected to tears," assured the meeting that "none of the partners had benefited in the remotest degree by any portion of its funds."[37] The government was equally generous with Tagore's sons, and in the case of one large estate, Mandleghat, which was not even a trust property, permitted them to delay revenue payments. In an unusually generous decision, the government held that, "from considerations of the peculiar pressure of the times, [the government] is unwilling to allow the sons of a man who deserved and enjoyed in so high a degree the respect of the government as the late lamented Dwarkanath Tagore to be sold of their patrimony in consequence of a comparatively small arrear of revenue."[38]

D.M. Gordon and James Stuart, as Gordon, Stuart and Company, assumed management of the Bengal Coal Company and the Calcutta Steam Tug Association, along with the commercial activities of the defunct house. They also inherited the enemies of Carr, Tagore and Company, foremost among whom was Captain Engledue, Calcutta agent for the P. & O. At the March 1848 meeting of the Steam Tug Association, Captain Engledue accused Gordon and Stuart of furnishing inflated reports on the capital position of the company, overpaying for coal and other provisions, raising dividends by promissory notes, and neglecting the maintenance of the tugs. [39]

Was this Association to go the way of all flesh—was it to go the way of all other companies in Calcutta? If there was any independence remaining in this place—any spark of public spirit, it would appear this evening, in the removal from office of the present Secretaries. The management was never secure in their hands. They belonged to the late Firm which had been the downfall of the Assam Company, the Salt Company, the Ferry Bridge Company, the Union Bank, the Tropical Insurance Company, the Inland Steam Company and the Coal Company:—and here they are now connected as secretaries with the Steam Tug Company, the property of which is disappearing rapidly. . . . Their connection with the Bengal Coal Company utterly disqualified them from the office. [40]

Those present at the May meeting voted seven in favor and six against the removal of Gordon and Stuart, but when proxies were counted, the final total was twelve for and forty-seven against. Dwarkanath's old mufassal constituency saved the day for his

37 *Bengal Hurkaru,* 5 Apr. 1848.
38 WBSA, Revenue Proceedings, Government of Bengal, 29 Mar. (100) 1848, letter dated 24 Dec. 1847.
39 *Bengal Hurkaru,* 28 Mar. and 19 May 1848.
40 Ibid., 19 May 1848.

successors,[41] and Gordon, Stuart and Company retained management of both the Bengal Coal Company and the Steam Tug Association until their retirement in 1867. Even the *Bengal Hurkaru* had sided with Engledue. "It appears to us," wrote the editor, "that the old system of making houses of agency secretaries to Joint Stock Companies is unsafe and impolitic."[42] But instead of disappearing, the "old system" proved its utility and, as the managing-agency system, became the model for the organization of almost all large business enterprise in India.[43]

Less is known about the disposal of Dwarkanath's personal debts. Debendranath, in writing that the total liabilities of "the firm" amounted to one crore of rupees, could well have been referring to his father's personal liabilities, which Debendranath pledged to discharge in full.[44] The family held onto Jorasanko, but they could not save Belgatchia, the symbol of Dwarkanath's civic leadership. The house and gardens were eventually sold to the Paikpara Raj family, and the Maharajah of Burdwan purchased most of the contents, including the fine glassware, cutlery, and artworks collected by Dwarkanath on his two trips to Europe [45] The amicable settlement, however, left virtually untouched the properties that Dwarkanath had placed in trust for his sons. They gave up their life interest in the property, but were permitted to retain one-third of the rents for their maintenance. Debendranath gradually assumed management of the estates, and by the time of his death in 1905 net income from zamindari had increased threefold.[46]

41 Ibid., 19 and 20 May 1848.

42 Ibid., 29 Mar. 1848.

43 Blair B. Kling, "The Origin of the Managing Agency System in India," *Journal of Asian Studies,* vol. 26, no. 1 (November 1966), pp. 37–47.

44 *Autobiography of Maharshi Devendranath Tagore,* p. 63. In the notes to Chakravarty's Bengali edition of Debendranath's autobiography it is suggested that the "crore of rupees" refers to Dwarkanath's personal debts. Dwarkanath had borrowed money from the descendants of Ramdulal Sarkar and from Raja Sukhamoy, Birnara Singha Mullick, Joyram Mitra, Rajchancha Das (Mar), Rani Katyayani of Paikpara, Raja Harinath of Kasimbazar, and Tilak Chandra, the Maharaja of Burdwan. Satischandra Chakravarty, ed., *Shrimanmaharshi Devendranath Thakurer Atmajibani* (Calcutta: 1927), pp. 333–39. Chakravarty takes his information from Nagendranath Basu and Byomkesh Mustafi, *Banger Jatiya Itihas, Brahman Kanda, Pirali Brahman Biberan,* vol. I, pt. 6, p. 355.

45 *Bengal Past and Present,* vol. 27 (June 1924), p. 221. *Bengal Hurkaru,* 4, 14, and 21 Sept. 1848.

46 *Bengal Hurkaru,* 6 Apr. 1848. KNT Collection, Case for Opinion, re: division of property of Debendranath Tagore requested by Hitindranath Tagore, opinion of B.M. Chakravarty, 23 Apr. 1907.

Important as these estates were, they were not as important as the spiritual legacy bequeathed by Dwarkanath to his descendants. By cherishing the freedom of mind and spirit he exemplified, the Tagores became the social and cultural pioneers of Bengal in the late nineteenth and early twentieth centuries. Although, of his own sons, neither Girindranath nor Nagendranath, who died childless at age 29, distinguished themselves, two of Girindranath's grandsons, Abanendranath and Gaganendranath, were precursors of the modern art movement in Bengal.[47] Debendranath, on the other hand, became the leader of the Brahmo Samaj and the prototype of the modern Indian religious teacher who creates a new religious synthesis and attracts disciples by his saintly bearing. Of Debendranath's fourteen children, Satyendranath became the first Indian to compete successfully for an appointment in the hallowed covenanted Indian Civil Service. Others earned fame as scholars, artists, and musicians. Rabindranath, the most gifted of all, was an enormously prolific artist, composer, novelist, dramatist, poet, and educational philosopher. His biographer, Edward Thompson, acknowledged the influence of his inheritance: "If he was fortunate in the time of his birth, when such a flowering season lay before his native tongue, in his family he had a gift which cannot be over-estimated. He was born a Tagore; that is, he was born into the one family in which he could experience the national life at its very fullest and freest."[48] Five and six generations after Dwarkanath, the Tagores have continued to produce men and women of talent. What most of his descendants share with Dwarkanath is his quality of bold creativity, breaking of new ground, defiance of convention, and rejection of provincialism in favor of a universal outlook.

Tagores have been entrepreneurs in the arts, in social reform, and in education, but among his hundreds of descendants, few have followed Dwarkanath's example and taken up business as a profession. In this, Dwarkanath's descendants reflect the declining role of the bhadralok[49] in the business life of their province. There have been many explanations for this decline, some involving internal

47 W.G. Archer, *India and Modern Art* (London: 1959), pp. 38 ff.

48 Edward Thompson, *Rabindranath Tagore, Poet and Dramatist* (London: 1948), p. 20.

49 Literally, "the respectable people." For a description of the bhadralok class see J.H. Broomfield, *Elite Conflict in a Plural Society: Twentieth-Century Bengal* (Berkeley: 1968), pp. 5–20.

values and others external pressures.[50] One factor often cited by scholars—including Karl Marx—is that the Permanent Settlement diverted Bengali capital from commerce and industry into land; but the case of Dwarkanath indicates that landholding was not necessarily a barrier to commercial activity, and, in fact, could help support it. Rather, one must look to the vast changes that occurred in the economy and society of Bengal in the second half of the nineteenth century. After midcentury the scale of economic activity in Calcutta greatly expanded. For Bengalis to compete successfully against British firms engaged in international trade and managing agency required access to the British capital market, knowledge of modern technology and business organization, and familiarity with overseas markets, all more readily available to Europeans than to Bengalis. In addition, Europeans received favored treatment in the use of railway and shipping facilities and found it easier to obtain credit from local and imperial banks. In Dwarkanath's day, when business operations were smaller and simpler, the British advantage was less obvious. Petty trade and small-scale industrial activities, such as iron founding and milling, were still open, but the bhadralok considered these to be low-status occupations.

Simultaneously, the expansion of British rule presented the bhadralok with alternative opportunities to achieve enhanced social status in a bureaucracy growing in size, professionalization, and prestige. The inauguration of the examination system in 1853 and the assumption of direct rule by the crown in 1858 created an aura around government service that extended to the lowly nonconvenanted ranks occupied by Indians. In the early nineteenth century, business had been the most accessible avenue of upward social mobility. Now, given the choice between government service and lower-status business activities, upper-class Bengalis chose government service, a choice, incidentally, consistent with the traditional status system of Bengal. Still another factor was the greater opportunities for higher education, especially in the liberal arts. The bhadralok who flocked to the colleges and universities received an education that prepared them for little else than government service or professions such as law and education. Nevertheless, though most Bengali bhadralok would have considered it beneath their dignity to

50 Blair B. Kling, "Entrepreneurship and Regional Identity in Bengal," in David Kopf, ed., *Bengal Regional Identity* (East Lansing: 1969), pp. 74–84. Nripendra Kumar Dutt, *Origin and Growth of Caste in India*, vol. II (Calcutta: 1965).

become petty traders, many would have been quite willing to work in
the executive offices of large British firms. But here they came up
against still another barrier—racial prejudice. British firms domiciled
in Calcutta preferred to recruit their apprentices in Britain from
among their own "race," and even Bengalis with technical degrees
from British universities were excluded from British firms.[51]

Although Bengali leadership in both commerce and industry
declined, Bengalis continued, until the twentieth century, to play an
important though subordinate role in commerce. In 1855, two of the
leading agency houses were Bengali—Ram Gopal Ghosh and Company and Ashutosh Day. The large British export-import houses
employed Bengali banian firms as middlemen between themselves
and the bazaar retailers or upcountry produce brokers, and the
Calcutta commercial directory for 1855 lists 50 banians and 150
"Bengali commercial traders."[52] By 1863 the number of Bengali
agency houses had increased to 7, and the directory for that year lists
35 Bengali banians and 31 "ships banians," primarily Bengalis.[53]

Despite their numbers, however, their position was not what it had
been in Dwarkanath's day, when many of the banians had been
independent merchants. For example, in 1839 Ram Gopal Ghose
wrote a friend in the government service that five of their Hindoo
College classmates had "all turned their attention to trading," and
that in a few years he himself expected to "become an independent
merchant—an honourable profession, the prospect of which thrills
me with delight."[54] As early as 1853, however, the Bengali daily
Samband Prabhakar noted the "shameful . . . retreat" of the Bengali
middle class from trade and commerce and criticized their preference
for working under foreigners to launching their own business
houses.[55] One indication of their declining status, as well as of the
increasing racial exclusiveness of the Europeans, is that the Bengal
Chamber of Commerce, which had five Bengali members in 1855,

51Amiya Kumar Bagchi, *Private Investment in India, 1900–1939* (Cambridge: 1972),
p. 205. Robert I. Crane, "Technical Education and Economic Development in India
before World War I," in C.A. Anderson and M.J. Bowman, *Education and Economic
Development* (New York: 1965).

52*Bengal Directory and Annual Register* (Calcutta: 1855), pt. VII, pp. 55, 58, 59. For a
description of the banian's work, see *Hindoo Patriot*, 11 Feb. 1858.

53*New Calcutta Directory* (Calcutta: 1863), pt. VIII, pp. 45–48.

54Ram Gopal Sanyal, *Bengal Celebrities* (Calcutta: 1889), vol. I, pp. 179–80.

55Quoted in Benoy Ghose, "The Economic Character of the Urban Middle-Class
in Nineteenth Century Bengal," in B.N. Ganguli, ed., *Readings in Indian Economic
History* (Bombay: 1964), pp. 146–47.

had none by 1860.[56] The late-nineteenth-century banians came mostly from the traditional merchant castes of Bengal. In time the successful ones purchased zamindaris, adopted the prevailing bhadralok cultural values, and lost "their mercantile instincts."[57]

Bengalis fared even worse in industrial enterprise. In 1842, aside from banks and insurance companies, there were six joint-stock companies, four managed by Carr, Tagore and Company and one by the Parsi, Rustomjee Cowasjee. The sixth was the P. & O., which, aside from the Assam Company, was the only firm in which majority shares were held in Britain. The situation had not altered significantly by 1847; and in 1855 a Bengali, Bysumber Sen, joined George Acland in establishing the first jute mill in India at Rishra, which they carried on together for three years.[58] By 1863, however, the number of joint-stock companies in Calcutta had increased to sixty-nine, the largest sixteen of which were sterling companies directed from Britain. There were fourteen steamer lines, twelve tea companies, twelve docking companies, seven transport companies, seven coal companies, four railways, three jute mills, one telegraph company, one iron works, and one gas company. Only a handful of Indians sat among the directors of rupee companies; three of the collieries were owned by Indians, and one steamship line was owned by Herra Lall Seal, the son of Motilal.[59] Thus, though Bengalis continued to participate on a modest scale in joint-stock enterprises, Calcutta, after the Mutiny, was engulfed by an influx of British firms. Bengal had entered a new, advanced stage of economic activity, and the Bengalis had been left behind in the economic race. In the countryside, Bengalis of traditional trading castes continued to have an important place in the production and trade in primary products and in some extractive industries. But by the end of the nineteenth century even they were rapidly being displaced by Marwari and other non-Bengali trading communities.[60]

Toward the end of the century, the Bengalis became increasingly concerned about their economic decline. Their response was the swadeshi movement which called on Indians to boycott British imports, to manufacture and use indigenous products, to develop

56 Bengal Chamber of Commerce, *Half-Yearly Reports* (Calcutta: 1853–1860).
57 Prafulla Chandra Ray, *Life and Experiences of a Bengali Chemist* (Calcutta: 1932, 1935), I, 446.
58 Ibid., p. 466.
59 *New Calcutta Directory,*
60 Ray, *Bengali Chemist,* pp. 440 ff.

indigenous industries, and to provide jobs for Bengali youth. Moved by idealism, young men with no business experience set aside their books and launched swadeshi enterprises, most of which failed. One of these young men was Dwarkanath's grandson, Jyotindranath, the talented older brother of Rabindranath, who tried without success to launch a match company, a powerloom, and a steamship company.[61]

Like Dwarkanath, the swadeshi entrepreneurs saw business, politics, and nation-building as a unified whole. True, Dwarkanath's "nation" was an integral part of the British empire, whereas the patriots of fifty years later conceived of India as a separate nation. But the same principle underlay both: a man could not separate his business activities from his civic, social, and political responsibilities. As a result, profits might suffer, business might be neglected for other duties, and the entrepreneur might not always base his investment decisions on rational economic considerations. Because civic or patriotic duties took precedence over business, and neither Dwarkanath nor his swadeshi successors made the most of economic opportunities, their success or failure must be measured in political as well as economic terms. Dwarkanath and the swadeshi entrepreneurs, each in his own way, presided over an "age of enterprise" in Bengal. The 1840s, like the first decades of the twentieth century, were a period of faith in the future, exhilaration, accomplishment, and civic spirit. Although in economic terms the achievements were modest, they were vital to the development of Indian nationhood.

61 Rabindranath Tagore, *Reminiscences* (London: 1954), pp. 146–47, 252–55. Concerning swadeshi, see Atulchandra Gupta, ed., *Studies in the Bengal Renaissance* (Jadavpur: 1958), pp. 203–23, 543–55; and Great Britain, *Parliamentary Papers,* 1919, vol. XVII, pp. 72–74, *Report of the Indian Industrial Commission, 1916–1918.*

CONCLUSION

Throughout most of Calcutta's 250-year history, outsiders rather than Bengalis have dominated the city's economic life. Until independence, the British controlled the city's major firms; after independence they shared control with businessmen drawn chiefly from non-Bengali trading communities. Yet, for a brief interlude at midpoint in the city's history—the 1830s and 1840s—Bengalis were the most active associates of the British in the modern sector of the economy. The era of Bengali participation coincided with the growth of interracial civic institutions and local community spirit. It also witnessed the introduction of the steam engine on a commercial scale, the development of new industries such as tea, steam shipping, and coal mining; and the application of new forms of business organization—the joint-stock company, the managing-agency system and commercial banking.

Presumably, the vitality of Calcutta's civic institutions was related to the participation of the city's largest ethnic community in the economic power structure. For a short period the Bengali elite found that the interests of their community and those of the city coincided and were willing to devote themselves to civic as well as community affairs. Calcutta was, however, a city of transplanted Britishers as well. It was founded by the British and its civic, governmental, and major business institutions were British in form and inspiration. It was as much an extension of Britain as it was a part of India and in closer communication with London than with, for example, Delhi. To build a polis, based on the solidarity of its inhabitants, called for a catalytic agent identified with both of the leading communities. The man who tried to fill this role was Dwarkanath Tagore.

Dwarkanath was the scion of a family that typified the cosmopolitan, *nouveau riche* Bengali landholding and commercial elite of Calcutta. As commercial intermediaries, the Tagores had trod their way adroitly between two contradictory worlds and in a pragmatic, piecemeal fashion had adopted some of the superficial trappings of western culture. But they did not take western civilization seriously. Instead, following the traditional path of upward mobility, they spent vast sums in an effort to acquire status within Bengali Hindu society.

Early in his life, Dwarkanath Tagore decided that the future lay with the West, that he would depart from his family's path and would aspire to acceptance in European society. It was a bold decision. Collaboration in business ventures with the British had long-established precedents, but acceptance into British society as an equal was unheard of. In his decision can be discerned the influence of his teacher and guide, Rammohun Roy. Rammohun led Dwarkanath beyond the superficialities of western civilization to an appreciation of European intellectual power and the need to incorporate Western political and ethical concepts into his own personal set of convictions. Through Rammohun, Dwarkanath was introduced to the small circle of enlightened Europeans devoted to utilitarianism, unitarianism, free trade, and civil liberties. In his enthusiasm for European art, technology, and political and social forms, Dwarkanath surpassed his teacher and extended Rammohun's synthetic approach into the realms of society and economics. Like Rammohun, Dwarkanath conceived of a prosperous, educated India taking its place in the modern world as part of the British Empire. The empire he envisioned was to be a racially and culturally heterogeneous collection of nations, each borrowing the fruits of the others' cultures, standing as equals, participating in the governance of the whole, and benefiting alike from the union. All of Dwarkanath's diverse activities were directed toward attaining that goal.

If Rammohun provided the framework for his enlarged views, recent developments in Calcutta appeared to bear out Dwarkanath's vision of the future. By the mid-thirties Calcutta was the political and economic capital of the Indian subcontinent. The East India Company, deprived of its trading function in India, was now encouraging British colonization, and the city had a growing population of British tradesmen, merchants, and professionals. As an offshoot of the recently enfranchised British middle class, and as custodians of a new industrial technology, the European business community had gained increasing pride and unbounded confidence in the future. Simultaneously, Indian businessmen were taking a larger role in international trade and joint-stock enterprises, and ever-growing numbers of Indians were receiving a Western education. By all indications the two communities were coming closer together. They were uniting on a number of common issues: the steam route to Europe, local control of banking and joint-stock enterprises, the extension of free trade, freedom of the press, and support for Western education. Furthermore, European merchants had become increasingly dependent on Indian capital and were paying for its use by accepting Bengalis into their firms. In addition to collaboration in business, Bengalis and Europeans were associated in such important public institutions as the Agricultural and Horticultural Society, the Managing Committee of Hindoo College, the Bengal Chamber of Commerce, and the Landholders' Association.

Dwarkanath realized that there were immense obstacles to overcome in building an interracial society. Racial tension had always been characteristic of Calcutta, a city of great social mobility with wide-open opportunities for aggressive individuals and families and with few traditional guidelines to soften the abrasive competition for money and status. The improvement of communications with Europe increased the tendency of the British to think of India in terms of a temporary exile from home. Indeed, Dwarkanath's own period of leadership only interrupted a trend that reasserted itself after his death. To Dwarkanath, however, the two societies appeared on the point of convergence, and he worked to facilitate the process. He promoted British settlement in India and the establishment of a civic loyalty based on geographic residence rather than on race and religion, encouraged the races to work as partners in business and civic organizations, invited them to mingle socially at his mansion, and encouraged them to attend the same theaters and read the same newspapers. By his own example he tried to embolden Indians to visit England and participate in British social and political life.

Dwarkanath's major economic achievements occurred within the favorable period of the business cycle between the two major depressions of 1830–33 and 1847–48. This "age of enterprise" was, in fact, a period in which the economic activities of the preceding era were intensified and amplified, and most of the new enterprises can be attributed to the extensive commercial application of steam power, introduced in the period before 1830. Even without the entrepreneurship of Dwarkanath Tagore new enterprises would have been launched. But if he did not create the "age of enterprise," he surpassed his contemporaries in bringing together the factors of production. His own activities demonstrated the potential of combining existing resources with the new technology. He developed his rural estates as sources for export staples—indigo, sugar, rum, and silk—and then integrated these products into the export business of Carr, Tagore and Company. To carry his products overseas, he assembled his own fleet of merchant vessels, and, when he saw the need to facilitate the financing of production and export trade, he took the lead in establishing the Union Bank. By his purchase of the Raniganj coal mines he complemented his commercial undertakings with industrial enterprises. To increase the market for coal and to expedite shipping, he formed the Calcutta Steam Tug Association, and to bring the products of the Ganges Valley to port, he promoted the India General Steam Navigation Company. He took over management of enterprises originated by the imaginative Prinsep brothers (the Bengal Tea Company and the Bengal Salt Company), encouraged the economically feasible but ill-fated ferry-bridge scheme, and, toward the end of his life, joined in the promotion of the Great Western of Bengal Railway Company.

In the operation of his companies he appears to have specialized in company relations and contracts, and he had a special talent for finance and organization. He persuaded the Marine Board by threats and pleas to use his coal; he coaxed the government to honor its professed commitment to indigenous development, and he took advantage of every opportunity to obtain special concessions, customs rebates, and advances on the hypothecation of his exports. His firm benefited from his wide contacts in the business community and among Indian zamindars. To control and manage his widespread enterprises he developed his house into the prototype of the managing-agency firm, and in the fashion of later managing agents, vertically integrated the various companies under his control. The tug and river-steamboat companies purchased coal from his mine and used the docking and repair facilities owned by his house. He was the first businessman in India to apply the joint-stock form on a large scale and by the sale of shares to tap both the savings of the Europeans and the wealth of his Indian friends.

Though brilliantly conceived, many of his enterprises failed or nearly failed as a result of poor management. Dwarkanath himself was too preoccupied to become immersed in business routine, and his partners came and went too quickly and spread themselves over too many projects to devote themselves to careful management. In this respect, however, Carr, Tagore and Company was no better or worse than its contemporaries. Poor management was endemic in Calcutta, and, in fact, in Britain itself, during the early nineteenth century. Yet, as a promoter, Tagore's record of success is impressive. Of the six joint-stock companies organized by his firm, four—the Calcutta Steam Tug Association, the Bengal Coal Company, the Assam Company, and the India General Steam Navigation Company—were long-lived. The first survived for over twenty years, and the latter three are still in operation under new names and corporate forms. Only two companies, the Bengal Salt Company and the Steam Ferry Bridge Company, failed while under the management of his firm. The salt company was an overambitious scheme based on inadequate appreciation of the technological problems involved. If it was ill-conceived, at least it had not been Dwarkanath's conception, but that of George Prinsep. The Steam Ferry Bridge Company, on the other hand, was a reasonable scheme, but failed because of the incompetence of its British agents, inadequate local financing, and governmental indifference. Dwarkanath's most conspicuous failure was the Union Bank, whose complex affairs he was not competent to direct. In sum, Dwarkanath was a shrewd, realistic, and imaginative businessman, and his idealism, rather than leading him astray, provided him with just the right amount of readiness to explore new economic opportunities.

This same idealism, however, blinded him to the ultimate futility of ever realizing his larger goal—a comprehensive Indo-British partnership. His fundamental error was to miscalculate the strength and to misread the nature of the British commitment to India. He believed that he could induce the British to reciprocate and embrace him and his country as he was embracing them and theirs. But all the overtures came from one side. Carr, Tagore and Company, for example, was not truly a partnership of equals. Dwarkanath established the house and invited Carr, Prinsep, and other impecunious British merchants to join him in the use of his capital. They had nothing to lose and everything to gain by accepting his offer, and they left for home as soon as possible.

Nor did the British reciprocate his bid for genuine social intercourse. It was at his home that they gathered to be lavishly entertained by their solicitous host; they did not return the invitation. If Dwarkanath wanted interracial cooperation, he had to provide the framework, whether it be a charitable society or a joint-stock company. True, he was received in Britain as an honored guest and undoubtedly believed he was making great strides for his countrymen by moving freely in court and government circles. But he was only receiving the treatment customarily accorded a charming and exotic foreign prince, and by calling him "Prince Dwarkanath" the British could pretend he was just that and not the more threatening personage he had meant to be—a fellow citizen of the empire. His son Nagendranath did not inherit his "title," and after Dwarkanath's death became only another job-seeking Bengali.

Dwarkanath paid a heavy price for his daring dream, not only in economic terms, but in psychic ones. He was cut off from intimate relationships with his own family and community, dependent on the friendship of strangers, and never certain whether he was loved for himself or his largesse. Only a profound loneliness could have driven him, on the eve of his final illness, from one social gathering to another. His light-hearted manner must have hidden an inner uncertainty as he explored new, untried paths for which there were no conventional rules of behavior. In rapid succession he played one role, then another: the rich, almsgiving Hindu, the governor-general's Indian counterpart, the exotic representative of his people at the royal court, the western-style entrepreneur, the crony among his British friends, and the daring breaker of caste taboos. Always on stage himself, it is no wonder that the art form he most appreciated was the theater.

Dwarkanath labored in vain, for the British would not accept genuine partnership with an Indian. The nature of investment depends on the investor's perception of economic opportunities in a political and social context. Whereas Dwarkanath conceived of India as a potentially modern, industrialized nation, the British, for the most part, saw only a vast agricultural dependency feeding raw materials to British industry. Their perception influenced the nature of their investments and made them unwilling to take risks in slow-maturing industrial enterprises. They saw no future for themselves or their children as settlers in India and considered India, instead, as a place where they could quickly enrich themselves and which they could then abandon. Many an enterprise foundered because the British capitalist in Calcutta, faced with the prospect of committing an extra sum that would have saved a company, preferred to remit his money home. The British lack of commitment precluded the establishment of a local, interracial citizenry founded upon an economic partnership. If, however, Bengal was not worthy of commitment, it was fair game for exploitation. Its tropical climate, resources, and location as the trade terminus of the Ganges Valley made it ideal for development as a complement to British industry, and Bengal failed to develop sufficient industries of its own to give employment to its youth and meet the economic demands of its increasing population.

In Dwarkanath's day, the Indian investor still required British leadership, and, so long as it was not forthcoming, was content to invest in land. Later in the century it was too late to reverse the trend. As the Bengalis fell behind economically, they compensated in other directions. Their entrepreneurs promoted new religions, social-reform organizations, and political parties, while their gifts of imagination were channeled into literature and politics. With partnership closed to them, the Bengalis, including Dwarkanath's son Debendranath, turned inward and probed deeper into the essence of their own traditions. Keshub Chundra Sen preached a new form of bhakti, Ramakrishna revived the cult of *shakti*, and Aurobindo deified the Motherland. In the twentieth century, Bengalis turned to revolutionary terrorism, to Marxism, and to the militarism of Subhas Chandra Bose. Because the British had rejected the Bengalis, their popular leaders rejected British liberal values, and the land that had spawned the internationalism of Dwarkanath Tagore became, in time, the fountainhead of neo-Hinduism, and the nursery of Indian nationalism.

GLOSSARY

amla	Plural of *amal,* manager
babu	Bengali word used as a title for a Hindu gentleman, equivalent to "sir" or "mister." Later in the nineteenth century, applied in derision to English-educated Bengalis.
baithak khana	Sitting room or parlor.
bania	Hindustani trader, shopkeeper, or moneychanger.
banian	In Bengal, an Indian businessman in the service of Europeans.
banik	The Bengali variant of "bania."
bhadralok	Bengali word meaning "gentlefolk." Applied especially to educated upper castes and to those who imitated their style of life.
bhakti	Devotional worship.
bustee	Hut.
dak	Relay station.
dal	A party or faction.
dalapati	The head of a party or faction.
crore	Ten million, written 1,00,00,000.
darogha	Police.
dewan	Financial manager.
gariwala	Cart driver.
gomasta	Steward.
gur	Raw sugar.
jhil	Shallow lake.
kusa grass	A kind of grass used in religious ceremonies.
lakh	One hundred thousand, written 1,00,000.

lathiyal	Warriors armed with sticks.
Kulin	A person of high birth.
molunghee	Salt-maker.
mufassal	Countryside as distinct from Calcutta; also, upcountry, or the area from Calcutta to Delhi.
mukhtear	Agent or attorney.
paribar	The extended family.
pathsala	Bengali school.
patta	Lease of property.
puja	Worship.
raiyati	Owned or managed by a *ryot*.
ryot	Peasant.
Sadr court	Chief court within jurisdiction of East India Company.
sanyassi	Religious mendicant.
sheristadar	Head native officer.
shetia	In Bombay, an Indian merchant.
shroff	Moneychanger.
sraddha	Funeral ceremonies.
swadeshi	One's own country; a movement to encourage the manufacture and use of indigenous articles.
taluk	An estate.
thakur	A person of rank
zamindar	Landholder.
zilla court	District court.

CURRENCIES, WEIGHTS, AND MEASURES

rupee	Usually refers to the *sicca rupee,* a coin equal to about two shillings, or fifty cents American, in use during the 1830s and 1840s. C.R. refers to Company's Rupee, a standard all-India rupee adopted in 1835 and equivalent to about 15/16 sicca rupee.
anna	One-sixteenth of a rupee.
pice	One-fourth of an anna.
maund	About 82 lb. av.
bigah	One-third of an acre.

BIBLIOGRAPHY

Comparatively few of Dwarkanath Tagore's own writings have survived intact. Among these are about fifty personal letters, written mostly to business associates, some official letters to government agencies, speeches and letters printed in the newspapers, and excerpts from the lost diary, kept during his trips abroad, which were printed in Kissory Chand Mittra's *Memoir of Dwarkanath Tagore* (Calcutta: 1870).

The major sources of information concerning his personal life are found in two archives: Rabindra Bharati University at Jorasanko, Calcutta; and Rabindra Sadhana at Santiniketan, West Bengal. Rabindra Bharati University holds a collection on Dwarkanath assembled by Kshitindranath Tagore (1869–1937). Kshitindranath challenged the will of his grandfather, Debendranath, in 1907 and built his lawsuit around the will of his great-grandfather, Dwarkanath. Later he became interested in the person of his great-grandfather and devoted the remainder of his life to collecting materials on Dwarkanath. Although he discovered some items found nowhere else, most of the collection consists of newspaper clippings and legal documents. Kshitindranath's problem is explained in a letter in his collection written by Kshemendranath Tagore, dated 11 November 1939. The letter states that Rabindranath Tagore removed all the personal papers of Dwarkanath from the home at Jorasanko and burnt them. Before doing so, however, he gave three volumes of Dwarkanath's business letters to Sir Ashutosh Chaudhuri, who in turn passed them on to Hitendranath Tagore, a brother of Kshitindranath. Thereafter, however, they too disappeared.

The second major Dwarkanath Tagore collection is situated in the Tagore family archives in Rabindra Sadhana on the campus of Visva-Bharati University, Santiniketan. Material on Dwarkanath is contained in seven thin folios of manuscripts and two volumes of typed duplicates of manuscripts. One of these typed volumes, entitled "Our Family Correspondence," was assembled by Gagendranath Tagore in 1905. A microfilm copy of the original letters of Dwarkanath is on deposit in the National Archives of India.

In contrast to the paucity of personal letters, abundant material exists on the joint-stock companies founded by Dwarkanath and his partners. The *Bengal Hurkaru,* a daily newspaper directed at the European business community of Calcutta, contains verbatim reports of shareholders' meetings. In addition, the papers of two of the companies founded by Dwarkanath's firm have been preserved in archives; those of the Bengal Coal Company are in the archives of Andrew Yule and Company, Calcutta; and those of the Assam (Tea) Company in the Guildhall Library, London. Finally, where government decisions were involved, material on the companies is preserved in the West Bengal State Archives at Calcutta, the National Archives of India in New Delhi, and the India Office, London.

A. Manuscript Sources

Andrew Yule and Company, Calcutta
Bengal Coal Company Papers, 1840, 1842–45

British Museum
Auckland Papers, *Additional Manuscripts* 37689–37718.
Broughton Papers (John Cam Hobhouse), *Additional Manuscripts* 36456–36480 and 43744–43748.
Charles Babbage, *Additional Manuscripts* 37205, 37192, 37200.
Robert Peel, *Additional Manuscripts* 40515.

Calcutta High Court Archives
Plea Side.
Civil Side.

Cambridge University Library
Jardine Matheson Archives.

Guildhall Library, London
Assam (Tea) Company Papers, 9924–9936.
Walter Prideaux Papers, 8794–8803.

India Office Library and Record Room, London
  Records: Home Miscellaneous 839–853, Broughton Papers; Home Depart-

ment, Railways, 4 PWD/3, nos. 19–25; Despatches to India and Bengal; Revenue Letters Received from Bengal and India, Board's Copies; Bengal Revenue Consultations; Financial Letters from India and Bengal, with enclosures; Revenue Despatches to Bengal and India, Board's Copies; Public Despatches to India and Bengal, Board's Copies; Board of Control Letter Books.

   European Manuscripts: C. 97, H.T. Prinsep, "Four Generations in India;" D. 443, "The Palmer Histories;" E. 123–24, Letter 6 of 1842 from Elisa Reade to her sister.

National Archives of India, New Delhi
Finance Department (Pre-Mutiny), India Finance, Proceedings 1835–46 Military Department, Marine Proceedings, 1843–44.

Oxford University, Bodleian Library
Palmer Manuscripts, English Letters, c. 67–125; English History, c. 301–2; English Letters, d. 105–7.

Public Record Office, London
PRO 30/12, Ellenborough Papers.

Rabindra Bharati University Archives, Calcutta
Kshitindranath Tagore Collection.

Royal Archives, Windsor Castle
Queen Victoria's Journal, 8 July, 1842.

Santiniketan, West Bengal
Rabindra Sadhana Collection.

Somerset House, London
Principal Probate Registry. "Last Will and Testament of William Prinsep," 3 March 1874.

University College Library, London
Brougham Papers.

West Bengal State Archives, Calcutta
Marine Proceedings, 1842–52; General Department, 1835–47; Education Department, 1842; Separate Revenue Department, Customs Proceedings, 1834–46; Separate Revenue Department, Salt Proceedings, 1837–45; Miscellaneous Revenue Department, 1836–37; Separate Revenue Department,

Board of Customs, Salt and Opium, 1846; Revenue Department, Tea Committee, 1839; Board of Customs, Salt and Opium, Miscellaneous, 1824; Board of Trade—Wards and Board of Customs, Salt and Opium—Wards, 1824–38; Board of Trade and Board of Customs, Salt and Opium, Salt, 1828–47; Board of Trade and Board of Customs, Salt and Opium—Customs. 1837–47; Revenue Proceedings, Governor of Bengal, 1835–48; Territorial Revenue Department, 1833–34; Judicial Department, 1816–46; Judicial Department, Criminal, 1840–41.

B. Documentary Sources

Bengal Chamber of Commerce, *Half-Yearly Reports, 1853–1860.* Calcutta, 1853–60.
Bengal, Government of. *Report of the Indigo Commission Appointed under Act XI of 1860, with Minutes of Evidence and Appendix.* Calcutta, 1860.
————. *Report of a Committee for Investigating the Coal and Mineral Resources of India.* Calcutta, 1838. (I.O. Record Department (26) 708/1.)
———— *Committee on Improvement of Mofussil Police, Report and Appendices.* Calcutta, 1838.
Great Britain, *Parliamentary Papers.*
1837, vol. 7,
1840, vol. 8,
1841, vol. 45.
1899, vol. 31, *Indian Currency Committee of 1899,* app. 10.
1919, vol. 27, *Report of the Indian Industrial Commission, 1916–1918.*
U.S., Congress, Senate, 35th Cong., 1st Sess. *Report of the Commissioner of Patents for the Year 1857, Agriculture.* Washington, D.C., 1858.

C. Books and Articles

Achievements of the Managing Agency System. Calcutta, 1954.
Ahmed, A.F. Salahuddin. *Social Ideas and Social Change in Bengal, 1818–1835.* Leiden, 1965.
Andrew Yule & Company, Andrew Yule & Co. Ltd. 1863–1963. Calcutta, 1963.
Antrobus, H.A. *A History of the Assam Company, 1839–1953.* Edinburgh, 1957.
Archer, W.G. *India and Modern Art.* London, 1959.
Ascoli, F.D. *Early Revenue History of Bengal and the Fifth Report, 1812.* Oxford, 1917.
Bagchi, Amiya Kumar. *Private Investment in India, 1900–1939.* Cambridge, 1972.
Bandopadhyaya, Brajendra Nath, ed. *Sambedpetry Sekaler Katha, 1818–1840.* 2 vols. Calcutta, 1949–50.
Banerjee, Tarasankar. *Internal Market of India (1834–1900).* Calcutta, 1966.

Barraclough, L.J. "A Further Contribution to the History of the Development of the Coal Mining Industry in India." Presidential Address, Mining, Geological and Metallurgical Institute of India, *Transactions.* Vol. 47 (April 1951).

Basu, S.K. *Industrial Finance in India.* Calcutta, 1961.

―――.*The Managing Agency System.* Calcutta, 1958.

Bearce, George D. *British Attitudes Towards India, 1784–1858.* Oxford, 1961.

Becher, Augusta. *Personal Reminiscences in India and Europe, (1830–1888).* Ed. by H.G. Rawlinson. London, 1930.

Bell, John Hyslop. *British Folks and British India Fifty Years Ago: Joseph Pease and His Contemporaries.* London, n.d.

Bengal District Gazetteers. *Murshidabad.* Compiled by L.S.S. O'Malley. Calcutta, 1914.

―――. *Howrah.* Compiled by L.S.S. O'Malley. Calcutta, 1909.

Bernstein, Henry T. *Steamboats on the Ganges.* Bombay, 1960.

Bhattacharya, Jogendra Nath. *Hindu Castes and Sects.* Calcutta, 1896.

Blanford, William T. "On the Geological Structure and Relations of the Raniganj Coal Fields, Bengal." *Memoirs of the Geological Survey of India.* Vol. III, pt. I. Calcutta, 1861.

Bose, Amalendu. "A Note on Dwarkanath Tagore." *Visvabharati Quarterly,* Vol. 31, no. 3. (1965–66).

Bose, N.K. *Calcutta: 1964, A Social Survey.* Bombay, 1968.

Bose, Shib Chunder. *The Hindoos As They Are.* Calcutta, 1881.

Bourne, John. *Railways in India by an Engineer.* (I.O. Tract 479) London, 1847.

Brame, Alfred. *The India General Steam Navigation Company, Ltd.* London, 1900.

Brimmer, Andrew F. "The Setting of Entrepreneurship in India." *Quarterly Journal of Economics,* Vol. LXIX (November 1955).

Broomfield, John H. *Elite Conflict in a Plural Society: Twentieth-Century Bengal.* Berkeley, 1968.

Buchanan, Daniel H. *The Development of Capitalist Enterprise in India.* New York, 1934.

Buckland, C.E. *Bengal under the Lieutenant-Governors.* 2 vols. 2d ed. Calcutta, 1902.

―――. *Dictionary of Indian Biography.* London, 1906.

Campbell, George. *Modern India.* London, 1852.

Capper, John. *The Three Presidencies of India.* London, 1853.

Chandra, R. and Majumdar, Jatindra Kumar. *Selections from Official Letters and Documents relating to the Life of Raja Rammohun Roy.* Vol. I, 1791–1830. Calcutta, 1938.

Chattopadhyay, Goutam, ed. *Awakening in Bengal in Early Nineteenth Century.* Vol. I. Calcutta, 1965.

Chaudhuri, K.N., ed. *The Economic Development of India under the East India Company, 1814–58.* Cambridge, 1971.

————, "India's Foreign Trade and the Cessation of the East India Company's Trading Activities, 1828–40." *Economic History Review,* second series, vol. XIX, no. 2 (August 1966).

Chowdhury, Benoy. *Growth of Commercial Agriculture in Bengal (1757–1900).* Vol. I. Calcutta, 1964.

Chuckerbutty, S. Goodeve. *Popular Lectures on Subjects of Indian Interest.* Calcutta, 1870.

Coates, W.H. *The Old Country Trade of the East Indies.* London, 1911.

Collet, Sophia Dobson. *The Life and Letters of Raja Rammohun Roy.* D.K. Biswas and P.C. Ganguli, eds. 3d ed. Calcutta, 1962.

Cooke, Charles Northcote. *The Rise, Progress and Present Condition of Banking in India.* Calcutta, 1863.

Correspondence and Documents relating to the Suspension of W.P. Grant, esq., from the Office of Master in the Supreme Court of Judicature, Fort William in Bengal, on the 6th June 1848. Calcutta, 1848.

Cotton, H.E.A. *Calcutta Old and New.* Calcutta, 1907.

Crane, Robert I. "Technical Education and Economic Development in India before World War I." In C.A. Anderson and J.J. Bowman, *Education and Economic Development.* New York, 1965.

Crawford, D.G. *Roll of the Indian Medical Service, 1615–1930.* London, 1930.

Crawfurd, John. *A Sketch of the Commercial Resources and Monetary and Mercantile System of British India.* London, 1837. Reprinted in K.N. Chaudhuri, ed., *The Economic Development of India under the East India Company, 1814–58.* Cambridge, 1971.

Das, Satyajit. *Selections from the Indian Journals.* 2 vols. *Calcutta Journal (1818–1820).* Calcutta, 1963, 1965.

Das Gupta, A.C., ed. *The Days of John Company. Selections from Calcutta Gazette, 1824–1832.* Calcutta, 1959.

Das Gupta, H.N. *The Indian Stage.* 4 vols. Calcutta, 1935–46. Vol. I.

De, Sushil Kumar. *History of Bengali Literature in the Nineteenth Century.* 2d ed. Calcutta, 1961.

Decisions of the Sudder Dewanny Adawlut, Recorded in Conformity to Act XII of 1843, in 1849. Calcutta, 1850.

Dey, Sumbhoo Chunder. *Hooghly Past and Present.* Calcutta, 1906.

Dharker, C.D. *Lord Macaulay's Legislative Minutes.* Madras, 1946.

Dimock, Edward C., Jr. "Doctrine and Practice among the Vaisnavas of Bengal," in Milton Singer, ed., *Krishna: Myths, Rites and Attitudes.* Honolulu, 1966.

Dobbin, Christine. *Urban Leadership in Western India.* Oxford, 1972.

Dutt, Nripendra Kumar. *Origin and Growth of Caste in India.* Vol. II. Calcutta, 1965.

Eden, Emily. *Letters from India.* 2 vols. London, 1872.

Evans, D. Morier. *The Commercial Crisis, 1847–1848.* 2d ed. London, 1849.

Everett, I. *Observations on India by a Resident There of Many Years.* London, 1853.

Field, C.D. *Introduction to the Regulations of the Bengal Code.* Calcutta, 1897.

Finch, C. "Vital Statistics of Calcutta." *Journal of the Statistical Society of London,* vol. 13 (1850).

Frykenberg, Robert E. *Guntur District, 1788–1848.* Oxford, 1965.

Furrell, James W. *The Tagore Family.* 2d ed. Calcutta, 1892.

Gadgil, D.R. *Origins of the Modern Indian Business Class, an Interim Report.* New York, 1959.

Ganguli, A. and Basu, N.D., eds. *A Glossary of Judicial and Revenue Terms of British India by H.H. Wilson.* Calcutta, 1940.

Ghosal, H.R. *Economic Transition in the Bengal Presidency, 1793–1833.* Patna, 1950.

Ghosh, Benoy. "The Economic Character of the Urban Middle-Class in Nineteenth Century Bengal." In B.N. Ganguli, ed., *Readings in Indian Economic History.* Bombay, 1964.

———, ed. *Samayek-Patre Banglar Samaj-Chitra 1840–1905.* 3 vols. Calcutta, 1963.

Ghosh, Lokenath. *The Modern History of the Indian Chiefs, Rajas, Zamindars.* 2 vols. Calcutta, 1879–81.

Ghosh, Manmatha Nath. "Friends and Followers of Rammohun." In Satischandra Chakravarty, ed. *Father of Modern India Commemoration Volume, 1933.* Calcutta, 1935.

Gibbon, Edward. *The History of the Decline and Fall of the Roman Empire.* 7 vols. 2d ed. London, 1926. Vol. I.

The Great Tagore Will Case. Calcutta, 1872.

Greenberg, Michael. *British Trade and the Opening of China, 1800–1842.* Cambridge, 1951.

Griffiths, Percival. *The British Impact on India.* 2d ed. Hamden, Conn., 1965.

Gupta, Atulchandra, ed. *Studies in the Bengal Renaissance.* Jadavpur, 1958.

Gupta, M.N. *Analytical Survey of Bengal Regulations.* Calcutta, 1943.

Habib, Irfan. "Potentialities of Capitalist Development in the Economy of Mughal India." *Journal of Economic History* (March 1969).

Hagen, Everett E. *On the Theory of Social Change.* Homewood, Illinois, 1962.

Hardinge, Viscount. *Viscount Hardinge and the Advance of British Dominion into the Punjab. Rulers of India Series.* Oxford, 1891.

Heatly, S.G. Tollemache. "Contributions towards a History of the Development of the Mineral Resources of India." *Journal of the Asiatic Society of Bengal,* vol. XI (1842).

Heber, R. *Narrative of a Journey through the Upper Provinces of India.* 3 vols. 4th ed. London, 1828.

Henderson, H.B. *The Bengalee.* 2 vols. Calcutta, 1829, 1836.

Hoskins, H.L. *British Routes to India.* Philadelphia, 1928.

The House of the Tagores. Calcutta, 1963.

[Hume, James.] *Letters to Friends at Home by an Idler from June 1842 to May 1843.* Calcutta, 1843.

————. *Letters to Friends at Home by an Idler from June 1843 to May 1844.* Calcutta, 1844.

Humphreys, H.D.G. "History of the Bengal Coal Company, 1843–1861," Manuscript in archives of Andrew Yule and Company, Calcutta.

Imlah, Albert H. *Lord Ellenborough.* Cambridge, 1939.

India, Government of. *Small Scale Industries.* New Delhi, 1971.

Johnson, George W. *The Stranger in India.* 2 vols. London, 1843.

Kannangara, A.P. "Indian Millowners and Indian Nationalism before 1914." *Past and Present,* no. 40 (1968).

Kaye, John W. *The Administration of the East India Company.* London, 1853.

Keynes, J.M. *Indian Currency and Finance.* London, 1913.

Kidron, Michael. *Foreign Investments in India.* London, 1965.

Kling, Blair B. *The Blue Mutiny.* Philadelphia, 1966.

————. "Entrepreneurship and Regional Identity in Bengal." In David Kopf, ed. *Bengal Regional Identity.* East Lansing, 1969.

————. "The Origin of the Managing Agency System in India." *Journal of Asian Studies,* vol. 26, no. 1 (November 1966).

"Economic Foundations of the Bengal Renaissance." In Rachel van M. Baumer, ed. *Aspects of Bengali History and Society.* Honolulu, 1975.

Kopf, David. *British Orientalism and the Bengal Renaissance.* Berkeley, 1969.

Lardner, Reverend Dionysius. *A Treatise on Silk Manufacture.* Philadelphia, 1832.

Larpent, A.J. de H. *Facts Explanatory of the Connection of the Late Firm of Cockerell and Company of Calcutta with the Union Bank of Calcutta.* London, 1848.

List of Merchant Ships, 1834–35. Calcutta, 1835.

Lokanathan, P.S. *Industrial Organization in India.* London, 1935.

Lubbock, Basil. *The Opium Clippers.* Glasgow, 1933.

MacBean, Alasdair I. *Export Instability and Economic Development.* London, 1966.

Maccoby, S. *English Radicalism, 1853–1886.* London, 1938.

Mackenzie, Compton. *Realms of Silver.* London, 1954.

Majumdar, B.B. *Indian Political Associations and Reform of Legislature (1818–1917).* Calcutta, 1965.

Majumdar, J.K., ed. *Raja Rammohun Roy and Progressive Movements in India.* Calcutta, 1941.

[Marshman, John.] "Commercial Morality and Commercial Prospects in Bengal." *The Calcutta Review,* vol. 9 (January–June 1848).

Martin, R.M. *History of the British Colonies.* 5 vols. London, 1834.

————. *Statistics of the Colonies of the British Empire.* London, 1839.

Mehrotra, S.R. "The British India Society and its Bengal Branch (1839–1846)." *The Indian Economic and Social History Review,* vol. 4 no. 2 (June 1967).

———— "The Landholders' Society, 1838–44." *Indian Economic and Social History Review,* vol. 3, no. 4 (December 1966).

Mehta, S.D. *The Cotton Mills of India, 1854–1954.* Bombay, 1954.

Mitra, Asok. *Calcutta India's City.* Calcutta, 1963.

Mittra, Kissory Chand. *Memoir of Dwarkanath Tagore.* Calcutta, 1870.

————. *Mutty Lall Seal.* Calcutta, 1869.

————. "The Territorial Aristocracy of Bengal. The Rajas of Rajshahi." *The Calcutta Review,* vol. 56, no. 111 (1874).

Mittra, Peary Chand. *A Biographical Sketch of David Hare.* Calcutta, 1877.

————. *Life of Dewan Ramcomul Sen.* Calcutta, 1880.

Moore, Charles. *The Sheriffs of Fort William from 1775–1926.* Calcutta, 1926.

Morris, Morris D. *The Emergence of an Industrial Labor Force in India.* Berkeley, 1965.

Mukherjee, Amitabah. *Reform and Regeneration in Bengal 1774–1823.* Calcutta, 1968.

Mukherjee, Amritamaya. "Thakur Barir Itikatha." *Samakalin* (Posh 1365, December–January 1958–59).

Mukherjee, S.N. "Class, Caste and Politics in Calcutta 1815–1838." In E. Leach and S.N. Mukherjee, eds. *Elites in South Asia.* Cambridge, 1970.

Müller, F. Max. *Biographical Essays.* London, 1884.

Mullick, Kissen Mohun. *Brief History of Bengal Commerce from the Year 1814 to 1870.* Calcutta, 1871.

Nigam, Raj K. *Managing Agencies in India.* Delhi, 1957.

"Notes on the Right Bank of the Hooghly." *The Calcutta Review,* vol. 4 (July–December 1845), pp. 476–520.

O'Hanlon, Patrick. *Mr. O'Hanlon's Remarks on Mr. G.J. Gordon's Publication.* Alipore, March, 1843.

"120 Years Ago—Janet Hare with Raja Rai." *Behala,* autumn number, 1371 (1964).

Orlick, Captain Leopold von. *Travels in India.* 2 vols. London, 1845.

Parks, Fanny. *Wanderings of a Pilgrim in Search of the Picturesque during Four and Twenty Years in the East, etc.* 2 vols. London, 1850.

Philips, C.H. *The East India Company, 1784–1834.* Manchester, 1940.

Phipps, John. *Ship Building in India.* Calcutta, 1840.

Plowden, Walter F.C. Chicheley. *Records of the Chicheley Plowdens, AD 1590–1913.* London, 1914.

Prinsep, G.A. *An Account of Steam Vessels and of Proceedings Connected with Steam Navigation in British India.* Calcutta, 1830.

————. *Sketch of the Proceedings and Present Position of the Saugor Island Society and its Lessees.* (I.O. Tract 146.) Calcutta, 1831.

Ray, Prafulla Chandra. *Life and Experiences of a Bengali Chemist.* 2 vols. Calcutta, 1932, 1935.

Reasons for Establishing a New Bank in India. London, 1836.

Redford, Arthur. *Manchester Merchants and Foreign Trade, 1794–1858.* Manchester, 1934.

Rendel, James M. "Particulars of the Construction of the Floating Bridge lately Established across the Hamoaze . . . . " *Transactions of the Institutions of Civil Engineers,* vol. II. London, 1838.

Roberts, Emma. *Scenes and Characteristics of Hindostan with Sketches of Anglo-Indian Society.* 3 vols. London, 1835.

Roy, Rammohun. *The English Works of Raja Rammohun Roy.* 6 parts. Kalidas Nag and Debajyoti Burman, eds. Calcutta, 1945–51.

Roy, Satindra Narayan. "Bengal Traditions of Trade and Commerce." *Journal of the Anthropological Society of Bombay.* Vol. XIV, no. 4 (1929).

Rungta, R.S. *The Rise of Business Corporations in India, 1851–1900.* Cambridge, 1970.

Sanyal, Ram Gopal. *Bengal Celebrities.* 2 vols. Calcutta, 1889.

Sastri, Sivanath. *Ramtanu Lahiri, Brahman and Reformer.* Roper Lethbridge, ed. London, 1907.

Scutt, S.P. Symes. *History of the Bank of Bengal.* Calcutta, 1904.

Semmel, Bernard. *The Rise of Free Trade Imperialism.* Cambridge, 1970.

Sen, A.K. "The Pattern of British Enterprise in India, 1854–1914: A Causal Analysis." In Baljit Singh and V.B. Singh, eds. *Social and Economic Change.* Bombay, 1967.

Sen, Dinesh Chandra. *History of Bengali Language and Literature.* Calcutta, 1954.

Sen, Sunil Kumar. *Studies in the Industrial Policy and Development of India.* Calcutta, 1964.

Singh, S.B. *European Agency Houses in Bengal (1783–1833).* Calcutta, 1966.

Sinha, Nirmal, ed. *Freedom Movement in Bengal, 1818–1904 Who's Who.* Calcutta, 1968.

Sinha, N.C. *Studies in Indo-British Economy Hundred Years Ago.* Calcutta, 1946.

Sinha, N.K. *Economic History of Bengal from Plassey to the Permanent Settlement.* 2 vols. Calcutta, 1956, 1962.

———, ed. *The History of Bengal (1757–1905).* Calcutta, 1967.

Sinha, Pradip. *Nineteenth Century Bengal: Aspects of Social History.* Calcutta, 1965.

Soltykoff, Prince Alexis. "Bombay and Calcutta in 1841." H.L.O. Garrett, trans. and ed. *Journal of the Punjab Historical Society,* vol. 2 (April 1933).

Spate, O.H.K. *India and Pakistan: A General and Regional Geography.* 2d ed. London, 1957.

Stephenson, Rowland M. *Report upon the Practicability and Advantages of the Introduction of Railways into British India.* London, 1844.

Stewart, J.C. *Facts and Documents Relating to the Affairs of the Union Bank of Calcutta.* London, 1848.

Stocqueler, J.H. *The Handbook of India.* 2d ed. London, 1845.

———. *Memoirs of a Journalist.* Bombay and Calcutta, 1873.

Stokes, Eric. *The English Utilitarians and India.* Oxford, 1959.

Sykes, W.H. "On the Population and Mortality of Calcutta." *Journal of the Statistical Society of London,* vol. I (1845), pp. 50–51.

Tagore, Debendranath. *Shrimanmaharshi Devendranath Thakurer Atmajibani.* Satischandra Chakravarty, ed. Calcutta, 1927.

―――. *The Autobiography of Maharshi Devendranath Tagore.* Satyendranath Tagore and Indira Devi, trans. Calcutta, 1909.

Tagore, Rabindranath. *Reminiscences.* London, 1954.

The Tagores of Calcutta. Calcutta, 1869 (?).

Thakur, Kshitindranath. *Dwarkanath Thakurer Jabini.* Calcutta, 1969.

―――. "Dwarkanath Thakurer Jabini." Manuscript copy in archives of Rabindra Bharati University, Calcutta.

Thompson, Edward. *Rabindranath Tagore, Poet and Dramatist.* London, 1948.

Thompson, George. *Addresses Delivered at Meetings of the Native Community of Calcutta and on Other Occasions.* Calcutta, 1843.

Thorner, Daniel. *Investment in Empire.* Philadelphia, 1950.

Tripathi, Amales. *Trade and Finance in the Bengal Presidency, 1793–1833.* Bombay, 1956.

Turner, Ralph E. *The Relations of James Silk Buckingham with the East India Company, 1818–1836.* Pittsburgh, 1930.

Tyson, Geoffrey W. *The Bengal Chamber of Commerce and Industry, 1853–1953, A Centenary Survey.* Calcutta, 1953.

―――. *Managing Agency.* Calcutta, n.d.

Vidyarutna, B. *A Brief Account of the Tagore Family.* (I.O. Tract 137.) Calcutta, 1868.

Watt, George. *A Dictionary of Economic Products of India.* 7 vols. London, 1885–96.

Westland, J. *A Report of the District of Jessore.* Calcutta, 1874.

Wilkinson, E. *Commercial Annual of the External Commerce of Bengal during the Years 1841–42 and 1842–43.* Calcutta, 1843.

Wilson, James. *Capital, Currency and Banking.* London, 1847.

Young, H.A. *The East India Company's Arsenals and Manufactories.* Oxford, 1937.

D. Directories, Periodicals, and Newspapers

Directories

Bengal and Agra Annual Guide. 2 vols. Calcutta, 1841.

Bengal and Agra Directory and Annual Register. Calcutta, 1840–50.

Bengal Annual Directory. Calcutta, 1822.

Bengal Directory and General Register. Calcutta, 1825–28.

Bengal Directory and Annual Register. Calcutta, 1840–51.

New Calcutta Directory. Calcutta, 1858, 1861.

Periodicals

Alexander's East India and Colonial Magazine. London, 1831.
Annual Register, 1846. London, 1847.
Asiatic Journal. London, 1832–38.
Calcutta Monthly Journal. New Series. Calcutta, 1833–41.
Fisher's Colonial Magazine. London, 1842.

Newspapers

Bengal Herald (weekly). Calcutta, 1829, 1841–43.
Bengal Hurkaru (daily). Calcutta, 1824–55.
Bengal Spectator (monthly). Calcutta, 1842–43.
Calcutta Courier (daily). Calcutta, 1832–42.
Calcutta Star (daily). Calcutta, 1842–50.
Englishman (daily). Calcutta, 1833–38.
Friend of India (weekly). Serampore, 1842–43.
Hindoo Patriot (weekly). Calcutta, 11 Feb. 1858.
Times (daily). London, 1842, 1846.
Moniteur Universal (daily). Paris, 1842.
Reformer (weekly). Calcutta, 1833.

INDEX